MW00460356

ATHEISM ADVANCED

ATHEISM ADVANCED

FURTHER THOUGHTS OF A FREETHINKER

DAVID ELLER

Foreword by Frank R. Zindler

2007
American Atheist Press
Cranford, New Jersey

ISBN10 1-57884-002-3
ISBN13 978-1-57884-002-1

American Atheist Press
P. O. Box 5733
Parsippany, NJ 07054-6733

www.atheists.org

Cover: Light Echoes from Red Supergiant Star V838 Monocerotis, December 2002, courtesy of NASA and STScI.

Library of Congress Cataloging-in-Publication Data

Eller, David, 1959–
  Atheism advanced : further thoughts of a freethinker /
  David Eller ; foreword by Frank R. Zindler.
    p. cm.
  Includes bibliographical references (p.   ) and index.
  ISBN-13: 978-1-57884-002-1
  ISBN-10: 1-57884-002-3
  1. Atheism. I. Title.

  BL2747.3.E54 2007
  211'.8—dc22
                2007049675

CONTENTS

ATHEISM ADVANCED

Foreword

The bad news is that it's going to be much harder to overcome religiosity than even the most pessimistic atheists have supposed. The good news is that Professor Eller has applied an anthropologist's powers of objective observation and a philosopher's analytical intellect to deconstruct all the phenomena broadly termed 'religion.' In the pages that follow, he reveals clearly for the first time the anatomy and physiology of the beast that threatens the survival of our civilization — indeed, even the survival of our species itself.

After reading this book it will become clear why atheists, agnostics, and freethinkers of all kinds have made so little progress in the struggle against the religions that multiply the miseries of our world. Not only have we allowed religionists to frame the questions we debate, we have permitted them to coin the very vocabulary with which we think. To rephrase that: we have allowed Christians and other believers to supply the thoughts with which we *think* we think. If one were to read no more than the chapter "Speaking Christian," it would justify the purchase of this book.

Religious behaviors are part and parcel of our evolutionary heritage as a social mammal. It is my opinion that religiosity in general — as contrasted with specific religious behaviors — was once adaptive and contributed to the group fitness of our kind. But what may have been adaptive in Pliocene forests and savannahs or Pleistocene glacial margins is now dangerously maladaptive as Spaceship Earth hurtles forward in its race around the Milky Way.

'Faith' and 'belief' are not going to help us on this cosmic journey. Only sober, objective knowledge of ourselves and our world can preserve us in a universe that has expanded from the three-storied cosmos of the ancient Hebrews to reach the inflationary dimensions of the multiverse now being mapped by cosmologists. Indeed, faith and belief now make it increasingly difficult to get to the truth relating to virtually all problems confronting would-be benefactors of the human race. They impede all who seek to safeguard life itself on this ever-less fair planet we call home — this nest that we have soiled. Belief has got to go. Wherever before we may have been content to rest upon belief, we now must eschew the habit and seek genuine knowledge to refill the gaping voids once filled by faith. We must eliminate the word *belief* from our active vocabularies.

As Dr. Eller argues so eloquently, atheism must advance not only in the political sphere but in the conceptual sphere as well. It must not only be a *gods*-free *Weltanschauung*, it must become a *belief*-free way of life. Atheism must advance into *discredism*, to use the apt new term our author has introduced in this book.

The advance of atheism or discredism will not be easy, given the morally appalling doctrines and dogmas of the world religions that sow the sorrows of so many lives and block so many paths to progress. There is hope, though, in the fact that almost every True Believer is ethically superior to the deity that he or she professes to worship.

Frank R. Zindler

Introduction

Over 2,400 years ago, Socrates was condemned to death for impiety toward the gods and corrupting the youths of Athens by encouraging them to question traditional beliefs. Atheism has not advanced much since.

In Socrates' time, the questions were whether the gods recounted in Homer and Hesiod were real, what the nature of those gods was, and what the proper emotional and ritual attitude of humans should be. The questions were serious enough to get you killed. No one today (well, virtually no one) even thinks about those gods anymore, except as historical and mythical oddities. But the questions remain essentially unchanged; only the names of the gods have changed. In America today, people argue over whether the god recounted in the Judeo-Christian texts is real, what the nature of that god is, and what the proper emotional and ritual attitude of humans should be. In other societies, they substitute the local god's name in the same questions.

Of course, one reason why atheism has not advanced much over the millennia is that theism has not advanced much. Greeks, ancient Egyptians, Norse, Hindus, Jews, Christians, Muslims—for all these, it is still gods and more gods. Nothing has changed except the names and numbers of the gods. In fact, theism, and religion more generally, *cannot* advance; the very idea of 'religious advance' is nonsense, since *advance* implies moving closer toward something, and theisms and other religions do not even agree on what the goal or object is, even while each asserts that it has already reached it. Advance from one religion's perspective is decline from another's: is *mono*theism an advance toward the 'truth' of one god, or a retreat from the 'truth' of many gods? Is theism itself a progression toward the truth of god(s), or a regression from the truth of something other than god(s)—or of no god(s)?

Let us be clear that religions do not and cannot progress the way that, say, science can progress. When science progresses, it abandons old and false ideas. Once we discovered oxygen and the principles of combustion, we stopped thinking that there was a substance called phlogiston. Once we discovered that the earth is round, we stopped thinking that it is flat. Science and reason are *substitutive* or *eliminative*: new ideas replace old ideas. Religion is *additive and/or schismatic*: new ideas proliferate alongside old ideas. For instance, the development of Protestantism did not put an end to Catholicism, and the development of Christianity did not put an end to Judaism. With science, we get *better*. With religion, we get *more*.

Since there are so many religions—and more everyday—that are not only different from but contradictory to each other, it makes no sense to talk about better or true religion. The only thing that makes sense is to talk about *local* religion, the religion that people follow in one place or time as opposed to someplace or sometime else. Atheism or irreligion therefore has generally taken the form throughout the ages of the rejection of the local cult; this is why atheism in majority-Christian societies generally assumes the shape and tone of a-Christianity or anti-Christianity. In India, atheism tends to become a-Hinduism or anti-Hinduism, in Muslim societies it tends to become a-Islam or anti-Islam, and so on. Each local atheism, in other words, seems to struggle with—and be shaped by—its local theism in isolation, as if that is what atheism is.

The point is that theists and atheists alike, co-existing in their local context, usually carry on as if they both equally know and care about one religion and its particular god(s) and/or other beliefs, beings, morals, *etc.* In the American/Christian version, this means arguing about Yahweh, Jehovah, or whatever you want to call the Christian god and his supposed manifestation as Jesus. It means wrangling over the Judeo-Christian writings, pointing out errors and contradictions. It means debating the relationship between and relative merits of science and 'religion,' which always and only means science and Christianity. It means struggling over the proper role of religion in politics and public life, which again only means the Christian religion in politics and public life.

Notice that the controversy and conflict between theism and atheism in America and the West in general seldom involves Judaism, only recently involves Islam, and virtually never involves Hinduism or Sikhism or ancient Greek/Egyptian/Norse/Babylonian or the thousands of other religions humans have invented. Theists do not defend, and atheists do not attack,

Introduction

Zeus or Odin or Vishnu or Osiris or any of the thousands of other gods and non-god supernatural beings that have stalked and haunted human minds over the eons. Partly this follows from an ignorance of other religions in the sense of lacking knowledge about them. But partly it follows from an ignorance of them in the sense of lacking *interest*, of literally *ignoring* them. Each religion ignores the gods and other entities of rival religions just as much as atheism does. For any particular theism or religion, the claims of all other religions are not even false but foreign, outside their own sphere of reality, incomprehensible, and unworthy of consideration. Christians, in other words, do not argue with ancient Greek pantheists or Hindu polytheists. They dismiss them and *ignore* them; they are indifferent to them. To paraphrase General Douglas Macarthur, old gods never get disproved, they just fade away from mind. For Christians, the pre-Christian gods have faded away, except as folklore, while their own god is still very much on their minds.

Atheism, one might think, would therefore dismiss, ignore, and be indifferent to *all* religions or at least all theisms—literally not have its god(s) on its mind. Instead, we find atheism taking not so much 'religion' as the local religion in its particular social setting just about as seriously as the local religionists do. Atheists in Christian-dominant societies argue with Christians about the *Christian god*, bicker over *Christian morals*, fend off *Christian creationist 'theories,'* resist *Christian symbols* in the public square, and criticize *Christian scriptures*. Atheists, whom one would think would be 'without god(s),' often know as much about—and seem to care as much about—Christian beliefs and doctrines as do Christians themselves. Sometimes it even seems that we fetishize their beings and their texts and their morals almost as much as they do. We certainly let ourselves live in their world and let ourselves get dragged into their concerns and debates. As a simple example, a good atheist friend of mine was being interviewed on a radio show some time ago, and the hosts asked him what his notion of god was. An earnest person, he proceeded to describe the Christian god, when what he should have done was say, "I don't have a notion of god—I am god-less—but I have heard Christians talk about their god this way...although I have heard other

ATHEISM ADVANCED

Christians talk about their god in other ways. Personally, 'god' is a word that has no meaning for me."

It is time for atheism to advance. For this reason I have written the book that I present here and have titled it *Atheism Advanced*. I seek to advance, and to encourage others to help advance, atheism in three ways.

First, naturally, I aim to advance atheism in the sense of promoting it. I want atheism to become better understood and better accepted. I want more people to hear it and to embrace it. An atheism which has advanced in this manner will be a more prominent and a more successful force in culture and politics.

Second, I aim to advance atheism in the sense of moving it in new directions, of making it more than it currently is. For much too long, atheism has trod the same ground over and over. I hate to say it, but atheists tend to write the same book again and again. Perhaps this has been necessary, and I would never suggest it has not been fun, in order to emphasize our position and bring it to the attention of each subsequent generation. However, we have done it already. We do not need to publish the proofs of the non-existence of god(s) again. We do not need to trash fundamentalism again. We do not need to belly-ache about how violent some or all religions are again. I call upon my fellow atheists to desist from writing yet another there-is-no-god or religion-is-so-bad text, unless they really have something original to add. What we need is new subjects and new ideas on those subjects. That is why, although I have included a chapter on 'religious violence' here, it is unlike the typical Religion-(especially Islam)-is-violent diatribe that excites us and sells copies but does not advance our understanding of religion or violence one single step.

Finally, I aim to advance atheism in the sense of moving *beyond* atheism as it is usually known. My second goal above initiates this process: if atheism becomes more than squabbling with Christians about the Christian god, it is already a different beast. Specifically, I see two ways in which I envision a 'new atheism,' an atheism that transcends the shackles with which it has allowed itself to be bound. One way involves putting atheism in a much wider context. As we suggested earlier, atheism has tended to be in practice a-Christianity, but that will not do. Atheism is the rejection of, dismissal of, or indifference to *all gods*, Christian and otherwise. At the same time, we often use the term *atheism* to mean opposition to all religion, but this is not quite right. As we will see in the first few chapters of this book, atheism cannot mean a-religion since most religions are already a-theistic in that they do not have god(s) either. Atheism strictly speaking only targets a certain 'level' of religion; one can easily imagine someone saying, "Oh, yes, I am an atheist, I only believe in nature spirits or ancestral spirits, *etc.*" Therefore, we need to perceive atheism as a good and valid position but one of limited scope. Atheism opposes theism, but something 'higher' must oppose all religions, theisms and non-theisms alike. And religions are themselves only a branch on the tree of irrational belief systems, so we must form and adopt something higher even than a-religion, something that criticizes all 'beliefs' that contradict evidence and reason. This is the destination of the final chapter of this book.

The other way that atheism can become more than it is — and has historically been — is to overcome its argumentative and propositional limitations. Atheism, in the conventional sense as a claim about the non-existence of god(s), is basically a matter of 'facts' — or a matter of a single fact, that there is no such thing as god(s). If we want it to be no more than this fact, then fine, but we will also have to accept its inevitably peripheral status. As I discussed in my previous book, and as I explore in more range and depth here, humans do not live by facts alone, and we need to begin the process of constructing an atheist worldview, an atheist culture, that is more than arguments and propositions. Part of this project will require dismantling and evicting religion from the reigning worldview and culture, where it has colonized and established itself as if it were not so much true as *natural and necessary*. To do this, we must understand the power of language, of action, and of the body itself. One of my central assertions in this book is that, in our eagerness to falsify the belief that god(s) exist(s), we have acquired the bad habit of over-emphasizing beliefs. Most of religion, indeed most of human life, has little to do with beliefs or with facts and everything to do with how people live their lives and shape their collective realities — talking, singing, eating, laughing, singing, telling stories, valuing, and above all *doing things,* acting in the world. A new atheism, a transcendent atheism, an atheism of the future—the kind of atheism that I want to live in and that will attract others—will have to find ways to incorporate these human activities, in order to incorporate humans into an atheist society.

These are the books we need to write. This is the message that we need to formulate and advance. This is the world that we need to create. This is the project to which I make my humble contribution.

Maxims and Reasons

In addition to being an effort and a plea to advance atheism, this book is also a tribute to the greatest atheist of the modern era and arguably the greatest atheist of all time, Wilhelm Friedrich Nietzsche [1844–1900]. The reader will encounter him and his thoughts throughout this work, and I am proud to admit that my own journey toward the recovery of my natural atheism began with the discovery of his writing.

Nietzsche's 1888 book *Twilight of the Idols*, subtitled *How to Philosophize with a Hammer*, opens with a section called "Maxims and Arrows" in which he offers a series of penetrating short, one- or two-sentence thoughts. Such terse literary jabs are known as aphorisms, from the Greek for 'to define' or 'to bound,' because they do precisely that—draw the boundary around and define a question or idea. Although he did not invent the device — Francis Bacon [1561–1626] used it in his *Novum Organum* in 1620 and Søren Kierkegaard [1813–55] occasionally employed it in the earlier 1800s — Nietzsche was a master of it. In fact, he seldom if ever wrote in sustained arguments, preferring a style of verbal strike and retreat that sometimes left his intention unclear but always made an impression on the reader. Many of his works, including *Beyond Good and Evil*, utilized the aphoristic style.

On occasion it is not possible to present a sustained case, and on some occasions it is not necessary. The goal of writing, as Nietzsche knew keenly, is often not so much to settle an issue as to raise a question, prod a complacency, or startle a familiarity. A quick and insightful thrust, a well-placed word, a concise and quotable summation is frequently a better stimulation for thought than a protracted and sometimes incomprehensible exposition. Nietzsche's aphorisms were not always 'true,' and they were often partial if not cryptic, but they acted like fireworks to momentarily shed light on complex notions in surprising ways.

As a tribute to Nietzsche, and because the aphoristic style allows the writer to succinctly express an idea that does not demand a protracted treatment or that cannot be treated as well any other way, I open this book with my own set of aphorisms. As Nietzsche himself would have approved, these are the *prelude* in the sense that they come 'before the song' that is the body of the book. They introduce the themes and set the motifs, as a musical overture would do. Readers may expect to meet these themes and motifs again as they advance through the text.

APHORISTIC PRÉLUDE

1

An atheist is not a person who knows too little about religion. An atheist is a person who knows too much about religion.

2

There is no such thing as religion — only religion-*s*.

3

There is no such thing as morality — only moralit-*ies*.

4

It has been said that if you don't believe in god(s)
you will believe in anything.
But the opposite is true.
If you will believe in a god, then you will believe in anything.
Belief is a habit that, once acquired, knows no limits.

5

You say your god is unknowable?
But the unknowable and the non-existent
are indistinguishable.

ATHEISM ADVANCED

6
A cult is a religion you disapprove of.
A religion is a cult that has gained acceptance.

7
A myth is somebody else's belief.
A belief is a myth taken seriously.

8
So many gods, so little reason.

9
The problem with religion in the public square is that
there are so many religions but only one public square.

10
If one has belief, knowledge is lacking.
If one has knowledge, belief is unnecessary.

11
The difference between science and religion:
When knowledge is inadequate,
science poses a question,
but religion proposes a belief.

12
The trouble with leaps of faith is that there are
so many directions to leap in—most of them wrong.

13
Groups are almost always irrational:
one reason why it is difficult to have atheist groups.

14
Order is not necessarily design.
Design is not necessarily good design.
Good design is not necessarily benevolent design.

15
If atheism is a religion, then bachelorhood is a marriage.

16
If atheism is a religion, then not collecting stamps is a hobby.

Introduction

17
The first reaction to human difference is usually conversion or
extermination. The second reaction is segregation.
Only the last reaction is toleration.

18
Religion is not so bad — unless you believe it.

19
If people say that atheism is a religion,
do they mean that as a compliment or an insult?

20
Most religions do not even have gods — they are a-theistic.

21
Science does not so much disprove god(s) as disregard god(s).

22
Tertullian said, "I believe because it is absurd."
Did he mean that
absurdity is a sufficient reason to believe something,
or that the only way to hold an absurd position is by belief?

23
The best argument against any religion
is all the other religions.

24
Faith is not different from belief,
nor is it the basis of belief.
It is the same thing as belief:
accepting the false or unfounded as true.

25
In the absence of evidence,
the scientist says, "I do not know,"
but the religionist says, "I believe."

26
Is a meaning only meaningful if it is universal?
Is a value only valuable if it is absolute?
Perhaps 'local' meaning or value is enough
— and must be, because that is all there is.

ATHEISM ADVANCED

27
'Spirit' is either a claim or a metaphor.
If a metaphor — not to be taken literally.
If a claim — not be taken seriously.

28
Great minds think alike.
Small minds believe all kinds of things.

29
America is not a Christian country; it is a free country.

30
If America is a Christian country
because it was founded by Christians,
is it also a white country because it was founded by whites?
A male country because it was founded by males?

31
The problem with organized religion
is not that it is organized but that it is religion.

32
One can ask, "How do you know?" and expect to get reasons.
One cannot ask, "How do you believe?" at all.
Belief *is* how you believe.

33
Spirituality is the alienation of humanity: the human
(and the best part of human) attributed to the non-human.

34
You cannot believe in a generic god or a generic religion
anymore than you can speak a generic language.
You can only speak a particular language
or believe in a particular god or religion.

35
Science not only produces knowledge but solves problems.
Religion neither produces knowledge nor solves problems.

36
Religion is not always wrong.
It just has no better chance of being correct than guessing.

37
Freethought is the only kind of thought there is.
If it is not free, it is not thought at all.

38
Tertullian again: If he believes because it is absurd,
how does he decide which absurdities to believe?
There are so many to choose from.

39
The question is not whether a thing is possible.
Many false things are possible.
The question is whether there is any reason
even to seriously consider the thing in the first place.
If not, its possibility means nothing.

40
One does not have to prove a negative.
One should *assume* a negative.

41
Some argue that it takes perfect knowledge
to prove a universal negative.
Actually, it takes perfect knowledge to prove a universal positive.
How would you know if a god knows everything or is everywhere
unless you yourself know everything or have been everywhere?

42
Theists sometimes say that their god is possible,
but no one goes to church to worship a possibility.

43
Every religion thinks it is true.
All religions cannot be true simultaneously,
but they can all be false simultaneously.

44
If power corrupts, and absolute power corrupts absolutely,
then wouldn't an all-powerful god be all-corrupt?

ATHEISM ADVANCED

45

The claim that "evolution cannot account for complexity"
is a universal negative — and religionists like to argue
that you cannot prove a universal negative.
So maybe evolution *can* account for complexity.

46

Religion is neither all good nor all bad.
It is all human
— and therefore diverse, ambiguous, and contradictory.

47

Old gods don't get disproved.
They get forgotten.

48

Since there are so many religions
and none of them can claim a majority of humanity,
whatever you believe,
you are in the minority.

49

If people are Christians because they use money with
"In God We Trust" on it, are they also Egyptians
because they use money with a pyramid on it?

50

Religion did not invent beauty or love or awe,
nor kindness, nor hope, nor generosity.
They are all human qualities,
and religion only appropriated them.

51

An extreme answer is usually simple, usually appealing
— and usually false.

52

Descartes should have said, "I think, therefore god isn't."

53

If the Christian god was a real human father,
he would be in jail for child abuse.

Introduction

54

War on Christmas?
Atheists are as interested in Christmas
as Christians are interested in Ramadan or Diwali or
Buddha's Tooth Day—which is not at all.
Atheists are not at war with Christmas;
they are indifferent to Christmas.
But to believers, indifference feels like war.

55

People argue over the religious beliefs of the "Founding Fathers."
But their religion is less important than their politics
— and their politics was to separate church from state.

56

If there is an Intelligent Designer, scientists only have to revise their
science books. If there is no Intelligent Designer, Christians have to
throw out their Christian book. Science could live with a Designer;
Christianity would die without one. That is why
Christianity fights so hard for what it claims is a scientific idea.

57

If there is no such thing as god(s), then theology is as futile and
meaningless as unicornology or leprechaunology.
You cannot study the non-existent.

58

If someone asks whether you believe in god
(or heaven or hell or soul or sin), do not say yes or no.
Say, "I don't know what you mean — and neither do you."

59

For those who would like to have prayer in school,
a few humble suggestions for prayers:
"There is no god but Allah, and Muhammad is his prophet."
Or "Hare Krishna, Hare Krishna, Krishna Krishna,
Hare Hare. Hare Rama, Hare Rama,
Rama Rama, Krishna Krishna."
Or "*Namo myoho renge kyo.*" Or "Om."
The moral: there is no such thing as a non-sectarian prayer.

60

Prayer is what you do when you can't do something useful.

ATHEISM ADVANCED

61
Kierkegaard once said that to believe, one must crucify the intellect.
Sadly, he was right. Even more sadly, he approved.

62
Jesus has been called a great teacher.
However, his own apostles often did not understand what he said,
few people today understand or follow his teachings, and many of his
teachings are absurd or would get you killed if you followed them.
That is the mark of a *failed* teacher.

63
"Let children acquire reason and critical thinking, then introduce
them to religion and let them choose for themselves."
What religion has ever said that?
They would not dare.

64
There are those who insist that atheism is negative, because it is
against theism. Atheism, they say, is not for anything, just against
something. If that were true, then anti-smoking campaigns are
negative, because they are against smoking. But anti-smoking
campaigns are not just against smoking; they are in favor of health.
True, if there were no smoking, there would be no anti-smoking
movement. But then everyone would be a non-smoker.
If there were no theism, there would be no atheist movement
— but then everyone would be an atheist.

65
The 'new atheism': 'Normal' theism operates on the god-paradigm,
but 'normal' atheism operates on the same paradigm,
only in the negative (arguing against gods).
The revolution in atheism, a truly new atheism,
will only come when we have a paradigm shift
—when we discard the god-paradigm
and stop speaking god-talk at all.

66
Religion is less about belief than it is about habit.
So atheism is not so much refuting a belief as breaking a habit.
And belief is a habit too—a habit of mind.

67
I do not disbelieve in god(s). I do not even disprove god(s).
I disregard god(s), dismiss god(s), discredit god(s).
I am disinterested in god(s).
Atheism is—or should be—freedom from god(s).

Chapter One

Atheism *versus* A Theism:
Rethinking the Religious Argument

The conventional debate over religion pits atheism against Christianity. The conventional debate is wrong. The problem with the common approach is that it gets both atheism and Christianity wrong. It over-extends and over-generalizes Christianity, and it simultaneously over-estimates and under-estimates atheism. In terms of Christianity, what I mean is that the debate effectively sees Christianity as the only religion in dispute, indeed as the *only religion*. It equates Christianity with theism and with religion itself. At the same time, it overlooks the tremendous diversity within Christianity. Christianity, as we will suggest shortly, is probably not 'a religion' at all but rather a category of religions that share a few core claims and beliefs (and a particular god and an allegedly historical figure bearing the title 'Christ'). The variation within Christianity is immense, from Roman Catholic to the numerous national Orthodox sects to the plethora of 'protestant' churches to new and 'non-denominational' sects including Mormonism, Seventh Day Adventism, and many even newer and odder groups. Some of these factions actively deny that others are Christian at all.

In terms of atheism, the standard debate similarly under-extends the position to appear to be mere opposition to Christianity; in effect, atheism becomes a-Christianity or anti-Christianity. That is understandable to a certain extent, since Christianity is the main theism or religion in the neighborhood of most Western atheists; it is the main religious force that we American atheists struggle against. However, the challenges for atheists in Saudi Arabia or India are quite different, and therefore the shape that atheism takes is quite different. At the same time, atheism commonly is understood as opposition to all religion—theism and otherwise—which is an admirable and probably correct position but not strictly the meaning or mission of atheism. Theism is a particular kind of religion, not religion itself, and therefore atheism strictly speaking is the rejection of a particular kind of religion, not of religion itself.

In this first chapter, I want to re-organize the debate by reorganizing the everyday notion of Christianity, theism, and religion. Readers who are reasonably familiar with the comparative study of religions will recognize this treatment, but many general readers may find it novel and unfamiliar. The goal I am trying to achieve here is to inform readers of the vast diversity of religions, to introduce them to the terminology and descriptions of these types of religion, and to situate Christianity far out on a limb of the tree of religions. The result will be to de-emphasize Christianity, to show that, even in the universe of religions — let alone in the universe of atheism — it is not the most important religion, surely not the only religion, and not the essence of religion. It is one theism among many theisms, and theism is one kind of religion among many kinds of religion. In the end (literally — in the final chapter of this book), I will return to place religion as one kind of belief among many kinds of belief — and suggest a broader approach to beliefs than atheism can or should represent.

Religions Without Gods

It has been observed that virtually all societies have religion. This is probably true, depending on how one defines religion; we will reserve that task until Chapter 3. However, in the sense of maintaining that there are non-human and super-human or super-natural forces at work in the world, this seems to be a human universal. Still, the forms that these beliefs can take are dizzyingly diverse.

Most modern citizens are familiar with one religion or at most a small handful of religions. All Americans know Christianity of course. Most know Judaism and Islam. Some know at least a bit about Hinduism and Buddhism. A few have some notion of Wicca or Satanism or perhaps 'New Age' religions (although not always a very accurate or positive notion of them). I am sure that most people, based on my experience of teaching college students about religions, assume that all religions include gods, even a single god. This is simply false.

Atheism versus A Theism

Most religions that have been identified and recorded by anthropologists, the social scientists who study cultural diversity, do not include gods, and those that do include gods usually do not include just one god. The belief in only one god (monotheism) is actually fairly rare, and it is also fairly recent. Furthermore, most religions that include gods do not include *only* gods. That is, even most — and I would argue *all* — religions that have gods also have other kinds of supernatural or spiritual entities as well. Christianity, which likes to fancy itself a strict monotheism, in reality contains an array of spiritual beings — angels, demons, saints, souls, and so on. Islam, which likes to fancy itself the most absolute monotheism, in reality contains, at least in some versions, angels and *jinns* and of course a Satan. Ultimately, there is no religion that contains only one supernatural being.

However, the vast majority of religions do not mention gods at all. Theism, then, is simply *not* the only or even the most common kind of religion, let alone the 'real' religion. Scientists who have investigated religion cross-culturally have developed a typology for this religious diversity, which we can visualize as follows.

Figure 1: Theistic and Non-theistic Religions

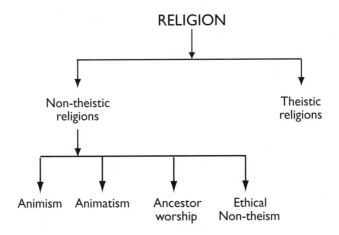

These are all ideal types, and it should be noted that (1) there are other real-world cases that defy simple categorization and that are in between these ideal types and (2) any or all of these types can co-exist.

Animism

By some accounts, animism is the oldest and most universal form of religion. Essentially everywhere observers have traveled, they have encountered some version of it. Derived from the Latin *anima* for 'soul,' 'breath,' or 'respiratory air,' it postulates that there is a non-material or 'spiritual' component to living things that makes them alive. Early anthropologists like E. B. Tylor (see Chapter 3) noted that there are certain basic questions that humans seek and tend to answer in certain ways. What is it that makes a living body different from a dead body? What makes some things move ('animated') while others are 'inanimate'? And what are those things that we experience in dreams and visions and other non-normal mental states?

The premise of animism is that some or all physical beings, objects, or phenomena have this non-physical dimension. 'Spirit' (from Latin *spiritus*, also meaning 'breath') may be attributed to animals (a word that also derives from *anima*), plants, rivers and mountains and other natural features, the sun and the moon, or phenomena like wind and rain, human-made objects, and even emotions or states of being like anger or love. The world can become a place teeming with spirits.

It would not be accurate to call these powers gods, since they often if not ordinarily do not have the qualities we associate with gods. They are not necessarily creators. They are not all-powerful, although they have specific and important powers. They are not particularly moral; it might be more precise to say that they are *interested* or have interests — some of which coincide with human interests and some of which do not. In fact, the most critical aspect of animism is that it reckons that non-human species and phenomena are much more like humans than may seem apparent. They have thoughts and feelings and wills and interests. They have personalities; they are persons.

The Warlpiri, an Australian Aboriginal society where I did anthropological fieldwork, possess a unique version of

Atheism versus A Theism

this animistic view. They believe that ancestral beings, who themselves were part-human and part-animal or part–plant, established the features of the world during their adventures in the beginning-time which they call *jukurrpa* or Dreaming. These ancestors, emerging from the earth (there is no explanation and no curiosity about how they originated — they were simply always there), traveled and lived and died on the land. Their actions, artifacts, and even bodies became trees, waterholes, riverbeds, mountain ranges, and such; each of those places is infused with supernatural, animistic power, which they call *pirlirrpa*. Members of the society would show me sacred places and say, "That tree (or waterhole or hill) is *jukurrpa*." They were not suggesting that all trees, or even all trees of that particular species, were spiritual but rather that this particular tree was. As the eminent anthropologist A. Irving Hallowell (1976) reported, he once asked a member of the Ojibwa (Native American) society if all rocks and trees were intelligent living beings, and the informant responded, "No, but some are."

Among the 'traditional' societies of humanity, this is a pervasive worldview. One of the most thorough-going cases was the Ainu of northern Japan. As described by Ohnuki-Tierney (1974), the Ainu believed that most beings or objects 'owned' a spirit aspect or soul. Humans certainly possessed an animistic element, but so did plants and animals as well as artifacts like tools and utensils. As would be sensible in a reality suffused with willful and powerful beings, the Ainu considered it critical to maintain proper relationships with the soul-owning beings. Hunting became, for instance, a semi-religious activity. A kind of social respect was due to the species that were hunted: they could not be killed in greater numbers than necessary, and correct rules and behaviors for hunting had to be observed. Hunters purified themselves spiritually before undertaking the task, and various taboos were followed, including the avoidance of certain words. A man who came in physical contact with an animal like a bear, especially if he was injured by it, became supernaturally associated with the animal for a time and had to be respected in the same manner. A final concern was the proper disposal of remains of soul-bearing beings. The bones of animals were placed in species-specific piles called *keyohiusi*, with a skull set on top of a ritual pole in the case of large animals. Even household objects like spears and pots and pans had their funeral piles since they too contained spirits, and rituals were practiced for the remains and their souls. Failure to treat the bodies of these spirits with respect or mistakes in the rites could result in illness, misfortune, or death.

In many religions, animistic spirits are attached not so much to species as to spaces. The Dani people of New Guinea believed in supernatural entities living in hills, rocks, ponds, and whirlpools (Heider 1979). The Anutans of the Solomon Islands spoke of spirits called *tupua penua*, some of which were associated with species like the shark, octopus, or sea turtle and others with natural features and places; according to Feinberg (1996), they had names, individual personalities, and power but were also amoral, egotistical, and dangerous.

In fact, wherever humans believed in animistic spirits, these entities were at least potentially dangerous. Since, as individuals, they have personalities, some were benevolent, some were malevolent, and others were merely capricious and indifferent. The world is a much more complicated and treacherous place with them in it: like all of our human social relationships, we must keep them in mind as we go about our lives. In an animistic worldview, humans cannot treat (at least certain) non-human beings and objects as sheer objects; we must treat them more like the persons that they are.

Animatism

Animism posits a personal kind of entity in the supernatural dimension — something that is not human but has many qualities in common with humans. Another religious form, though, refers to non-personal and even impersonal spiritual forces that exist in and perhaps pervade the universe. This belief has been dubbed *animatism*.

Animatistic forces are akin to spiritual electricity; they have a nature of their own, although not necessarily a personality. They follow their nature like water follows its nature, flowing downhill and along the path of least resistance. Many people are familiar with versions of animatistic forces, although they may not know them as such. The most familiar is the Chinese concept of *chi*. As depicted in classic texts like *Tao Te Ching* and *Chuang Tzu*, *chi* is an energy that permeates and occurs in all things. It is an animating force. Lao Tzu, the semi-mythical author of *Tao Te Ching*, literally likens the force to water, which flows along its own course, its *tao*, and accomplishes great things without any striving at all. Like a swimmer or boater, we do best to learn the currents and allow them to carry us; to struggle against the *tao* is to invite difficulty and dissension.

The *chi* in Chinese philosophy occurs in two states or modes, known as *yin* and *yang*. They are complementary and mutually necessary. Yin is the slower, darker, damper, more female mode; yang is the faster, brighter, drier, more male mode. All things contain some balance of the two, male humans more yang than yin, female humans more yin than yang. The sun is the most yang object, the moon the most yin. The proper balance of yin and yang leads to conceptions of health and diet, and the general notion of flowing energy takes shape in practices like martial arts and *feng shui*, the arrangement of living space in conformity with the currents flowing through that space.

Other manifestations of animatistic forces abound. The Polynesian concept of *mana* is one. In such cultures, people believed that *mana* is a finite energy that certain individuals understand, possess, or control and others do not. Those who have and know how to use it become successful, powerful, and great; those who do not have or know how to use it never achieve greatness. Chiefs, warriors, hunters, and of course religious specialists are the masters of *mana*, and the sign of one's diminishing or absent *mana* is defeat and failure.

Less well-known examples include the Dusun idea of 'luck,' the Apache concept of *diyi*, and the !Kung (pronounced *click*-Kung) bushman notion of *n/um*. The Dusun of Borneo (Williams 1965) considered luck to be a finite spiritual resource of each individual: if a person spends his or her luck in one area of life then it is unavailable in other areas (*e.g.*, acquisition of property, success in disputes, *etc.*). Also, luck was finite in society, making one person's gain another person's loss. This naturally led to arguments about surreptitious efforts to steal or damage each other's luck. The Apache power known as *diyi* came in infinite supply (Basso 1970). Individuals who possessed or controlled *diyi* were identifiably different from those who did not. Many forms of this power were recognized, related to different animals or natural phenomena. In a twist on the animatistic theme, *diyi did* have some personal attributes, including the ability to seek out people to attach to (individuals can also seek *diyi*) and to experience anger, which could of course be harmful to humans.

Among the !Kung bushmen of the Kalahari desert, religious healers used a power called *n/um*, which was a "substance that lies in the pit of the stomach of men and women...and becomes active during a healing dance. The !Kung believe that the movements of the dancers heat the *n/um* up and when it boils it rises up the spinal cord and explodes in the brain" (Lee 1984: 109). Almost every person possessed this energy, although not all could master it, and those who did became healers or shamans (*n/um kausi* meaning 'master/owner of *n/um*'). This was a transferable force, which senior shamans could inject into apprentices by snapping it from their fingers in invisible arrows.

If we expand the meaning of animatism somewhat, we can also include within it 'principles' that are not exactly energies or forces. An instance, then, would be the Hindu concept of *karma*. *Karma* is certainly not a being, nor is it quite an energy. It is more like a principle or a relationship, a kind of spiritual cause and effect.

A religion as old, large, and diverse as Hinduism embraces much diversity, but generally *karma* is a negative spiritual condition that is exacerbated by wrong-doing and neglect of ritual and social obligations (*i.e.*, whether there is such thing as 'good *karma*' is debatable). As individuals move through multiple lifetimes, their burden of *karma* ideally lightens as they obey rules and fulfill responsibilities. An improvement in one's karmic condition leads to a better rebirth until one achieves the highest human state — the Brahman caste, one of the 'twice-born' levels and spiritually purest — and after that, superhuman states and eventually escape from the cycle of rebirth altogether. Naturally, disobedience or irresponsibility causes spiritual impurity and social demotion, to lower castes, the outcaste or untouchable status, and on down to animals, plants, and lower forms of life.

Atheism versus A Theism

In certain traditions related to Hinduism, such as Jainism, *karma* is believed to be a near-physical substance, a literal rust or dirt on one's soul that weighs it down and drags it to lower spiritual and physical conditions.

Ancestor Worship

It only stands to reason that if non-human species and things have spiritual or non-material parts then humans would have such a part as well. Stretching this reasoning a little further, it is not hard to imagine that some cultures and religions might believe that the human spiritual/non-material part, freed from its physical body, might continue to linger near and interact with living humans. This idea is conventionally referred to as ancestor worship, although we should caution that not all societies that believe in the ongoing existence of dead ancestors necessarily worship them or even like them.

The key concept in any system of ancestral spirits is the surviving, non-mortal spirit of individual humans, known to Christians and other English speakers as the *soul*. In Christianity and English, the word 'soul' has a rather specific (but not *too* specific — nobody knows what it looks like or exactly how it interacts with the body) meaning. In the familiar tradition, a soul is eternal, immortal, non-material, *personal* (that is, it retains its personality or identity after death), and *unitary* (that is, it is a single 'piece'). These are not notions that are shared by all religions that speak of human spirits.

The Hindu correlate of soul is *atman* which is a personal bit of the total universal soul, the *brahman*. The spiritual goal in Hinduism is to break the *atman* out of the cycle of incarnation (birth into a flesh body) and reunify it with the *brahman*, creating a single *brahmatman*. At this final stage, the individual soul would not be an individual at all but rather a drop in the cosmic ocean. In at least some variations of Buddhism, the message is the same: the goal is *anatta*, 'no soul/self,' and the ultimate state of *nirvana* would not be a heavenly existence but a spiritual non-existence, a snuffing of the candle of the soul.

As should be expected by now, beliefs about souls and ancestors are yet more diverse. The Tausug of the Philippines believed that humans consist of four parts: the body, the mind, the 'liver' or emotion, and the soul. The soul in turn consists of four parts: the transcendent soul, which is all-good and always in the spiritual realm, even while you are alive; the life-soul, which is related to the blood and attached to the body but which wanders from the body in dreams; the breath, which is the essence of life and always attached to the body; and the spirit-soul, the person's 'shadow' (Kiefer 1972).

The Mandinko of Africa also talked of a four-part human nature, including the body, breath, intelligence (located in the heart), and the soul; both the intelligence and the soul continued on in the afterlife (Schaffer and Cooper 1980).

The Aymara believed that humans have three souls, named *animo, ajayu,* and *coraje* or courage (Buechler and Buechler 1971).

The Huron of North America talked of two souls or *atisken*, both of which were the same size and shape as the body; one remains with the body after death while the other leaves (Trigger 1969).

The Konyak Nagas of India are reported to have believed in several different soul-parts that separate at death. The *yaha* contains the individual's personality and goes off to the land of the dead, while the *mia* stays attached to the skull (which explains their practice of headhunting), and the *hiba* becomes a ghost if the person dies a violent death (Von Fuerer-Haimendorf 1969).

Finally, the Dusun of Borneo believed in seven soul-parts, one inside the other. The smallest was the width of the little finger and the largest the thickness of the thumb. They were not 'born' full-sized but grew as the body grew. The six 'outside souls' or *magalugulu* were visible in human form, but the innermost soul or *gadagada* was formless and invisible.

Along with these widely varying conceptions of human spiritual existence comes wide variety in the relations between the living and the dead. Many cultures revered and celebrated their dead, but most if not all also feared them to some extent. For instance, the Navajos said that all ancestral spirits that haunt the living are evil by definition, since the 'ghost' is the evil part of the deceased person (Downs 1972). The Dani of New Guinea too claimed that most ghosts were malevolent.

Atheism versus A Theism

The Burmese villagers studied by Spiro (1978) asserted that the spirits of their dead, called *leikpya*, were a potential source of trouble, especially former government officials who did not like giving up their power. As in many cultures, the spirits of those who lived wicked lives constituted a special class of evil ghosts, *tasei* or *thaye*. These evil ghosts resided at the edge of villages, especially near burial grounds, eating corpses or sometimes the living.

For the !Kung, the dead, known collectively as either the *//gauwasi* or *//gangwasi*, constituted a danger to humans not because they were malicious but because they were lonely; they would try to bring the living to the land of the dead to be with them, with undesirable results for the living (Katz 1982). Clearly we should not call any of these examples ancestor worship.

Ethical Non-theism

One remaining category of religious expression does not have a formal name but can be referred to with some accuracy as ethical non-theism. The best example is Buddhism, particularly in its original or Theravada ('way of the elders') form. According to tradition, the historical Buddha, Siddhartha Gautama, was a spiritual seeker looking for the path to enlightenment. Coming out of the Hindu tradition some 600 years before the Christian era, he tried many different disciplines and exercises. One such discipline was the asceticism and self-mortification of some of the more extreme teachers and gurus (see Chapter 5 on self-inflicted religious violence). He had previously rejected a life of ease and plenty. His enlightenment came when he realized that neither path led to wisdom and, even more, to the escape from suffering and rebirth. He subsequently advocated a middle path, neither self-mortification nor self-indulgence.

The Buddha is said to have taught that every person had to achieve enlightenment — become a *buddha* or enlightened one — on his or her own. Other people could not help you. Teachers, gurus, and previously enlightened ones who remained in the world to lead the way (*boddhisatvas* or those whose being is enlightenment) could not do it for you; they were not saviors but rather instructors and doctors. A doctor cannot take your medicine for you or heal your sickness with his body; he can only give you the information and techniques to help you heal. You must do the work yourself. Even the gods, if there are any, cannot do it for you. The Buddha said that he did not know if there were gods or not and that it was ultimately irrelevant. Even if there are gods, they are on their own individual salvation quests (although much further along) and cannot give salvation to others. They would be models at best, advanced teachers but not saviors. Even they cannot change the laws of *karma* or remove an individual human's karmic load.

Thus, Theravada Buddhism at least is a system based on specific supernatural or spiritual principles but not relying on gods in any real way. What this version of Buddhism requires of the individual is not belief and certainly not worship of the Buddha. Again, one does not get healthy by worshipping one's doctor but by following his or her strict regimen. So the Buddha offered not a belief for humans but a discipline and a code. This code, summarized in the Eight-fold Path, included correct thinking, action, and so on. These rules have been elaborated in Buddhist literature ever since, for the lay seeker as well as for the professional or full-time devotee or monk. Some of the strictures emphasized sexual chastity, nonviolence, and vegetarianism, and two of the central values were compassion and doing no harm (*ahimsa*).

The Theravada path is an austere road, one that few will walk successfully. It has been called, somewhat condescendingly, the *hinayana* or small vehicle since few will be saved by it. A later development known as Mahayana or 'great vehicle' promised to deliver more people by making the path seriously less demanding. In Mahayana traditions, one can be saved in a number of ways, including devotion to or worship of the Buddha or other supernatural figures (including various gods), giving gifts and alms to monks, subsidizing a temple or monastery, or sending a son to a monastery where he can 'make merit' for the whole family. What Gautama would think about these developments we can only imagine. Still, his original teachings and the early history of the Buddhist movement demonstrate that a complex and successful religion can exist without any specific claims about or even reference to gods at all.

Atheism versus A Theism

Theisms and Their Gods

Many or most religions have functioned quite well without any notions of god(s) at all, and others (as we will see later) have mixed god(s) with other beliefs such that god-beliefs are not the critical parts of the religion. However, more recently in history, gods have become increasingly common and central elements in religions, until today most modern people virtually equate religion with god(s). We know now that this is false, but even so, once gods enter and dominate the religious picture, religion is not the same as before.

We have one major and overlooked problem. What exactly is a god? There are many kinds of spirits that are not gods; gods are spirits, but not all spirits are gods. Again, to the mundane Western Christian mind a god is a particular thing or has particular characteristics. These usually include omnipotence (all-powerfulness), omniscience (all-knowingness), creativity, immortality, and morality (omnibenevolence or all-goodness). However, as we look around the world at gods, not all of them have all of these qualities. In other words, we cannot take one religion's notion of god(s) as *the* universal or absolute notion.

One set of authors has attempted to settle the distinction between gods and other types of spiritual beings. Levy, Mageo, and Howard (1996) suggest that spirits and gods stand at the opposite ends of "a continuum of culturally defined spiritual entities ranging from well-defined, socially encompassing beings at one pole, to socially marginal, fleeting presences at the other" (11). Apparently, gods are intended to be the former, spirits the latter.

The four variables along which gods and spirits differ are structure, personhood, experience, and morality. By *structure* they mean that gods are the focus of more detailed social institutions, including priesthoods, shrines, and festivals, as well as specific territories; spirits are not the subject of such elaboration, being more "fluid," "emergent, contingent, and unexpected" (14). By *personhood* they mean that gods are more physically and socially human, while spirits are "vague...only minimally persons" (15). By *experience* they mean that gods are actually more remote and less directly experienced, whereas spirits are more commonly encountered and often more immediately the objects of human concern. Finally, by *morality* they mean that gods are more likely agents and paragons of moral order than spirits, who tend to be "extramoral" or evil. Gods, they argue, "are clear models for social order" (21) who establish and sanction human morality, but spirits "are threats to order and frequently must be purged so that order may be re-established" (16).

Unfortunately, the cross-cultural evidence does not support this analysis. Some of the non-god spirits that we have already encountered are not vague at all but are quite well-defined, with names and known personality traits and histories. Some have complicated and important cults and rituals associated with or directed toward them. Some are evil and some are good.

As we look around the world of gods, we find just as much diversity and just as little continuity as in all other religious domains. Some religions that refer to or focus on gods believe them to be all-powerful, but others do not. Some consider them to be moral agents, and some do not; more than a few gods are downright immoral. Some think they are remote, while others think they are close (or both simultaneously). Some believe that the gods are immortal and eternal, but others include stories of gods dying and being born.

To begin, not all gods are creators, nor is creation a central feature or concern of all religions. The Kaguru of East Africa spoke of a god named *Mulungu* who was a universe creator, but the people did not know the story of this creation nor care very much about it (Beidelman 1971). The islanders of Ulithi in Micronesia made claims about several gods, none of whom were creators, and their religion contains no creation story at all (Lessa 1966).

Further, not all gods are moral agents or guarantors of human morality. The Konyak Nagas believed in a sky god called *Gawang* or *Zangbau* who is a highly personal being and is invoked in daily life and the main social occasions in culture; he is the protector of morality and punishes wrongdoing. On the other hand, the Azande of Africa had a god named *Mbori* or *Mboli*, who Evans-Pritchard (1962) tells us is morally neutral and not really interested in human affairs. The ancient Greek gods are renowned for their questionable ethics, involving themselves in seduction, rape, deception, and many other immoral actions.

Finally, there is not even always a firm boundary between humans and gods; humans can become gods, and gods may be former humans. The Tewa of the southwestern United States explained that there are six levels of humans with different spiritual destinies. When a person in the lowest tier of humans dies, he or she becomes the lowest tier of spirits; when members of the highest tier of humans die, they become and join spirits or gods of the highest tier. These gods are the remote, detached types of deities who are not discussed much or known in much detail. Commonly, leaders of ancient kingdoms and empires were deified at their death, and some — like the Egyptian pharaohs — were believed to be living gods. Julius Caesar was elevated to godhood after his death. Augustus and some of the succeeding Caesars were worshipped as gods during their life times, with temples being erected and priesthoods created.

Amidst all this diversity, some subtypes of god-belief or *theism* can be distinguished. The most fundamental distinction is between religions that include only one god and religions that include two or more gods. Of the two major subtypes, multiple-god belief or *polytheism* is by far the more frequent and ancient. Single-god belief or *monotheism* is comparatively recent (the first known historical experiment with it occurred under the Egyptian pharaoh Akhenaton and was quickly crushed by the polytheistic priesthood). Within each of these major divisions, though, are some interesting variations.

Polytheism

Theism in general is a minority version of religion (most religions have not been theisms at all), but within the minority, polytheism is historically and cross-culturally the most common. To rephrase, the vast majority of theisms have been polytheisms. Theisms tend to be associated (although not exclusively) with centralized societies and governments; people do not seem to develop the notion of a consolidation of high supernatural power until they experience a consolidation of high social and political power. And since most pre-modern societies and states were more or less loosely integrated, it stands to reason that most pre-modern theisms would be more or less loosely integrated, with multiple gods sharing power in some hierarchy or council of gods.

The most famous *pantheon* or gathering of gods in the Western world is the ancient Greek one. Gods (all of them second-generation or later, since even Zeus was the son of more primordial gods, and some of the Greek gods were his offspring) sat in an assembly that evinced both a local and a functional division of labor. Some gods had specific portfolios — Ares (Mars) was a god of war, Aphrodite a goddess of love, Poseidon a god of the sea, *etc.* — while others were associated with particular places or cities (Athena was the goddess of Athens). They might bicker and compete and betray each other, and they might interfere in the affairs of humans, not always for the better. The Norse pantheon resembles the Greek in many ways, with a father god Odin and then departmental gods like Thor, the god of thunder. The ancient Romans and Egyptians had their own pantheons, and Hinduism is a religion of literally thousands of local gods, often organized as manifestations or incarnations or avatars of three main gods — Brahma, Shiva, and Vishnu — who in turn are avatars of the one godhead.

Polytheism is not limited to ancient societies or imperial ones. The islanders of Ulithi practiced a polytheistic religion with a high god and many lesser and more specialized gods. The high god *Ialulep* is described as very large, old, and weak, with white hair, who holds the thread of life of each person and decides when a person will die by breaking the thread. Under him are numerous sky gods and earth gods, including his son *Lugeilang*, who likes the company of human women and gave birth to the trickster god *Iolofath*. The earth gods include ones with more or less specific natural and social jurisdictions, like *Palulap* the Great Navigator, *Ialulwe* the patron-god of sailors, *Solang* the patron-god of canoe-builders, and so on. Even the Ainu whom we met above believed in multiple deities or *kamuy* in several categories including gods of the shore, of the mountain, of the sea, and of the sky. Among the shore *kamuy* are God of the House, Grandmother Hearth, and God of Ground; among mountain *kamuy* are *iso kamuy* or bear god, *horokew kamuy* or wolf god, and *sumari kamuy* or fox god.

Atheism versus A Theism

Monotheism

Monotheism, the belief in only one god, is the rarest and, in most cases, the most recent of all theisms and of all religions. This is not to say that no traditional societies ever developed monotheisms; the Azande above appear to hold a monotheistic position. However, we see monotheism coalesce and expand mostly in the last few thousand years, not only in a comparatively few locations but in a comparatively few religions. These are the religions that we tend to know best and that have tended to spread the farthest, raising the issue of the competitive advantage of monotheism over other types of religions (to which we will return in a later chapter).

Then, since monotheism is a later evolution of religion, we note two things. First, monotheism in most cases evolved from and in a context of multiple gods and multiple non-god spirits and had to dissociate itself from them. We see traces of this process in the most ancient literature that monotheism can offer, such as the Hebrew Torah and related writings, also known by Christians as the Old Testament. There it is quite clear that the god Yahweh or YHWH was one of many gods known by the writers. When Yahweh refers to himself as *elohim*, he is speaking in the plural, since this Hebrew word means 'gods,' not 'god.'

In Genesis 3:22, Yahweh says that humans after the Fall have "become as one of us," speaking about (and to) other gods. Repeatedly through the early books of the scripture, there is no assertion that Yahweh is the *only* god but rather that he is the only god *for the Hebrew people*. This is why they are told to avoid other gods, not to worship or sacrifice to other gods, and to prevent their children from marrying into families that worship other gods. Why make such rules unless there really are other gods?

This position, which is probably ordinary in most monotheisms, is called *henotheism* or *monolatry*. The idea is that we as a group or a society are only to worship one god, however other gods there may be. It is not a categorical denial that there are other gods. Other peoples, other gods. The Athenians did not deny that other Greek gods existed; they simply focused their attention on Athena. The Azande theoretically would not say that *Mbori* is the only god in the universe but that he is *their* god, and other people may and probably do have theirs. Such gods are 'local' in the physical and social sense. They relate to particular places and particular human groups. Your god does not negate our god nor *vice-versa*. Such local monotheisms are potentially and actually more or less tolerant of other religions and gods, since those others have little to do with it: one god here, a different god there.

Monotheism can take other, even more interesting shapes. For instance, it can solve the morality problem or what is called *theodicy* — the problem of evil in the world given an all-powerful and all-good god — by taking the position of deism. Deism, the preferred view of many of the founding fathers of the American republic, posits a god who is relatively impersonal; it has been compared to a clockmaker god who is only necessary to set the universe into motion. It is not a moral agent, let alone a moral arbiter. In that sense, Azande monotheism appears to be a form of deism; *Mbori* does not punish or reward humans, presumably does not perform miracles, and generally remains detached from human affairs. Clearly such a god would appeal to the kind of people who take a more technical approach to the world, who are skeptical about miracles and who see morality as a human matter, not a divine one.

Some monotheisms take the position, or are compelled to the position, that the god and the world are radically different things. The god stands apart from the world, *transcends* the world, even opposes the world. Others, however, take an unlike stance, asserting that the god and the world — the creator and his/her creation — are one and the same thing. This attitude is known as pantheism (*pan* from Greek 'all' or 'inclusive'). This view, most famously held by Spinoza, maintains that the universe *is* 'God,' and that that god is the sum total of all existence. It is not entirely clear what this adds to the understanding of the universe or of the god, and it has been condemned as heresy by the more absolutist monotheistic traditions where it has sprung up.

This brings us to the main monotheistic traditions. Monotheism, as we have seen, is rare and recent. It can emerge potentially in any time and place, but it is most prominent in the last two millennia or so and in certain geographic locations. It may even be that most monotheisms really are not monotheistic at all: often they speak of one *god* but allow for or crucially include a counterpart who is not a god in name only. Zoroastrianism purported to be a radical monotheism, but the god Ahura Mazda was opposed by an equally powerful and essentially god-like evil figure in Angra Mainyu. Christianity and Islam both call themselves monotheisms, but both refer to and depend on a character who is virtually as powerful as the god—a Satan or devil—and who is actually probably *more* dominant in contemporary human life, from their perspective. In other words, most monotheisms are still dualisms in the end, with two more or less evenly-matched supernatural beings locked in combat. Perhaps only ancient Judaism was a true monotheism in the sense we are using here, where the one god, as Isaiah 45:7 said, forms the light and the darkness and makes peace and evil.

At any rate, except for the occasional traditional monotheism as among the Azande (and the occasional new monotheism, as in Sikhism, which tends to be inspired by one or more of the old monotheisms), this particular religious variation is best represented in the Middle Eastern tradition that gave the world the three 'Abrahamic' religions—Judaism, Christianity, and Islam. Each claims to be a monotheism, in fact the *same* monotheism, only a truer version than the others. Each bases itself on a single god known by various names — Yahweh, Adonai, God, Allah — and tells similar stories and establishes similar rules and regulations.

Each, of course, considers the others to be something between corrupt and false. Islam, for instance, regards the Christian notions of the Trinity and the divinity of Jesus to be wrong at best and blasphemous at worst. God is one, the Qur'an proclaims; there is none like him, and he neither begets nor is begotten (Sura 112).

Each, as not only a monotheism but a totalistic monotheism — which says that it not only worships one god but insists that there only *is* one god and that its claims about that god are true — is inherently absolutist and intolerant. If there is only one god, all other god-beliefs are false, and if there is only one correct path to this god, all other paths are futile or worse.

ATHEISM ADVANCED

Religious Hybrids and Schisms

One thing is patently clear: *religion* is not the same thing as *theism*. Theism is one type of religion, a branch of a religion. Any particular theism is a branch of a branch. However, as we said before, religion does not exist in perfect exclusive types. First, the various types can mix and blend and co-exist. Second, within the various types there are subtypes and sub-subtypes. In other words, one seldom sees—if there even is such a thing—a pure theism, and any theism is not a single homogeneous thing but rather an assortment of more or less related sects that share a small core of central beliefs.

Hybrids

As complex as the religious picture appears so far, it is actually much more complex in reality. This is because any actual practiced religion tends to be a hybrid of various *types* of religion, as well as a hybrid of various religions and even non-religions. It might be more accurate to say that these types of religion are bits or building blocks out of which an actual religion can be constructed, rather than being closed, mutually exclusive religions. The building blocks of religion can be combined in various ways, and they can be combined with bits from sources other than religion as well.

Thus, there are two kinds of religious hybridization. The first encompasses the schema that we have already developed. We seldom if ever see a pure theism or a pure animism, *etc.* The two supertypes (nontheism and theism) along with their specific types (animism, animatism, ancestor worship, ethical nontheism, polytheism, and monotheism) can be combined in any and all possible arrangements.

For instance, we just saw above that Ainu religion includes both animistic spirits and multiple gods. Hinduism obviously comprises multiple gods along with an impersonal supernatural principle (*karma*). The Tallensi of Africa believe in an animatistic force like 'destiny' which is mixed with and partly controlled by ancestor spirits (Fortes 1959). The !Kung may represent the most complete amalgamation of religious materials: their religion contains natural spirits, dead ancestors, a supernatural force, and some gods. Their main focus is the ancestral *//gangwasi* or *//gauwasi*, and they employ the force of *n/um* in their healing rituals (often to combat the effects of the ancestors). They also believe in two main gods, the great god *Gao Na* and the lesser god *Kauha*. Each has a wife and children and lives in the sky. The great *Gao Na* has the form of a human and brings both good and bad to humans, via the dead ancestors and other intermediary spirits. Gods, forces, ancestors, and other spirits all inter-operate in a vast religious system that we could not properly call animism *or* animatism *or* ancestor worship *or* theism. It is all of those at once.

Religions hybridize in another way as well. They may internalize part or all of other religions, or they may borrow and integrate elements from non-religious sources. The 'world religions' are clear examples of the former, since they tend to spread and diffuse more widely than other kinds (which is why they are world religions). Religions like Hinduism or Buddhism or Christianity or Islam have spread so far and commingled with so many previous and subsequent religious systems that each is noticeably different in different parts of the world and it is almost pointless to attempt to describe the 'real' version of each. Each religion has its own unique set of claims about spiritual matters; however, when it penetrates a new territory, it encounters other beliefs already in place.

Melford Spiro's study of Buddhism in Burma makes the point well. The Burmese villagers merged Buddhist ideas with indigenous ones to produce a unique local version of Buddhism. Not only did they believe in Buddhist 'deities' (a non-traditional aspect of Buddhism) called *devas* but many other beings as well. *Devas* were inherently good and benevolent beings. The higher *devas*, called *byahma devas*, played little or no role in belief and ritual; the lower ones, *thamma devas*, were the focus of attention. Some of them were gods in the Western sense, with supernatural powers and infinite (or at least indefinite) existence. Others were former particularly pious humans, constituting a bridge between gods and humans via ancestors.

They also believed in more animistic spirits called *nats*, some of whom were associated with specific objects or locations, such as "trees, waterfalls, hills, paddy fields, and so forth" (Spiro 1978: 42). Each lived in and guarded its place, leading to names like *taw-saun* and *taung-saun* for 'guardian of the forest' or 'guardian of the hill.' Prominent among the *nats* were the so-called 37 chief *nats* (*thounze khunna min nat*) that were responsible for much of the evil in their world. Each had a known name and story, and they tended to be spirits of humans who died under violent circumstances.

As if these are not enough, our Burmese Buddhists also believed in demons like *tasei* and ogres or *bilus* that attack and eat the living. The *tasei* in particular stood on the margins of Buddhist and non-Buddhist belief, as former living beings who had committed evil in life and been reborn in a non-material condition until they worked off their *karma*. Finally, human agents of evil, *soun* or what we might call witches, were a source of sickness and death. Most were believed to be women, although the master witches were all men, and they could work their malice through evil spirits by apprenticing themselves to a spirit or manipulating the spirit with gifts of food. The Buddha would probably not have recognized or approved of most of these additions to his teachings.

All around the modern religious world we observe the same phenomenon. In areas that are ostensibly Christian or Muslim, *etc.* we see remnants or admixtures of prior religions. The Tausug of the Philippines were Muslims, but Muhammad would not have liked what he would see there. The people observed the Five Pillars of Islam concerning prayer and alms-giving and pilgrimage, and they listened to Muslim teachers and followed a Muslim ceremonial calendar. The monotheistic god *Tunan* was their "ultimate religious concern" (Kiefer 1972: 112). However, they had numerous lesser concerns, including evil spirits called *saytan* and others called *jin*. The *saytan* were classic animistic spirits, attached to fearsome animals or anomalous places or things. Some of them were known by name, and all of them were responsible for human misfortune and death. A particularly feared one was the *barbalan*, which flies and eats the livers of corpses. The *jin* were more closely associated with Islam; in fact, there were two classes of *jin*, those who obey Islam and those who do not.

As we noted above, the Tausug also believe in a force like fate or luck. Actually, this force or principle took two forms, 'theological fate' or *kadal* and 'empirical fate' or *sukud*. *Kadal* was the god-predetermined life and death of the individual. *Sukud* was more like luck (good and bad), the reason behind particular events and phenomena. *Kadal* was attached to the person's soul, but *sukud* was a matter of the body.

We could multiply examples indefinitely. This process is eminently clear in the history and development of Christianity, where it has mixed with and absorbed local traditions, sometimes incidentally and sometimes intentionally. Many aspects of Western and American Christianity have little or nothing to do with 'traditional' or 'primitive' or scriptural Christianity. There is no basis for a Christmas celebration and certainly no authority for December 25 as the birthday of Jesus. Christmas trees and Easter eggs are appropriations from non-Christian traditions (even the name *Easter* refers to a Germanic pagan goddess of spring), and some of the more purist groups — like the Massachusetts Puritans — were actively opposed to such jocularity and paganism.

In other parts of the world, not only have European/pagan influences been passed along (people in Africa and Asia know about Christmas trees and Santa Claus), but local traditions, concepts, and practices get embedded as well. The final product is a unique, and sometimes unrecognizable, 'local Christianity' — like the local Tausug Islam or Burmese Buddhism — that is no more, but also no less, authentic than any other.

Of course, religious processes are not limited to religious resources alone. Religious formation and hybridization can and does pick up any material in its environment. The deism that we mentioned above, at least in the early modern Western case, was largely influenced by the new reigning mechanical model of the universe. If the cosmos is a machine, all that it needs is a machinist to construct it and start it, and it can operate from there on its own principles. In more recent times, we see religions soaking up any kind of influence, from technology to psychology to UFO-logy. Many of the new religious movements that we observe have this nature: from Scientology to Heaven's Gate to Raelianism, religion seems to have the capacity to ingest and integrate virtually any kind of idea or practice.

ATHEISM ADVANCED

Schism

If there is a religious process that is equal to or maybe greater than hybridization, it is schism. Religions, claiming to offer the truth, differ widely on what that truth is. Within each type or named variety of religion, then, there is some — often much — diversity of opinion and practice. In fact, all that unifies any particular religion or cluster of religions is a (potentially quite small) set of core claims or concepts.

Obviously, within animism or animatism or ancestor worship, *etc.*, there is a stunning array of diversity. Our interests turn more to the right side of our chart, however. Within theism there are two major branches, polytheism and monotheism, with some sub-variations. Each of these demonstrates enormous diversity: Greek polytheism, while identifiable as part of the family, is quite distinct from Hindu polytheism in its specific gods and its general operating principles. Likewise, the various monotheisms, while conceptually — and in the case of Judaism/Christianity/Islam, historically — similar, are distinct as well. Within each of these sub-types of monotheism, we find further diversity and disagreement. Judaism has settled into a number of approaches, from Reform to Orthodox to Hasidic. Islam has two major divisions, Sunni and Shi'ite, with any number of specific schools of thought, leaderships, and agendas. But let us follow the Christian line with more attention.

Christianity can and must be resolved into at least three major sub-lines based on doctrinal, organizational, and historical premises. These are the Catholic, Orthodox, and Protestant lines. Catholicism (deriving its name from the adjective *catholic* simply meaning whole or universal) was the first sustained Christian church to emerge from the new message of the Gospels and the first to achieve political power and stability by the early 300s CE. Questions and controversies of authority, doctrine, and practice divided this allegedly universal institution and religion. Was its god one or three? Was Jesus the 'same substance' as 'the Father' or not? Were the other bishops, especially the eastern ones in Constantinople, Athens, and elsewhere equal to the Roman one? Should baptism be done in infancy or adulthood? Should icons and images be used in worship or not?

Atheism versus A Theism

The Church has fought against dissension (that is, dissension from *its* authority and doctrine and practices) from its first days, but the first great and permanent schism in Christianity occurred in 1054, when the disagreements between Rome and eastern leaders became too great. Roman and eastern bishops excommunicated each other, opening the way for Eastern Orthodox Christianity to develop separately. In Roman Catholicism the bishop of Rome (the Pope) was the head of an international religious institution; in Eastern Orthodoxy, each bishop or patriarch was accorded equal status, leading to a national organization of Christianity, with a Russian Orthodox church, a Greek Orthodox church, and so on. It was only 600 years later, in 1963, that Eastern Orthodox churches formally opened relations with Rome.

Meanwhile, other dissensions were dividing the Western/ Catholic family. The Unitarian heresy continued to pop up periodically, denying the Trinitarian doctrine of the official church. Disputes about the timing of baptism could not be settled: the Catholic church insisted that baptism was a ritual for infants, while others—re-baptizers or 'ana-baptists' or simply *Baptists* — demanded that only adult baptism had any meaning, since only adults could choose to accept the religion.

Various heresies sprouted, most squashed by the official church and its 'inquisition' into heresy, which were collectively known as *protests* and their advocates as *Protestants*. Many would-be Protestant leaders were banished or killed, until one finally managed to make his protest stick. Martin Luther, a Catholic monk and teacher, was deeply concerned about the doctrine and the purity of his church, and in 1517 he published his seminal *Ninety-five Theses* criticizing church practices. He did not intend to found a new church but merely to restore the existing church to correct belief and ritual. Rejected by Catholic officials, his movement eventually evolved into a distinct institution, the Lutheran church, rejecting the authority of the Catholic Church and replacing it with the sole authority of scripture. He denied the doctrine of transubstantiation in which the wine and wafer literally transform into Jesus' blood and flesh, and he disputed the possibility of any effort or work of humans (even the Pope) to achieve salvation. Only God's 'grace' could ever redeem a creature as flawed as humanity.

The specifics of Lutheranism are not the point here. The point is that Christianity was irrevocably split by the early 1500s into three major divisions. Under the Catholic division was a fairly unified, hierarchical institution, although local bishops (from the United States to Africa) did not always agree with the men at the top (not to mention the laity, who often did not agree with either). Eastern Orthodoxy was never so unified nor aimed to be; 'Eastern Orthodoxy' is not actually a religion but a category of religions, including the various eastern national churches, with diverging leadership, organization, and doctrine and practice. If this is so for Orthodoxy, it is doubly so for Protestantism. Protestantism is not a religion but a tremendous assortment of religions. At first one (Lutheranism), then two (Lutheranism and Calvinism), the category grew over time as new schisms within the original schism appeared. Methodism, Baptism, Quakerism, Shakerism, Unitarianism, and too many others to name eventually emerged. Many of these sub-subtypes of Christianity further divided into local or doctrinal splits, giving us the Southern Baptists or the Evangelical Lutherans, *ad infinitum*. In recent years and decades, new protestant sects and denominations have continued to be invented, from Mormonism and Seventh Day Adventism in the mid-1800s to Christian Science to contemporary Pentecostalism and the 'non-denominational' movement (which is of course a denomination of Christianity — certainly not of Islam or Hinduism!).

Atheism, Theisms, and Religions

In view of this investigation, we need to revise and extend our chart of religions. The tree of religions does not cease to branch at the bifurcation of mono-/polytheism nor of Christianity and the other theisms nor even of the major schools or variations of Christianity. It continues right down to the sects or denominations of the major schools — perhaps on down to sub-sects and local variants of those sects and denominations.

Figure 2. Religion, Sub-Religions, Denominations, and Sects

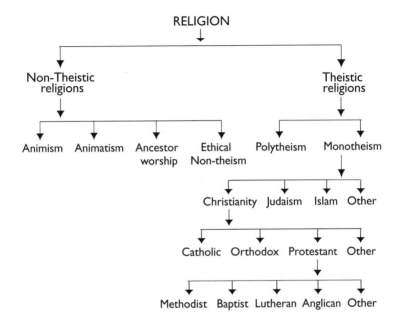

The result of all of this analysis brings us to two significant conclusions.

First, religion is much more diverse than most people conceive. 'Religion' does not equal 'theism' and certainly not 'Christianity,' let alone any particular sect of Christianity. Indeed, there is no specific religion or type of religion that is *really* religion, the very essence or nature of religion. Religion exists in its diversity, not in any central or essential or true variation or expression. Theism is no more religious than non-theism.

Not only that, there is no central or essential or uniquely authentic theism but rather an array of theism*s*. Monotheism is not more theistic than polytheism. Going further, there is no central or essential monotheism: Christianity is not more monotheistic (and of course not more religious) than Judaism or Islam. And there is no central or essential Christianity:

ATHEISM ADVANCED

'Christianity' consists of a collection of Christianities including Catholic, Orthodox, and Protestant. And there is no central or essential Protestantism: it is a type of Christianity/monotheism/theism/religion with many branches. No one Protestant sect is more Protestant or more religious than any other. No one is more authentically Christian than any other — or than any other denomination of Catholic or Orthodox Christianity. In fact, there is no 'real' Christianity at all, only a range of Christianities.

Second, because Christianity (and all other monotheisms) and monotheism and religion itself is a complex hierarchy (and combination) of religious types, no one can claim — or attribute to anybody else — 'religion itself' or 'religion in general.' One cannot believe or follow 'generic religion,' any more than one can believe or follow 'generic theism.' But to pursue this reasoning, one cannot believe or follow 'generic Christianity' or 'generic Protestantism.' At best one can believe or follow a particular sect, like Baptism, or perhaps only a particular subsect, like Southern Baptism. (It might be possible — and valuable — to chase this particularity all the way down to the particular congregation and individual member; religion is *that* diverse.) In other words, whatever religion you believe and follow, you are way down at the bottom and far out on a branch of the tree of religions. So people who talk about Christianity as if it is one consistent, monolithic thing are wrong; how much more so those who talk about — and claim for themselves — monotheism or theism or religion itself?

Religion, theism, monotheism — even Christianity — may not really exist in the sense of being particular things. Rather, they may all be generalities, categories, classes and kinds. As an analogy, think of the Linnaean classification or taxonomy of living species. At the highest or Kingdom level (in the old system: there have been some refinements and some major rethinking of the traditional system) is the animal kingdom — Animalia — along with several others. Below and within the animal kingdom are the phyla, among which we find Chordata, or animals with a notochord. Below and within each phylum are various classes, of which Mammalia is one. Below and within each class are various orders, of which Primates is one. Below and within each order are various families, of which Hominidae is one. Below and within each family is the genus, of which there are several genera including *Homo*, and each genus exists as one or more species — which is where the 'real' individuals exist. Now, these species are grouped together based on common characteristics into genera, and the genera are grouped together based on common characteristics into families, *etc.* The smaller and lower the category, the more the actual beings in them have in common, but even at the kingdom level, the beings have *some* things in common.

If we were to look at a cat and say that it is an animal, that would be true but not very informative. And it would only be true in a certain sense: when we say, "A cat is an animal," what we mean is "A cat is a member of the animal kingdom category" or "A cat has animal characteristics." But *animal* is not a thing to be; it is a *type* or *class* of thing to be. Only a 'cat' is a thing to be, a real kind of existent. On this logic, to say that "Christianity is a religion" is really to say that "Christianity is a member of the religion kingdom category" or "Christianity has religious characteristics." Just as *cat* is not equivalent to *animal*, *Christianity* is not equivalent to *religion*. I would consider going still further, and I do not see how the logic can prevent it: Christianity is not a thing, not a religion either, but rather a category of religions. If *religion* is the kingdom, then *theism* would be one phylum under it, *monotheism* would be one class under that, and *Christianity* would be one order under that. If this is valid, then Christianity is not a species or particular religion at all. Roman Catholicism, Russian Orthodox, or Southern Baptist would be particular religions, which we could group together in higher and higher categories based on (more and more diminishing) similarities. But there would be no such thing as generic Christianity any more than there would be a generic mammal.

Where does this leave atheism? What level of religious phenomena does it apply to? It is critical to understand immediately that atheism is not an alternative to or refutation of all religion. In fact, as we can clearly see from the diagram and clearly comprehend from the discussion above, 'atheism' and 'religion' are not opposites. A religion can be a-theistic in the sense of containing or making claims about no gods at all and still be a *bona fide* religion; it appears, to be honest,

ATHEISM ADVANCED

that *most* religions have been a-theisms. They do not *deny* the existence of gods — they are not religious denial-systems — they simply make no reference to gods. They are 'without gods.' Even more so, it is entirely possible and actually entirely consistent that an a-theist might believe in all kinds of other non-god supernatural beings. An animist who believes in interactive nature spirits is, in every real sense, an atheist. An animatist who believes in important supernatural forces and organizes his or her life in accordance with them is, in every real sense, an atheist. Theravada Buddhists, with an elaborate, organized, and literate religious tradition, are in every real sense atheists. So, in any meaningful way of thinking, atheism is not a-religion or anti-religion. Most religions *are* atheisms.

I assume — and hope — that this is not what most atheists mean when they ascribe the term to themselves (although I know that atheism does not necessarily inoculate one against other, non-religious irrationalities). In the debate mentioned at the start of this chapter, most American atheists — and most American non-atheists — understand or act as if they understand that atheism means non-Christianity or anti-Christianity. But if 'Atheism equals non-religion' is too broad, 'Atheism equals non-Christianity' is too narrow. Christianity is merely one kind of theism, not theism itself. One could be a non-Christian and still be a theist; most theists in the world *are* non-Christians. They are Jews or Muslims or Hindus, *etc.* Of course, it is true that most theisms have used the term 'atheist' at some point not as an analytical term but as a term of opprobrium: Christians have called Muslims atheists and *vice-versa*, on the assumption that, if you do not believe in the right god, you do not believe in any god at all, since only the right god exists. We cannot and will not play that game: for us, anyone who professes a belief in god(s) is a theist. So only a person who professes no belief in god(s) would be an atheist.

In this case, then, 'atheism' relates to an intermediate position in the hierarchy of religions. It does not apply to the highest level — as a-religion — since many religions are atheisms. Nor does it apply to the lowest levels — as a-monotheism or a-Christianity or a-Protestantism, *etc.*—since if it opposed merely one of those categories it would leave other theist categories unopposed: one could be, again, an a-Christian and be a Muslim or Hindu, theists all. Therefore, *atheism* applies at one and only one level of analysis, the level of theisms or theistic religions. It would then represent an alternative or refutation at that point in the hierarchy, as follows:

Figure 3 Atheism in Relation to Religions

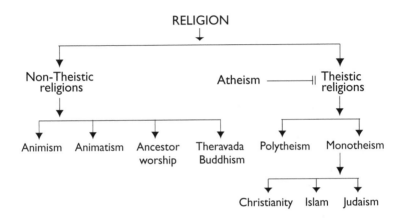

Any other claim about atheism would be a tactical and/ or intellectual error. If we convey that atheism is only about Christianity or only anti-Christian, we misrepresent atheism and risk being seen as hostile to one religion more than others. If we convey that atheism is about all religion or a-religious or anti-religious, we misrepresent most religions. Perhaps as bad, we end up playing on theism's and Christianity's field and speaking their language: it is theisms like Christianity that deny that non-theisms are religions in the first place. The only thing that counts as religion for theists is theism. But they are wrong, and we cannot follow them in their error.

So atheism is a rejection of god(s) — all gods, no matter how many are believed in or what their specific nature is alleged to be. That is all the term can usefully mean. But is that all that atheists want to assert? I certainly hope not. If atheism is arrived at by the correct process — that is, by reason — then this process rejects not only the existence of god(s) but of other and all unsubstantiated and irrational claims. All religions make such claims; in fact, that is what distinguishes religion from other systems of human thought. It would be my hope and aspiration that rational atheists extend their rejection of belief to all speculative and evidence-deprived supernatural claims. But for that we would need a term different from and bigger than 'atheism.'

Finally, does the positing of unsubstantiated, empirically inadequate and unjustified, and irrational claims distinguish religion from all other human thought systems? Actually, it does not. One could rid oneself completely of religious or supernatural beliefs and still hold irrational beliefs — and many do. Beliefs in UFOs, Big Foot, unicorns, beings from higher dimensions, and various 'alternative cures' do not necessarily entail any religious element at all but are every bit as unsubstantiated and irrational as any religion. This is not to say that they are categorically false; as I wrote in my previous book, someone can stumble across a truth accidentally. However, it is my hope and my aspiration that atheists, and all people of rational mind, would resist such beliefs until those beliefs are supported by some irresistible evidence. That, however, is a much bigger project than atheism can or should undertake — and it is where we will arrive in our final chapter.

Chapter 2

Speaking Christian:
Atheism and the Language of Religion

Imagine that an Australian Aboriginal from the Warlpiri tribe comes to the United States to study American religion. He walks up to typical Christians, or to Christian specialists like priests and ministers, and inquires about their religion. The questions he poses include "What is your belief about *jukurrpa?*" or "How does *pirlirrpa* work in your religion?" or "Tell me about your conception of *kuruwarri.*" How would Christians respond? They would certainly not offer an exposition on *jukurrpa, pirlirrpa,* and *kuruwarri.* They would probably not even insist that they disbelieve in these things. Presumably they would say, "I don't have any belief about *jukurrpa, etc.* In fact, I have never heard of them. I have no idea what they mean."

Imagine now that a Christian goes to Australia to study Warlpiri religion. He walks up to typical Warlpiri, or to Warlpiri specialists like shamans, and inquires about their religion. The questions he poses include "What is your belief about God?" or "How does sin work in your religion?" or "Tell me about your conception of soul." The Warlpiri would certainly not offer an exposition on God, sin, and soul. They would probably not even insist that they disbelieve in these things. Presumably — and actually, as I can assure you — they would say, "I don't have any belief about God, *etc.* In fact, I have never heard of them. I have no idea what they mean."

Is there a god? Does the soul exist? Is heaven a real place? These are the kinds of questions that atheists ask just as surely as Christians do; the only difference is that we ordinarily answer them in the negative. But why — or how — do we answer them at all? Why are atheists and Christians in the United States arguing about 'God' and soul and heaven and sin instead of *jukurrpa* and *pirlirrpa* and *kuruwarri*? Or for that matter, why not about Hindu concepts like *karma* and *samsara* and *moksha*? And why are we trying to settle the debate rather than simply stating, "I have never heard of them. I have no idea what they mean." Or declaring, "They mean nothing at all."

In the first chapter, we discovered how incredibly diverse religion really is, as well as what a minority the Christian religion(s) is/are within this sea of diversity. Accordingly, it is incumbent upon us not to take Christianity more seriously than any other religion. There are understandable practical reasons why we do: it is the dominant religion in our particular context, and it is the one with which we are most familiar. But familiarity is not a strong reason for taking any religion seriously: after all, Athena and Zeus and Apollo were familiar to the ancient Greeks, but we do not worry about trying to prove or disprove their existence today. Nor do we argue about the truth or falseness of *n/um* or *diyi* or *tupua* or *gadagada* or any of the other notions that we encountered in the previous chapter.

Admittedly, we atheists actually have heard of Christian beliefs like God and soul and sin — but then the Greeks had heard of Athena and Zeus and Apollo. This does not entail, however, that we atheists know what they mean. Christians themselves seem to be unclear as to what their words mean. A recent cover story about heaven in *Newsweek* illustrated this point. The article claimed that 76% of Americans believe in heaven but have no consensus on what it is. Some 71% of heaven-believers think that it is an actual place, leaving 29% who do not (Miller 2002:47). Many heaven-is-a-place believers imagine it as a garden, others as a city (with golden streets), others as mere light. Ann Graham Lotz, daughter of Billy Graham, apparently even asserts that heaven is specifically a cube 1,500 miles on each side: "It could easily accommodate 20 billion residents, each having his or her own private 75-acre cube or room or mansion. This would still leave plenty of room for streets, parks, and public buildings" (50).

There is a difference between honest disagreement and sheer nonsense talk. Scientists may disagree about how the universe originated, but at least they are reasonably sure a universe exists and are in reasonable agreement on the properties of said universe. If people could not agree on what a cat is, or whether a cat even exists, we would be tempted (and justified) to doubt that there is any such thing, and we would certainly be wise to be leery of any claims about cats. And if people could not agree on what a *blork* is, or what the characteristics of a *blork* are, or whether a *blork* exists — and if we found that many people did not even possess a word or idea for *'blork'* — we would be foolish to make any affirmations about it.

The problem for us atheists is that we allow the familiarity and pervasiveness of Christianity to lure us into its issues and debates. We take words like *God* or *heaven* or *sin* as seriously as we take 'cat,' when perhaps we should take them as unseriously as we take *blork*. Maybe if we were to de-familiarize the apparently familiar by putting Christian terms in italics as we do with foreign religious terms, so that we would discuss *God* and *soul* and *heaven* and so on, then we could see, and get others to see, that we are not talking about things but about concepts — and specifically about concepts that some religions have (or merely one religion has) and that other religions lack. We would establish the fact that Christian religious concepts are not universal religious concepts but nothing more than Christian ones — concepts that most human beings, not only atheists but all the non-Christians too — do without. We would arrive at a new understanding of atheism in relation to Christianity: atheism is not *disbelief* in Christian concepts but rather *absence* of them, which is not all that difficult to grasp *since most religions are absent Christian concepts*.

What we are trying to say is that in the United States and other Christian-dominant societies, there is a habit of speaking and thinking in Christian terms which is not shared by the rest of the world and its religions. In India, they speak and think in terms of Hindu terms and concepts, in Saudi Arabia in terms of Muslim terms and concepts, in Thailand in terms of Buddhist terms and concepts, and in Warlpiri society in terms of Warlpiri terms and concepts. As atheists we are not interested in refuting one theism or religion and ignoring, let alone supporting, others. Yet we find in practice that atheists in Christian-dominated societies speak and think in Christian terms just as surely as Christians do. We let Christianity set the agenda, identify the questions, and provide the language of the debate. We quite literally 'speak Christian' just as fluently and just as un-self-consciously as they do. This chapter is dedicated to exploring the dangers of this practice, specifically the damage it does to our thought and to our activism, where we too unintentionally but effectively promote and perpetuate Christianity by participating in their language. We need to stop speaking Christian so as to loosen the grip of Christian language on our thinking. We further need to impress upon Christians that they are speaking Christian, not talking about all religion and certainly not about the real world. This would not automatically defeat Christianity but would automatically *demote* it — and demoting a religion is halfway to defeating it. But even these steps are not enough: we must begin to craft our own language in which it is easier, more natural, and ultimately unavoidable to 'speak atheist' — and to generate an atheist reality.

Religious Language, or Religion *as* a Language

The central thesis of my previous book *Natural Atheism* was that that all humans are born atheists, since humans are born without any knowledge of, concept of, or belief in any god(s). By birth, humans lack god(s) and are a-theists. Despite the philosophical and theological contention that humans have some innate god-idea (see Chapter 9, specifically the discussion of Descartes), there is not only no evidence to support this contention but plenty of evidence to refute it. If you never mentioned the term *god* to a child, it is highly unlikely that he or she would spontaneously arrive at it; many other cultures and religions *do not* arrive at it. Likewise, children raised in Christian environments who have never been exposed to the term *jukurrpa* do not spontaneously arrive at it nor hold any belief about it. Some honest Christian thinkers have even acknowledged this fact, most notably John Wesley, the founder of Methodism, when he said in his Ninety-fifty Sermon (significantly entitled "On the Education of Children"):

> After all that has been so plausibly written concerning "the innate idea of God"; after all that has been said of its being common to all men, in all ages and nations; it does not appear, that man has naturally any more idea of God than

any of the beasts of the field; he has no knowledge of God at all; no fear of God at all; neither is God in all his thoughts. Whatever change may afterwards be wrought...he is, by nature, a mere Atheist.

In other words, the very *idea* of a god must be acquired. In this sense, religion is like language. No particular language is innate (no one is born speaking English or Japanese or Warlpiri, *etc.*), although all humans normally do acquire one and have a capacity or a set of capacities (some say an instinct) to acquire one. In a sense one might insist that humans are natural language-speakers, but it would be more accurate to say that we are natural language-*acquirers*. Which *actual* language a human acquires depends on his or her social environment.

We might summarize the situation with language as follows. First, while there may be an inborn capacity to learn language, *no particular language* is inborn. Therefore and second, there are very many particular real or potential languages. Third, a person acquires a particular language simply by and because of being raised among others who already speak it; generally, people speak whatever language is spoken around them. And fourth and most critically, no speakers of a particular language would ever claim that their language is 'true.' The very notion that, for instance, English is true while Spanish is false is nonsensical. A language is neither true nor false.

Interestingly, religion is like language in a number of ways — none of them fortunate for those who want to take religion seriously. First, while most humans end up believing some religion (and there may even be an inborn tendency to acquire certain kinds of beliefs that we commonly call religion, as we will explore in the next chapter), *no particular religion* is inborn or natural. Therefore and second, there are very many particular real or potential religions, as we explored in the previous chapter. Third, a person normally acquires religion simply by and because of being raised among others who already do speak it; generally, people practice whatever religion is practiced around them. The profound difference between language and religion, however, is that *all members of a religion think that their religion is true.* The very notion that, for instance, a person would say, "I am a Christian, but I don't think Christianity is true" is contradictory and ridiculous. A religion is a set of truth-claims. Therefore, the claims of a religion are either true or false.

The Vocabulary of Religions

One cannot put forth and accept or defend claims except in some specific terms. If physics, say, wants to make claims about atomic processes, it must employ terminology like *nucleus* and *electron* and *atomic forces* and *electrical charge* and *quarks.* Such terminology — whether it is a matter of physics, car repair, or religion — constitutes its vocabulary, which is, or is part of, its particular 'language.' These specialized technical languages are of course not completely independent of everyday natural language: there are forces and electrical charges outside of the professional context of physics, just as there are wheels and transmissions outside of the professional context of automobile repair. And there are rituals and morals and symbols outside of the context of religion, as we will examine in later chapters. Nevertheless, each specialized context not only uses certain everyday terms in non-everyday ways — *transmission* means something different in relation to cars than to radio — but each technical language also invents and uses distinct and unique terms to express things that cannot be expressed in mundane speech. There are no quarks outside physics-talk, no distributor caps outside of car-talk, and no gods outside of religion-talk. So Kai Nielsen (1982) is right to argue that religious language is not a complete, independent language but instead a manner of speaking that piggybacks on (some particular and fuller) natural language. But he is wrong to insist that therefore there is no such thing as 'religious language.'

Religious language is a subset — but a very distinct subset — of some complete language, one that uses many of the terms and conventions of the broader language but also adds its own vocabulary that is specific to its interests, just as physics and car repair do. So, any religious utterance that humans can make will consist of many words that occur in non-religious utterances too, like 'is' or 'the' and so on, but also of words that occur in no other kinds of utterances but religious ones. English words like 'heaven' and 'hell' and 'sin' and of course 'god' have no source and no application other than religion. Religion, in conclusion, has a unique technical vocabulary even as it incorporates much of the vocabulary of secular language to produce religious talk. Therefore, even though religious talk shares many characteristics with other kinds of talk in any natural language (*e.g.*, religion, physics, car repair, and vernacular English can all talk about forces and can all say things like "The force is great"), religion presents its own special terms and concepts. One could not make religious claims or recognize a religious utterance from any other kind unless there were recognizable religious terms to use. We have just identified a few such terms — *heaven, hell, sin,* and *god*. It is essential to grasp two things. First, a religion like Christianity has a much more extensive vocabulary than this. To list even a fraction of this vocabulary would take too much space, but it is worth mentioning a few: *messiah, anointing, angel, devil, salvation, soul, saint, transubstantiation, baptism, holy, divine, divinity, sacred, gospel, priest, Pentecost, Pentecostalism,* and *Mariolatry*, not to mention unfamiliar terms like *agape, kerygma, kenosis, filioque*, and of course all of the ordinary words that it uses in non-ordinary senses (as if they were technical terms) like *grace, election, tribulation*, and so on.

Second — and this is our basic point — each religion has its own set of such vocabulary. Understandably, not all religions talk about messiahs or baptisms or *filioque*. These are religious terms and concepts, yes, but they are specifically *Christian* religious terms and concepts. Another religion may share one or more terms with Christianity or with each other, or they may use the same or similar terms in very different ways, or they may have their own completely separate terms.

One example will have to suffice. Buddhism obviously has its own religious language, with words and ideas like *nirvana* and *anatta* (literally, no-soul or no-self) and *bodhisattva*, etc. In Stanley Tambiah's (1970) study of a Thai Buddhist village, he discovered a much more elaborate and unusual universe of terms and meanings. First of all, in their religious view the universe passes through an infinite number of *kalpas* or cosmic cycles. All of reality is divided into 31 planes of existence, with three planes making up *laukika* or 'this world,' including *kama loka, rupa loka,* and *arupa loka. Kama loka* in turn contains eleven *lokas*, six for the gods and five for various levels of sub-divine beings including humans, animals, ghosts, demons, and tormented souls. The lowest godly *loka* is the home of the four 'guardians,' especially the *Nagas* who are shaped like serpents and friendly to Buddhism; the very highest of the heavens is *Tusita*, where the bodhisattva resides. In the lower *lokas* dwell humans, *asuras* or demons, and *pretas* or ghosts, who are huge with dried skin, big bellies, hot, and hungry. So, what Christians might consider the universe — heaven, earth, and hell — are all part of *kama loka*. *Rupa loka* is a further 'dimension' of physical form but no pleasure or pain, and *arupa loka* is the 'higher dimension' without form or sensation (and of little interest to the villagers). Yet, all of these *lokas* are contrasted against *lokattara*, the hypercosmic realm beyond sensation and thought, where even personhood ends.

Meanwhile, the quality of an individual's life is measured in terms of *bun* ('merit') and *baab* ('demerit'). If a person dies with surplus of *bun*, the person's *winjan* goes to heaven until the merit is used up and is then reborn. If a person dies with a balance of *bun/baab*, the *winjan* goes first to hell and then to heaven and is then reborn. If the person dies with surplus of *baab*, the *winjan* goes to hell or wanders as a *preta* and is then reborn. Of course, *bun* can be acquired by acts like sponsoring a temple, becoming a monk or sending a son to become a monk, paying to support/repair a temple, feeding monks, or obeying Buddhist rules. This *winjan* is a spirit essence residing in the body; it is permanent and leaves the body only at death. Humans also have a *khwan* or 'personal essence' in their bodies. Composed of thirty-two separate essences associated with different body parts (and also present in animals and paddy fields), it can become detached from the body during life, and it leaves permanently at death and dies. Rituals called *sukhwan* are performed to prevent the loss of *khwan* and the resulting sickness or bad fortune. Finally, a *winjan* can turn into a *phii*, a disembodied spirit which may be attached to places, free-floating, or trapped in hell and may be benevolent, disciplinary, capricious, or malevolent (although most are malevolent). The *khwan*, on the other hand, can become a *thewada* or benevolent being or angel, which is eternal and lives in one of the *kama loka* heavens.

Speaking Christian

Without doubt, it is going to be exceedingly difficult to 'do Christianity' in Thai Buddhist terms, and *vice-versa*. In fact, we can say with reasonable certainty that most of the Thai terms just discussed have no Christian equivalent — in other words, you cannot translate straight across from Thai Buddhist to Christian — and again *vice-versa*. In regard to religious language, then, you cannot say Thai Buddhist things in Christian language nor say Christian things in Thai Buddhist language. Clearly, 'speaking Christian' is profoundly different from 'speaking Thai Buddhist,' which is profoundly different from 'speaking Scientologist' (with its *thetans* and *anatens* and *clears* and *engrams* and such). Finally, it seems that every religion has, or better yet *is*, its own language. In this sense, Nielsen was right: there is not *a* religious language but rather many religious languages. Most people speak one — and all the others are like a foreign language.

Words and Things: The Meaninglessness of Religious Language

Based on the preceding discussion, you cannot say *soul* in the Christian sense in Thai Buddhist, nor can you say *winjan* or *khwan* in Christian, and you cannot say *thetan* in either. The question before us now is, when you say *soul* or *winjan* or *khwan* or *thetan*, what are you talking about? Clearly, *soul* and *winjan* and *khwan* and *thetan* are not synonyms; they are not different names for the same thing. They are, according to their definitions and uses, different things. So, when you are speaking Christian or speaking Thai Buddhist or speaking Scientologist, you are not just saying different words for things, *but you are saying different things*. Or, are you talking about anything at all?

This is the basic issue of the meaningfulness of religious language. Michael Martin opens his formidable *Atheism: A Philosophical Justification* with the following question: "Is God-talk meaningful?" (1990:40). That question raises another one: what does it mean to be 'meaningful'? Clearly we can give a meaning to the word *god*, and many people — Christians and atheists alike — do. In fact, it is one of the main contentions of this chapter that atheists *do* find the word *god* meaningful

ATHEISM ADVANCED

— at least meaningful enough to argue about it. However, just because one can give a definition of a word does not make that word meaningful in a more valuable sense, as 'referring to something real.' We can define the word *unicorn* or *leprechaun*; we can even make up nonsense sounds and assign definitions to them. But the definition, hopefully, is not the meaning. The meaning must be, if it is worth talking about, something *out there*, something *other than mere words*. That is to say, we could posit that 'unicorn' means a horse-like animal with one long pointed horn on its head, and then move to the more interesting matter: is there any such actual thing as that? But the ability to utter a word, and even the ability to define and use a word, does not make the word meaningful.

There are two insurmountable problems for theists when it comes to 'god-talk.' The first is defining the term. The contemporary Christian theorist Richard Swinburne has attempted to fill this requirement by defining *god* as a "person without a body (*i.e.*, a spirit) present everywhere, the creator and sustainer of the universe, able to do everything (*i.e.*, omnipotent), knowing all things, perfectly good, a source of moral obligation, immutable, eternal, a necessary being, holy and worthy of worship" (1977: 2). It would appear that he has solved the first problem, except for the fact that not all Christians necessarily accept this definition; even worse, it contains a number of other problematic terms, like *omnipotent* and *immutable* which themselves call for definition.

But the second and bigger problem is that this definition does not accurately account for all of the god-concepts out there. Many religions contain gods that do not fit this description at all, lacking one or more of the putative qualities. Not all of the Greek gods were creators, nor were they all-knowing or all-powerful. The Norse god Thor had power over thunder only. The Azande god Mbori is not all-good; in fact, he is not morally interested in humans at all. The Piaroa tribe in Venezuela believed that at least one of their gods, Kuemoi, was an ugly, insanely violent cannibal (Overing 1986). Many religions include trickster gods who cause mischief and hardship. Not all gods are eternal: some are born (some gods are second- or third-generation gods), and some die. They are not all immutable. And not all religions with gods adopt a worshipful attitude toward them, like the !Kung who are more likely to chastise their gods Gao Na and Kauha than praise and adore them.

Thus, the primary objection to Swinburne is that his is not a definition — not even a bad definition — of *god*; it is not a definition at all but rather *a description of a particular god*, namely, Yahweh, Jehovah, the Christian god. It would be like offering the following as a definition of 'human': five feet ten inches tall, male, brown hair, blue eyes, atheist, with a Ph.D. in anthropology. That is not a definition either but a description of me.

As not only atheists but thinking human beings, we have a conundrum here. What do we make not only of Christian god-talk — which is only one species of god-talk — but of god-talk as a whole? There are evidently many different gods to talk about. Yahweh/Jehovah, Mbori, Keumoi, Gao Na and Kauha, not to mention Zeus (and his pantheon), Odin (and his pantheon), Vishnu and Shiva and Brahma, Osiris and the other Egyptian gods, and the thousands upon thousands of others — what are they? Are they different names for the same thing? After all, that can happen: 'dog' may be *perro* in Spanish or *chien* in French or *Hund* in German and still mean the same thing, that is, refer to the same entity. And it would be stupid to argue about the real word for dog (and even more stupid to kill people over it). But it is impossible that all of these god-words could be local names for the same entity, since each religion/language has its own different and often enough incompatible definition and characterization of the concept. Are they then terms for different entities? That is possible, although it would firstly make the world a very crowded place for gods, and secondly this multitheistic approach contradicts the assertion of at least some of the gods, who claim to be the only god. So we can safely reject the different-term-for-a-different-god position. Finally, are they, like 'unicorn' and 'leprechaun,' words without referent — literally, sounds that we make with our mouths but that have no meaning?

There are probably two ways to determine if a word refers to anything real. The first is to identify, produce, or point to the thing that it refers to. If I say the word 'cat' and show or indicate a cat, I can demonstrate the reference of the word. If someone could identify, produce, or point to a god, then the reference and reality of the term would be settled. However, virtually everyone, theist and atheist, agrees that this cannot be done; indeed, sometimes the theist revels in the fact that his or her god(s) is/are hidden or mysterious or unknowable — even, as Tertullian or Kierkegaard argued, absurd (see Chapter 9). So the 'demonstration' of *god* is unavailable and perhaps impossible. The other way to determine if a word has a reference is more indirect but still useful: does the word have a consistent definition or application? That is, every time the word is spoken, do people mean the same thing by it? However, as we just observed, god-talk fails this test too. Christians cannot even agree among themselves exactly what this *god* is or does. And other cultures and religions have very different conceptions of god(s). Talk about god(s) is utterly inconsistent, often contradictory. It would be like some people using the word 'cat' to designate a small furry four-legged creature, others a large fire-breathing eight-legged creature, others an immense invisible being, and others insisting that no such being exists at all. We would be within our rights to doubt that the word 'cat' actually means anything. We would, therefore, also be within our rights to doubt that the word 'god' actually means anything. It is just a verbal sound, a cultural concept — which, as we have seen, some cultures and religions get along fine without. And if *they* can, *we* can.

According to Michael Martin's critique of god-talk, if the word *god* has no actual meaning or referent, then any sentence containing or making claims about *god* must also necessarily be meaningless or empty. To say such a sentence, whether it is 'God exists' or 'God is good/all-powerful/moral/*etc.*' is to say precisely nothing; we could just as easily say 'Unicorns exist' or 'Dragons are all-powerful.' "Consequently," he concludes, "if belief in God is factually meaningless, then having no such belief is justified" (47). Having no belief in god(s) is atheism; therefore, atheism is justified. However, we must remind ourselves that god-talk is not the sum or essential part of religion. Even in theism, not all religious talk is god-talk: there are many other things that theisms talk about, such as *heaven* and *hell* and *devil* and *angels* and *demons* and on and on. Each of these terms must be evaluated separately.

That is, proving that god-talk is meaningless does not yet prove that demon-talk is meaningless. However, each of these terms fails the two tests we proposed above. Even worse for theism, most religions, as we have learned, do not include god-talk at all. Animism, animatism, ancestor-spirit systems, and ethical non-theisms do not talk about god(s) in any way. They are not *against* god(s), they are simply *without* god(s). They are a-theistic. Nevertheless, they have their own local religious talk, whether it is about plant or animal spirits, or supernatural forces, or dead ancestors or whatever. Each of these claims must be evaluated independently, but again, each fails the tests. All such talk is meaningless; it is just cultural concepts, not references to anything real. And each religion does fine without the terms and concepts of the other. Atheists like us are just people who do fine without any of them.

Words of Power

We do well to begin our debunking of religion with a debunking of religious terminology, since any religion inevitably starts with a set of terms for its beliefs and concepts. However, we cannot end our debunking there because — and this is critically important — *no religion is only a vocabulary or terminology*. We atheists, we rationalists and literalists, tend to overemphasize the empirical or cognitive, that is, the factual, part of religion at the expense of the other, and arguably more vital, parts. We tend to think, and to act, as if we have done our job once we have 'proven' that god(s) do(es) not exist. The evidence that our job is not finished is that religion survives.

Much of the remainder of this book is designed to illustrate that religion is not only, maybe not mainly, ideas or beliefs or fact-claims (false ones as they may be). To treat religion as nothing more than a set of (false) beliefs or fact-claims is to misunderstand it and to misdirect one's effort against it. Of course, this is true of all language: uttering propositions, or factual statements, is merely one of the things humans can do with words — and probably not the most common, the most interesting, or the most powerful. At the very least, we can also utter questions, imperatives (orders or commands), and expletives, none of which are true or false but all of which are crucial to the real everyday performance of language and social interaction. As we will now investigate, language — including religious language — can do much more.

Effectiveness without Understanding

As people of reason and of science, we typically insist that the function of words is in their meaning and therefore speakers must necessarily understand the meaning of words in order to get anything out of language. As appealing as this position is, it is not accurate. People use words all the time with only a vague notion of what they mean (how many Catholics really know how transubstantiation works, and how many ordinary Americans know how an electron really works?). Descartes (see Chapter 9) insisted that the best argument for the existence of a god is that people have a clear and firm idea of a god, but nothing could be further from the truth. Most Christians and other theists have the fuzziest of notions of god, and many include 'unknowability' as one of their god's qualities (a remarkable contradiction, but when has contradiction ever bothered religion?). Since religious ideas need be no more clear and firm than factual ideas or political ideas or social ideas (few Americans can draw an accurate map of the United States, and yet they are still fairly sure that the United States exists), we do wrong to discount religious ideas that are vague, variable, unavailable, or just plain non-existent.

One of the outstanding features of religious language is that it need not be understood to be powerful; in fact, sometimes it is more powerful if it is not understood. That is one reason for specialized religious dialects, like Latin in Christianity. Most medieval Christians had little or no knowledge of Latin, and the fact that the priests did and that the language of the Church was a 'high' or 'secret' language conferred not less but more status on it. In most religions of the world, there are special ritual idioms, containing esoteric if not sacred or secret words, phrases, grammars, and tones of voice. Audiences of such linguistic performances will understand little or none of it, but they are nevertheless convinced of the efficacy of the speech. Accordingly, Tambiah mentions the chants performed by Thai monks in front of a lay crowd, in which the words "are meant to be heard but paradoxically they are not understood by the majority of the congregation (nor by some of the monks themselves), because the sacred language is the dead Pali language." Yet, the villagers are "emphatic that through listening to the chants the congregation gains merit, blessings, and protection" (1970:195). Tambiah aptly calls this "the virtue of listening without understanding" (196). In fact, as he indicates, there may also be a virtue of "speaking without understanding" in the priests, who do not understand their own words.

In many religious traditions, lay people may not even get to hear the religious speech at all. It may be conducted in cloisters and other segregated gatherings of religious specialists. Ordinary citizens are not invited and never experience the words in any way. Yet, these secret chants and verbal rituals are often the most important and supposedly efficacious ones of all: if the monks or priests did not perform them, the consequences would be devastating.

At the extreme, religious words may not be spoken at all but accessed in some other manner. The best example comes from a Muslim tribal society called the Berti in Sudan (Holy 1991). As most Westerners may know, Islam takes its scriptures unusually seriously, not just the words and ideas but the very physical form of the book itself, which is to be revered and respected. The Berti think that all of the Qur'an is sacred but that particular parts are effective for particular purposes; one verse may be good against sickness, another verse against drought, *etc.* But the words need be neither uttered nor heard in order to work. Two non-verbal uses of religious language are amulets and *mihai.* Amulets (*hijbat*) are made by writing lines from the Qur'an and/or names of Allah on paper and sewing these texts into leather or cloth pouches to be worn like charms and talismans. The Jewish practice of wearing phylacteries is similar. *Mihai* is an even more fascinating practice, in which religious leaders write Qur'anic verses in chalk on a slate, wash the writing off with water, and have a person drink the fluid. As Holy explains, the Qur'an "is considered to have an immense power which guarantees the well-being of those who have internalized it" (33) — whether that internalization comes through the ears or the mouth.

Thus, as Tambiah reminds us, religious words are not just acoustic symbols of meaning. They are, very often, 'objects' in their own right — and objects of profound power. Whether it is intoning a sound or phrase (like *Om* or *Namo myoho renge kyo*), hearing a chant or sermon, *not* hearing a chant or sermon, or wearing or drinking the words, the language is effective just the same.

Words that Change Things

We rationalists and literalists usually focus on the meaning of statements and the facts that these statements allegedly describe. That is why we are so obsessed with propositions or sentences that describe factual states of affairs ('The cat is on the mat' or 'God does not exist'). However, many kinds of language are not propositions, such as interrogatives ('What time is it?' or 'is everybody happy tonight?'), imperatives ('Shut the window' or 'Thou shalt not kill'), or expletives ('You dirty bastard' or 'Oh, no'). We can usually tell a question or imperative or expletive when we hear one. Some utterances, however, are more mysterious, for they are not propositions — although they may have the grammar of propositions. For example, if I say, "You are a married person," that is a proposition and either true or false. However, if I say, "I now pronounce you man and wife," that is not a proposition despite its resemblance to one. The first person to identify this distinct and vitally important quality of language was J. L. Austin, whose small book *How To Do Things with Words* (1962) exposed a previously unappreciated power of speech.

Austin used the term 'performatives' for utterances that do not describe circumstances but rather *achieve* circumstances. When, for instance, a judge says, "I find the defendant guilty," he or she is not describing the defendant's legal status but *making the defendant guilty*. Other examples would include a king saying, "I knight thee" or a police officer saying, "You are under arrest." Each of these speech-acts accomplishes the social status of which it speaks. Many of these performative utterances require not only special occasions but special performers; they are ritual acts that only work if they are performed correctly. In other words, if I walked up to two people on the street and said,

"I pronounce you man and wife," they would not be married. Even if an ordained minister spoke those words on the street or in a wedding rehearsal, they would not result in a marriage. They must be said properly, in the right social or ritual context, or they are ineffective. Not all performatives require specialized personnel, of course. Some are acts that ordinary folks can do in their regular lives. When people say "I'm sorry," they are not making a propositional statement or offering testimony about their internal state; they are performing an apology. Likewise, "I love you" is a performance of love, "I forgive you" is the act of forgiveness, and "Thank you" is giving thanks.

The efficacy of performatives is limited. For instance, a performative can fail. If I say, "I apologize" with a smirk on my face, the other person may respond, "That was not sincere, you did not apologize at all." Or if a man says, "I love you" to a woman as he hits her, his profession of love can (and should) be rejected. Performatives can be faked, that is, we can even lie in our public performances. And from a rational standpoint, verbal performatives can only effect changes in *social* circumstances: we can change social relations and statuses with our words (turning a commoner into a knight, a single person into a married person, a juvenile into an adult, an innocent person into a guilty person). We do not ordinarily think that our words can change nature. For example, we cannot make it rain just by saying, "Let it rain."

It should be obvious that much of religious language is not propositional at all and that arguably the most important utterances in religion are not factual references. For example, when a priest is ordained with ritual words and gestures, the performative effect is to turn the novice into a priest. Marriage ceremonies, for many people, are religious performances that transform individuals into married couples, with verbal formulas like "With this ring I thee wed": the words here do not describe the action, *they are the action.* But priesthood and marriage are still, religious opinion notwithstanding, social statuses. Religion also includes, in fact depends on, using language to affect the natural, non-human, and super-human world as well. Prayer is a form of speech intended not only to communicate with religious beings but to *influence* those beings, namely to achieve some result (much like saying "I'm sorry" to another human — in fact, one thing that Christians at least are supposed to say to their god is that they are sorry). In other religions, humans may speak to plants, animals, natural objects, or natural forces and not only expect those things to understand but to respond. When priests or shamans say, "Let it rain," or perhaps, "It rains," they hope — and presumably expect — that the outcome will be rain. We refer to this application of human speech to the non-human world as *magic*.

Much of religious speech indisputably is of the performative sort; it is not *describing* a state of reality but *achieving* one. And it is doing so either through the inherent power of words themselves (*i.e.,* say it and it is true) or through the social interaction implied by speaking the words *to* a super-human being or force. Curing rituals are one clear manifestation. The goal is not to describe the illness, nor to symbolize it, but to change it; curing rituals are as practical as any medical procedure (if not as 'true'). As an illustration, the Navajo ceremony known as the *Enemyway* is intended to rid a victim of negative external influence, such as a curse placed on him or her by an enemy. Among the phrases spoken in the ritual, one may find repeated references to health and well-being (Gill 1981:106–7):

> By which he is long life, by that I am long life,
>> By which he is happiness, by that I am happiness,
>> By which it is pleasant at his front, thereby it is pleasant
> at my front,
>> By which it is pleasant in his rear, thereby it is pleasant
> at my rear,

>> Long life, happiness I shall be, pleasant again it has
> become,
>> pleasant again it has become, pleasant again it has
> become,
>> pleasant again it has become, pleasant again it has
> become.

Obviously, the victim is not happy and pleasant now; the words are not descriptions. They are goals which the speaker believes can be accomplished through words.

Speaking Christian

A Mighty Fortress is my God: Metaphors

There is a class of linguistic acts that is often indistinguishable from propositions grammatically but that is less like proposition than like poetry. When I say, "A rose by any other name would smell as sweet," that sounds propositional, but it is not an invitation to conduct an experiment on the names and smells of roses. It is honestly quite irrelevant if it is false, since it was never meant as a factual account of the relation between names and smells. It is a metaphor, intended to invoke an image and establish a relation between one thing (a rose) and some other thing, depending on the context.

Some metaphors are obvious. When someone says, "He has the heart of a lion," we are not supposed to conclude that doctors have transplanted a lion's heart into his chest. "Heart" here is a metaphor for courage, and "heart of a lion" is a double metaphor for very great courage. When someone says, "Time is money" or "Life is a dream," we would be wrong to try to deposit the first in the bank or wake up from the second. When someone refers to the "faith of a mustard seed," that should not lead us to try to identify and quantify the mustard seed's faith. Understandably, many metaphors are employed in the wisdom of a culture in the form of figures of speech, proverbs (like "A stitch in time saves nine," which is not really about sewing), riddles, and other specialized but familiar and popular speech forms.

Rationalists and literalists tend to overlook the pervasiveness and power of metaphor; we see it as trivial, fun perhaps, but not serious and literally false. George Lakoff and Mark Johnson (1980), however, have demonstrated just how ubiquitous, and how subtle, metaphorical thought and speech is in ordinary life. For instance, when we say that the future is "ahead of us," we are using a spatial metaphor to express something about time. Time does not really occupy space at all, but the image conveys a meaning — and a feeling. When we say that we are "under pressure," again we are translating an experience into a spatial metaphor. One of the regular — and perhaps especially appealing — qualities of such metaphors is that they express a vague or intangible phenomenon, like an emotion or impression, in a more concrete, tangible, even visceral and bodily way: having a variety of different emotions about something is real, but being on 'an emotional rollercoaster' is much more immediate and substantial.

The recurring example that Lakoff and Johnson use is "argument is war." With this model, they show that any metaphor plays on the similarities between two things, which may be more or less extensive but never total. Argument is not war in the sense that anyone gets killed (usually) but in the sense of winners and losers and 'attacks' and 'defenses' and 'weapons' — each of these a sub-metaphor of the main metaphor. We may 'advance an argument,' 'parry the thrust' of an opponent, 'demolish' an opponent's case, and so on. The power of a metaphor, then, rests on our knowledge of the predicate in the statement (in other words, knowing what a war or a lion is like) and extending those notions to the subject. But — and this is critical — it would be silly to attempt to prove whether or not 'argument is war' or 'he has the heart of a lion.' The statement is not propositional; as a metaphor, it is *neither true nor false*. It is instructive, evocative, or picturesque. We might disagree about whether he really is all that courageous, but fighting about the truth of the metaphor itself would be a profound waste of time.

It is surprising just how common metaphor is in our language, including the language of reason and science. In fact, Den Boer (1998) measured written texts from poetry to scientific books and papers and found that 19% of the overall words used were metaphorical, with an astounding 25% of scientific words being metaphors. We can see them if we look for a moment: the depiction of an atom as a tiny solar system is a metaphor, as is the term 'natural selection' (as if nature is intentionally selecting anything, a notion that causes trouble, since it sounds like intelligence). Humans engage in metaphors for a variety of reasons: they actually are informative (if not taken too literally), they are interesting, they are creative and fun, and they express things that cannot be expressed better in any other way. To say that one's child or spouse is "the light of my life" is poetic and beautiful and, in a sense, quite meaningful. Humans would be diminished without the power of metaphor. This does not mean that metaphors cannot get out of control, or that we must not be cautious in handling them. As Max Mueller commented over a century ago, taking one's metaphors and poetry literally leads to a "disease of language" — specifically, a disease called religion. Language and culture are full of conventional metaphors, but some are more fundamental and effective than others. Sherry Ortner referred to the deep and influential metaphors in a society as "root metaphors," which are a class of what she called "elaborating symbols." Elaborating symbols are more than cute and thoughtful things to say; they "work" in the society that utters them by "providing vehicles for sorting out complex and undifferentiated feelings and ideas, making them comprehensible to oneself, communicable to others, and translatable into orderly action" (1973:1340). Root metaphors elaborate knowledge and experience by providing a model or representation of what experience, the world, or reality is "really like." They offer "a set of categories" for conceptualizing and organizing life; they formulate "the unity of cultural orientation underlying many aspects of experience, by virtue of the fact that those many aspects of experience can be likened to it." The metaphor "shapes" our experience and makes it "hang together" in meaningful ways (1341). Some examples of root metaphors might be "the cosmos is a battleground" or "America is a shining city on the hill" or "life is a test."

No doubt, religion is a context in which metaphor is going to be particularly common ('God is a fortress,' 'Heaven is like a thousand orgasms,' 'Jesus is the lamb of God,' and so on *ad infinitum*). They are self-evidently not literally true: Jesus was not a lamb, and God is not a fortress. Still, they are 'good to think' in that they convey impressions and associations that are comprehensible and powerful. But they are more than that. Metaphors, like other linguistic forms such as hyperbole (extreme exaggeration, such as the heaven-as-orgasm remark, or 'Iraq is the axis of evil' or 'God is all-knowing'), are part of *rhetoric*. We are very wrong to confuse reason and rhetoric — and to underestimate the power of rhetoric. Rhetoric is not factual description, and it is more than argumentation. It is, as Kenneth Burke once put it, "the use of words by human agents to form attitudes or to induce actions in other human agents" (1969: 41). It is, in other words, not just about getting people to think in certain ways as to get them to *feel and act* in certain ways. It is motivational. Clearly, if people think that the cosmos is a battleground, then they are motivated, and encouraged, to act like soldiers.

It is fascinating to ponder not only how many standard metaphors there are in a culture, but how many of these metaphors originate in religion. Christianity is naturally the source of a vast body of cultural metaphors, from 'my cross to bear' to 'a Jezebel' to 'like David against Goliath' to 'being my brother's keeper' and many, many others; Richard Dawkins lists two pages of such images in his latest book (2006:341–3). Non-Christian religions have also contributed metaphors to our language and culture, such as Greek references like 'caught between Scylla and Charybdis,' 'crossing the river Styx,' 'a Herculean effort,' 'narcissistic,' 'flying too close to the sun,' 'Achilles' heel,' and so on. Humanity, it seems, cannot live by facts alone but is prone to invent and live in meaningful systems assembled over history out of the bits and pieces of various cultures and religions.

Now Say This: Scripts

The vocabulary of a language provides the raw materials, the elementary bits, out of which speech can be constructed; the elements can be combined in almost endless ways to produce possible and intelligible utterances. But a language is not just possible things to say but a ready-made assortment of standardized things to say. In other words, when you meet a person for the first time in the morning, you could potentially say any number of things — many of which have never been said before — but actually you are likely to say one of a small list of prefabricated, traditional things, like "How are you?" or "Good morning," which are most likely to receive a standard response. Any language is full of these standard things to say, which we can call scripts.

Scripts include the conventional utterances we make in specific situations, like greetings or farewells. They also include a number of other kinds of conventional speech, like proverbs, folk sayings, famous quotations, and such. Learning to speak a language well and fluently involves learning and mastering these regularized interaction forms: if you did not know what to say to someone first thing in the morning, or did not know and give a proper response, people would be confused and displeased. Likewise, if you gave one of these routine speeches in the wrong context — say, said "Good morning, how are you?" every time you saw the same person throughout the day, people would doubt your sanity.

So, when we acquire and use a language, we also acquire and use a battery of pre-established linguistic scripts. It is interesting to think about how much of our speech is scripted and unoriginal in this sense, the proper performance of pre-determined interaction patterns. And speaking the correct script in the correct situation *is* a performance; it demonstrates mastery both of the language (including the history of the language) and of the relevant social situations in which to say them. It also demonstrates a degree of *acceptance of* and *conformity to* these social expectations.

Similarly, subcultures and other specialized communities (professional, regional, ethnic, and of course religious) have their own set of these conventionalized utterances. Learning to be a member of that community is learning to say the things that other members of the community routinely say — to talk like them. And obviously, these patterned utterances are not meant to be, or at least not primarily to be, propositional, or even literal. The question, 'How are you?' is not asking for a literal accounting of your physical or moral condition. It is asking, as we specified earlier, *for a response*, usually and ideally another script. Scripts in this sense are interactional routines or social rituals (see Chapter 10 on interaction code behavior).

Further, scripts are specific to particular genres within the broader language. A conventional phrase like 'Once upon a time' or 'Dearly beloved' or 'Hear ye, hear ye' announces what genre of speech (and of social interaction) is being done — a fairy tale, a wedding, or a trial. Religion too has its own collection of linguistic scripts, some of which have penetrated everyday speech, as when Americans say "God bless you" when you sneeze, or when French or Spanish invoke God to say goodbye (*adieu* or *adios*). In fact, a religion is, to a large extent, nothing but a collection of verbal and behavioral scripts. A ritual like a mass is entirely scripted, as are prayers, chants, songs, spells, myths, and other oral speech genres (some more inflexible than others). Such religious language is almost purely conventional, that is, it is public and traditional and provided for the member in advance. To know a religion, to practice a religion, is to master its verbal routines and perform your part in them at the right place and time.

Religious scripts are ultimately part of a much larger and more comprehensive body of linguistic material which we might rightly call the literature of the religion. For oral traditions, this encompasses the total of stories, songs, myths, prayers, proverbs, *etc.* that is known to the culture, which is not to say that every individual knows every item. There may be a division of knowledge such that some members know or specialize in some components and not others. In literate traditions, some of this literature will be settled in and committed to writing, constituting the *canon* or *scriptures* of the religion. Two things are worth noting. First, the Christian Bible, foundation of the Christian canon, contains all sorts of linguistic genres, from history to allegory to ritual instruction, moral commandment, song, proverb, poetry, sermon, and correspondence. It is hardly only 'myth' and it is definitely not all fact-claim and proposition. Second, the Christian Bible, although standing at the center of the canon, is by no means the whole of it. There are commentaries, apocryphal writings, church documents and doctrines, lives of saints and martyr's tales, hymnals and songbooks, published sermons, and a mountain of other writings. Not all members are fluent in all of it; most Christians have probably never read — or even heard of — Augustine or Tertullian or the thousands of others who have crafted the contemporary literature. All the same, being a member of a religion means more than accepting a certain set of religious propositions. It means belonging to a linguistic community that possesses a corpus of literature and thus saying and doing the expected things to enact and reproduce that literature and that community. This does not, we must stress emphatically, require understanding or assenting to every 'proposition' in the religion.

Religion in Mind and in Control

> Who controls the past controls the future. Who controls the
> present controls the past.

> —George Orwell, *1984*

Language, including religious language, is partly about
propositions, fact-claims, or what we might call "truth-talk."
However, as we have amply demonstrated, it is not *only*
about saying factual things or accurately describing the
world. Speaking is also *doing*, and there are many things to
do when one speaks. One can inform but as the discussion of
performatives shows, one can also transform. One can entertain
or motivate or manipulate. One can misinform and disinform,
obfuscate, and lie. What difference does it make if a religion is
a language that the members speak? And more importantly,
what difference does it make if non-members, even non-
believers, even opponents of the religion join in speaking it too?
The answer is that it makes a profound difference. *Speaking*
religion is *doing* religion, and saying the proper religious things
is not only to inform but to transform, motivate, manipulate,
and often enough to obfuscate on religious subjects. How, after
all, in Orwell's tale, did the regime control the past? They did
so by controlling the language; he even had them invent a
language, Newspeak, in which it was possible and easy to say
certain things and difficult or impossible to say others.

Frames of Speech:
Whose Language are We Speaking?

Everyone knows that there is a 'home field advantage' in
any struggle; more saliently, many people — especially those
involved in crafting and influencing popular opinion — know
that there is a dramatic advantage in getting other people to
use your words and phrases, even when arguing against you.
Various observers of modern culture, from Douglas Rushkoff
in his *Media Virus* (1996) to Chip and Dan Heath in their new

book *Made to Stick* (2007), have taught the persuasive force of language — how getting people to 'speak your language' can induce or compel them, if not to adopt your position, then to reproduce your position in their very refusal to adopt it. As Rushkoff stresses, certain words, concepts, phrases, metaphors, scripts, and such can be viral in the sense that they take over the discussion and replicate themselves on both sides of a debate.

To illustrate this essential point, consider the work of psychologist Daniel Wegner, whose *White Bears and Other Unwanted Thoughts* (1989) examines the question of language and attention. He asked subjects in an experiment not to think of a white bear, and what he found was that they almost obsessively thought about one; merely introducing the notion, and trying to control it, sent it on a rampage in their minds. He relates the phenomenon to what he calls "incrimination through innuendo" in which people are inclined to concentrate on messages, whether those messages have been explicitly stated, indirectly implied, or even denied. Innuendo occurs, he suggests, "when we communicate disavowal along with our ideas [and] attach comments that are meant, at least on the surface, to qualify, question, deny, or even apologize" (103). One example would be to say, "I am not claiming that my opponent is a murderer but..."; the speaker is in fact not claiming it, but he or she is implanting the thought in people's minds just the same. Why else mention it? If the opponent swallows the bait and answers, "I am not a murderer," that actually *reinforces* the association between him or her and murder. Those of us alive in the 1970s recall Richard Nixon's insistence that he was "not a crook" and how all that many people carried away from that remark was a connection between 'Nixon' and 'crook.'

"Rather than denial removing or neutralizing the incrimination, and thus acting as one expects denials to act, here it *caused* incrimination" (102). This is because the denial or disclaimer of the original claim was still in the terms and language of the original claim. In other words, by attempting to refute an assertion in the language of the assertion, we may inadvertently cause the original assertion to have more force and more sticking power. We keep it in the public eye, and we make it, like a white bear, available to — if not compulsively present in — people's minds. If 'I am not a crook' is like 'There is not a god,' then both disavowals only tend to remind the hearer of crooks or gods and potentially to strengthen the thought of them.

George Lakoff offers some explanation for this counterintuitive process. In his *Don't Think of an Elephant* (2004), he reminds us that any verbal exchange, discussion, or debate must be conducted in some terms. *Whose* terms are used matters very much. He refers to the effect of language use as "framing." A frame is a cognitive or conceptual structure within which thought and discourse occur; it is the "box" that people think and talk in. Within that frame, words and actions have meaning, and some frame of thought is always necessary for shared meaning. Even more, the frame is a powerful constraint on what *can be talked and thought about*, in the following ways:

- Every word comes from some frame. You cannot speak in a generic language. You must speak some particular language, so that every word you use derives from and relates to some — and somebody's — language.
- Words understood within the frame evoke the frame. Words, concepts, *etc.* from one frame or language bring along the whole rest of the frame or the world view that it builds.
- Evoking the frame reinforces the frame. Every time we use the frame or speak the language, it strengthens the frame or language. It becomes more cognitively real and compelling to the participant.
- Negating a frame also evokes the frame, since negating it is still evoking it. And since every evocation is a reinforcement, then even a negation is a reinforcement: we are still talking about their things in their words.

If so, then talking about god(s), even saying there is no such thing as god(s), *is still talking about god(s)* and therefore is evoking and reinforcing the idea of god(s) and with it the entire edifice of theism. This is probably one reason why theists love to engage us in debates about their god: it makes us take their nonsense word seriously and puts us in the public eye talking about their nonsense word. They have even been so savvy as to insist that the atheist ability to dispute god(s) proves that we too have a concept of god(s).

The Dark Side of Language

As we have acknowledged, language is just as easily employed to confuse and mislead as to clarify and enlighten. It can convey meaning or be utterly meaningless — or, more sinisterly, it can invert and pervert meaning. For instance, the regime's slogan in *1984* was "War is peace, Freedom is slavery, Ignorance is strength." While we rationalists might simply dismiss such talk as false and contradictory, such an attitude fails to grasp the goal of the talk, which uses calculated absurdity precisely to dazzle and stupefy (in Chapter 9, we will see again how Tertullian and others utilized overt absurdity to *convince* people that Christianity was true). Politicians are renowned for this sort of deception. Religions take fullest advantage of the mystifying quality of words and may depend on it most essentially. When Islam says that submission is freedom (the very word *Islam* means 'submission'), that is an Orwellian inversion. Many religions like Christianity and Hinduism say that life is really death, and death is really life. They may teach that matter is unreal and that reality is immaterial. Others believe that suffering is pleasure and that pleasure is suffering. We see this too in the debates between religion and atheism, where atheism is asserted to be a religion. Knowledge, religionists will argue, is belief, and therefore belief is a kind of knowledge. Science is a religion, and therefore religion is a science. A theory is an opinion, and therefore an opinion is a theory. The point of these sentences is really not to argue at all but rather to undermine and discredit: atheism is *nothing more than* religion, knowledge is *no better than* belief, and so on. They are really *attacks*, not statements at all, although they have the grammar of propositions.

Savvy professionals who understand the psychological and social force of language can and do use this insight to persuade and motivate, to engineer thoughts and emotions and to maneuver others into acting in certain ways, whether that be buying a particular product, voting for a particular candidate,

Speaking Christian

or supporting a particular policy. The 'right words' can be highly persuasive or motivational, while the 'wrong words' on the same issue can be unpersuasive or even aversive. Some words have positive or negative associations, and their use can polish or tarnish a subject. Some words are like bombs to be dropped on the opposition: *racist* is one example, as well as *unpatriotic* or *terrorist* or *evil*, Interestingly, the Left was formerly expert at manipulating language in this way, whether it was crafting slogans like 'New Deal' or 'War on Poverty' or assassinating characters with charges of 'counter-revolutionary' or 'enemy of the people.' But recently the Right has become the master of it, with such terms and phrases as 'defense of marriage' (a code for anti-gay measures), 'activist judges' (a code for any judge who rules against them), 'liberal media' (a code for any medium that questions them), and 'family values' (the ultimate code for all of Christian 'morality'). Perhaps the two most important manipulation words in modern jargon are 'tradition(al)' or 'moral(ity).' These words are not descriptions and are not intended to be; they are, and are intended to be, rhetorical devices and weapons.

Anyone who pays attention to current American political discourse realizes how words are deployed to shape public opinion; in fact, modern political and social discourse is little more than a war over words. Note how hard both sides fought over the term 'civil war' in reference to Iraq in 2006. Lakoff, in his book mentioned above, insists that the Left understand the power of words and take command of the language, but the Right already has its guru of language in Frank Luntz, who literally ran a consulting company to test terminology for its social and political effect. It was he who urged the use of 'death tax' to refer to the estate tax and 'climate change' to take the place of 'global warming.' His memo entitled "14 Words Never to Use" made other concrete recommendations of words for conservatives to avoid, such as *government, privatization/private accounts, tax reform, inheritance tax, estate tax, global economy, globalization, capitalism, outsourcing, undocumented workers, foreign trade, drilling for oil, tort reform, trial lawyer, corporate transparency, school choice,* and *healthcare 'choice.'* Curiously, he has recently gone quite public with his methods by publishing a book called *Words That Work: It's Not What You Say, It's What People Hear* (2007).

61

ATHEISM ADVANCED

Speaking Atheist,
Not Speaking Christian

> The Atheist does not say, "There is no God," but he says, "I
> know not what you mean by God. I am without the idea of
> God; the word "God" is to me a sound conveying no clear and
> distinct affirmation."
>
> —Charles Bradlaugh

The understanding of religion as a language has grave
implications for atheism and its confrontation with theism. As
we established in the first chapter, theism is not even identical
to religion but is merely one form or variation of it. Theism
speaks a particular dialect of religion, one with god-terms in
it. Other religious dialects do not engage in god-talk at all (and
likewise theisms do not talk about, or at least emphasize, the
things that non-theisms talk about). Each particular theism,
such as Christianity, is then nothing but a sub-dialect of the
dialect of theism, and each sect or denomination of Christianity
is a sub-sub-dialect, with its own vocabulary (Protestants
seldom talk about Eucharist or extreme unction or saints, *etc.*),
metaphors and literature. So, before we can even criticize or
refute religion, we must determine *which particular* religion
and religious language we are questioning. There are so many,
although in America and in Western societies we automatically
assume that we are talking about Christianity. But even if
we were to defeat Christianity, there would be several other
theisms and hundreds of other religions ready to fill the
vacuum. Must we — can we — fight each one in succession?
That would fill a lifetime of swatting at religions.

We must, therefore, first liberate ourselves from the
assumption that Christianity *is* religion and that religion *is*
Christianity, and then from the assumption that the Christian
language is a neutral and necessary way of talking — about
Christianity, other religions, and the world in general.
Christianity, like each religion, is trapped in its own little
language box, its own small terminological and conceptual
universe. Most Christians are not even aware that there
are other religions with, more significantly, other ideas and
concepts than their own. At best, most probably presume that,

although there are other religions, every one of those religions has a god and a heaven and a soul, *etc.* They do not. It appears that Christianity, like every religion, is an introverted, self-referential system of thought, depending on and running wild with the fact that humans can create imaginary worlds and live in them — perfectly content and confident, it seems, that their imaginary world is real and is the only one.

We atheists, who like Bradlaugh are not even *against* god(s) but *without* god(s), absolutely must escape the box of religious thought and language. Then, we must emphasize and at every turn point out to religions that *they* are in boxes and that their ideas and concepts are not only uninteresting but quite literally nonsensical to anyone outside their box—which is, in every case, the vast majority of the human species. Exposing a religion as a language is a sure way to deflate it, since no Christians want to admit that they are not describing the world but simply speaking Christian. Perceiving Christianity as nothing more than speaking a certain language would deny it, and every other religion, the status of truth, since languages are not 'true.' If your religion is *just* a language, why would you bother? What is the point of a language that does not refer to anything? Why would you get agitated and mobilized about a metaphor? No, religion depends for its existence on its (supposed) truth status. The result, in every case, is some degree of literalism: the words, concepts, stories, symbols are real. We belittle literalism, but it is the beating heart of every religion. For religious literalists like James Kennedy (an ardent atheist-basher), the Bible, except where it is expressly figurative, is literally true. There was a real Tree of the Knowledge of Good and Evil, not a metaphorical one, although what Good and Evil look like hanging on a tree is hard to say.

Toward an Atheist Language

Therefore, I warn atheists to be circumspect about the way we talk about religion, and not merely as a tactical issue. We should stop speaking Christian partly because it is an inadequate and biased way of talking about religion itself: Christian language is *not* a neutral objective rational language for discussing religions but rather only one religion's language treated as if it is neutral and objective and real. To try to talk about other religions, or religion in general, in Christian terms is to get them wrong. As scientists, we simply cannot describe one religion in the language of another.

But neither can we describe — or do — atheism in the terms of religion. We do not want to inhabit their linguistic box, where god(s) and heaven and hell are things worth talking about. And we most assuredly do not want to reinforce and support their box, which, if Lakoff is correct, is exactly what we do when we dignify their vacuous terminology with our attention. What we need is a distinct atheist discourse—to 'speak atheist.' We need words and concepts that convey our meanings in own terms, and not just as negations of their terms. Fortunately, some non-religious types have begun this process in small ways, offering terms like 'Bright' and 'Universist' to designate the idea and identity. But the process will have to go much further.

I am not suggesting inventing a completely new language, although I would not be against it either. Like religions, we will obviously piggyback on ordinary everyday English, with twists and additions. At the same time we should not be afraid to introduce new terms. Everyone who has ever studied a new subject knows that one major aspect is learning a new technical language or jargon. We could not do physics, say, in the language of religion, or of philosophy, or even of biology or chemistry. Nor can we do democracy in the language of monarchy; modern democracy required creating a language for new ideas like 'popular sovereignty' or 'election' or 'impeachment.' We often forget that many of the familiar freethought terms that we use today were created quite recently. For instance, in his study of the secularization of England, John Sommerville tells us that words like 'skeptic,' 'deist,' 'rationalist,' 'investigate,' 'criticism,' 'analyze,' 'consciousness,' and yes even 'atheist' were only introduced in the sixteenth and seventeenth centuries, giving people for the first time "a vocabulary which could express real unbelief" (1992:44). Imagine trying to do twenty-first-century atheism and freethought without those words — or doing religion *with them*.

We can also use, sometimes with slight modification, words in common parlance. We can even appropriate — or in many cases, *re*-appropriate — words from religion that were appropriated by religion in the first place. After all, we must face, and advertise, the fact that religion has already pervaded and commandeered everyday English as part of its comprehensive colonization of experience. Therefore, we must evict religion and reclaim the language for freethought (see Chapter 8 for much more on this suggestion). On the other hand, there are some words that are so poisoned, or else so thoroughly religious, that we do not want to speak them and, frankly, have no occasion to speak them.

For instance, we should never again use the word *spirit* or any of its forms. As I argue in *Natural Atheism*, 'spirit' is a metaphor for life or vitality or energy. If we mean that, we must say that. If we mean emotion or feeling, say that. If we mean immaterial beings, then we can say 'spirit,' but since I hope that we never mean that, we would never have a reason to say it. We should never use the word *belief* or *believe* in regard to ourselves (see Chapter 11 below), since its only concrete reference is to unsupported or counter-factual claims, and I hope we have none of those. We should not even use the word *religion*, and certainly not if we mean Christianity specifically; that is the most grievous error that everyone in America makes. We should replace it with *religions* or, if we *are* talking about Christianity, 'the Christian religion.' Even more fun would be to speak of 'a system of claims without evidence or in contradiction of the evidence.' I would not be averse to using the terms 'superstition' or 'imaginary thought systems' either. Likewise with *church*: there is no such thing as 'church,' only church-*es*, and to speak the plural is to remind any particular set of believers that they are not the only group in town. If we mean a Christian church, we should say "a Christian church," which will force listeners to think about why we make the distinction. *And we should never, under any circumstance, call atheism a religion or a church.* We should never say "Bible" or "Scriptures" but only "Judeo-Christian writings," which confronts believers with the reality that all religions have their own sources and most have their own writings. And of course we should never use any words that are specific to any one religion or only to religion; this includes *heaven, hell, sin, devil, angel, soul, pray, worship, sacred, bless, holy, divine, anoint,* and on and on. If we need to talk about them, we can specify "the Christian concept of heaven, hell, sin, *etc.*" because as we have seen, these are simply not universal and objective religious — let alone scientific — notions.

Finally and most important of all, we should stop talking about 'God.' We should *never* use the term with a capital G; when we are talking about the Christian god in particular, we should say "the Christian god" or "Yahweh" or "Jehovah." We should always say "god(s)" to remind them that there is more than one god-concept in the world. Again, I am not opposed to using the term 'imaginary being.'

So, when a theist asks us, "Is there a God?" we should not rush to say yes or no. Rather, we should demand that they define the term for us and tell us why they defined it that way. We could even explain to them that not all religions define god that way or have gods at all. Or better yet, we could simply say, "I have no idea what you are talking about — and neither do you."

Chapter 3

What Is Religion?
Getting Beyond the Theistic View

It is unfortunate, and almost inevitable, that when we talk about religion we quite literally do not know what we are talking about.

—Pascal Boyer

It is impossible to understand, let alone to advance, atheism without understanding theism, and it is impossible to understand theism without understanding religion broadly. The problem so far, for atheists and theists alike, is that almost no one has actually comprehended religion in a meaningful way.

As we have already established, for instance, religion is not a single thing or kind of belief and certainly not just theism. There are many *religions*, with some aspects in common — enough aspects to recognize them all as religions. But what precisely is it that makes an idea or behavior or institution religious? What is the function of religion, that is, why do humans have such a thing, especially when apparently other beings do not? And ultimately, where does religion come from? One simple answer would be that it comes from reality, from the discovery by humans or the revelation of spirits to humans of religious facts. This answer is singularly unsatisfactory, though, since the discoveries by or revelations to different human groups are so profoundly different and contradictory. If it were possible to determine any particular religion as true, then our problems would be solved. There would also be no more atheism (well, that is not quite true: if a non-theistic religion were determined to be true, then the true religion would be a-theistic), but there would be no other religions either. The final arrival at the 'true religion' would render all other religions false and therefore not worth holding.

67

ATHEISM ADVANCED

There are many reasons why the understanding of religion has not advanced much over the centuries. One is that there has been a strong and natural tendency to perceive one's own religion *as* religion. This was best expressed by the character Parson Thwackum in Henry Fielding's novel *The History of Tom Jones*: "When I mention religion I mean the Christian religion; and not only the Christian religion, but the Protestant religion; and not only the Protestant religion, but the Church of England." But this cannot be; since religion is a tree with many branches, it would be taking one branch as the entire tree. Substituting some other religion or category of religion fares no better: every religion is a minor branch on the tree of religions. Even using Christianity to represent religion is inadequate, for two obvious reasons: there is little that all Christianities agree on (in other words, there is no such thing as 'Christianity'), and there are so many other religions besides Christianity. Even using theism to represent religion is flawed, for the same two reasons: there is little that all theisms agree on, and there are so many other religious types besides theism.

Another reason why most people, including atheists, fail to grasp the nature of religion is that they think about it in the language of their own or the most familiar or locally-dominant religion, as discussed in the previous chapter. But it is not only religion that can obfuscate religion. Scientific or theoretical approaches can do the same. If a particular discipline or school of thought stresses one aspect of religion or human nature over others, then it can generate a view that is every bit as one-sided and inadequate as any religion. Interpreting religion as merely unconscious wish-fulfillment or social organization or pre-scientific question-answering is insufficient; it is once again mistaking the part for the whole. It is an instance of what is called *reductionism* — the explaining and explaining-away of a phenomenon as nothing more than a manifestation of one other, more basic process.

Atheists and other critics of religion often are guilty of their own kind of reductionism, a typically thin and derisive one: religion is often described, and ridiculed, as ignorance or fear-mongering or power-abuse. It may be any or all of those things, but it is not *just* those things. A system of thought and institution as pervasive and powerful as religion could not be so simple.

Moreover, many religions have little or nothing to do with fear or power: Warlpiri religion and those of other hunter-gatherer societies are not about fear at all (the spirits or ancestors are overall benevolent, and the general worldview is positive), nor do they recognize power (political or supernatural) in the same sense that we do. Here as elsewhere we are imposing familiar but local concepts and experiences on others who do not have those concepts and experiences themselves.

Our first project in this chapter, then, is to examine the conventional explanations or theories of religion and to consider why they are not so much wrong as deficient. Having done so, we will turn to a new attitude that is coalescing in regard to religion and other phenomena as well. Finally, we will return to think about our initial question — what is religion? — and its relation to society, human action, and (virtual) reality.

Theories of Religion

Over the centuries and millennia, people could not help but notice that religion is a curious and internally-diverse thing (that is, that any particular religion has many different aspects, beliefs, and practices, not all of which are entirely consistent with each other), that there are many other religions than one's own, and that religions do not always quite conform to empirical facts (for instance, bad people do not always suffer, and rain rituals do not always make it rain). Some have been inspired to suggest explanations or theories about religion.

Before we can analyze them, we need to consider what a theory is. It is more than a description: if we studied and summarized every religion in the world, even created a catalog or encyclopedia of religions, we would not have explained anything yet. A theory does not so much ask *What?* as *Why?* Why do religions have the general qualities that they do? Why do different religions and classes of religions have the particular qualities that they do? And why do religions exist at all?

A theory should offer some process or mechanism by which phenomena — in this case, religions — emerge and work, as well as change. It should be testable in some way, so that we can judge if we have the *correct* theory; we should be able to imagine some observation that our theory could not account for, which would challenge and falsify it. (For instance, if we theorized that all or any single type of religion grows out of castration anxiety, then finding a society without castration anxiety but with religion would disprove our theory.) Finally, ideally our theory should stimulate some predictions or other practical insights: what would happen to religion if this or that circumstance or variable were to change, or can we use religion or our model of religion to solve some problem or shed light on some other, non-religious question? The one thing that a theory cannot do is to take its subject matter for granted, to say, "Well, it is just true, and there is nothing more to say about it." There is always more to say, whether it is true or not.

As a consequence, a variety of types of theories of religion have appeared. Each has focused its attention on some particular aspect of religion, and many if not all have developed their own terminology and conceptual framework for dealing with it. Some of the main approaches to religion have included the historical, psychological (including intellectualist, emotionalist, and unconscious), sociological, and biological. Each makes some contribution to the ultimate understanding of religion, but each also falls short of a total explanation. Notice, however, that no major serious theory attempts to explain religion *in terms of religion* but always in terms of something else — and something quite human. As we will see, they are not usually motivated to prove that religion is true — that practice is known as *apologetics* and is not a theory of religion but a *part* of religion — but rather, as we will see in Chapter 6, often have the intended or unintended effect of *disproving* it.

Historical Theories

Historical theories of religion take the form of connecting religious beliefs and practices to the evolving history of humanity. One of the oldest versions, known as Euhemerism after the classical scholar Euhemerus, suggests that the gods of religion are nothing more than deified human heroes, perhaps great warriors or kings. As he wrote:

> With respect to the gods, too, our ancestors believed
> carelessly, credulously, with untrained simplicity; while

worshipping their kings religiously, desiring to look upon them when dead in outward forms, anxious to preserve their memories in statues, these things became sacred.

This is not a flippant notion: many ancient religions actively fostered the belief that leaders became powerful spirits or gods after death or even that they were powerful spirits or gods during life. Much more recently, Julian Jaynes (1976) argued that prehistoric people continued to hear (in their minds, of course) the voices of influential dead people and to confer supernatural status on them. Neanderthals, we know, as long as 60,000 years ago sometimes buried their dead with symbolic objects that indicate some meaningful (we hesitate to say religious) perception of death. By the Neolithic age (around 10,000 years ago), humans were living in settled communities with village leaders or chiefs. Jaynes describes a burial site called Eynan in the Middle East dated to around 9,000 years ago where the 'first god' was interred. This deceased king and a woman (his wife?) were placed in specific positions and decorated with shell jewelry, and the whole tomb had been painted with red ochre. He writes:

> I am suggesting that the dead king, thus propped up on his pillow of stone [to face east toward Mount Hermon], was in the hallucinations of his people still giving forth his commands.... This was a paradigm of what was to happen in the next eight millennia. The king dead is a living god. The king's tomb is the god's house, the beginning of the elaborate god-house or temples...prescient of the multitiered ziggurats, of the temples built on temples, as at Eridu, or the gigantic pyramids by the Nile... (142–3).

Jaynes has been criticized for the speculative quality of his theory, but we do not have to look far for later manifestations of the same mindset, as where Mayan kings were often left to sit on their throne for days or weeks after death, still giving royal orders and treated like gods. Pharaohs of Egypt, as he alludes, were gods in their own lifetimes.

A different historical approach has emphasized the evolution of religion over time. Ancient Greek religion itself told of a progression (or a regression) of religion, from the Golden Age of gods and human heroes to the Silver Age of regular humans to the Iron Age of current and inferior life. The philosopher Hegel in the early nineteenth century developed a theory of history and religion in which the Spirit (*Geist* in German) came to know itself more clearly over time, first through religion, then through philosophy, and finally through science. Later in the century, scholars of comparative religion like the ethnologists Lewis Henry Morgan and E. B. Tylor formulated an even more articulate stage-theory of religion and culture, in which culture progressed from "savagery" (hunting and gathering) to "barbarism" (settled farming) to "civilization" (urban life), and religion evolved from the "lowest" stage of animism or "nature worship" to the higher stage of polytheism and then the highest stage of monotheism. Notice that, in this line of thinking, the "highest stage" is their own culture's religion.

A final historical theory that could just as well be placed among the sociological theories is that of Karl Marx. Marx was not interested in religion as such; in fact, he was quite disdainful of it. His view was that practical, economic, "productive" activities were the source of ideas, rather than *vice-versa*. Any set of ideas, any worldview — which he called an ideology — was a product of its historical context and tended to mirror that context.

One kind of religion would emerge as a symbolic representation of the primitive, prehistoric social order. In ancient (*e.g.* Greek or Egyptian) times, a different religious formation would appear, reflecting new social realities — say, a pantheon of gods echoing the formal but decentralized politics of Greece. In medieval Europe, religion — namely, Christianity — took yet another shape, consistent with the static, hierarchical, and class-bound nature of its society. And in the modern capitalist era, religion would again reflect economic and social realities, particularly the consolidation and monopoly of power and wealth in the hands of a single class, church, and god.

However, in a starkly capitalist world, religion had no function, Marx argued, since it produced nothing. It was rather a parasite on production, creating a non-productive class (the clergy) who lived off the work of others. Worse yet, religion actually had a negative or exploitive function — to keep the working classes distracted from real, practical concerns by redirecting their attention to an afterlife where social relationships would be inverted and the poor would be rich and the rich would be poor. Marx was adamantly in favor of the abolition of religion, or more accurately he expected religion, like the government itself, to "wither and die" when real human material needs were met. When this world was perfected, the other world would have no appeal.

Psychological Theories

Psychological theories of religion relate it to human mental capacities and tendencies, which means (1) an emphasis on individuals and their experiences and (2) usually one particular capacity or tendency from among all of human mental function, since the mind does more than one thing and has more than one interest or need.

Among psychological approaches, one could be dubbed *intellectualist* or *rationalist* in the sense that it stresses the problem-solving or question-answering function of mind. Humans are motivated to understand and explain things, and some events or experiences are more elusive than others.

E. B. Tylor, for instance, suggested that religion grew to answer questions about uncanny phenomena like dreams, visions, out-of-body experiences, and of course the mysteries of death (what is it that distinguishes living bodies from dead ones?). According to Tylor and other intellectualists, humans are fundamentally questioners, and religion is a kind of primitive philosophy or science. For instance, one way to explain these paranormal experiences is with a concept of 'spirit' that is detachable from the body. According to the religious view, a dream may be an actual journey in the spirit world or the projection of the spirit to a faraway place; death occurs when the spirit is permanently dissociated from the body.

James Frazer, the early comparative religionist and author of *The Golden Bough*, went further in suggesting that religion is like science in that it formulates answers to questions and even does so rationally; the difference is that religion reasons from false premises (for example, that inanimate objects have mind or that words can cause physical changes in nature). Religionists, he opined, understand cause and effect; they just have the causes wrong. So, religion is not radically distinct from science, it is just pseudoscience or bad science. Religion, or more specifically magic, is a "technique" although a faulty one.

Bronislaw Malinowski, an anthropologist in the early twentieth century, agreed that religion (again, mostly magic) was a "tool" in the toolkit of religionists, but this toolkit also contained practical and effective techniques as well: no person, no matter how primitive or religious, expects crops to come out of the ground from prayer alone without putting some seeds in the soil too.

Another approach to psychology and religion de-emphasizes the intellectual side of us and highlights our emotional nature. In the emotionalist view, humans have feelings or sentimental needs that provide the basis for religious experiences or attitudes. Two of the founding thinkers of religious emotionalism were Max Mueller and Rudolph Otto. Both linked religion to the transcendent sensation, the feeling of vastness or oneness with the universe — what Freud once called the "oceanic feeling." For Otto, this experience of contact with something outside of and bigger than the self — perhaps infinitely big — gave rise to *The Idea of the Holy*, as his major book was titled. "The Holy" was how humans made sense of this transcendent feeling, which also felt "wholly other." It engenders additional complex emotions, including both fear and fascination, love and dread. From there, other ideas and interpretations would flow, but the feeling was the ultimate source of religious experience and thought.

Mueller started from a similar premise, that humans long ago had encountered these sentiments of vastness and overwhelming power but had been unable to express them clearly. Giving them names like 'the divine' or 'the infinite,' people could not quite capture their ineffable quality and symbolized them in mundane forms like the sun and the moon, the rain and the wind, and the animals and plants. As we saw in the previous chapter, when these metaphors or poems started to be believed, the result was religion.

Malinowski, whom we classified above as an intellectualist, also had an emotionalist streak in his work. His own approach to culture he called "functionalism": every aspect of culture had a function or else it would not exist. He located the function of most of culture in the organic needs of human individuals, such as food, shelter, warmth, sex, and so on. Religion does not seem, at least ordinarily, to fulfill these needs, and there would be other much more practical ways to achieve the same goals. Rather, he stated that religion filled more emotional needs, such as the need for comfort, security, hope, love, and a sense of control; he noticed that Trobriand Islanders brought out their religion in times of danger or uncertainty — such as fishing in the deep sea — but not in regular times when human knowledge and skill were adequate. As I often tell my students, they are much more likely to pray on test day than on normal class days.

A third version of psychological theory comes directly from the work of Sigmund Freud and the various psychoanalytic schools spawned by it. Freud's thinking focuses on the parts of the mind that we know the least, the so-called "unconscious." He argued that all humans have a set of instincts and drives that are impossible to bring to consciousness or too unacceptable to bring to consciousness or both. Yet, although they are unconscious, they are powerful and undeniable: unconscious drives shape our behavior as much as if not more than conscious ones. We try to "repress" them but they return nonetheless.

One (and remember that Freud's theories essentially focused on male psychology) is the desire to replace the father and have the mother all to oneself — his famous 'Oedipus' instinct. But the father is large and powerful and frightening, and the son has to repress this desire out of practical and psychological concerns. In one of his more speculative moments, Freud actually offered an ostensibly historical account of the sons of a pre-historical 'primal horde' rising up to kill their father and claim all the females for themselves. However, their guilt and remorse led them to forbid parricide and incest in the future, and the dead father was integrated into the unconscious — specifically the *superego* — as a judgmental and punishing figure. This powerful psychological figure became the template for god(s).

This led Freud, as the title of his book *The Future of an Illusion* indicates, to condemn religion as infantile wish-fulfillment, a neurosis that humans would outgrow when they got in better contact with and control of their unconscious drives.

ATHEISM ADVANCED

Some apostles of Freud, like Carl Jung, had a more positive attitude toward religion but still translated it into deep psychological processes. For Jung, religious symbols were really symbols of the mind and its instincts and drives, especially the drive for mental "wholeness" or "self-actualization" — bringing all of the parts of the mind into integration, balance, and control. But religious ideas were not true, they were externalizations of internal processes. Even alchemy, he famously insisted, was not about changing lead into gold but about changing the unconscious and unrealized self into a conscious and realized one.

Sociological Theories

Another approach to religion has placed the burden not on the individual and the mind but on the group and the culture. Of course, no theory — even Freud's — exclusively points to one at the expense of the other. Freud was aware that our interactions with external reality (what he impersonally called "objects" including the mother or at least the mother's breast) shaped our internal reality and even generated the conscious part of the mind called the 'ego' which operates on the 'reality principle.' But sociological theories, by which we mean those from both sociology and anthropology, locate most of the important religious processes in human collective existence.

One of the oldest modern sociological theories of religion is that of Marx, which we introduced above. Sometimes called "historical materialism" or "dialectical materialism," it suggests two factors that explain religion: (1) society is continuously changing through the dialectical evolution of practical, productive relations and the social relations that they engender — dialectical because the conditions established in any historical period create the terms for the destruction of that system and the development of a new one, which in turn will establish the conditions of its overthrow, *etc.*— and (2) each productive and social system spawns an idea system or ideology that supports it. Even more, he finds that in virtually every period in history, there existed a differentiation of society into groups of unequal wealth and power (masters and slaves, patricians and plebeians, lords and serfs, or industrial owners and workers).

What Is Religion?

The ideology of the age does more than support the system; it explains and justifies the system, keeping the various groups in their places and thus guaranteeing the power and wealth of the powerful and wealthy. As he said, the dominant ideas of an age are the ideas of the dominant class. Religion, then, would be part of a much more comprehensive social system, one based on social inequalities and in which religion serves the practical interests of the superior group by appearing to serve the 'spiritual interests' of the inferior group. That is why he called religion "the opium of the masses" and "the heart of a heartless world." Religion in his view was not even false but manipulative and exploitive.

Another very influential social theory of religion comes from the work of Emile Durkheim, a French theorist who helped to build modern sociology. His most complete discussion of religion can be found in his *The Elementary Forms of the Religious Life*, first published in 1912. He started from the same question that Tylor, Otto, and others did: what is the source of religion, where does the very idea of religion originate? He pinned religion to the distinction between two incommensurable realms, the "sacred" and the "profane."

The sacred is the powerful, the set-apart, that which we cannot approach at all or at least not casually; it is comparable to Otto's or Mueller's notion of the holy or the divine. The profane is that which cannot touch the sacred, that which would pollute or corrupt or "profane" it.

Thus his definition of religion is "a unified system of beliefs and practices relative to sacred things, that is to say, things set aside and forbidden — beliefs and practices which unite into one single moral community called a Church, all those who adhere to them" (1965:62). But this still does not solve his problem: where would humans ever get the concept of the sacred in the first place? His suggestion is that there is a real, palpable source of the impression that there is something bigger and more permanent than the individual, something that is external to and formative of the individual. It is not simply some oceanic feeling but an empirical force and reality. It is society itself.

Every human, he notes, is born into a society and into a specific position within that society. Groups are real, and the power they have over individuals is real. Humans cannot help but sense that they are a part of something much bigger than themselves — something that existed before them and will exist after them.

Society is the model of the sacred. And he means this quite literally: he finds, as we continue to find, that the organization of a religion reflects the organization of a society. If clans or classes or whatever groups and roles exist in society, they are expressed in religion too. What is important in society is important in religion. Only it is society that exists first; religion is a symbolic expression of those social realities. But religion does not merely represent a society; it functions to maintain, strengthen, and perpetuate that society. Particularly during ritual, the collective identity of the group, and its beliefs and values, are recreated by being impressed on the minds of the members:

> When they are together, a sort of electricity is formed by their collecting which quickly transports them to extraordinary degree of exaltation. Every sentiment expressed finds a place without resistance in all the minds, which are very open to outside impressions; each re-echoes the others, and is re-echoed by the others. The initial impulse thus proceeds, growing as it goes, as an avalanche grows in its advance. And as such active passions so free from all control could not fail to burst out, on every side one sees nothing but violent gestures, cries, veritable howls, and deafening noises of every sort, which aid in intensifying still more the state of mind which they manifest.... So it is in the midst of these effervescent social environments and out of this effervescence itself that the religious idea seems to be born (247).

So, in a circular process of generation and regeneration, society is the original source of religion and religion is the continuing source of society.

A third sociological theory of religion, known as 'structural functionalism,' is attributed to the anthropologist A. R. Radcliffe-Brown. In ways it builds on Durkheim's insights and constitutes a response to Malinowski's version of functionalism.

Malinowski had theorized that religion functions, like everything else, to fill the needs of individuals; in his view, individuals are the only real thing in society. Radcliffe-Brown disagreed, for two reasons. First, he insisted, like Durkheim, that group and roles and institutions were real as well and therefore could and would have their own needs apart from the individuals who composed them. Second, he noticed the obvious fact that religion does not always fill the needs of individuals. For instance, if a religion leads the society to sacrifice children or slaves or captives, it certainly does not fill the needs of the victims; it might even be difficult to perceive how it fills the needs of the sacrificers. Further, religion does not always have the effect that Malinowski described, of making people happier or more hopeful or less afraid. People who believe in an eternal and fiery hell may be *more* afraid than those who do not; people who do not believe in a hell *cannot* be afraid of it in principle, any more than Christians are afraid of *hekura* or *bilus* or any of the frightful beings we encountered in other religions.

Instead of an individual, psychological, emotional function, Radcliffe-Brown claimed that religion has a collective, social, structural function: the function of religion or all other aspects of culture was "the contribution that they make to the formation and maintenance of a social order" (1965:154). These included functions like enculturation of members into the group, the integration of subgroups and classes and genders and so on into a single social system, conflict resolution within the group which might otherwise blow it apart, means for collectively responding to crises both natural and social (such as the death of important members), and punishment of violation of the norms and standards of the group.

Biological Theories

Our final set of theories places stress on human biological characteristics, usually either the brain or genes. Some have gone so far as to propose a "god spot" in the brain or a "god gene" in cells that makes religion possible or inevitable. An entire field called neurotheology has even emerged recently, exploring the connection between religion and the nervous system.

Arguably the launching point for a modern biological, evolutionary perspective on religion was E. O. Wilson's *Sociobiology: A New Synthesis*. To counter the 'blank-slate,' ultra-cultural approach of much of social science and to give human behavior a naturalistic foundation, Wilson proposed sociobiology as "the systematic study of the biological basis of all social behavior" (1975:4). Thus his project was to explain the evolutionary processes behind social behaviors like altruism and aggression. He did not propose and has not subsequently defended a simplistic view in which there is a single gene for each such behavioral tendency, but in his original book and in his later *On Human Nature* he did insist that humans, as material and evolved beings, must have material and evolutionary bases for their behaviors. His latter book suggested that religion in particular was not only natural but "in all probability an ineradicable part of human nature" (1978:169). In a much more recent interview, he expanded on his previous views to claim that "Religious belief itself is an adaptation that has evolved because we're hard-wired to form tribalistic religions" (Paulson 2006).

The key to the sociobiological, evolutionary approach to religion is the notion of adaptation, that is, that religion, like any other trait — physical or behavioral — must have some adaptive value to the species. Followers of this line of thinking point to the *universal, complex, and costly* qualities of religion as evidence of its biological foundations. All humans, or at least all human societies, appear to possess religion: humans everywhere seem to do it, it seems too complicated and intricate to be a mere learned phenomenon, and it often makes such burdensome demands on practitioners that they would presumably stop doing it unless there was some benefit or advantage to it. And if religion is biological and adaptive, then it must heritable — there must be some way for religion to pass from generation to generation — and if it is heritable then it must have a genetic component.

The two goals of sociobiological, adaptationist researchers therefore have been to define the benefit or advantage that religion confers and to identify the genetic basis. Supporters have advanced a variety of possibilities as to benefit. There are essentially two kinds of advantages that any adaptation can provide, individual ones and collective ones; in other words, a trait can increase the individual's fitness or the group's fitness. Bulbulia, for instance, expresses the view that religion enhances individual health and survival: he likens religion to a placebo and claims that "religiosity evolved as a mechanism of self-healing" (2006:67), while elsewhere he insists that "if believing in supernatural causation helps us to recover from illness or meet the terrors of life, then tendencies to fall into such deceptions will be conserved and more intricately articulated" (2004:680). Note he considers religion to be a deception, specifically a *self*-deception, but a useful one.

There are other conceivable individual advantages in religion, but collective, group benefits have been even more controversial, since many evolutionists reject the very idea of group selection. Despite this resistance, probably the dominant position in the sociobiological, adaptationist theory of religion is that it helps the group, even if it costs individuals. David Sloan Wilson (2002) champions the group-selection perspective, that religion is an "adaptive belief system" with "secular utility" for groups in terms of group cohesion, social control of members, and the regulation of mundane affairs like the management of resources. However, neither he nor anyone else can ignore the fact that religion is also patently inefficient, that it wastes vast amounts of time, effort, and wealth in empirically unproductive activity.

One common solution to this problem is what many group-adaptationists call "costly signaling theory." Religion is effective *precisely because* it is expensive and superficially wasteful. Bulbulia as well as Sosis and Alcorta and many others make the argument that social living depends on cooperation and mutual trust. However, there is always the potential of deception and "freeloading" in the group. Thus, lazy deceivers find themselves in "an evolutionary arms race" with their comrades who, as deceiver-detectors, erect ever-more demanding tests of honesty and commitment. "The result of such escalation would be increasingly complex ritual behaviors as senders attempt to deceive receivers and receivers seek to determine the truthfulness of the sender's signal" (Sosis and Alcorta 2003:266). In a word, religion is not useful because it is *true* but because it is *difficult*: only whole-hearted members would accept the burdens religion entails. This might help explain some of the extreme difficulties that religionists put on themselves and each other, including sacrifice and self-injury (see Chapter 5).

Finally, sociobiological, evolutionary scientists seek the specific genetic substrate of religion. That there is such a substrate at all is of course debatable, but research by D'Onofrio finds that there is. Reviewing a number of previous studies and analyzing data on a sample of 30,000 experimental subjects, he concludes that there is some, but only some, genetic component to religiosity, as measured by behavior like church attendance.

> Additive genetic effects...explain between 18% (women) and 19% (men) of the total variation in church attendance. If we included the apparent contribution of dominance to the genetic variation, we find that genetic factors account for approximately 30% in women and 23% in men. The balance of the variation is due to environment factors (1999:970–1).

In other words, as he confesses, his results show "that religious affiliation is primarily a culturally transmitted phenomenon, whereas religious attitudes and practices are moderately influenced by genetic factors" (953). Nevertheless, some scholars have tried, or even claimed, to find one or more genes that produce religion. Dean Hamer, in his recent *The God Gene* (2004), appears to announce exactly this discovery. Somewhat misleadingly named, what Hamer studies is the "spiritual" or "mystical" or "transcendent" experience (see below) and what he actually says is that there are probably many, even hundreds, of genes involved in the production of religious behavior. However, he does place special emphasis on a gene called VMAT2, which seems to play a role in the brain chemistry of mystical experiences.

This leads us to the other main locus of interest in the biological basis of religion, the brain. The brain (human and otherwise) is a complex composite organ with many physiological and functional specializations (see below). Researchers have discovered that certain areas of the brain seem to be implicated in 'religious experience,' which only makes sense. Andrew Newberg and Eugene d'Aquili (2002) undertook a more systematic investigation of this fact, observing the brain activity of people during meditation. They discovered that the temporal lobes were active during meditative states but that the parietal lobes were almost completely inactive. From other work we know that the parietal lobes play a role in our sense of time and space, even more crucially in our experience of 'being in our body.' The sensation that meditators — especially master-meditators — often report, the 'transcendent' or 'one-with-the-universe' or 'disembodied' feeling, would logically be associated with the deactivation of the brain functions that give us our grounded, embodied experience in the first place. In other words, there is evidence that the condition that meditators describe, and that Mueller and Otto stressed, is a brain state.

If religious experiences can be studied, it is conceivable that they could be experimentally reproduced. Michael Persinger (1987) has for years been stimulating the temporal lobes of subjects with a mild magnetic field, and he has announced that 80% of those people tell him that they get the impression of "not being alone," of sensing a presence around them. The magnetic stimulation that he applies simulates temporal lobe epilepsy, and it has been noted that such epilepsy often results in religious experiences or obsessive-compulsive behavior. Robert Sapolsky goes so far as to indicate that a specific kind of brain damage following epilepsy leaves patients with a compulsive interest in religious matters.

There are two ways to interpret these data. Religious apologists have latched onto them as proof that religious conceptions are real: the brain, they conclude, could not have produced such experiences unless there was something real to experience. The brain, in this view, is like a receiver, an antenna, picking up the true religious signals from a supernatural source. But the first part of their argument is patently false, and the second part is fatally hasty. We know that the brain can have all kinds of non-objective experiences, like dreams and hallucinations. No sane person would demand that all psychological or mental phenomena are real. If we use a probe to stimulate a spot on the brain that causes the subject to 'hear a sound,' there is no real sound there — only the brain function that produces the sensation of sound. More significantly, none of these experiments or clinical observations has yielded any *particular* religious knowledge. Subjects and patients report a kind of generalized mystical experience, but not the experience of any specific god or spirit. Even worse, their experience is not even distinctly religious: a sensation of 'presence' or 'disembodiedness' could be understood in any number of ways, religious and non-religious. It is clear that what is going on here is that people are interpreting those experiences *as* religious. If Mueller and Otto are correct, they are the source of the very impression that there is something 'out there' to explain, and religious explanations rush in to fill the void.

The fact is that the mundane experiences of being bound by space and time, of having a body, and of being a self appear to be accomplishments of the brain. This becomes evident when these accomplishments fail. For instance, in a condition known as Capgras syndrome, also termed 'mirror self-misidentification,' sufferers do not recognize their own face in a mirror. They think that they are looking at someone else. This self-foreign-ness can transfer to property and pets as well: some patients say that they believe someone replaced their cat or dog or shoes with other, identical objects. (Another condition called prosopagnosia leaves victims unable to recognize other people's faces.) There is an increasing awareness of a syndrome called body dysmorphic disorder in which people have an unrealistic vision of their own appearance, even when they are staring directly into a mirror. People with perfect skin can see themselves as pocked and scarred, and perfectly normal and attractive people can see themselves as hideous. If a human being's experience of self can be so detached from reality, and if that sense of self is a product of brain activity (and not reality), then under- or over-stimulated brain activity could produce all sorts of anomalous perceptions that we only falsely take as real let alone religious.

There is No Such Thing as Religion: The Emerging Modular View

All of these theories and more purport to explain religion, both its source and its function. None of them is wrong, but none of them is perhaps quite right either. Most interestingly, despite their conspicuous differences, they are all quite similar in certain regards. First, each attempts to explain religion in a

What Is Religion?

single way, sometimes with a single word, like 'feeling' or 'wish-fulfillment' or 'ideology' or 'integration.' Here as elsewhere, this is not so much incorrect as incomplete: religion certainly does have emotional and intellectual and social dimensions, but it cannot be reduced to any *one* of these dimensions. The continuing and stubborn desire to understand religion in one simple way may be the greatest reason for misunderstanding; as the sociologist Georges Simmel put it in 1957, "The ambiguity which surrounds the origin and nature of religion will never be removed so long as we insist upon approaching the problem as one for which a single word will be an 'open sesame'" (quoted in Glasner 1977:12). It is a symptom of the same kind of simultaneous overgeneralizing and undergeneralizing that we have already marked as a habit in the discussion of religion.

Another problem with these theories is that they all tend to take one kind of religious experience — or even one religion — as the paradigm for all. In a word, since they are all products of Christian scholars or at least of scholars in predominantly Christian society, they all tend to speak Christian in their sense of what religion is and what it does. In some ways the writers cannot help but use terms like 'sacred' and 'church' and even 'belief,' since they must write in some language, but there is often little sensitivity to the fact that these theories might be an imposition of one religion's language and experience on others — an assumption that all religions are like Christianity. We know that they are not.

A third and most subtle problem is that these theories of religion see religion as 'a thing in need of explanation,' in fact as 'a thing' at all. What I mean is that they present religion as a distinct, distinguishable phenomenon with its essential and unique characteristics. It appears to be unlike anything else that humans do, to be an identifiable and real thing with its own nature and properties. Exactly what separates the religious from the non-religious or at least the other-than-religious is not always stated, but it is always presumed. There is *something* that makes religion 'religious.' There is an essence of religion. There is such a *thing* as religion.

However, a growing and convincing consensus is that religion is not a thing at all, and in two senses. First, there is nothing that *all* religions share and that *only* religions share. Other phenomena besides religion can answer questions, produce feelings, fill needs, and integrate society. Other phenomena can be speculative and unfalsifiable (like UFO beliefs, astrology, or certain alternative medical ideas). In other words, there may be no unique essence of religion; religion is like other psychological and social phenomena in some ways and unlike them in others. Second, religion is not a singular, unified, monolithic phenomenon. It is, among other things, incredibly diverse, as we have seen. It also seems to have multiple and disparate parts or elements that can be combined in any number of ways. This is why we had to reject the notion of 'types of religion,' since any particular religion can have any or all of the types represented in it (gods, nature spirits, ancestors, *etc.*). A religion seems more like a system — a collection or congeries of modules — than a uniform substance. And a religion seems to be built out of elements that are not inherently or exclusively religious but that also can and do have other-than-religious manifestations and functions.

Introduction to Modular Thinking

The idea of theoretically-stubborn phenomena being systems constructed out of modules or subsystems rather than unitary and homogeneous things is not a new one, and it is not one that has been applied only to religion. Actually, it has only lately been applied to religion, due to the certainty that most people — religious and non-religious alike — that religion really is a 'thing.' A system by definition has (1) distinct parts (2) in some specific arrangement or order or structure. The parts themselves may be subsystems made of even more basic parts in structures, and so on. The real action may not be at the level of the total system but at the level of the parts and their structure. That is, the explanation may not reside at the top level but at lower levels; at the top level — in this case, 'religion' — there may be little or nothing to explain. Further, the parts and structures that are found in the top-level system may not be unique to the top-level system (that is, they may also figure into other systems too), and therefore they may not be *for* the top-level system. What I mean to say is that the parts of any system — from a mouse trap to a brain to a religion — may not originate or exist *for* the mouse trap or brain or religion but rather be combined so that the result is what we call a mouse trap or a brain or a religion. The parts may certainly be changed by being integrated into the system, but the parts existed prior to and apart from the system, not *vice-versa*.

This perspective sees what we often consider things as actually systems of systems of modules. Each module is a structural and functional unit, a component that does something. It contributes to the functioning of the whole, but its modular function is often lost to the observer within the functioning of the whole. One of the most obvious modular systems is the brain itself. We have known for some time that the brain is functionally and anatomically specialized; the entire brain does not perform every function of the brain, but specific functions are located (more or less) in specific areas. For instance, we know that there are areas of the brain that perform motor or movement functions, while other parts perform autonomic functions like regulating heartbeat and breathing. The evidence of this anatomical specialization comes from brain injuries, lesions and tumors, as well as intentional experimental research (stimulate a certain part of the brain and the subject has a certain sensation or experience). As we saw above, particular regions of the brain apparently even control our experience of self and of time and space. We know especially clearly that skills like language are localized (for most humans, in the left temporal lobe), and even more so that linguistic subskills are still more localized. One spot, named Broca's area, appears to be involved in speech production (literally, moving the mouth and tongue) and perhaps in grammar generally; people with damage there speak slowly and haltingly. Another spot, called Wernicke's area, seems to control meaning such as the names of objects; damage there can produce fluent but nonsense speech. And not only do the areas provide their particular functions but they cooperate to provide other functions: damage to the connecting tissue between the two regions causes patients to be unable to repeat what they hear (Pinker 1995:311). What seems to us in our everyday lives as a single linguistic ability, in other words, is actually an elaborate organization of linguistic modules each with its own contribution to make to the whole.

ATHEISM ADVANCED

Other skills and abilities that were formerly assumed to be unitary are now regarded at least by some as sets of modules. This includes more abstract concepts like intelligence. Most of us feel confident that we can declare someone intelligent or unintelligent in general (perhaps with some gradient of intelligence in between). Intelligence is a *thing*, a single property or quality, we think. However, the work on intelligence by Howard Gardner starting in 1983 suggests otherwise, and it fits our day-to-day experience of ourselves and others. Gardner argues that intelligence is really a bundle of intelligences, each of which can be independently advanced or underdeveloped in any individual. In his original formulation, he identified seven distinct intelligences: linguistic, musical, logic-mathematical, spatial, bodily-kinesthetic, interpersonal, and intrapersonal. (He has added two extra intelligences — naturalist and existentialist — in later versions.) We all know people who are really good at some mental activities like math but just average or really bad at others, including interpersonal relations. In the past, we had to judge a person as a whole as either intelligent or unintelligent; now we can make finer distinctions. It has even become common practice to distinguish between 'IQ' and 'EQ' or 'emotional quotient,' which would capture one or two of Gardner's intelligence modules. But, insofar as this new view is correct, it becomes meaningless to call someone intelligent or unintelligent in general. Intelligence is no longer a thing but a union of multiple skills and abilities.

We could go on offering examples. An economy is not a single thing but a complex and even ambiguous and contradictory assortment of factors: it is not just production or GNP but also employment, wages, spending, savings, and many other sub-systems. An ecosystem is certainly not a thing but, as the name suggests, a system of environments, species, *etc.* in a particular arrangement and balance. Even the self, it appears, may not be a unitary, homogeneous, and immutable thing but a bundle of experiences, perceptions, and capacities that seems monolithic most of the time (when it functions normally) but that can break down into its component parts and expose its modular functioning. A culture is absolutely a system of modules — families, classes, institutions, and the like — and each subsystem of a culture (language, economy, politics and, yes, religion) — is further constituted of modules that collectively give it its 'nature' but also potentially contribute to other domains as well.

Religion as a Modular By-Product

The idea that religion is a product, even a by-product, of an amalgamation of disparate and not uniquely religious traits or processes is not a brand new one, although it has gained traction and adherents lately. One of the first modular analyses of religion was given by the anthropologist Anthony Wallace forty years ago. In his discussion, religion begins with a basic "premise" and then elaborates more and more inclusive systems of systems to build up the recognizable "religions" that we find in the human world. The basic "premise of every religion — and this premise is religion's defining characteristics — [is] that souls, supernatural beings, and supernatural forces exist" (Wallace 1966:52). It is the same premise that E. B. Tylor started with, when he wrote that the "minimal definition" of religion is "belief in spiritual beings." Of course, Wallace's position begs the question of what a "supernatural" being or force is, but we will allow it for now. It seems that all religions have some fundamental commitment to beings or forces that are not the garden-variety kind, and when we talk about non-garden-variety beings and forces, we are talking 'religion.'

But the supernatural premise is far from a religion yet. Upon that premise is assembled some combination of the 'elementary particles' of religious behavior, of which he lists thirteen. These particles or building blocks or modules include (1) prayer, (2) music, dancing, and singing, (3) physiological exercises or rigors like mortification, sensory deprivation, drug ingestion, sleep deprivation, *etc.*, (4) exhortation, that is, commands, threats, comforting words, and such, (5) myth and narrative, (6) simulation or imitation, in which category he places ritual, magic, and witchcraft, (7) "mana" or the notion of power and powerful things that can be touched, (8) taboo or things that cannot be touched, (9) feasts, (10) sacrifice, (11) "congregation" or communal gatherings, (12) "inspiration" such as mysticism, hallucinations and visions, often achieved by way of #3, and (13) symbolism and symbolic objects (Wallace 1966:56).

There are two things to note. Not all religions will include all of these components, nor will they equally elaborate the ones they do include. Some religions may leave out sacrifice or physiological trials and ordeals, and some may have more intricate prayer practices or taboo notions than others. However, most of these will be found in most religions. At the same time, it is apparent that many of these modules are not exclusive to religion. Religion is hardly the only human activity that entails music and dancing. There are non-religious exhortations, non-religious exercises and rigors, non-religious stories and narratives, non-religious symbols, non-religious congregations and assemblies, non-religious feasts, even non-religious sacrifice in some senses. It is as if religion is exploiting and riding on otherwise generally human, not specifically religious, qualities and potentials to construct a religious system. We will return to this idea shortly.

Next, Wallace sees these particles or modules being integrated into complexes and sequences of religious action, which constitute rituals — along with cognitive and linguistic rationalizations or beliefs concerning these actions. Beliefs are absolutely secondary in his opinion, being a kind of spontaneous interpretation, a creation of meaning by the performers. At an even higher level of integration, religious/ritual sequences are bundled into "cult institutions," defined as "a set of rituals all having the same general goal, all explicitly rationalized by a set of similar or related beliefs, and all supported by the same social group" (75). A church would be a cult institution in his sense, as would more specific ritual complexes like a wedding or a mass, *etc.* A religion, at the ultimate level, is a bundle of these bundles, "a loosely related group of cult institutions and other, even less well-organized special practices and beliefs" (78). This leads him to the determination that a religion is not a thing, as we have said, but the name for a particular cluster of more elementary bits. Religion is, in the final analysis, "essentially a summative notion and cannot be taken uncritically to imply that one single unifying, internally coherent, carefully programmed set of rituals and beliefs characterizes the religious behavior of the society or is equally followed by all its members" (78).

The emerging contemporary view is similar to Wallace's in that religion is a summative product of multiple parts that are not necessarily tightly integrated or consistent, *and not necessarily religious*, but it is different in two major ways: it puts even less emphasis on religion as a unique thing, and it links religion more concretely to evolutionary psychological and social characteristics of humans. A clear illustration of these points can be seen in the work of Paul Bloom, a psychologist who has studied very young children, even infants. From his research, he concludes that the basic premise of religion is not anything as religious as a belief in spiritual beings but rather an inherent "dualism." His evidence indicates that, from the very earliest age, humans "are natural Cartesians — dualistic thinking comes naturally to us. We have two distinct ways of seeing the world: as containing bodies and as containing souls" (2004:*xii*). His choice of the last word is too overwrought and prejudicial, another case of importing not only one religion's term for all religions' experience but of importing a religious word for an essentially non-religious experience. What he more precisely means is that humans, even the tiniest babies, seem to have the concept that objects and people are different and that the key difference between them is mind or intention.

It has been known for a long time that babies are uniquely tuned to human faces; faces are their favorite things to look at. Bloom used this fact to study babies by examining the other things that they like to look at, on the assumption that the more a baby looks, the more interesting or surprising the sight is. He found, for instance, that babies around a year old prefer to look at shapes that are moving relative to each other than to ones that are moving independently and randomly. "When 12-month-olds see one object chasing another, they seem to understand that it really is *chasing*, acting with the goal of catching someone else — they expect it to continue its pursuit along the most direct path, and are surprised when it does otherwise" (18). In another experiment, one-year-olds were shown a film of a circle moving up an incline; in one version, there was a triangle below the circle as the circle ascended the hill, while in another there was a square on top of the circle as it climbed more slowly. We adults do not see these actions as random but as meaningful: the triangle is "helping" the circle, while the square is "hindering" it. Then the youngsters were shown a movie in which the circle would approach either the triangle or the square; they were more surprised when it approached the square. These children "seem to expect the ball to approach the one that helped it and to avoid the one that hindered it. My own interpretation of this behavior — admittedly a bit exuberant — is that the 12-month-olds assume that the circle *likes* the triangle and *hates* the square" (18).

Bloom's basic premises are more general and relevant to our discussion. First, humans, even very young humans, seem to attribute states of mind to things, including other humans (which we consider appropriate) and non-human objects (which we normally do not). If there is the slightest bit of intelligible behavior, we tend to perceive intentional behavior, an act of mind or will. Second, we are able to understand or empathize with the state of mind of others; we can imagine how a circle, a dog, or a person feels or thinks. We are, as Bloom puts it, congenital mind-readers — or perhaps mind-attributers. These two facts are fundamental to our social nature: in social groups, individuals *must* be able to attribute and understand mental states in others. It is just that we are not sure *which* others have mental states and which do not. We tend to overextend intention to objects or events that do not necessarily have it. The almost inevitable conclusion from this natural tendency is to see *objects* (physical things that do not have mind or intention) and *persons* (physical things that *do* have mind or intention) as different because the latter has a second component that the former does not.

Bloom calls this "soul," but we could just as well call it "personality" or "life" or "mind" or "spirit." It is a very small step to decide that the intentional component, which is not the same as the physical part, can exist separately from it and survive its destruction. With that, the supernatural premise of Wallace is set, and religion follows. But Bloom insists that the observations do not mean humans are born "with any capacities or dispositions that are special to religious ideas. There is no religion module or innate notion of a god, nothing akin to the 'language organ' proposed by Noam Chomsky" (222). The "religious instinct" is really nothing more than a "social instinct" widely applied; religions, like many of our other "most interesting mental traits are best understood as unexpected by-products of our evolved capacity to understand and respond to the minds of other people" (5).

What Is Religion?

Pascal Boyer pushes this attitude much further. He starts from the same place: humans are inherently social, and our psychological processes evolved in a social environment. In fact, he refers to our primary mental skill as "hypertrophied social intelligence" (2001:122), an overgrown and intensely sensitive attention to interpersonal information. He gives a much more nuanced description of mental processes, suggesting that the mind is not a single thing but "a whole confederacy of different systems" or modules, each providing some function and influencing the outcome of the whole. He refers to these modules as "inference systems," each of which is specialized, like parts of the brain, to handle "a limited aspect of the information available about our surroundings but produces very smart inferences about that aspect" (98). Among these are two that Bloom also discusses: agency detection and essentialism. Agency detection (or "hyperdetection" from Boyer's perspective) is the inclination to look for and attribute intentionality or mind or will to happenings. Essentialism is the notion that there is some 'essence' to things, both individual things and groups or classes of things, that makes them a particular kind of thing — in other words, a 'dog essence,' a 'tree essence,' and of course a 'human essence' (see Chapter 9 below).

Inference systems operate on the basis of concepts or even deeper generalities called *templates*, that provide the criteria by which we assign things to categories and make assumptions about their nature and behavior. 'Dog,' for instance, would be a concept, and it would be one particular manifestation of the template 'Animal.' He likens a template to a blank form with specific "fields" or spaces to fill in. All animals have a bundle of common traits: they eat, they have legs, they have life-spans, *etc*. For 'Dog,' we fill in the details: what they eat (meat), how many legs they have (4), how long they live (around twelve years or whatever). But being in the template 'Animal,' we import an assortment of assumptions that do not need to be catalogued or proven.

As the categorizing beings that we are, human mental processes are acute when it comes to violations of our expectations; like the babies who stare at exceptional or surprising things more than ordinary ones, we attend to exceptions to our concepts and even more so to our templates.

A talking dog is more compelling than a mute dog — or than a dog with five legs. 'Five' as a value for the field 'number of legs' in the template is not so exotic, but there is no field in the Animal template for language at all. Thus, what he calls "counterintuitive" ideas — dogs that talk or beings that do not have bodies or die — grab our attention and remain in our memory.

Add to these mental processes the modules of causality, social exchange (humans enter into and expect others to enter into reciprocal relationships of give and take), moral interest (human agents are aware of and interested in the effects their own actions on others and assume that others are too), and narrativity (connecting a series of events into stories or meaningful sequences), and you have all of the material out of which to build a religious viewpoint. Religious ideas and concepts, he notes, are those that violate intuitive expectations, but only in certain limited ways. Religious beings are not usually depicted as having six fingers (not exceptional enough) or only existing on Tuesdays (too exceptional), but as immaterial or immortal (just exceptional enough). Above all, in all other ways, they are rather conventionally *people*: they have likes and dislikes, they interact with us, they have language, and so on. They often eat and have families and homes and villages, *etc.* In fact, he argues that there is a fairly limited number of supernatural templates, which explains why religions around the world are not so widely different. "Persons can be represented as having counterintuitive physical properties (*i.e.* ghosts or gods), counterintuitive biology (many gods who neither grow nor die), or counterintuitive psychological properties (unblocked perception or prescience). Animals too can have all these properties. Tools and other artifacts can be represented as having biological properties (some statues bleed) or psychological ones (they hear what you say)" (78). It is easy to observe that the qualities of the Christian god are merely extensions or negations of normal human qualities — *all*-knowing, *all*-good, *im*-mortal, *im*-material,.

The power of religious concepts lies in a general mental power, which Boyer calls "decoupling." That is, mental modules and the functions they perform can be detached or decoupled from their everyday and evolved sources and functions. Many

What Is Religion?

familiar psychological phenomena — dreams, imagination, fantasy, make-believe, conditional (if/then) thinking, and art to name a few — arise from this same potential. This means that mental systems can be used for other than their original evolutionary/adaptive purpose (to detect the workings of other humans in the world and to decipher their intentions in relation to us) and can be combined in unexpected and unprecedented ways. In other words, a mental module or any other quality can evolve for one reason and be put to use for others, singly and collectively, spinning out by-products even as they work exactly as they evolved to work. Boyer's conclusion is that religion is just such a by-product, the result of "mental systems and capacities that are there anyway" (311). The mental modules and habits evolved originally for completely human/social purposes, and "we can explain religion by describing how these various capacities got recruited, how they contribute to the features of religion.... We do not need to assume that there is a *special way* of functioning that occurs only when processing religious thought" (311). Religion is in a very real way a side-effect or spin-off of normal mental activity.

Scott Atran is another contemporary thinker who arrives at the same conclusion. "Religious beliefs and practices," he writes, "involved the very same cognitive and affective structures as nonreligious beliefs and practices — and no others — but in (more or less) systematically distinctive ways" (2002:ix). The upshot is that "there is no such entity as 'religion'" and therefore nothing to explain other than the regular functioning of the human mind and its evolution (15). Much of Atran's analysis of mental modules resembles Boyer's in many ways. He identifies four classes of modules, operating relatively independently:

(1) perceptual modules, for input and processing of information about faces, objects, colors, and other perceptual qualities;

(2) primary emotion modules, which are the more "primitive" and "non-cognitive" states, even physiological states, associated with fear, anger, sadness, pleasure, disgust, and the like;

(3) secondary affect modules, which implicate cognitive processing along with primitive emotions, such as grief, guilt, love, pride, and anxiety; and

(4) conceptual modules, which access inputs and processing from other parts of the nervous/mental system to build up higher-level experiences and structures (57–8).

He also highlights the role of agency, finding that "supernatural agents" are simply a special case of agency as such, "by-products of a naturally selected cognitive mechanism for detecting agents — such as predators, protectors, and prey — and for dealing rapidly and economically with stimulus situations involving people and animals" (15).

Two aspects that Atran stresses more than some other writers are the high "cost" of religion and of social "deception" in general and the role of unintended or "accidental" or emergent characteristics in complex systems. Religion "is costly, counterfactual, and even counterintuitive," he grants, but this is not necessarily a problem and can be a positive advantage (5). Because it is difficult to do, it is difficult to fake doing. This plays into a notion that other modern analysts of religion as a social activity have advanced, namely, deception-detection. Humans are not only able and highly inclined to "read" the minds of others, but they are also liable to attempt to trick others by misrepresenting their own minds and intentions, that is, lying. In social contexts, lying can be a profitable but also a destructive thing: if I can get others to believe that I am working hard so that they feed me, great for me, although if everyone does so, no work will get done and no food will be produced. Social deception is a potentially serious issue. One way, some have asserted, to test and confirm the honesty and commitment of others is to give them expensive tasks to perform; fraternity hazing or other initiation rituals would suffice as examples. The more expensive (in time, money, effort, *etc.*) and the more difficult to fake, the more reliable the test. Thus, Atran defines religion as "a community's costly and hard-to-fake commitment ... to a counterfactual and counterintuitive world of supernatural agents ... who master people's anxieties, such as death and deception" (4).

The other important point in Atran's (and others') description is the unintended but often usefully employed outcomes of a system, which he and others call "spandrels." A spandrel, most famously invoked by Stephen Jay Gould in his discussions of biological evolution, is "an architectural term that describes the structural form or space that arises as a necessary concomitant to another decision in design and is not meant to have any direct utility in itself" (43). Atran offers the example of the space created under a stairway: no architect designed the space intentionally, but the nature of stairs leaves a space underneath them which can be used in ways that were not planned or sought. Another example might be earlobes: human earlobes did not evolve for the purpose of hanging rings from them, but as ears evolved the lobes appeared, in such a way that they are good for placing rings on. Noses evolved for breathing and smelling, but they are good today for propping up eyeglasses.

Biologists and paleontologists regard many of the physical features of species to be non-designed spandrels of real evolutionary processes (so much for the 'intelligent design theory'). Likewise, we can conceive of religion as a mental and social spandrel, an unintended and not-necessarily adaptive outcome of other processes that do have evolutionary histories and adaptive value. Religion in this sense would be a parasite or hanger-on of other, non-religious capacities and tendencies.

For one last quick example, the psychologist Lee Kirkpatrick places most of the attention on the psychological process of attachment. In his book *Attachment, Evolution, and the Psychology of Religion* (2005), he agrees that religion is best "conceptualized as the by-product(s) of numerous adaptations that evolved in early humans...for other mundane purposes" (336). He acknowledges many or all of the processes we have already seen, which he divides into two categories, "cognitive building blocks" and "psycho-emotional building blocks." The cognitive modules include essentialism (the presumption of "inherent differences"), anthropomorphism (the attribution of human-like qualities to the non-human), and psychological animism (the presumption that certain things, especially things that move, are 'alive' in ways that other objects are not). Among the psycho-emotional modules, he gives pride of place to attachment, the critical process by which humans, especially very young humans, develop preferential emotional bonds to specific care-giving adults. Psychologists have long observed that children around two years of age form powerful attachments to key others (especially and ordinarily parents) and seek them out in times of fear or need. Part of the motivation of attachment has been shown to be practical (getting food), but another part appears to be independent of physical needs and seems to be instinctive — a desire for closeness, comfort, and physical contact with another person. Religion in Kirkpatrick's analysis is another case of the "decoupling" of a human and natural process — seeking out the comfort and safety of a nurturing power-figure, a strong parent — from the natural/human dimension to the supernatural/superhuman one. Religion is a case of attachment writ large — attachment to the *most* nurturing and powerful figure (although, of course, this analysis does not withstand cross-cultural criticism, since not all religions have nurturing beings).

Kirkpatrick mentions other psychological and emotional factors as well. Some of them are the "coalition effect" (the preference for "one's own kind" or one's in-group), altruism, and social exchange and reciprocity. In the end, he agrees that religion is a kind of spandrel — not something that evolved on its own or for which we have an instinct or 'god spot.' Rather, he presents the colorful analogy of cheesecake: humans did not evolve to eat cheesecake, because no such thing existed in our prehistoric environment. We did, however, evolve to like fatty foods and sweets and fruity flavors, and cheesecake contains all of these. Religion, he admits, "is a kind of socio-emotional-cognitive cheesecake" (237) — we do not need it or have a natural drive for it, but it fits all too well our naturally-adapted tastes and needs.

Religion, Reason, and Reality

The new emerging consensus on religion, then, is that it is not a 'thing' at all but a compound, an epiphenomenon, a by-product, and a side-effect of more basic, human, and perfectly natural mental and social processes and abilities. Religion is what happens when otherwise not-religious or pre-religious instincts and tendencies operate in a particular manner. The very fact that the human mind is 'free' in unique ways means that it has become free from (decoupled from) the reality and the 'facts' in which it evolved and in which it currently lives.

What Is Religion?

The powers and potentials of the human mind can run wild, and one way that it runs wild we call *religion*. The modular, by-product approach to religion, in conjunction with the diversity between and within religions, allows us to deconstruct religion completely. We know that there is not any one thing that can be called religion and now perhaps that there is nothing that can be called *distinctly* religion. Yet we cannot help but acknowledge the pervasive power of religion, whatever it is, in the human world. Religion may be the derivative of a complex of not-uniquely religious cognitions and intuitions, but like any spandrel, once it is there, it is there.

Additionally, as important and accurate as the afore-mentioned evolutionary-psychology approaches to religion are, they fail to consider one critical factor: religion is not *just* a psychological phenomenon. It is not merely inside the heads of individuals. It is also *practiced* and even more so *institutionalized* among groups or societies of people. Religion is as much social as psychological, as much objective as subjective: once a religion is invented, it is real in the sense that it is an active social force, a palpable phenomenon that individuals encounter in their daily lives. Each individual, therefore, does not have to reinvent religion in his or her lifetime; each can, usually does, and ultimately must *learn* it from their peers and predecessors. Religion may not be part of the environment in which early humans evolved, but it is almost always part of the environment in which present humans mature.

This traditional Western or Christian focus on the psychological or the private or internal is partly responsible for the focus on the ideas or doctrines or beliefs of religion. What, after all, do individuals have in their heads except ideas or beliefs? These come then to be seen as the essence or core of religion. As we will see at the end (Chapter 11), this emphasis on belief is not shared by all religions, and to the extent that we single-mindedly stress it we also miss the social, institutional, and practical power of religion. Indeed, as Robert Hefner has phrased it, specifically in relation to world religions but equally applicably to all religions, their real force "lies in their linkage of these strict transcendental imperatives [the beliefs] to institutions for the propagation and control of religious knowledge and identity over time and space" (1993:19). That is to say, the significance of religion is "something both doctrinal and social-organizational." To overlook or underestimate this critical aspect of religion is to fatally misunderstand it.

To return to our initial question, then, what *is* religion? How should it be defined and comprehended — particularly so that we, non-religionists, can address and oppose it? It involves certain kinds of ideas, to be sure, but it is not those ideas themselves that are important. It is how those ideas lead humans to think about, and more vitally *act toward*, each other and the world around them. At the center of the religious perspective is what Wallace called the "supernatural principle" or what E. B. Tylor called the "minimal definition of religion": that other kinds of beings, often called "spiritual beings," exist in addition to and with distinct similarity to humans. The key similarity, as Atran and Boyer and others note, is *agency*, the possession of mind or will or intention, *etc.* Such spiritual beings are effectively persons — like us and unlike us in interesting ways. As Graham Harvey expresses it in his recent rehabilitation of the concept of animism,

> Persons are those with whom other persons interact with varying degrees of reciprocity. Persons may be spoken *with*. Objects, by contrast, are usually spoken *about*. Persons are volitional, relational, cultural and social beings. They demonstrate intentionality and agency with varying degrees of autonomy and freedom. That some persons look like objects [or do not have visible appearance at all] is of little more value to an understanding of [religion] than the notion that some acts, characteristics, *qualia*, and so on may appear human-like to some observers. Neither material form nor spiritual or mental faculties are definitive (2006:*xvii*).

Clearly, living in a world populated by non-human and ostensibly super-human persons is profoundly different from living in a world without such entities. Yet both worlds are *human* worlds: the models for religious behaviors and relationships are human and social behaviors and relationships. Toward other humans, we show approval or disapproval, like or dislike, respect or disrespect, and various kinds and degrees of reciprocity and obligation. Our interactions have a moral character in that there are proper and improper, good and bad, ways to act toward each other. Religion is not a deviation from or contradiction of these principles *but an extension of them*. Harvey gets it right when he states that religion is like culture in general in that both "are all about learning to act respectfully (carefully and constructively) towards and among other persons" (*xi*) — human persons and nonhuman or superhuman persons equally. In fact, careful and constructive action toward non-super-human beings might be more imperative, since those beings are more potent.

This presents an opportunity and a necessity to consider two definitions of religion. One comes from Robin Horton, an expert in African religions. He suggests that

in every situation commonly labeled religious we are dealing with action directed towards objects which are believed to respond in terms of certain categories — in our own culture those of purpose, intelligence, and emotion — which are also the distinctive categories for the description of human action. The application of these categories leads us to say that such objects are "personified." The relationship between human beings and religious objects can be further defined as governed by certain ideas of patterning and obligation such as characterize relationships among human beings. In short, religion can be looked upon as an extension of the field of people's social relationships beyond the confines of purely human society. And for completeness' sake, we should perhaps add the rider that this extension must be one in which human beings involved see themselves in a dependent position *vis-à-vis* their non-human alters — a qualification necessary to exclude pets from the pantheon of gods (1960:211).

What he tells us is what we have just discovered: that religion seems to mean those "personal" and "social" characteristics we usually attribute to humans attributed to (at least some) non-humans as well. But if non-humans have human-like qualities, then humans will tend to, if not be required to, interact with them as we interact with each other. These interactions, which we conventionally think of as religious, will convey all of the social meaning of normal inter-human behaviors, such as respect, cordiality, an assumption of mutual communication, and a hope or expectation of reciprocity (exchange or give-and-take). Additionally, the nature of the social interaction between humans and their spiritual counterparts will obviously share the qualities of the interactions between humans in the particular local society: in other words, if there is rank and hierarchy or gender inequality or hostility between humans, then there will be rank and hierarchy or gender inequality or hostility between humans and nonhumans or superhumans. The one consistent difference, which is itself actually an extension too, is that human-to-non/super-human behavior will be marked by an extra dimension of deference and dependence — like that of a child to an adult or a peasant to a king, but magnified exponentially.

The second definition to consider comes from the renowned American anthropologist Clifford Geertz, who offered one of the most-quoted accounts of religion in modern social science. According to him, religion ought to be conceived as

> (1) a system of symbols which act to (2) establish powerful, pervasive, and long-lasting moods and motivations in men by (3) formulating conceptions of a general order of existence and (4) clothing these conceptions with such an aura of factuality that (5) the moods and motivations seem uniquely realistic (1973:90).

Two things are strikingly and originally important about this definition. The first is its attention to the *effects of religion on humans*. Notice that Geertz does not even refer to beliefs, and whether any such beliefs might be true or false is quite moot. Instead, the central factor is that religion generates "moods and motivations" in humans. By *moods* he means tendencies to feel certain ways, to have certain typical experiences (see Chapter 9 below). In Christianity, for instance, one typical mood is *guilty* or *sinful*. Even more importantly, by *motivations* he means tendencies to *act* in certain ways, to have certain typical behaviors.

Naturally, a mood can be a motivation: if people feel guilty, or elated, or sad, or whatever, they will tend to act accordingly. And people will be motivated in other ways as well: if people are taught to believe in heaven, they may well be motivated to seek it. If they are taught to believe in reincarnation or nirvana, they will act in other ways. More specifically, if they are taught that they can guarantee a favorable afterlife by sponsoring a temple ceremony, buying an indulgence, paying a tithe, or following a set of rules and injunctions, they are more likely to do so. In short, religion in Geertz' view is about *producing the kinds of people who will do the kinds of things that the religion demands that people do.*

The second interesting element of his definition regards *the means by which religion achieves this powerful goal.* Surely many things are mood-enhancing and motivational to people, including money, food, sports, and patriotism. What is unique about religion, Geertz suggests, is that religious claims and ideas appear, or are presented as, true or real — even what he has called "really real," more real than anything else including reality. Whether or not religious ideas are true (and we non-believers hold that they are false by definition), the members of the religion hold them as true, or as more than true, as self-evident, natural and taken-for-granted. It is, for instance, because heaven and hell are real to Christians that they are mood-inducing and motivational. It is because reincarnation is real to Hindus and *hekura* spirits are real to Yanomamo that these 'beliefs' are attitude- and action-altering. But from the outside, including from the perspective of the non-member, what is important about the whole religious project is not the beliefs, let along the truth-or-falsity of the beliefs, but the *practical effectiveness* of the beliefs — that the religion induces people to behave in particular ways. These behaviors, sufficiently supported and sufficiently repeated, constitute the institutions of the society and literally make the society what it is. This brings us ultimately to Durkheim's description of religion, in which the crucial component is not "the sacred and the profane" nor the "beliefs and practices" themselves but rather the process by which the beliefs and practices "*unite into one single moral community* called a Church, all those who adhere to them" (*emphasis added*).

The Message for Atheism

The discussion in this chapter should be at once familiar and unfamiliar, heartening and disheartening. Religion is a human product, even by-product. It is a projection of human qualities onto the non-human, not a discovery of those qualities outside of humanity. It is not simple anthropomorphism, but it is made possible by inherent mental and social habits in humans, traceable down to the brain and explicable in terms of evolutionary advantages to social living, intersubjectivity (the ability to understand the minds and feelings of others), deception detection, and emotional attachment. Religion is, in a real sense, these naturally human propensities run amok.

However, this realization does not allow us to take religion any more lightly. In fact, because the skills and habits that make religion possible are deep in the human brain, religion is also likely, perhaps even inescapable; as Newberg and d'Aquili insisted, "God" will not go away. More than that, religious conceptions represent some of the most compelling notions that humans can have, and they are some of the most satisfactory solutions to human concerns that we could imagine. This leads us to ask what is unique, or uniquely elaborated, about religion. The answer includes the following:

1. It personalizes the non-human realm. It gives us agents like ourselves to understand, relate to, and interact with.
2. It links our existence and that of our societies, our norms, and our institutions to something outside of ourselves and greater than ourselves.
3. It establishes a purportedly super-human reality that transcends the flux of mundane, contingent reality and on which mundane contingent reality depends.
4. It is believed to be true.

It is no wonder that most humans live under the spell of such a system; it at least grabs the attention.

But the news is much more sobering than that. As atheists, hopefully having arrived at our conclusions by reason, we like to think that we can dislodge theists from their position by reason. This is why we engage in argument and debate and other rational activities. No doubt, we have all been frustrated by the imperviousness of religious belief to what is demonstrably true. We must face the fact, though, that reasoning — in the sense of empirical observation and logic — is only one of the modules of the human mind. 'Truth' in the rational sense is not the only or most influential consideration in the mind of the believer. As Radcliffe-Brown counseled us, "the social function of a religion is independent of its truth or falsity, [and] religions which we think to be erroneous or even absurd and repulsive... may be important and effective parts of the social machinery" of a community or society (1965:154). Worse still, religions can not only survive but actually thrive on factual contradiction and absurdity (remember that Tertullian believed *because* it was absurd). If Boyer is correct, religion is founded on violations of intuition and experience, so presenting them with more violations is unlikely to move them.

For people like us, the discovery that religion is not a thing at all but a by-product of various not-specifically-religious mental and social processes lends credence to the rejection of religious claims. Religion is not an accurate depiction of non-human reality; it is not even *about* non-human reality. It is like looking at the insides of your eyelids. However, we cannot take much comfort in this discovery — that religion is decentralized or distributed across the human mind and society — because therein lies its persistence. As Boyer warns us, "The intuitive plausibility of [an] idea... becomes greater as more and more different systems produce intuitions compatible with that general interpretation" (316). An idea or conception "is likely to have direct effects on people's thought, emotions, and behaviors if it is distributed among different systems of the mind" (316). In other words, the more mental and social systems that are activated by a concept, the more stubborn and intractable it will be.

This helps to explain experiences that we non-believers cannot help but have. One is that argument and debate seldom shake believers, at least in the short term. Even if we could dislodge one point of connection between religion and their mind, there are many other points of connection still locking it in place. The other is that we seem to have nothing else that is as compelling or satisfying to offer in substitution. If various religious 'plugs' are removed from a mind, something else must fill them. This is why Atran avows that *our* kind of explanations — scientific, theoretical, rational ones, that is impersonal, agentless, and intention-less ones — "are at a serious disadvantage in the struggle for cultural selection and survival" (146). Answers that we give — to questions from origins to morals — are human answers, factually convincing perhaps but lacking in the persuasive features we just outlined. They are new or recent, they come from no source other than ourselves, they are changeable and transient or at least tentative, and above all else they provide no 'mind,' no 'personhood' to relate to. What Atran calls such "purely ideological commitments" he goes on to say "lack interactive aspects of personal agency — and the emotional intimacy that goes with it" (146). A not only factually true but socially successful atheism must, in all likelihood, offer — in consideration of the nature of human minds and societies — a more complete and satisfying program than it currently does, and all of that without falling once again into the mold of religion.

Chapter 4

Making Gods:
The Continuous Creation of Religions

Many if not most of the scholars of religion have been preoccupied with the question of the origin of religion — when and how religion began. This is probably not the right question to ask and may actually be an impossible question to answer. The notion of origin presupposes that one day humans did not have religion and then the next day they did. It gives the (not necessary but typical) impression that religion is something that 'originated' from nothing (no-religion) to fullness in one moment. It is the same error that has been multiplied by thinkers like Hobbes, Rousseau, and Freud on the matter of culture in general: at one time in the past, they claim, humans had no culture at all, and then one day humans created it totally formed.

E. B. Tylor is an example of this thinking applied to religion. Once upon a time, humans had no religion. But they had some mysterious experiences, like dreams and hallucinations and altered states of consciousness, and they invented religion to explain those mysteries. Other theories seem to imagine, if not depend on, a religionless past out of which mature religion sprang. But this is wrong in a number of ways. For one, there was probably never exactly a religionless past. For another, religion did not spring forth full grown in one swoop. Rather, religion probably and almost certainly emerged gradually, a bit at a time. We know that anatomically modern humans were painting mystical-appearing images on cave walls 20,000 years ago. We know that Neanderthals were sometimes burying their dead in ritualistic poses with flowers and artifacts more than 60,000 years ago. Whether or not these gestures indicate a complete religion (and what that religion might be) we do not and cannot know. That they had something on their mind that strikes us as religious concern is clear enough.

If, as we established in the last chapter, religion is a phenomenon or even epiphenomenon of various mental systems or modules, and if those mental systems developed in the course of human biological and social evolution, then it stands to reason that as these systems evolved, religion would have evolved gradually into a recognizable form. In other words, if religion depends on, say, ten mental systems, then one day in the past nine of these systems had matured, and before that eight, and before that seven, and in the distant past the first one appeared. And these systems are not unique to humans: obviously all animals understand some basic cause-and-effect relations and some basic qualities of objects. Primates are highly social, which requires being able to intuit the mental state of group members. The upshot is that humans were not the first beings to possess some of the critical mental faculties that produce religion, but possessing one or two of them is not sufficient to ignite religion. How many *are* sufficient? We do not know, but we can safely assume that at a certain 'critical mass' of mental systems something vaguely like religion emerged, and that as more of these systems came online, what we call religion today slowly took shape.

So, in a very real sense, as humans evolved into their contemporary form, religion evolved into its contemporary form. We know enough by now to reject the notion that our familiar kind of religion is the only kind of religion and that it is either this religion or none at all. The modular approach to religion (and most everything else) suggests that it materializes progressively as its subsystems develop and connect; rather than a sudden explosion of religion onto the human scene, there was probably a slow and vague appearance out of the mists of pre-religion. At what moment religion came to exist in the modern sense may be an impossible and meaningless question.

If religion evolved from pre-religion, just as humans evolved from pre-humans — with no sharp dividing line between the two states — then it is also true that this evolution has not ended and cannot end. This is the reason why it may be an unimportant or vacuous question to ask when religion originated. There is no doubt whatsoever that, the day religion finally evolved into a recognizable shape, *Christianity* did not evolve, nor did any other religion that we know today. Christianity and every other contemporary religion stands at the recent end of a very long path of historical development, long after humans had settled into their physical and mental form and after religion had settled into its psychological and social form. In other words, the origin of *religion* tells us nothing about the origin of *any particular religion*, and to presume otherwise is to commit the mistake that we vanquished in Chapter 1 — that the religion that one knows best (as friend or foe) *is* religion.

If religion originated thousands or tens of thousands of years ago, Christianity originated at most less than two thousand years ago. Hinduism originated earlier, and Islam originated later. We cannot even pin down a precise moment or year for the origin of Christianity: it was not the year that Jesus was (allegedly) born, since nothing new and Christian had happened yet. It was not when he was thirty (as the story goes), since he had not started preaching yet. It was not even at his death (somewhere supposedly around 30 CE), because at that point his followers were simply Jews of a particular messianic persuasion. It was not for some years or decades after his death, as many continued to be messianic Jews and others began to carry the mission in new directions. By the second or third Christian century, there was not one monolithic Christianity but many local and differing (and often clashing) Christianities. In 325 the Council of Nicaea decided some lingering issues of the faith, laying down an orthodox and ideally 'catholic' Christianity, but in reality Christianity continued to be a diverse and contentious bundle of beliefs and practices. 'Orthodox Christianity' as a separate entity did not originate until 700 years later, and Protestantism — or at least Lutheranism — until 500 more years after that. Methodism, Baptism, and other subreligions appeared still later.

Even then, religions continued to originate. Mormonism came together in the early-middle nineteenth century in the United States. Seventh Day Adventism was established in mid-late nineteenth century, and Scientology in the 1950s. All of these were taking shape in the American context, while other religions, from Baha'i to the Unification Church to Cao Dai and Soka Gakkai were forming in other parts of the world. The point here is that we cannot answer the question 'When did religion originate?' without specifying which particular religion we are referring to. The propensity to 'have religion,' to 'be religious,' may have originated tens of thousands of years ago, but any actual religion originated a few thousand years ago or a few hundred years ago or a few decades ago — or tomorrow. And within each of these religions, evolution and schism has continued. We cannot really even ask when Christianity originated as much as when Catholicism or Orthodox Christianity or Protestantism originated. Moreover, we cannot really ask about Protestantism as much as Lutheranism or Methodism or Quakerism, *etc.* Finally, the answer to any of these questions is not ultimately very meaningful: we can affirm that Catholicism originated in 325 CE or whenever, but that does not mean that everyone in Europe, let alone the world, then became a Catholic. Catholicism may have originated in Rome in late antiquity, but it did not originate in certain parts of Europe until hundreds of years later and in the non-Western world until at most a few centuries ago. By then it was a very different religion, and it continued to diversify as it spread to new regions and societies.

Furthermore, the process of religious origination has not stopped. If anything, it has accelerated. According to one source, there are almost 10,000 recognized religions in the world today, with two or three new ones added *per day* (Lester 2002). The newest of these religions are technically referred to as 'new religious movements' or NRMs, although many people call them "cults." While *cult* is a popular term, it is one that specialists have essentially stopped using altogether for two reasons. First, it has a negative connotation: religions are good, but cults are bad. As students of religion, it is not our job to judge religions against each other but to understand the whole phenomenon of religion. Besides, a cult is only bad *according to someone.* You may think that Moonies or Hare Krishnas (formally, the Unification Church and the International Society for Krishna Consciousness, respectively) are crazy and bad, but obviously they think they are quite sane and correct. Second, 'cult' is not a useful term since there is nothing concrete that distinguishes a cult from any other kind of religion. Cults tend to be new, *but all religions were new at their origin.* If 'cult' just means 'new religion,' then Christianity was a cult in its early period — and of course it was. The Romans, for instance, viewed Christianity was a new, crazy, false, and anti-social religion. When did it — when does any religion — cross the line from a cult to a religion? This is essentially a nonsense question. If cults are new, small, and unpopular, then a cult becomes a religion when it gets older, bigger, and more popular. Someone once said that the difference between a cult and a religion is a hundred years and a few thousand members, and that might be all we can say.

Religion and the Illusion of Immutability

The idea that religions change and that new religions burst onto the scene may strike us as strange, and it certainly seems to contradict the typical claim of religion itself that it is eternal and unchanging. Christianity clearly holds up a god that, they say, is unchanging, change being an imperfection: if something changes, it is either becoming less perfect (and thereby less god-like) or more perfect (which means it was not god-like before). Not all religions, as we have seen, claim perfection for their gods or spirits or forces, and it is not clear what 'perfection' even means, if anything, so we cannot use that as the benchmark for understanding all religions. Even so, it is characteristic if not universal among religions to assert a timeless, immutable truth. Religions tend to posit a transcendent, timeless reality — one that was established 'in the beginning' and has not varied since and cannot vary without being corrupted and lost altogether. I experienced this attitude firsthand on the island of Groote Eylandt off Australia's north coast when I sat one evening with a group of Aboriginal men. They asked me if the law could change in my country, and I said yes, of course; in fact, it is the job description of a group of people (politicians, the government) to change the law. They looked at me and responded that this was crazy: the law cannot change, since it was set down by the ancestors.

One key term that is frequently applied to religion is *traditional*; in fact, in contemporary American (and not just American) discourse, the word 'tradition' is commonly employed far beyond religion, for instance in regard to 'family' or 'values' (or both). I would suggest, as we considered in Chapter 2, that *tradition* is so much a descriptive word as a power word. It does not mean anything in particular, but its use is a rhetorical device to convince people to think something, to accept something, and to do something.

To clarify my point here, when people talk about "American traditions," what exactly do they mean? One firm implication of tradition is continuity with the past; if it is traditional, it must have been done before. But how long and how many times before? Most people, when they talk this way, probably have some diffuse image of the 1950s in their heads; for many Americans, traditional America is *circa*-1950s America. But why that specific moment in the past? Why not 1850s? 1750s? 1650s? We know why not 1550s or 1050s: there was no 'America' that far back. So an idea like 'American traditions' has a limited meaning; it can only go back so far into the past. Not only that, but I safely assume that most Americans do not relish *everything* about that past. For instance, the 1950s was a time of official racial segregation; I assume that people who lionize tradition do not include that particular tradition (although I know that some do). And if the 1950s is traditional, then the 1850s ought to be even more traditional. But in the 1850s slavery was still practiced and had been for some two hundred years, making it an established American tradition. I assume that most people who revere tradition do not want to revive that institution (although I know that a few actually do). And in 1650 the settlers in Massachusetts wore hats with big buckles on them, but most Americans do not want to restore that 'tradition.' Finally, except for the most radically traditional types, people do not want to practice *only* traditions; they want to mix some traditions with some modern behaviors and objects too. They might like more 'traditional' families, but they still want those families to have a cell phone, a microwave oven, and a car.

In other words, 'tradition' is not an absolute concept but a relative one. America has its traditions, France has its, Egypt has its, Japan has its, and the Warlpiri have theirs. So, tradition is relative to the particular society one is talking about. Second, each of these societies has a more or less long history to draw from and to revive; tradition is relative to the particular time-period of the past of the society that one is talking about. Third, any particular moment of the past contains some things that we admire and some that we condemn; we do not want to revive it lock, stock, and barrel. Fourth, no one wants to return to the past completely, and even if they could it would be impossible. They want some aspects of the past blended with some aspects of the present. Tradition, then, is relative to some particular items from a particular moment of the past of the particular society that one is discussing, combined with some particular items from the present. Even the Amish, whom many Americans regard as uniquely traditional, have frozen aspects of a specific time and place — sixteenth- century or so Holland (Pennsylvania Dutch) or Germany. They would be *more* traditional, I suppose, if they lived the life of the fifteenth century or twelfth century or fourth century; they would be still more traditional if they did not use the wheel or fire.

So, 'tradition' is a word without any distinct referent. It is more like *big* or *old* — not specifying *how* big or how old, just bigger and older than some other things. Or perhaps the best comparison is between traditional and *important*. Who, in the end, cares if something is traditional or not? The polio vaccine was not traditional when it was invented, but it was definitely beneficial. *Traditional*, as it is regularly used, does not mean exclusively old. Many old traditions, like slavery, are gone and good riddance. Yet when most people use it, especially in political, social, and religious contexts, the term 'traditional' tends to mean 'better' or 'preferable' or 'more authentic.' *Traditional values*, they imply, are *superior* values, and *traditional religion* is *truer* religion — or just plain *true* religion.

There is no disputing that some traditions are older than others and that all traditions started at some point in time. Even the tradition of making stone tools began once upon a time, although it was a very distant time. Thus, every tradition is new when it first appears — and by definition 'unorthodox' if not vilified. Christianity was not a traditional religion in Jesus' time, nor in Paul's time, nor in Constantine's time. Lutheranism was not a traditional religion in Luther's time; it was a patently obvious innovation in his time, a *break* from tradition. This means that *all traditions were invented*; it is only a matter of how far back. Some traditions were invented long ago, others more recently — and some have not been invented yet. In the year 1 CE, Christianity was still a religion of the future.

ATHEISM ADVANCED

Religious traditions, then, are not the only kind, nor is religion the only human institution that values longevity and stability. Notice how American people of all political persuasions often invoke the 'founding fathers,' as if what *they* did or said or thought is somehow critical to what *we* should do or say or think. They are the paradigms, the models, the charters for present-day behavior. And notice that the founders themselves anchored their practices and values to older and even timeless ones: they held certain truths to be "self-evident," and they spoke of "natural rights." These were not opinions that they were inventing; rather, they insisted that these were *facts* inscribed in nature itself. And if their opinions and values were natural and self-evident, how can anyone argue against them?

While any thought- and social-system can, and is likely to, exploit antiquity and naturalness in support of its claims, religion depends on these alleged qualities more completely and essentially — and can assert those qualities most effectively. No one thinks that the U.S. Constitution always existed or that it was revealed by gods or found in nature. It was the creation of humans in a (fairly recent) historical period. How much *more* authentic and authoritative would be the claims of a system that was much older (maybe even *as old as time itself*), *not* created by humans, and given by the most powerful agents or forces in all of reality? Not only would such beliefs and imperatives be compelling, even ultimate, but they would be inescapable and unchangeable. We mere mortals can amend the Constitution, or we could scrap it and start over again. No Christian would seriously endorse that idea about the Bible: we did not create it in the first place, they would say, so we cannot change it.

The fact that the Bible was written by human hands notwithstanding, a crucial part of the power of religion is to be found in its pretense to immutability: it does not change because it *cannot* change. It describes what is 'really real,' and that is permanent. To modify it would be to falsify it. It further comes from outside of us, from that which has the authority to give it (gods, ancestors, nature spirits, or whatever); it is not ours to alter. And because it is real and given, it is ancient: as it was in the beginning, so it is and ever will be. This is a case of what the historian of religion Mircea Eliade called "the prestige of the past": the past was a period of power, and the deeper the past, the more potent the power. The more ancient, the closer to the original source: theoretically, in Jesus' time, followers did not have to ask "What would Jesus do?" They could observe him or ask him directly. The ancients, the spirits or gods, or nature itself set the precedents, established the institutions, and revealed the truth. Those precedents and institutions are valid, and those truths are true, at least in part because they *are* ancient and because they *have not changed* in all the ensuing time.

The immutability of religion is one of its greatest strengths, one that few if any non-religious systems can claim. There is no better reason to do something (in certain minds) than the authority of antiquity and the absolute and unvarying factuality of it. But the immutability of religion is an illusion. Religion is not immutable. If it were, Methodism would never have existed, since it was a new form of Protestantism when it first appeared. And Protestantism would never have existed, since it was a new form of Christianity. And Christianity would never have appeared, since it was a new form of theism. And theism would never have appeared, since it was a new form of religion. The reality is that each religion, and sect and denomination and cult of religion, avows immutability or authenticity for itself, even when it is brand new. Immutability, when the fact of change or invention stares the believer right in the face, is an ideology. It is part of the belief system: *Here is a belief, and it is and always has been true.*

There are a number of ways of getting around the pesky innovation problem. One is to deny the past, to simply assert that what we believe and do now is what we have always believed and done. This is more difficult in the days of writing and recording but not impossible. Another is to regard the novelty as a 'further revelation,' not a change in truth but an addition to our limited knowledge of that truth. A third is to consider the novelty to be not a modification and certainly not an invention but a *restoration*, a revival of what was always true but was lost or corrupted over time, a purification and return to the 'fundamentals' or 'roots' of the religion. A subtype of restoration might be *completion*, in which a religious tradition that others view as closed and settled is reopened and amended in a way that more or less drastically changes it but is interpreted as merely extending and finishing it — 're-closing' it again, until the next amender comes along. Islam sees itself in this manner, as amending and completing the revelations begun in the Judeo-Christian scriptures.

It is easy and worthwhile to identify examples of these approaches to preserving the illusion of immutability in the face of conspicuous religious change. One of the best places to look is at the so-called 'tribal' or 'primitive' religions. We know without dispute that Christianity started (as innovation, new revelation, restoration, or completion) in recent historical time, but it has been tempting to accept the illusion of permanence in the case of small and apparently unhistorical religions. Of all tribal religions, Australian Aboriginal religions have often been perceived as the oldest and most static. When the first European settlers and explorers landed in Australia in the late 1700s, they assumed that they were witnessing 'Aboriginal tradition,' religion as it had been since primordial times, unchanged and unchangeable. The Aboriginals themselves fortified this perception: even in contemporary times, as Françoise Dussart wrote in reference to the same society where I did my fieldwork: "If one asks the Warlpiri whether the *Jukurrpa*...is susceptible to change, they will say, point blank, that it is not" (2000:23). So newcomers, predisposed to think in terms of religious immutability and eager to see a real 'primitive religion,' accepted this ideology uncritically.

The fact is that Aboriginal religions have not only transformed since Western contact but were in the continuous process of transformation long before. However, Aboriginal societies had ways to embrace and even seek novelty without viewing it as change. First, in Warlpiri and other societies, the source of religion is referred to as *Jukurrpa* or Dreaming. Literally, in dreams one sees eternal things, visions of the spiritual dimension. But they never assumed that any living person, or all living persons collectively, possessed complete spiritual knowledge. There was always more to the spiritual world that one could learn, and a conduit to that learning was dreams. A person might dream a new song or design or story or entire ritual which was not really new at all; *it was always there, it was just that humans were only now accessing it*. After discussion among knowledgeable elders in the society, such new content could be integrated into the canon of religion.

A second principle of Aboriginal religion is that, since knowledge is potentially and probably actually infinite, different individuals and groups (family groups, local groups, ritual groups) possess different pieces of it. Religious and every other kind of knowledge is distributed, and other individuals always know and do things that you do not. Even more, some people, by right of birth or expertise, have a right to know and perform certain things; knowledge is like property. Men know things that women do not. Elders know things that youths do not. And there are various levels of depth of knowledge, from more public to more private and esoteric. The Warlpiri refer to the levels of understanding, in English, as 'cheap,' 'halfway,' and 'dear,' reflecting the degree of sacredness and therefore of secrecy of the insights. So access to knowledge and the meaning of that knowledge is unequal in society, but there is always the possibility of acquiring both. Youths will age into elders, and men and women alike may be keen to learn what others know. Aboriginal people would trade or teach each other sacred things, and this attitude extended to the innovations of Christian missionaries. Rather than a contradiction of traditional religion, many Aboriginal people considered Christian knowledge to be an untapped vein of religious secrets which they could acquire and integrate with their own.

The third principle, building on this process of exchange of information, is a conscious and sometimes extensive trade network of myth and ritual. Religious knowledge was not only distributed but also diffusible. Religious truths such as adventures of the ancestor-spirits were not limited to just one society but laced the countryside connecting various tribes' territory. With prior and often elaborate preparations, tribes could exchange stories, songs, symbols, and entire myth and ritual cycles, occasionally over a period of years. Poirier, for instance, describes an exchange of ceremonies between women of two different societies. In March 1988 thirty women from Balgo transferred the Tjarada ritual to women of the Pintupi community in trade for another ritual, the Walawalarra, which had been passed to Pintupi country from the opposite direction. Poirier reports that the women who were handing over the rituals felt sad at losing their old familiar knowledge but also excited about receiving new content in return. The real point, though, is that circulation of 'traditional' religion was the norm; in fact, she argues that "the very possibility of long-term 'ownership' or 'accumulation' of such bodies of knowledge appears to be ruled out, and groups seem to insist upon an ongoing circulation" (1993:771). So, if observers had arrived in Pintupi country before 1988 they would have seen one traditional religion, but after 1988 they would have seen a quite different one. We can comfortably conclude that this would be so, whatever two time-periods we compared. That is, there is no such thing as *the* traditional Pintupi or Warlpiri or other Aboriginal religion.

Any religion about which we have historical information presents the same situation. Looking at the history and evolution discernible in the ancient Judeo-Christian scriptures, it is quite clear that Hebrew/Jewish religion went through a series of changes. In the first phase (early Genesis), the picture is one of a fairly non-descript Semitic religion, without specifics about the nature of god or rules and morality or social order. (For instance, when Cain killed Abel, there was not yet a law against murder.) In the second phase, starting perhaps with Abraham, the picture is one of a typical pastoralist religion; the people are nomadic cattle-herders, practicing very normal pastoralist behavior (male domination, war, notions of pollution, animal sacrifice, *etc.*). In the third phase, the society had evolved to a centralized state and kingdom, and religion evolved with it: religious observance had become focused at a single site, the Temple in Jerusalem, and a sophisticated cult of priests overseeing complex sacrificial rituals had coalesced. The fourth phase comes after the defeat and destruction of the kingdom, when prophets interpreted the disaster as a divine punishment and when belief began to shift toward more extreme, apocalyptic, and otherworldly interests. Each of these phases represents a distinct religious formation, but they are all linked by history and a few central beliefs and concepts (like a god and sin and prophecy); they could just as easily have been four different religions.

Christianity, as we will see below, is both a continuation of these trends, a break from them, and a reinterpretation and supposed fulfillment of them. Moreover, it was hardly the only one. Christians are inclined to think that Jewish history ended with the final book of the Old Testament, but of course it did not. Long before the movement that developed into Christianity, there was another failed political/military movement of the Maccabees: starting in 165 BCE, it was an attempt to establish political independence and religious purity in the face of foreign domination. Other movements preceded, followed, and were contemporaneous with the Jesus movement, including the well-known Essene and Zealot ones.

Christianity does not end this evolution. True, the origin of this religion comes from a new revelation and a new 'covenant' or arrangement between a god and certain humans, following in the path of but radically breaking from the previous Mosaic one. For them, the job is done; the evolution of religion is complete. However, Islam, appearing gradually some 600 years later, purports to continue the story with still newer revelations — which are really ancient revelations clarified and perfected. Islam references the same god (simply called by his Arabic name, al-Lah or 'the god') and the same historical characters and events. It is seen, however, as the most comprehensive revelation yet — including social and legal regulations — and as the absolutely final one. Muhammad is viewed as a prophet in the tradition and line of the Judeo-Christian prophets but as the last and greatest one, the "seal of the prophets," closing forever the canon. Nevertheless, other religions continued to form, some in the line of Judeo-Christian-Islam and others in totally different lines.

Religious Dynamics and Revitalization

So it is eminently clear that religions never started changing and that they have never stopped changing and never will. Religion evolves, and the analogy between religion and biological evolution is really more than a mere analogy. Like any system — living, ecological, psychological, or social — religion mutates over time in particular ways for particular reasons. Religion is not fixed and static but mutable and dynamic. Even when it is reproduced without change over time, it is done so actively, just as a biological species is actively reproduced. Religions can interact with each other and borrow elements from each other (a kind of religious gene flow); again, if a religion is a constellation of discrete but integrated blocks, then blocks can be added to or subtracted from a religion, leaving it the same in some ways and different in others. Under certain environmental pressures, religions can transform in unpredictable ways or adapt. They even speciate giving rise to entirely new religions. Religions can and do compete with each other. And in the final analysis a religion can become extinct. Two things are true about the process of religious evolution. First, while religions have never been static, they have in times and places been relatively steady, with gradual or minor change. Second, while the conditions for faster and more radical change have always existed, those conditions have become more common and more urgent in recent history. Anthony Wallace, the anthropologist who contributed so much to the understanding of religion, provided one of the most important studies of this accelerated type of change in his essay on revitalization movements. Note that not all religions are movements in the technical sense, nor are all cases of religious change. When a Warlpiri man dreams a new song and includes it in his or the society's song-book, that is not a movement. Exchanging stories or ceremonies between societies is not a movement. A movement is more intentional and organized, a kind of directed change in which someone or some group is overtly attempting to change belief or practice. Nor are all movements religious. There are political movements, economic movements, social-reform movements, environmental movements, and many others. However, religion is a particularly ripe source or genre for movements, and when religion and movement coincide, dramatic but consistent things happen.

Wallace defined revitalization movements as "deliberate, conscious, and organized efforts by members of a society to construct a more satisfying culture" (1956:265). This of course presupposes some perceived and serious dissatisfaction with the reigning culture. He proposes that the process of revitalization is preceded by a condition of relative tranquility and satisfaction, which he calls the "steady state." While it may be and generally is dynamic, for the most part the beliefs and practices work for most members of society. There are no major crises or threats that established tradition cannot handle adequately enough. When, however, circumstances alter so greatly that traditions are felt to be failing — no longer providing the successful solutions or adaptations for people — a crisis emerges. What would create these problematic circumstances? One of the most obvious reasons is contact with another society or religion. Even contact with a comparable or weaker one can induce troubling questioning and self-examination: who are these people, why do they believe and behave so differently, and how are they related to us? In cases where the contact is with a much larger, more powerful, or more successful (say, richer, more urban, more literate) group, the problems are deeper. When the contact is sustained over time, and especially when it takes the form of invasion, conquest, and domination, the problems are acute. Other factors can also cause dissatisfactions. Economic or technological change can create imbalances and challenges. Environmental change (for instance, prolonged drought or sudden disasters like floods or hurricanes) can threaten life and destroy religious artifacts and upset religious practices, all the while casting doubt on their efficacy. Simple change of membership over time can have major impact, as new individuals interpret old beliefs and practices in unprecedented ways.

There is no denying that conquest and colonialism have been the most important motors for religious change, especially in the last few centuries. When European Christians appeared in other parts of the world, and when they began to actively proselytize their religion and suppress the native ones, while introducing foreign economic, social, military, and legal institutions — and firmly demonstrating the wealth and power inequalities between themselves and the native peoples — a crisis for the conquered peoples was inevitable. Native rituals to expel the invaders, to give themselves wealth and power, or to bring back the dead all failed. Deprivations — economic, political, religious, and psychological — caused stress for locals. Some individuals experienced these privations more keenly than others, in what Wallace called the "period of increased individual stress." As more and more people felt the pressures, a "period of cultural distortion" began, marked by social disorder, alcoholism, violence, apathy, and usually many deaths. Many societies and religions never recovered from this state, and they are long since gone. Some, however, made a productive response to it and survived but in a very altered form.

Out of the cultural distortion, a period of revitalization might appear. It usually begins with a single individual or at most a small set of people. The individual takes the stresses particularly personally, sometimes having a near-death experience or dreams and visions. The role of such altered states of consciousness cannot be emphasized enough. The visionary then shares his or her experience with others, often construed as a religious revelation or divine encounter. The person's own biography — especially living through a near-death or supernatural encounter — can give the message authority. He or she may actively preach the message or merely model it. This communication process is followed by organization. Others join; they are converted. The visionary becomes a leader and begins to reassemble the members into new social relationships with new social goals — to stop drinking, to stop fighting or acting immorally, to push out the white devils, to bring back the dead, or whatever. A new and active community is born.

The diffusion of the message and movement through society is usually not automatic or unopposed. Foreign administrators do not want to see the conquered people mobilized for action. Traditionalists in the native society may disagree with the doctrine or practices of the new group or simply resent the threat to their own power and prestige. And, we cannot forget, other movements may rise with competing messages, doctrines, and incipient communities. In conditions of sufficient stress, there are almost certainly going to be multiple movements, each with a different answer, leader, membership, and organization. Beyond that, the personal and charismatic leadership of the founder may give way to more formal and even bureaucratic relationships as the movement grows. New members may have their own interpretations and agendas and take the movement in other directions. Circumstances may demand a change in strategy. And of course if the original leader dies while the movement is still active, other leaders must step forward, often with ideas of their own.

Not all movements survive this adaptation process. Most religious and other movements perish early in their development. Those that succeed continue to spread and to put their message and plan into action. In this cultural transformation stage, the movement begins to have its effects on the group or the wider society, changing behaviors and creating new institutions. A new culture, a new way of life, comes together. If it is successful, it may spread to the entire society, becoming a new 'universal' and 'tradition' for the whole; in other cases, it may get lodged at a lower level of generality, becoming a niche group or one of the accepted alternatives in the society. At any point, it may still start to fade, eventually disappearing. However, if it can entrench itself firmly and permanently, it enters the stage of routinization. When the movement becomes routine, it becomes less like a movement and more like an establishment, with its rules, its officers, and perhaps its bureaucracy. It loses some of its more fiery and charismatic features and settles into normalcy. If all goes well, a new steady state is achieved, with a new tradition and a satisfied — or at least orderly — populace. Of course, this new steady state may itself be unstable, or it may face subsequent threats and challenges (internal and external), commencing the entire cycle over again.

Types of Revitalization Movements

The details of any movement and the course of its development will be historically particular, depending on the pre-existing culture or religion, the specific culture or religion that contacts it, the nature of that contact, the ideas and decisions and actions of the leaders, the actions of outside forces and opposition, and so on. Despite all of these variable details, centuries of experience with — and a growing historical knowledge of — these movements has led us to identify a set of typical forms that they can take. These are 'ideal types' which may vary in real cases and which can combine and interact in numerous ways.

Syncretism

Probably the central process in all religious and cultural change is *syncretism*. Syncretism is the more or less intentional blending of two or more sources or traditions to create a new and presumably better one. In the case of religious syncretism, this means mixing elements of two or more different religions. For instance, non-Western, non-Christian tribal peoples who were exposed to Christian beliefs often fused bits of Christian doctrine or practice (frequently imperfectly understood) with bits of their own religious traditions. This is why African or Latin American or Asian Christianity is different from European and American Christianity in so many ways. At the same time, Western peoples introduced their own beliefs and practices into the Christianity they inherited: that is where Santa Claus and Christmas trees (there are no pine trees in the Middle East) and even December 25 as Jesus' birthday came from. Other religions have had the same experience: the scriptural ethical non-theism of Buddhism that spread to Burma or Thailand or Vietnam commingled there with local spirit beliefs and integrated into them in locally-unique ways. In the contemporary global context, recent and modern movements may mix items from multiple world religions, for instance, Christian with Buddhist or Hindu or Taoist, *etc.* Aum Shinrikyo (Japan) is a good example, as is Cao Dai (Vietnam). In ancient times, the same processes were at work, as movements might conjoin aspects of Hellenistic culture and religion with Egyptian or Persian or Hebrew.

Because religion is a system of modules, none of which are uniquely religious, the parts that enter into the syncretism process need not be distinctly religious. The 'New Age' movement melds various combinations of religions old and new with astrology, tarot cards, and all sorts of other materials. The infamous Heaven's Gate group (more formally known as TELAH or The Evolutionary Level Above Human) amalgamated Christian-like concepts with science-fiction elements, computer technology, and UFO ideas. In fact, UFOs or extraterrestrials play a part in several movements, from the ill-fated flying saucer cult in Leon Festinger's study *When Prophecy Fails* (1964) to the 'atheistic' new religion of Raelianism. The women's spirituality movement draws not only from Christian and indigenous (especially Native American) religious traditions but, as Cynthia Eller (1993) describes, the New Age movement, the psychology of Jung, the therapy/self-help movement, the feminist movement, and sometimes the gay and lesbian movement. Scientology attaches psychological and technological components to religious ones, with a dash of science fiction.

Millenarianism

A second form or characteristic of revitalization movements is *millenarianism*. The term comes from Western and Christian thinking, but the approach is not original or unique to either. The millennium literally refers to 'thousand,' even more specifically to the thousand-year era that is believed to comprise the present and unsatisfactory — indeed, wicked and sinful — period of human history. At the end of that thousand years, the current fallen world is to end and a new reality to be substituted in its place. While the first and second (depending on how you count) Christian millennia have come and gone, the idea that the world — either the world as we know it or the world as a material existence — will end is still axiomatic in Christian thinking.

Not all cultures and religions reckon in terms of a thousand years (not all even reckon in base-ten), but many share a vision of an end to the 'present age' and the arrival of a new and better age. A millenarian movement, then, organizes people to prepare for this event — often if not always a cataclysmic event, since the old world will not pass quietly — and more than occasionally to help bring it about. For, while there is a certain dread of the end, there is a thrill about it too, as anyone who has ever watched Jack Van Impe on television knows. He is positively jubilant that the evil world will pass and soon, no matter how many people have to die in the process. At any rate, Hinduism also posits a destruction of the present world or *kali yuga*, although its cyclical view of reality holds that the destruction will be followed by another creation and a whole new cycle of decline, destruction, and creation. Also, the cycles are much longer than Christian history can comprehend — millions of years each. Ancient Norse religion predicted an apocalyptic finale to the contemporary world, as did Mayan religion. Many newer religions, inspired both by the teachings of Christianity and by the desperation of their own cultural situation, advanced similar notions. The Native American Ghost Dance and the various cargo cults (see below) expected and eagerly awaited at least the end of things as they were, if not the end of all things.

Irredentism

Some movements get involved in more specific and mundane kinds of goals, like *irredentism*. Irredentism is a style of revitalization, entirely compatible with the previous two, that expects or works toward the recovery of a lost homeland. Many irredentist movements are more or less purely secular, such as the Serb drive to reoccupy Kosovo (although there can be some 'spiritual' content even there). However, others are overtly religious and, as a legitimation system, religion can help bolster the authority of any such movement. If the group can substantiate a historical and spiritual claim to the land, that is better than a purely secular claim. The best recent example of a religious irredentist movement is the so-called Zionist movement, or the struggle to re-establish a Jewish homeland in the Middle East. While not all Jews or their supporters saw this as a religious mission, others did and do, and both Christianity and Judaism see it not only as a justified move — based on the divine promises made to the people in their scriptures — but as a necessary precursor to the millenarian events to come. Both agree, based on religious beliefs again, that the occupation of Jerusalem and the rebuilding of the Temple are requirements before the awaited messiah can arrive or return. Interestingly, an irredentist movement may not necessarily entail recovering a land that one has physically lost but also restoring a land that has lost its religious way to the straight path. In this sense, we could regard the present-day Christian Exodus movement (www.christianexodus.org) — to "rebuild" a government and society in America "founded upon Christian principles" by migrating to and taking control over one of the states — as an irredentist movement.

Vitalism or Modernism

A fourth type or style of movement is known as *vitalism* or sometimes *modernism*. Confronted with the reality of their own religious, political, economic, *etc.* inferiority, some movements aim more or less completely to solve their problems by abandoning their traditional or pre-contact religion and culture. If the foreign society or religion is superior, then it might make sense to imitate them, since whatever they do seems to work. One dimension of cargo cults was the willing abandonment and sometimes destruction of traditional religion as well as economics. In fact, this seldom means merely an embrace of religious beliefs and behaviors alone but usually of an entire way of life. When Japan first felt the force of Western power in the late 1800s, there were serious discussions about jettisoning all of Japanese culture — clothing styles, religion, language, and all — in favor of the 'modern' one. They certainly did learn lessons about industrial production and military technology. If a society totally modernized, of course, it would cease to be a distinct society at all but be assimilated into the outside society. In most cases, a society or religion will partially modernize and partially resist modernization: the Catholic Church, for instance, periodically raises a cry against modernity while it uses computers and cell phones and the Internet to accomplish its work.

Nativism and Fundamentalism

A fifth and final mode of revitalization is *nativism*, the conscious and deliberate rejection of foreign or modern influences. The philosophy behind this attitude is that the foreign or modern is bad, corrupt, decadent, *etc.* and/or that the strength and virtue of one's own culture or belief lies in its traditional and fundamental principles. A society in crisis, like nineteenth-century China, could ask itself why it was declining from the onslaught of Western invasion; the answer they arrived at was that they were not Chinese enough. China had been great in the past, so to be great again, they had to be more purely Chinese. Rather than welcome Western styles and technologies and values, China attempted to promote more traditional and exclusive ones.

A particularly intense and often combative kind of nativism is what we know as *fundamentalism*, the movement to return to the fundamentals or deep, abiding, and unique characteristics of one's identity and group. Fundamentalism is especially associated with religion, but it is not unique to religion by any means. One can be fundamentalist about anything, from politics to economics to baseball to cuisine. And of course, fundamentalism, while best known in the context of Christianity and Islam, is not unique to those faiths; there are Jewish and Hindu and Buddhist and many other fundamentalisms as well (*see* Eller 2004, Chapter 11). The main difference between fundamentalism and nativism in general is that the former is usually more literalist (especially in regard to a written tradition or text) and more militant. Fundamentalists, by their own admission, frequently see themselves locked in a battle with foreign, false, or liberalizing forces.

The Great Transformation: Local and World Religions

It is evident that religion has evolved in many ways in many different times and places, making any typology of religions, let alone any generalization about religions, difficult to sustain. Like all evolution, the course of splitting and mixing and rising and falling has produced not a line or a few discrete types but a bush of tangled religious species and subspecies. Some classifications have been attempted, most notably the theism/nontheism or Western/Eastern ones, but these dichotomies do not help much and are becoming increasingly meaningless. There is, however, one decisive, even monumental, split between religions that is seldom identified and appreciated — between *local* versus *global/universal* or 'world' religions.

Until fairly recently in history, human beings lived in a certain kind of social arrangement that is unfamiliar to most of us today. We often dub such societies *tribes*, although 'tribe' is a technical term that only fits some of them. Robert Redfield characterized this way of life, which he called "precivilization," as based on communities that were small (sometimes as little as a few dozen, and seldom over a few thousand), isolated and self-contained, homogeneous, decentralized, informal, and non-literate. The essential structure of society was provided by kinship bonds, giving people a "strong sense of group solidarity" (1957:8). There were few if any full-time specialists, and the roles that did exist were determined more by personal status that a formal "division of labor." He suggested that the central order of society, "the nexus which held people together, was moral" (15) — not morality as we ordinarily think of it, but shared sentiments and judgments, what Durkheim called a "collective conscience."

For such people, religion is a key source and support of their moral reality. As Redfield put it, "'Moral order' includes the binding sentiments of rightness that attend religion, the social solidarity that accompanies religious ritual, the sense of religious seriousness and obligation that strengthens men, and the effects of a belief in invisible beings that embody goodness" (21). While not all religious beings embody goodness, humans who live in this social condition will produce a particular kind of religion. The details can and will vary widely, but the form is fairly consistent. Ernest Gellner (1988) argues that this form was

1. Concrete, with a lack of speculation and philosophical introspection. Religious conceptions, as well as social institutions, were taken for granted, the truth of their beliefs and the efficacy of their behaviors seen as self-evident.
2. *Ad hoc* and particular, dealing with specific spiritual or practical problems when they arise rather than establishing a permanent abstract orthodoxy.
3. Non-codified, especially not written down and settled into a canon of official dogma.
4. 'Patently social,' in the sense that religion and society are tightly interwoven. The point of religion is not so much to declare absolute truths that all humans are to believe as to establish and justify patterns of interaction. *Belief*, as we have seen, is not a crucial or even familiar notion.

Given these traits, perhaps the most important thing we can say about such religions is that they are inexorably *local*.

A local religion is one that applies, or is understood and felt to apply, to a particular people and place. The religion of such a precivilized society is profoundly about *their* lives and experiences, even their homeland. The Warlpiri are a shining example. Warlpiri religion is undetachably rooted in their land and their history. Their religion is about *their* ancestors, *their* country, and *their* social and ritual practices. They would never expect that other societies, especially ones so far away and so different as European societies, would have the same beliefs and rituals (although they would assume that we have *our* ancestors and country and practices too). But theirs do not relate to us, and ours do not relate to them. Even more so, they could not 'do' their religion anywhere else but in their homeland, since that is where the creative beings and dead ancestors are, and the stories and songs and ceremonies of that land are the ones they know and are responsible for. Bluntly, *they have their religion and we have ours.* The idea of proselytizing their religion to other groups would make no sense: what do Warlpiri ancestors have to do with the Pintupi or the Luritja, let alone the English or French? Therefore, the notion of fighting about whose religion is "correct" would seem like nonsense. Such religions are not so much "tolerant" of each other as disinterested in each other.

Starting around five or six thousand years ago in a few locations on the globe, a new social organization, with a new associated religious attitude, appeared. Redfield called it "civilization," emphasizing the existence and dominance of cities in this changing system. Civilization is the opposite of precivilization in almost every way: large (reaching millions and hundreds of millions ultimately), interconnected and interdependent, heterogeneous (composed of many different kinds of people, of diverse language, ethnicity, race, religion, class, *etc.*), centralized, formal, and especially significantly *literate*. The essential structure of such societies is provided by economic necessities and political power, not by kinship. The bonds of society are practical, even technical, and group solidarity may be weak. There are many full-time specialists and an extensive division of labor with positions defined by wealth, power, and prestige.

These features lead to and maybe even require a different kind of religion. There are new, and usually unequal, social relations (like class or government) to explain and legitimate. There are professional religious figures who have more time to articulate and formalize religious belief and practice. Religion becomes one of the institutions of the society, tied to but distinct from others. And writing changes everything. Myths,

Making Gods

genealogies, moral and legal rules, and ritual instructions are written down, creating the first religious texts or scriptures, which become settled and fixed: a *canon* is established, over which people can now argue about the true wording and the true interpretation. A formal priesthood, in collusion with a formal government, seeks to impose orthodoxy on the population and to monopolize religious activity in the process.

Some of these early civilized religions were still ostensibly local: not only did Greece have its local religion, but each city had its own gods and cults. Even early Hebrew religion sounds local: Yahweh chose the Israelite people as *his* people, never negating the possibility that there were others gods choosing other peoples; the only requirement was that Yahweh's people not worship other gods (which seems to imply that there *are* other gods). However, in the course of time, two phenomenally important developments occurred: a few religions became detached from their particular place and people, and they started claiming to apply to *all* people in *all* places. We can call such religions *world religions*. This name suggests that such a religion insists that it is true for the whole world and aspires to be true for the whole world, whether or not it has achieved its aspirations. The fact is that there are many such world religions but that none has reached its goal of global universal acceptance — and none seems likely to.

There are two major problems created by such universally ambitious religions, which flow from the same source — the absolutist nature of its claims, that there is only one true religion. The first is internal: disputes, schisms, and heresies about what the religion really means or really should do. Despite the fixity of the canon, individuals and parties could still disagree, and occasionally individuals or parties could demand the insertion of new items in the canon. But such developments would threaten and falsify the unity of the religion and must be suppressed. The second is external: disputes and conflicts with other religions, both local and global. For, if one religion is true, then all other religions must be false. Small, tribal, precivilized religions face sheer eradication from world religions in the form of missionization and conversion. Other allegedly global or universal religions present more of a challenge, since they are all trying to do the same thing — namely, dominate the world and eliminate rivals. There is an inevitable competition and hostility between them, as each says that *it* is the one true and universal religion. But of course, there cannot be more than one true and universal religion, so they are pitted in a struggle that, while not always active, is always mortal.

Toleration is not natural to or even consistent with such religions. While local religions appear tolerant, they are mostly just irrelevant to each other. World religions cannot adopt this stance. Everything is relevant to them, and their intolerance can be white hot. If they remained unaware of each other, trouble might not follow. But since such religions are expansionist, even colonial, they are bound to bump into each other eventually. When they do, the frontiers between them — like, say, the Middle East — are likely to grow into battlegrounds, what Samuel Huntington aptly called "clashes of civilizations." In an environment of modern and global economy and politics and technology and culture, it is understandable that new religious movements would more often take the global than the local form. Additionally, since many draw resources from overtly world religions like Christianity or Islam or Buddhism, they have global or universal ideologies built into them. Today, after centuries of religious movements, the human world is deluged with universal religions that are not highly inclined to peaceful co-existence.

Tomorrow's Truths:
Studies of New Religious Movements

As we noted above, as many as two or three new religions may start *every day*. Many of these religions will never get out of the basement or living room of the founders, which is probably just as well. Most of the others — as many as 90% according to Wallace — will fail over time, some growing to prominence before reversing and fading away. Some, though, will survive and stick, at least as minority religions in a broader society, and a few will succeed to the degree of becoming the dominant or 'universal' religion of a society or beyond. They will become the new tradition, the new orthodoxy. Some of these religions have been growing quietly in the shadows and will burst on the scene some day. Others were just born yesterday. Still others will be born tomorrow. The most useful way to end this chapter is with a sampling of new religious movements (NRMs). As we will see, they are very diverse, blending traditional and modern religions and often mixing in non-religious elements as well. They tend, as we have warned, to evade simple classification as syncretism or millenarianism, *etc.*, and to overlap these categories. They are all quite contingent, shaped by specific local historical and cultural factors and even the personality of the founders and early members. Yet, they present some common characteristics, most importantly the plasticity of religion to adapt and mutate to changing circumstances. If religion was ever a fixed and immutable thing, it is not today.

Cargo Cults

Among the most colorful religious revitalization movements are the so-called cargo cults that swept through the Pacific Islands, particularly Melanesia and the southwest regions, between about 1900 and 1950. The first half of the twentieth century was a time of upheaval for many societies, in many places but especially the Pacific, where colonialism and even contact with Westerners had been sporadic to minimal previously. However, the two World Wars brought foreign men and foreign goods to these areas in quantities never seen before. Thousands of odd-looking and odd-acting soldiers came ashore, and even more remarkably they unloaded hordes of valuables the likes of which no had ever imagined. Islanders could have had no idea where these people and their wealth came from; the one thing they knew was that the strangers had a lot of 'cargo' and that they never seemed to work for any of it.

Cargo cults were an indigenous attempt to make sense of this new situation and to get some valuables for themselves. One of the first and best-known examples is the 'Vailala madness' that broke out in 1919 among the Elema people of Papua. Missionaries, particularly the London Missionary Society, had been active on the island for a while, at least some of whom had criticized and suppressed traditional religion. Economic relations were also unfavorable to the locals. Soldiers and missionaries sat on vast caches of supplies, and land had been expropriated from the natives and native labor conscripted. Peter Worsley (1968) points out that most of the adherents of the Vailala movement had been "indentured laborers" and were at least partially acculturated, often speaking English. Even worse, in the gold rush of 1910 nearly one-fourth of the native workers had died in the first half of the year, and the discovery of oil near Vailala River in 1911 only aggravated conditions.

The precise origins of the movement are difficult to pinpoint, but they represent a syncretism of native and foreign elements as interpreted by one or two key founders. Melanesian cultures already had a traditional concern for the dead ancestors, as evidenced by rituals in which recently-deceased family members were welcomed back to the village (in the form of masked dancers) and celebrated with feasting. Also, the political institution of the 'big man' meant to islanders that a rich man should be a generous man, who gives away his surplus rather than hoarding it. More recently, the natives had been introduced to Christian doctrine, especially the notion of Jesus and his resurrection, which seemed sound enough from a Melanesian point of view. Traditional ideas, Christian ones, and economic concerns united to give shape to the movement.

The founding of the Vailala madness, or what the followers called the *kava-kava* or *kwarana giro, kwarana aika,* or *haro heraripi* ('head-he-go-round' in pidgin English, indicating the dizzying nature of the experience), or *iki haveve* ('belly don't know,' another local expression for dizziness or ecstatic trance-like feelings), is usually attributed to a man named Evara, an elder who both enjoyed some degree of acculturation and some talent for trance and dissociation. When his father died, he had experienced his first 'madness.' He experienced it again when his younger brother died, and this time he told others about it and it spread. Naturally, it was not the dizziness or madness alone that captured his and others' imaginations but the specific revelations acquired then. He learned while in trance that a steamship would be coming for the natives, carrying their dead ancestors as well as stashes of cargo. When these ships arrived, the whites would be run off, and the indigenous folk would be restored to independence and rightful ownership of resources.

Making Gods

Although the movement resonated with certain traditional attitudes, it was also overtly anti-traditional; Evara went so far as to claim that "brown skins were no good...he wanted all the people to have white" (Worsley 1968:82). Over time, it developed a more elaborated doctrine with a visibly Christian aspect. Many members referred to themselves as "Jesus Christ men," and garbled notions of heaven and the Christian god emerged. God was called *Ihova*, and heaven was named *Ihova kekere* or Jehovah's land. Others occupying heaven with *Ihova* included *Noa, Atamu, Eva, Mari* (*Atamu*'s daughter), and two of *Ihova*'s children, *Areru* and *Maupa*. An old worn-out picture of King George V was offered as the likeness of *Ihova Yesu-nu-ovaki*, that is, Jehovah the younger brother of Jesus.

The result of the Christianization of the movement was an opposition to the old rituals: masks and other tools of the ancestral ceremonies were deliberately banned and collected and destroyed. New behaviors and rituals were established in their place. Tables with benches around them were set up in the center of villages. At these tables villagers sat for feasting to the dead ancestors, men sitting on the benches and women and children sitting on the ground around them. Additionally, ceremonial houses were constructed, also with tables and benches inside. Only practitioners of the movement entered the houses, which were seen as meeting places for the dead and the members as well as places for the members to retire for inspiration, waiting for that characteristic feeling in their stomach to indicate the onset of the madness. Finally, a pole or flag pole played a prominent role, which apparently was used as a communication device with the ancestors: energy or revelation would pass down the pole, into the ground, and then up into the bellies of the communicants, inspiring their trance experience. There were also ethical or moral proscriptions associated with the cult. These included rules against stealing and adultery and violating the sabbath. However, in keeping with tradition, the worst behavior of all was neglecting the dead and the feasts that they needed or demanded. Some of the leaders of the movement also claimed or were claimed to have powers of divination, especially to see the causes of illness.

Many other cargo-type movements broke out in the region before and even more so after the Vailala. A few even still persist today, such as the Jon Frum movement, which believes that a messiah named Jon Frum ('John from America?') will come someday. All represented and continue to represent an attempt to make sense of and make a response to the crisis created by the novel situation they found themselves in. Julia Zamorska suggests that these cults "were ways of adaptation, adjustment to a new situation, attempts to find a new place in the changing world and ways of searching for a new definition of Melanesian culture and a redefined cultural identity of the native people" (1998:7). In particular, she characterizes this attempt as a kind of "magical leveling" — restoring parity, or even superiority, to the local people through religious or spiritual agencies.

The Taiping Rebellion

New religious movements are not always so quaint and harmless. By some accounts, the Taiping Rebellion in China (1850–64) cost up to 20–30 million lives. It was one of a number of such movements during the carve-up of China by colonialists, which caused great instability in the country. As enormous and destructive as it was, the movement (named from the Chinese *Taiping tien-quo* for Heavenly Kingdom of Great Peace) began with one man, Hung (or Hong) Xiuquan (or Hsiu-chuan), who had a vision of the religious future and his role in it. Hung's is the story of a typical social failure who found his calling in religion. He came from an immigrant class who were outsiders in their own homeland. In 1836 he took the all-important Chinese civil-service exam and failed it. However, while in the city of Canton, he received a Christian tract entitled "Good Words for Exhorting the Age." Jonathan Spence (1996) insists that he would have noticed that his own surname (*Hung*, meaning 'flood') occurred in the tract and that his personal name (*Huo*, meaning 'fire') was also the middle syllable of the name for the Christian god, Ye-huo-hua.

After a second failed test, he collapsed into a coma, in which he had a dream or vision: he was about to die, and the minions of death cut him open and replaced his old organs with new ones; they also unrolled a scroll, which he read carefully. He then met his mother and father — not his biological parents but God and His Wife. God explained to him how the "demon devils" had misled people, and Hung offered to lead the battle against them. Armed with a divine sword and a seal, he fought the demons until he faced the very king of the demons, Yan Luo, and won. He lived then for a time in heaven with his wife, the First Chief Moon, and had a son. However, God sent him back to earth, where the demons still reigned, giving Hung a new name (*quan* or *chuan*, meaning 'wholeness') and a new title ('Heavenly King,' 'Lord of the Kingly Way,' *Quan*). As a result of his experience and his study, he realized that he was the second son of God, the younger brother of Jesus.

Hung set out to spread the word of his new revelation — that people must resist the demon devils among them, whether they take the form of evil-doers, Confucians, or the Emperor himself. By 1846–7 his *Bai Shangdi Hui* or God-Worshipping Society had grown into a sizeable though still small local rural movement. As the movement began to institutionalize, he enumerated six rules of conduct: obey your parents, do not lust, do not kill, do not steal, do not engage in witchcraft and magic, and do not gamble. As the movement became openly intolerant and anti-establishment, the authorities grew concerned, accusing them of teaching false beliefs, desecrating shrines, and disobeying the law. Encountering resistance not only from the government but from local bandit groups, in 1850 he began to talk about reshaping the movement into an army. Like many a group since, they started to stockpile not only food but weapons and gunpowder. Fighting units were assembled, with generals leading divisions of 13,155 troops organized down to the 4-man squad level. A system of signal-flags was invented. Perhaps most importantly, Hung himself was finally elevated to Heavenly King, began to wear imperial robes, and was instructed by Jesus himself to "fight for Heaven" and to "show the world the true laws of God the Father and the Heavenly Elder Brother"(Spence 1996:126). Accordingly, in March of 1851 Hung ultimately decreed the existence of the Taiping Heavenly Kingdom, with 1851 CE being Year One of the new age.

On September 25, 1851, the movement conquered its first major city, Yongan. However, this was only the seed of the heavenly kingdom promised in revelation. Heading generally northeast, they finally reached and conquered Nanjing in March 1853. Nanjing served as the capital of the new Heavenly Kingdom for eleven years, until it was at last defeated by the Chinese authorities with European aid. Within the city-kingdom, the life ordained by God and Hung was instituted. All land was divided among the people — one full share for each adult man and woman, one half-share for each child. Units of 25 families were organized under a corporal who saw to it that each family fulfilled its needs and that the surplus was sent to the public treasury. Opium smoking was outlawed, as were gambling, tobacco and wine, polygamy, slavery, and prostitution. Gender equality was fostered, with an end to female footbinding and the selection of women as administrators and army officers. However, homosexuality was punishable by death. Sabbath observance was mandatory, and young boys were commanded to attend church every day. Meanwhile, Taoist and Buddhist temples and statues were ransacked and ruined, and priests were defrocked or killed. Taiping was the obligatory religion of the land.

The Taiping continued to conduct an unsuccessful and exhausting campaign against the imperial city of Peking until the central government mobilized to squash them. By mid-1863 Taiping armies were being defeated repeatedly at great cost. Hung could not even imagine failure; as he responded to one plea from a general: "I have received the sacred command of God, the sacred command of the Heavenly Brother Jesus, to come down into the world to become the only true Sovereign of the myriad countries under Heaven. Why should I fear of anything? ... You say that there are no more troops; but my Heavenly soldiers are as limitless as water. Why should I fear the demon Zeng? You are afraid of death and so you may as well die" (Spence 1996:322). In April 1864 Hung became ill and eventually announced that he was going back to heaven with the Father and the Elder Brother. On June 1, he did. The city of Nanjing fell to the Chinese imperial army in July 1864, and the Heavenly Kingdom — at least this time — was vanquished.

Seventh Day Adventism

The United States has of course seen more than its share of new religious movements; it may well be the modern home of

NRMs. The mid-nineteenth century was a particularly fertile period for birthing new religions, sometimes called the Second Great Awakening of religion in the U.S. One such fledgling movement came to be known as Seventh Day Adventism. It itself grew out of the failed movement of Millerism, which predicted the end of the world in the 1840s some time. William Miller, its founder, had begun preaching conventional apocalyptic messages in the 1830s at age 50. Contemporary newspapers attacked and ridiculed him and his group, which probably never numbered more than about 5,000 hard-core believers. However, as successful movement leaders often do, he attracted a wealthy benefactor, in this case Joshua Himes. In 1839 he assisted Miller in printing the first Millerite newsletter, *Signs of the Times*, and eventually managing a press that pumped out Millerite pamphlets and books, including *The Second Advent*, a compilation of Miller's views and writings. Reading rooms were established around the region, and even a collection of Second Advent songs and hymns was prepared. Late in the movement (1842–3) a second newspaper, *The Midnight Cry*, was inaugurated.

The first date that Miller had set for Armageddon was August 11, 1840, when he and others expected the Turkish Empire to collapse and God's "probation" for the world to close. When it did not, Miller revised the date for the Second Coming to 1843. Again nothing happened. Eventually other dates were identified (whether by Miller himself or by his admirers), first March 21, then April 3, and finally October 22, 1844. All of these dates passed uneventfully, which is remembered in the history of Millerism as "The Great Disappointment." Many followers, some of whom had sold or given away their belongings in anticipation of the event, drifted away, while others drifted into other sects and movements like the Shakers. A few die-hards refused to give up, however, and reinterpreted the prophecy, eventually spawning the Seventh Day Adventist movement.

Hiram Edson, a former Millerist, received a vision that the date (October 22, 1844) had been correct but that the event had been misunderstood: the important change on that day was not the arrival of Christ but his 'cleansing of the sanctuary' of heaven and closing of the door of salvation. This 'shut door doctrine' meant that the opportunity to save any additional souls had passed; only those who were believers already, who were in the sanctuary with God, would be saved. So they had not been totally wrong, and even more, they were the 'elect,' the chosen ones. Until 1852–3 they held to this position, thus ruling out any possibility of missionizing and proselytizing. In an important way, the world *had* ended. The single most central figure in the Seventh Day Adventist version of Millerism was Ellen Harmon White (born 1827), who as a child had been injured so badly that she had been unconscious for three weeks. She joined the Millerite movement and suffered through the Great Disappointment. Then she had her own vision of God and Jesus entering the inner rooms of heaven and closing the door, supporting Edson's view. She continued to have visions — five to ten times a year of a few minutes to a few hours duration.

In 1855 White's visions told her to move the church westward to Michigan, where a world headquarters eventually evolved in Battle Creek. But more importantly, the group was developing its own doctrines, practices, and institutions. In 1863 the General Conference of Seventh-Day Adventists was established, with twenty-two ordained ministers and 125 church locations. An Adventist press took the place of the informal Millerite publishing efforts, producing *Second Advent Review and Sabbath Herald*. One of the key doctrinal innovations was the 'return' to seventh-day (Saturday) sabbath observance, which was part of an overall emphasis on Old Testament law. Another was the prominent place given to health and medical issues. In 1866 the Western Health Reform Institute (also called the Battle Creek Sanitarium) was opened, incorporating vegetarianism, exercise, and spiritual education, along with water cure. Adventist medicine avoided drugs in favor of clean living, fresh air, and rest. Seventh Day Adventist health interests grew into a medical school, accredited colleges to produce medical students, and seminaries to advance spiritual as well as practical education. Today, Seventh Day Adventism persists, with more than five million members and a world headquarters in Washington, DC. It is interesting to note that the Branch Davidians, the infamous group led by David Koresh in Waco, Texas, was an offshoot of the Adventist church.

Making Gods

Scientology

New American religions are not limited to the past. If anything, they pop up more regularly today and have more resources at their disposal to promote and diffuse themselves. One example of a twentieth-century NRM is Scientology, the creation of the science-fiction author L. Ron Hubbard. Born Lafayette Ronald Hubbard on March 13, 1911, he published his seminal religious work, *Dianetics: The Modern Science of Mental Health* in 1950 It follows in the well-trod tradition of American 'new thought' and 'mind cure' that typically takes the form of an alloy of psychology, spirituality, popular belief, and hard science. *Dianetics* is defined in the book's glossary as "spiritual healing technology."

It addresses and handles the effects of the spirit on the body and can alleviate such things as unwanted sensations and emotions, accidents, injuries and psychosomatic illnesses (ones that are caused or aggravated by mental stress). *Dianetics* means "through the soul" (from Greek *dia*, through, and *nous*, soul). It is further defined as "what the soul is doing to the body" (Hubbard 1999:579).

Hubbard quickly institutionalized the new psychological 'theory' into a string of clinics and eventually a church. The movement that grew out of the concept and doctrines of Dianetics was dubbed *scientology*, literally 'the study of science' or 'knowing about knowing.' In 1954 the first Church of Scientology was opened in California, and in 1955 Hubbard centralized and internationalized the movement with the Founding Church of Scientology in Washington, DC.

According to the teachings of scientology, the human mind consists of two parts, the analytical and the reactive. The analytical mind is basically the familiar consciousness; the reactive mind is akin to the unconscious, only much more negative. The reactive mind not only makes us sick; it makes *all* the ways in which we get sick. The point of the discipline, then, is to free ill people from the torment of their reactive minds and the *engrams* of which they are made. Engrams are the data of the reactive mind, defined as "a moment of 'unconsciousness' containing physical pain or painful emotion and all perceptions, and is not available to the analytical mind as experience. The engram is the single source of aberrations and psychosomatic ills" (581). The patient cannot access his or her engrams alone but only with the aid of an 'auditor,' a therapist or minister who listens to the person and identifies the negative 'moments.' At one point in the history of the church at least, this was done with the use of a machine that measures and displays the energies — an E-meter or 'electropsychometer' — as a picture or chart of a person's engrams. Persons still under the influence of engrams are called 'preclears'; once freed from their powers they become 'clears.'

The movement has evolved to identify other processes and goals that one can use to advance in one's spiritual, human improvement. The first formulation identified four 'dynamics' or urges or impulses or 'wills to survive' — through self, through family and sex, through group or friends or society, and through species or all of mankind. Later, four more dynamics were found — individual biological or animal, material universe, spiritual universe, and eternity or 'God.' By now, we have left the realm of mental (and physical) health and entered a dimension of spiritual awakening or achievement of a higher consciousness or reality. The goal thus evolved from becoming a clear — a happy and healthy human in the normal world — to becoming a *thetan*, a being of pure thought or soul. Humans are not really mind or body but soul or *theta*. A clear can progress to being an 'operating thetan' whose essence is no longer limited to his or her body. An operating thetan knows immortality and functions beyond life and death, making this condition somewhat similar to heaven but much more like the Buddhist notion of nirvana. The Church maintains no specific dogmas on 'God."

Scientology has developed a sophisticated system of institutions and attracted a large following. Among its specific programs are Narcanon International (for rehabilitation from substance abuse), Crimanon International (for rehabilitation of criminals), The Way to Happiness Foundation (a non-religious morality system), and Applied Scholastics International (for reforming education). Many people still find scientology cultish, partly due to the very secretive stance the Church takes toward its texts and doctrines and the energetic attacks it mounts against its critics. Individuals who have published secret writings have been sued, as have those — inside or outside the movement — who have said or written unflattering things about it. In September 1998 the Church won a $3 million suit against a person named Grady Ward for posting their documents on the Internet. Scientology is particularly disfavored in Germany, where it is regarded as a business, not a church (it received tax-exempt church status in the US in 1993) and is looked at suspiciously as a threat to society.

Heaven's Gate— The Evolutionary Level Above Human

For many Americans, Heaven's Gate is the very model of a dangerous and wacky doomsday cult. It is also a textbook case of syncretism — an ersatz mix of Christianity, UFO talk, computer-speak, spirit-possession, and birth or maturation analogies —yet it bears most of the marks of a classic religion. The deceased head of the group, Marshall Applewhite, who referred to himself as "Do" (pronounced *doe*), claimed to be the incarnation of a being from The Evolutionary Level Above Human who had to gather up his crew and prepare themselves and as many humans as possible to return to that higher realm. In fact, he suggested that this was not the first such visitation among humans but that the visits occurred at roughly 2,000 year intervals. Their Web-site posted the following:

Two thousand years ago, a crew of members of the Kingdom of Heaven who are responsible for nurturing "gardens," determined that a percentage of the human "plants" of the present civilization of this Garden (Earth) had developed enough that some of those bodies might be ready to be used as "containers" for soul deposits. Upon instruction, a member of the Kingdom of Heaven then left behind His body in that Next Level...came to Earth, and moved into...an adult human body (or "vehicle") that had been "prepared" for this particular task. The body that was chosen was called Jesus.

Do writes: "Our mission is exactly the same. I am in the same position to today's society as was the One that was in Jesus then."

ATHEISM ADVANCED

The process of evolution to this higher level of existence, then, involves the incarnation of a higher being into a human body through occupation or possession of that body. A 1995 statement from TELAH explained that previous missions to Earth selected and tagged specific bodies for insertion of a 'chip.' Presumably like a computer chip, the device is the 'soul' of the incarnated double-being (human and TELAH) with "a program of metamorphic possibilities." As the 'Next Level mind' fills, it expands and takes up more of the space that the human mind was originally taking, until it displaces and replaces it. Humans therefore come in two varieties: those with TELAH chips have souls, and those without chips have no souls. The latter are "simple 'plants,'" mere physical, human bodies. Those with chips are potential but not yet actual higher beings, since they may be actively filling their hard drives through instruction from the present representative of TELAH on Earth and thus progressing toward "metamorphic completion," or they may be not progressing either because they are not in communication with the representative or may "have chosen not to 'pursue.'"

The urgency behind all this is that the present civilization of the Earth is about to be "recycled" in order that the planet might be rejuvenated. The world is not salvageable any more and has become inadequate for its designed purpose, which was as a giant greenhouse for growing "human plants" that could become vehicles for TELAH souls. So, the beings of TELAH are coming to end the experiment, and it was believed that they were coming in a spaceship that was hidden on the other side of the Hale-Bopp comet that swung near Earth around that time.

In preparation, members were supposed to be detaching themselves from their lower, human nature. This nature included not only materialism and sexuality but gender itself. TELAH beings, without physical bodies, did not have gender, which explains the auto-castration of the male members of the group. As if this were not enough, TELAH saw enemies out there, in the form of a competing population of evil beings called "Luciferians." Consequentially, the Luciferians used not only material comfort, sexual pleasure, and increased sexual behavior to keep humans drugged and ignorant, but 'religion' as well. All of the human religions were conspiracies of the enemies to distract us from the truth and to prevent us from achieving our higher nature. As their website put it:

the Next Level abhors religions, for they bind humans more thoroughly to the human kingdom, using strong misinformation mixed with cosmic or universal consciousness of Creation, about which, in truth, they know nothing.... Only the Luciferians could have Christians believing that Jesus promoted family values, becoming better humans, establishing professional religious institutions, and looking for the Second Coming of some flowing-robed, peace-and-love manifestation of their artists' conceptions.

"If you have grown to hate your life in this world and would lose if for the sake of the Next Level, you will find *true* life with us — potentially forever. If you cling to this life — will you not lose it?" Those are the words that empowered sacred suicide.

Cao Dai

While America has been creative in the religious arena, other countries have cranked out their NRMs too, with some of the same raw materials and the added energy of response to the destabilizing effects of colonialism. For instance, Vietnam was a French colony when Ngo Minh Chieu was born in 1878 as the only child of a poor family. Exposed early in life to Chinese religion, in particular the teachings of Confucius, as well as to French culture and Christianity, he stood at the crossroads of cultures and religions. He also practiced spiritism and séances; at one of these events, he received a spiritual message that supposedly cured his mother of her illness. At a séance in 1920, he was visited by Duc Cao Dai, the Supreme Being, who launched a series of revelations that would lead to a new religion, Cao Dai.

After three years of preparation, Chieu began to proselytize around Saigon. He had great success, especially among the lower class and peasants; Susan Werner (1981:4) concludes that the new religion "claimed more followers within a year of its founding than Catholicism had gained in over 300 years of proselytization." On October 7, 1926 when the "Declaration of the Founding of the Cao Dai Religion" was written, 247 members were present. Originally named *Dai Dao Tam Ky*

ATHEISM ADVANCED

Pho Do or 'The Third Great Universal Religious Amnesty,' the movement conspicuously saw itself as related to and continuing other, older religious traditions.

Chieu soon withdrew from daily administration, and Le Van Truang came to act as the 'Pope' of the church. The new church appropriated other structural characteristics of the Catholic Church, with the *Giao-Tong* ('Pope') presiding over a college of church administrators (*Cuu-Trung-Dai*), considered to be the executive branch. Three *Chuong Phap* or 'Legislative Cardinals' headed up the three 'legislative branches,' one for each of the old Asian religions (Confucianism, Buddhism, and Taoism). Underneath that, 36 *Phoi-Su* or 'Archbishops' (twelve for each branch) held authority over 1,000 *Giao-huu* or 'priests' each, with *Le-Sahn* ('student priests'), *Chuc Viec* ('lay workers'), and *Tin-Do* ('adepts' or followers) arrayed in an elaborate order.

Doctrinally, Cao Dai is a classic globalist-universalist syncretism. Although resembling Catholicism institutionally, its explicit agenda is to unify the great Asian religions. It is monotheistic, believing in 'God the Father' (*Duc Cao Dai*) but also a 'Universal Mother.' It recognizes a number of divine beings including Siddhartha, Confucius, Lao-Tzu, and Jesus, but its cosmogony and theology are probably closest to Taoism. From Taoism it borrows notions of matter, energy, and soul plus the 'five elements.' From Confucianism it imports the 'three duties' (social relationships) and 'five virtues.' From Buddhism it inherits the 'three refuges' and the 'five prohibitions' or moral regulations. And the goal of the religion is basically that of Buddhism: to achieve enlightenment through the careful management of one's karma, by avoiding bad action and engaging in good, including the teaching of others about the right path. Reincarnation in a higher state or ultimate escape to a better reality, heaven or nirvana, is the reward.

Ritual services can take place at home or at a local temple. The focal site of ritual activity is the Mother Temple located at Tay Ninh. The temple, called the Holy See, was constructed in 1928 and houses a mural of the Three Saints of Cao Dai, who are Trang Trinh (a fifteenth-century Vietnamese nationalist poet), Sun Yat-sen (the leader of the 1911 Chinese nationalist revolution), and Victor Hugo (the French writer). These three figures not only represent the 'Third Alliance' of Vietnam, China, and France but speak to followers during séances. Séances, in keeping with Chieu's early personal experience, make up a critical part of religious practice, using Ouija boards or calling on spirits to tap out messages on tables or write them with ritual pens. Mediums are necessary officiates at such events.

Like many NRMs, Cao Dai met with initial official resistance, but by 1935 they were tolerated as a religion. In 1941 the French administration closed the Holy See and tried to eradicate the movement, and the coming of Communism in the 1940s only steeled the faithful more. On February 7, 1947 a Cao Dai army was introduced under the rubric of the "Great Community for Guarding Righteousness and Humanity"; followers were recognized as "Soldiers of the Heavenly Path." The Cao Dai militia grew to 10,000 men and fought both the French and the Communists. The end of the Vietnamese war in 1975 with the victory of the North Vietnamese Communists meant the abolition of all observable religion and the 're-education' of religionists as socialists. Even so, Cao Dai claims some five million believers internationally, with at least 1.5 million in Vietnam, making it the third-largest religion in the country.

Aum Shinrikyo

If Heaven's Gate is the epitome of an American suicidal doomsday cult, the Aum Shinrikyo is the Japanese version, with its violence turned outward. On March 20, 1995, the group released a nerve gas called sarin into the subways of Tokyo, killing twelve and injuring over 5,000. The NRM was led by a blind guru named Shoko Asahara, born Chizuo Matsumoto in 1955, who had been a religious seeker since early in life. He had tried out various New Age and Eastern beliefs and groups, picking up ideas about natural foods and Chinese medicine and karma along the way, until he found and joined the Japanese new religion called *Agonshu*. Agonshu taught that bad karma blocked believers from true enlightenment and that this karma could be alleviated through meditation and suffering — including the imposed suffering of others.

147

ATHEISM ADVANCED

In 1984 Asahara formed his own group, and in 1986 while in India, he supposedly achieved enlightenment. The following year he named the new group Aum Shinrikyo — *Aum* after the Hindu mantra *om*, *shinri* which is Japanese for 'supreme truth,' and *kyo* for 'religious teaching.' The movement met immediately with controversy and disapproval, and the group saw these challenges as the reactions of a hostile world against their truth; the result was to make the sect more militant. A militant Aum Shinrikyo was not destined to be a pleasant thing, given its belief structure. These beliefs focused on two areas: the person of Asahara as a unique being, and the eschatological predictions it made and the plans it proposed. Asahara claimed, for instance, that he possessed special DNA and that he had even done blood tests to prove it. Further, he maintained that he was a higher being, an inhabitant of a super-human non-material plane of existence. Therefore, he could see and know things that other mere humans could not, including the unfolding of the end-time.

The eschatology of Aum Shinrikyo was a syncretism of Christian and Hindu-Buddhist beliefs mixed with the prophecies of Nostradamus. It predicted an apocalyptic end of the world, which was referred to as Armageddon or World War III. The expected apocalypse was at least partly a consequence of a vast international conspiracy involving the Freemasons and the American government. Early in the sect's history, the goal was to prevent this event from occurring. The work of the group was to intercept the negative energy in the world and transform it into positive; for this work, 30,000 members were needed, who had achieved their own enlightenment through the teachings of the guru. However, as prevention began to seem more and more unlikely, the goal shifted to survival through and beyond the inevitable end of the world. The only path to survival was Aum Shinrikyo. By 1990 the sect was building communes and bomb shelters where they could isolate themselves from society and prepare for and be saved from Armageddon. These sole survivors of the mass destruction could then emerge to rebuild civilization — Aum Shinrikyo civilization. (The similarity to American survivalist doctrines and practices— especially but not exclusively surrounding Y2K — should be clear.)

The conflagration and the future world-to-be were vague in description, but it was understood that evil forces would attack the world with their ultimate weapons, including nuclear, biological, and chemical weapons; gases like sarin would be among those weapons. The group even began manufacturing, stockpiling, and testing its own supply of these weapons, using sarin gas on the population of Matsumoto Nagano prefecture in Japan a year before the Tokyo attack (June 1994), with almost equally deadly results — seven fatalities, 600 injuries. The Tokyo subway attack might have been an effort to jump-start Armageddon; on the other hand, it might have been an attempt to make their prediction appear true, perhaps as a recruiting effort. That latter interpretation seems likely in view of Asahara's claim immediately following the attack that it was actually committed by the United States, which had allegedly begun its war against Japan and already seized the government.

One follower of the sect, interviewed by Mark Juergensmeyer, thought that the action was orchestrated by Asahara to give himself a feeling of power, or perhaps was a reaction to the pressure he felt from authorities who were increasingly attentive to the sect's movements (that the end of the group was near and he wanted to go out with a bang). One other suggestion was that the master wanted his chance to appear to be the last hope for humanity, that he "wanted to be seen as a savior" and "wanted to be like Christ" (2000:112). Either way, the plan failed. Armageddon did not start, and recruits did not rush to the religion. Yet, Aum Shinrikyo could and did still justify the plan by appealing to spiritual conceptions. By twisting a Tibetan Buddhist term, *phoa* or the transfer of consciousness from the living to the dead to elevate their spiritual merit, Asahara could argue that some people were better off dead for the benefit of the living. In fact, Asahara wrote about the moral acceptability of "mercy killing," maintaining the "right of the guru and of spiritually advanced practitioners to kill those who otherwise would fall into the hells" (quoted in Juergensmeyer: 114).

International Raelian Religion

Not all revitalization movements are religions, and not all religious revitalization movements are alike. Some are actually 'atheistic,' since we know that religions need not be theisms.

ATHEISM ADVANCED

And because religions are conglomerations of items, virtually all of which also have their non-religious form, not all of the elements of a NRM need be religious. Religious movements can ingest elements from any and all sources, including secular, technological, and pop-cultural ones — such as notions about UFOs and space aliens. Perhaps one of the most curious such movements, one that has been in the news lately for its claims about human cloning, is the Raelians.

On December 13, 1973 a French journalist named Claude Vorilhon (born 1946) decided not to drive to work and instead ended up driving himself to a volcanic crater near Auvergne. As he tells it in his book *The Final Message* (Rael 1998), he saw a flying saucer descend from the sky, out of which stepped four-foot tall "greens" with long dark hair. One extraterrestrial — significantly named Yahweh — told him to write down what the being was about to tell him and to spread it to others, although Vorilhon was urged to be wary about the readiness of people to hear the message and the objections he was likely to face. Over five subsequent meetings the outer-space beings explained their identity, their role in human history, and their plans for us: that they would return to earth when world peace had been achieved and an embassy for them had been built, of all places in Jerusalem. They also gave him a new name — *Rael*.

According to the Raelian Web-site (www.rael.org), the message to humanity included the surprise that 'God' does not exist; rather, the aliens had created humans and all life on earth through DNA technologies. It so happens that the name of the race of aliens is *elohim*, one of the biblical terms for God — or literally, 'gods,' since the word which appears in Genesis is plural — which had been distorted by humans into some kind of supernatural entity. The Raelian religion is thus self-consciously atheistic, since what we thought were gods are really just extraterrestrial beings. The various world scriptures are garbled and confused. At the same time, they say, all of the great world religious prophets have been in communication with the *elohim* race, which has continually tried to reach and instruct us. They have finally decided that we humans have matured to the point when they can reveal greater knowledge and power to us, such as the secret to world peace and to longer life, perhaps even immortality. Peace will come through a world government and currency, and life and immortality from technology, especially cloning. The alien creators, we learn, are ready to return. For them to do so, two things must occur: the human race must be prepared for them and convinced of their reality and their good intentions, and an embassy must be built for them, a landing spot and meeting ground, specifically, as we said, in Jerusalem. The new philosophy that they will establish, a confluence of religion and science, will also lead to universal happiness. Unlike Scientology which identifies engrams as our biggest enemy, Rael identifies social institutions as the main obstacles to natural human happiness. The "organized brutality" that has marked human history, together with the deliberately misleading behavior of leaders, distracts us from our true destiny. The Raelian Web-site tells us:

Governments and religious institutions don't have your interest at heart, they are just fronts to make money and maintain power, the puppets of economic giants acting behind the scenes. They lie behind their smiles and benedictions before the elections but behind your back they are laughing all the way to the bank. They use the media as their obedient little liars to manipulate public opinion with their politically correct propaganda and maintain the illusion of legitimacy while deliberately cultivating an atmosphere of fear.

However, science, the "great democratic leveller," will free us from this exploitation. It will also free what Raelians call our "sensuality," but by this they mean a disciplined sensuality through "sensual meditation," which "teaches us how to awaken our potential and bring these into our lives, so that we each become gardens of fulfilment [sic] with all our flowers blossoming." This meditative technique seems to be the main product that Raelianism is selling for now, offered through books, CDs, and most importantly conferences and training seminars. Finally, in 1997 the Raelian Religion founded a technology company called Clonaid to further its scientific, specifically DNA-related, researches. This technology, the original "creation method" of the *elohim*, is believed to be a gift to us and a virtual religious duty, as well as a way of participating in the creative process of making more and better humans and ultimately humans that realize their infinite and eternal potential.

Chapter 5

Religion and Violence:
The Virtue of Hurting

It is impossible and undesirable to ignore the pervasive violence of our modern world and the pervasive role of religion in that violence. Indeed, there is a veritable industry of books on religion and violence, with titles like *When Religion Becomes Evil* (Kimball 2002), *Sacred Fury: Understanding Religious Violence* (Selengut 2003), *The Demonic Turn: The Power of Religion to Inspire or Restrain Violence* (Lloyd 2003), *Fighting Words: The Origins of Religious Violence* (Avalos 2005), and several that explicitly link violence and 'God' like *Terror in the Mind of God* (Juergensmeyer 2000), *Terror in the Name of God* (Stern 2003), and *Violence in God's Name* (McTernan 2003). Each of these volumes, and many others, makes some more or less meaningful contribution to the overall understanding of religion-inspired violence. However, none has come close to seeing the entire picture and real relationship, and some are further from ever seeing it than others.

All of these efforts are limited by one or more of a number of perspectives, some of which we have already raised in this book. For instance, all of them without exception operate with an inadequate and sometimes patently false notion of religion. Kimball and Selengut are particularly guilty on this count. Kimball asserts, "At the heart of all authentic, healthy, life-sustaining religions, one always finds this clear requirement [to love God and each other]" (39). That is simply wrong, because, as we have discovered, most religions never even had a concept of god(s), and most of those that do have such a concept do not place love at the center of their religious experience. The relationship with god(s) may be fear, obedience, annoyance, or plain indifference.

Selengut makes an assortment of more specific false claims. One is that "the earliest and most elemental expression of religious violence [is] holy wars" (17). This is untrue: most religions never had and could never have such a thing as a holy war because they lacked a proper notion of 'war' to begin with and because their religions, as local and tribal matters, were nothing to go to war about. He also insists that "the center of all religions is the yearning for the *eschaton*, an end-time when all peoples of the world live together in peace and harmony, without war or conflict" (1). That is false since many religions have no ideas about an end-time at all, and not all of those that do have the idea romanticize it as a time of peace and harmony; Hinduism, for one, expects existence to end completely and to be replaced with another incarnation of reality that will follow the same cyclical pattern as the present one.

Finally, Selengut says that "All religions have versions of an eternal life for their religious martyrs who die a sacrificial death on behavior of the tradition" (7). But of course most religions never had a conception of martyrdom in any way, and not all of those that did necessarily had a concurrent belief in eternal life and associated the two.

The problem here is obviously that these authors are assuming a particular *kind* of religion and extrapolating it to *all* religions. They have a completely insufficient understanding of what religion is and how incredibly diverse it is. In short, they are focusing on two or three familiar religions — almost always Christianity, Islam, and Judaism — which are undeniably important but are absolutely not the only religions or types of religion in the world.

Thus limited in their vision, they proceed to select one or two familiar kinds of violence to analyze over and over again. The most-often treated expressions of violence are 'terrorism' and 'holy war' which are, again, very important and particularly prominent at the present moment but are by no means the full extent of religion-based violence. That is to say, they are also operating with a deficient conception of violence. Violence is much more diverse, and much more complex, than they perceive.

Finally, almost all of them come from one of two extreme positions in regard to the relationship between religion and violence. McTernan sees this clearly when he observes, "They either exaggerate religion's role, denouncing it as the root cause of all conflict, or they deny that 'real' religion could be responsible in any way for indiscriminate violence" (20). That is, they tend to see religion as all innocent or all guilty. Kimball

Religion and Violence

falls most conspicuously in the former camp, or in a way in both camps: for him, there are really two distinct kinds of religion, "authentic" and "corrupt." Authentic religion never commits "evil," while corrupt religion does. When religion "remains true to its authentic sources" it is a positive force, he opines, not realizing that sometimes violence is *part of, even central to*, the authentic source of a religion. Christianity, as a prime example, locates suffering at the very heart of its belief and encourages believers to accept if not seek suffering as a religious experience (see below). And all religions that fancy themselves as the one *true* religion, especially when they fancy also a cosmic struggle between the (supernatural) forces of good and evil in which humans must participate, establish violence against non-members as at least a strong possibility if not a religious duty. It is plain to see, in the end, that Kimball's "five warning signs" of corrupt and violent religion — absolute truth claims, blind obedience, the idea of an end-time, the attitude that the ends justify the means, and the concept of holy war — *are the core and the source of certain kinds of religion*, among them Christianity.

Other writers, not coincidentally often the atheist and freethought ones, describe religion as the whole problem, as violent and evil by essence. James Haught is a good example of this approach: in his books *Holy Horrors: An Illustrated History of Religious Murder and Madness* (1990) and *Holy Hatred: Religious Conflicts of the '90s* (1995), he offers an undiluted litany of complaints against the violence that religion does. Many non-religionists and anti-religionists enjoy or even gleefully applaud such recitations of the violent resumé of religion. While we should take no real pleasure in religious violence, any more than any other kind of violence, it is also really quite irrelevant whether or not religion breeds violence for determining the truth-status of religion: the effects of a position do not change the truth or falseness of the position. But more than anything else, it also perpetuates a one-sided view of religion, in which critics of religion engage advocates of religion in a "yes it is, no it isn't" kind of pointless argument.

In this chapter I want to bypass all of the conventional debates and perspectives in the discussion of religion and violence, on the premise that they have so far been unproductive and continue to be unproductive. They fail to understand the

155

real connection between religion and violence because, for one thing, they fail to understand religion as well as violence. We have said enough about religion in the previous chapters to set our approach firmly in place: religion is much more diverse and complicated than most analysts ever admit. Our first project in this chapter will be to explore the diversity and complexity of violence, with a special emphasis on the characteristics conducive to greater and more intense violence. Then, we will turn to a description of the usually overlooked diversity of religious violence — well beyond the typical repetition of holy war and terrorism. We will also make the point that religion is hardly the only source of violence in the human world — and of course never the source of violence in the non-human world — and that virtually every form of religious violence has its counterpart in the mundane or non-religious realm (*i.e.*, there is holy war and secular war). Even more, in many incidents of violence, religion is one component or module in a more mixed and varied violent situation

Understanding Violence

If there is one recurrent theme in this book, it is that it is impossible to speak coherently about any subject if our words and concepts are vague and confused. *Violence* is one of those words and concepts. Everyone thinks that they know what violence is — and that it is a universally bad thing. Both notions are false. As I have argued in a previous work (Eller 2005), the definition and measurement of violence is extremely elusive and subjective, and violence is only a problem when it becomes a problem.

To tackle the first issue here, for most people violence is like pornography in the famous phrase, "I can't define it, but I know it when I see it." If they were pressed for a definition, it would probably entail some reference to physical harm. But 'behavior that causes physical harm' is neither a necessary nor a sufficient characterization of violence. What if the harm is emotional or psychological rather than physical? By that definition, it would not count as violence. What is 'harm' anyhow? How much damage must be done? An action can

Religion and Violence

cause pain without causing harm precisely: such behavior, like spanking, is violence to some people and discipline — even loving care — to others. 'Pro-family' spokesmen like James Dobson of Focus on the Family advocate physical punishment for children, often on a biblical basis. Summers and Hoffman tell us for instance that in Italy the official definition of spousal abuse demands that the woman "must show physical proof and her injuries have to take forty days to heal" (2002:xv). Whether it is forty days or four or fourteen or four thousand, there must always be some, at least implicit, sense of what makes an action violent as opposed to not-violent.

It is futile to attempt to establish *the* definition of violence; the issue is that how you define it affects how you measure it and how you react to it. In other words, a narrow definition leads to few cases of it, since few things qualify. A wide definition leads to more cases of it, since more things qualify. This makes it vexingly complicated to compare violence across history and culture, since different groups and historical periods count different actions as violent: until fairly recently, few Americans would have counted spanking as violence, and many cultures today still would not. Likewise with 'marital rape': such a concept did not exist until twenty or thirty years ago, so there were zero cases of it until then, and many cultures around the world still lack such a concept.

Rather than craft yet another flawed and relative definition of violence, let us consider some of the issues that go into our judgment about whether something is or is not violence. One concern, for instance, is intention. In some situations, the exact same action and outcome can be violence or not-violence (or at least criminal violence versus not-criminal violence) depending on the intentions of the actor: a gun fired with intent to injure is different from a gun fired by accident. In accidental harm, there is no intention to do violence, although the harm may be the same. In self-defense, there *is* an intention to do violence, but it is often an acceptable kind of damage. Defending your property or your family — or defending your country (as in war) — can be positively *noble* intentions for violence.

Another concern is the 'personhood' of the parties. The question is this: must the victim — or the perpetrator — be a person, a human agent? In other words, when one human kills another human, that can be (although not necessarily in all cases) construed as violence. If a human kills a lion, is that violence too? If a lion kills a human? If a lion kills another lion or a gazelle? Most of us kill and do other types of harm every day: we swat mosquitoes, chop down trees, slaughter (or are accomplices after the fact) cows or chickens for food — and vegetarians are not better, since they contribute to the killing of living plants — and gargle bacteria to death. At the present moment, humans around the globe are exterminating millions of birds to contain the avian flu. Isn't that violence? Yet how many people object to it? And if we did not kill the avian flu at the point of contagion, we would take vaccinations to kill the virus itself, most of us without a moment's regret for the 'life' of the virus.

A third concern is the innocence or guilt of the party suffering the harm. We tend to make a distinction between those who deserve injury and those who do not. No doubt, putting someone in prison — and clearly, executing them — is injurious, but we find such punishments appropriate and moral most of the time (notwithstanding those who are opposed to the death penalty). In fact, to label an action 'punishment' or 'justice' rather than violence is to move it from one category (a negative one) to a different category (a positive one). That is to say, at least some kinds of harm, even deadly harm, are judged as *legitimate* by some societies or members of society.

This takes us to a second consideration when pondering violence: some violence is acceptable while other violence is not. It is pointless to insist that all harm in every form is bad and wrong and must be eradicated. Even the most adamant pacifist (except perhaps for the Jain: see below) would defend himself or herself against injury and would gladly kill bacteria and viruses, not to mention killing thousands or millions of people to win a war. 'Violence' as such is not a problem. Violence is only a problem when it crosses a certain 'tolerable' or 'legitimate' threshold and/or when it is perpetrated against 'the innocent.' Contact-sports are clearly violent, but it is acceptable violence as long as players commit it within the rules. Likewise, there are rules of justice and rules of war. Contrary to the prejudice that all violence is out-of-control and irrational, most violence is very much rule-governed. It is only when we violate the rules of violence — say, kill non-combatants or torture prisoners of war — that people's moral indignation rises. Of course, we must remember that not all groups and cultures participated in forming these rules or agreed to abide by them — and that we ourselves will apparently break them when it is in our interest.

So violence is only a social problem, a cause of objection, when it reaches a certain level or crosses a line. The questions for us would then be, naturally: where is this line, who set it, and how and when does it change? The fact is that different societies, and even different factions within a society, set the line differently. For pacifists, any violence or war is objectionable; for most of us, there are good wars and bad wars. As we mentioned above, in our own history the bar has moved over time: involuntary and even coercive marital sex was acceptable and normal just a short while ago, but it is violent and even criminal today. Capital punishment has gone in and out of fashion. Spanking, a common and official punishment during my youth, is unsavory to many and illicit to some.

In American society, killing your own daughter is wrong and illegal in pretty much every circumstance, but in some societies when it takes the form of honor killing — avenging the honor of the family which has been tainted by the actions of the girl, due to premarital sex or just dating the wrong person — it is normal, acceptable, and actually admirable. In many cultures, infanticide has been and is acceptable. Wife-beating and child-directed violence have been common historical and cultural practices. Women of the Kaliai tribe in New Guinea expect to be beaten by their husbands during their lives. They do not enjoy it, but both they and the men "uphold the right of a husband to hit his wife for cause" (Counts 1999: 76), which can include adultery or just flirting, publicly shaming the man, fighting with co-wives (in a polygynous society), or merely failing at her normal domestic duties. Even the most intimate of violence, suicide, is regarded as scandalous and immoral in American society but noble and virtuous in traditional Japanese culture; there were even elaborate standards for when and how one should commit a good suicide.

I am not arguing here, of course, that all of these behaviors and values really are acceptable and normal. They are not acceptable and normal *to me*, but apparently they were acceptable and normal *to them*. The point is not whether or not a woman beaten in Kaliai culture feels any less pain than a woman beaten in American culture; doubtless she does not. The point is that the Kaliai did not see wife-beating as a *problem*, and therefore they were disinclined to fix it. Likewise, a few decades ago Americans did not see marital rape as a problem (in fact, the term 'marital rape' would have been viewed as a contradiction), so they felt no inclination to fix it. The most profound point for us is that humans can and do regard specific types of behavior that are harmful and injurious by any standard as *actions that they not only consider acceptable but sometimes necessary, valuable, and praiseworthy*. In other words, the issue is really not the actions themselves but rather the value systems and cultural norms from which they emerge. And religion is a critical aspect of value systems and cultural norms.

How to Be Violent and Feel Good —or Feel Nothing at All

Without having claimed to settle the question of what is and is not violence, we turn to the circumstances and characteristics that lead to greater violence, either quantitatively or qualitatively. However a society or community defines violence, what kinds of things lead to more of it?

Scholars from a number of social science fields have studied the nature of violence. The two basic approaches that have emerged locate violence either in the personality of the violent individual or in the social circumstances in which the individual finds himself or herself. There is no doubt that there are violent and otherwise destructive and undesirable individuals out there, and some of the worst violence — psychopathic violence — may well have a biological foundation in the brain. Significantly, Roy Baumeister, a psychologist and author of the book *Evil: Inside Human Violence and Cruelty* (2001), finds that most people attribute their own violence to external forces but attribute other people's violence to their deviant personalities. This is highly unlikely and only perpetuates what he calls the "myth of pure evil," which views evil as something that comes completely from the "outside" of people and that is wholly

Religion and Violence

"other" and foreign: it cannot be *me*, so it must either be *you* or *my surroundings*. You are a bad person; I am just a good person in a bad situation.

Again acknowledging that it sometimes really is the individual and his or her personality, research has shown that we do not have to be a bad person to do bad things. The most famous experiment, one that probably almost everyone has heard of, was conducted by Stanley Milgram (1963), who asked normal people off the street to administer painful and potentially lethal electric shocks to other normal people as part of an ostensible "teaching study." He discovered that two-thirds of the subjects were willing to give the highest level of shock, even though the 'victim' screamed in pain and then fell silent. Of course, there was no actual victim or even actual shocking, but the subjects thought there was. His finding was that regular people will consciously hurt others if they are in a situation where an authority figure pressures them to do it and takes responsibility for it.

The psychologist Philip Zimbardo (2000) has extended this argument, suggesting that social factors are much more important than psychological ones. In particular, he identifies five factors that are effective in making good people do bad things:

1. indoctrination into a thought-system that rationalizes or legitimizes violence;
2. obedience to authority, with no opportunity for dissent;
3. anonymity and deindividuation (*e.g.* getting lost in a crowd or having one's individual decision-making powers taken or suppressed);
4. diffusion of responsibility (*e.g.* "just following orders" or dividing the violent behavior among a group of people);
5. gradual escalation of violence;
6. dehumanization of the enemy or the victim.

Of these six, he concludes that blind obedience to authority is the most dangerous.

Roy Baumeister compiled his own list of characteristics that generate violent action, which overlaps partially with Zimbardo's. Baumeister thinks that the key social and psychological components are diffusion of responsibility, deindividuation, division of violent labor (that is, separating the violence into small tasks and distributing them among an organization of violence), dehumanization or demonization of the victim, separation of decision-makers from those who actually carry out the violence, egotism, and idealism. These last two are the most original additions. Most of us think, for instance, that people do harm and crime because of low self-esteem; of course, we like this answer, since it makes the perpetrator seem inferior and damaged. The truth is, Baumeister argues, that violent offenders often have *high* self-esteem, feeling themselves to be superior to others, especially their victims. Either the victims deserve their treatment, or else the perpetrator does not care about their pain at all.

We should clarify that high self-esteem alone is not a bad thing, but when it is *fragile* and easily challenged, as when a violent man feels that he is better than his wife but does not get the proper respect from her, that is when the trouble starts. Idealism may be the single most important contribution here: when people feel like they are acting — even acting violently — for a good reason, for a cause, for an ideal, they are most likely to act extremely violently and to have no qualms about it. After all, an 'ideal' is by definition the highest and best goal, and everything is worth less — if not worthless. If this ideal is perfection itself, then everything else is imperfect, or worse, a real obstacle to perfection. Obstacles are meant to be removed.

Zimbardo's and Baumeister's analyses of violent behavior — sharing an emphasis on deindividuation, dehumanization, and gradual escalation — strongly indicate that one of the essential characteristics in committing injurious actions is a lack of empathy for potential victims. In an empathetic response, we feel the suffering of the others around us. It is a central aspect of our human intersubjectivity, our ability to read the minds of our peers. We know for ourselves what it feels like to be hurt, and we know what a hurting person looks like. When we are empathetic, it really does 'hurt me as much as it hurts you' (see Chapter 10). It is considerably more difficult to cause pain to another if it causes simultaneous pain to oneself. However, if one can give pain without getting pain, it is much easier. And if one thinks that the other *deserves* pain, or that the other does not matter at all, one can actually feel good at the prospect of punishing or eradicating the other.

Religion and Violence

Surveying all that we know about violence and its motivators, I have arrived at a model of the expanding scope of violence based on six degrees or sources of violence. Each of these alone can be a basis for acting in harmful and destructive ways; in combination, they are deadly. The more of these six degrees any situation or system possesses, the more likely and more intense the violence will be. The only question for us then would be: which kinds of situations or systems meet these conditions the most fully?

First Degree: Individual Nature or Instincts

Certain kinds of beings have violent capabilities in their nature. Nature itself is a violent thing: life kills life, and 'nature' destroys life wantonly. Lions kill gazelles, cats kill mice, and so on. Some species simply have more violence in their instincts than others. It is critically important that, when it comes to violence against their own kind (what scientists sometimes call *intraspecies* or *intergroup* aggression), primates demonstrate a uniquely high level of such behavior. We are not talking here about violence committed in search for food or competition for mates but rather in confrontations between groups of the same species *as* groups. Primates are by no means the only species that act this way: ants, dolphins, lions, and wolves among others have been observed engaging in group-*versus*-group aggression (say, one colony of ants literally waging war on another). However, of the 64 species for which intraspecies aggression has been documented, 54 are primates. Chimpanzees, the most human-like of primates, have been observed patrolling their territories, apparently looking for chimps from other troupes to attack — and when they find them, attacking them savagely, in a sustained and fatal way. One particular troupe was watched as it systematically exterminated another over months. Chimps have even been referred to as "xenophobic" and "nationalistic" in their dislike and aggression toward other groups of their own kind.

Humans, descendants of remote ancestors of these creatures, have inherited much of this behavior. Humans have aggressive and violent instincts. We do not act on them continuously and unselfconsciously, but we do act on them. We

163

have the capacity to hurt others of our own kind, or we would be unable to do so. We also have the tendency to be xenophobic and nationalistic: we will sometimes attack and harm those closest to us, but we more often and happily attack and harm those remote from us.

Second Degree: Integration into Groups

If humans have violent potential as individuals, that potential is multiplied in groups. And it is not a simple linear increase: twice as many individuals producing twice as much violence. Groups seem to have their own dynamics — not the least of which is creating an 'out-group,' an 'other,' a 'not-us' against whom we can commit violence more extravagantly — which increases violence exponentially. Many commentators have noted the violent tendencies of groups. Sigmund Freud suggested that groups have their own distinct psychology, characterized by heightened emotionality and irrationality, increased excitability and agitation, and a kind of "suggestibility" found in hypnotic states. It is almost as though, he opined, a sort of "group mind" emerges.

More recently, Howard Bloom (1995) took this notion much more seriously, offering a view in which groups and other collectivities (nations, parties, movements, *etc.*) are literal organisms, even "superorganisms," with their own natures and tendencies; we individuals are mere "cells" in the body social and are swept along with it the way that a fingernail cell is swept along with our body when we run. Much of the history — especially the violent history — of humanity can be understood, he says, as a clash between these huge social organisms. Any explanation of violence, at least large-scale violence, will be incomplete without the inclusion of these super-individual processes.

Others have agreed. Eric Hoffer, in his short but provocative study of mass movements, writes that

> All mass movements generate in their adherents a readiness to die and a proclivity for united action; all of them, irrespective of the doctrine they preach and the program they project, breed fanaticism, enthusiasm, fervent hope, hatred and intolerance;

Religion and Violence

all of them are capable of releasing a powerful flow of activity in certain departments of life; all of them demand blind faith and single hearted allegiance (1966:*xi*).

Masses have many sources of integration — imitation, persuasion, coercion, leadership, joint action, suspicion — but the single most integrative one, he argues, is hatred, namely, hatred of those outside the group and particularly of those who were formerly members of the group but have left it, the apostates.

Gustave Le Bon gives an equally negative assessment of the effect of groups. The problem with groups is that they

> do not reason, that they accept or reject ideas as a whole, that they tolerate neither discussion nor contradiction, and that the suggestions brought to bear on them invade the entire field of their understanding and tend at once to transform themselves into acts. We have shown that crowds suitably influenced are ready to sacrifice themselves for the ideal with which they have been inspired. We have also seen that they only entertain violent and extreme sentiments, that in their case sympathy quickly becomes adoration, and antipathy almost as soon as it is aroused is transformed into hatred. These general indications furnish us already with a presentiment of the nature of the convictions of crowds (1896:62–3).

Whether groups, then, unleash something dormant in humans or add something absent in them, mere participation in a group has a profound and often malignant effect. Baumeister actually dubs this the "group effect," according to which groups "tend to be more antagonistic, competitive, and mutually exploitive than individuals. In fact, the crucial factor seems to be the perception that the other side is a group. An individual will adopt a more antagonistic stance when dealing with a group than when dealing with another individual" (193). We will return to this issue in Chapter 7.

Third Degree: Identity

Studies have shown that merely considering oneself in a certain category can make people more positively inclined toward members of the category and more negatively inclined toward non-members. Henri Tajfel's 'minimal group' experiments found that humans prefer their own kind even when they have never met them and when they do not really exist: subjects were assigned randomly to fake groups like 'reds' and 'blues' and given tasks to perform and then asked to evaluate their group and the other, and they typically judged 'their group' more favorably despite the fact that the group was imaginary and had not interacted at all (Tajfel 1981; 1978).

If human beings prefer and attach to their groups on such a flimsy basis, consider the consequences of significant and sustained interaction with members and of a shared sense of identity among them. That is, if people can get excited about being 'a red,' the effect is only multiplied when they regard themselves as 'an American' or 'a Christian' or 'a Republican' or 'a white.'

An identity in this sense typically has four elements. The first is a name: a group needs to think of itself as 'the Xs' in order for the member individually to identify *as* an X. The basis for the name can be anything — common language, territory, history, religion, race, or what have you. The second is a shared set of values or beliefs, that is, a shared culture. These are things that individuals will learn and internalize as they grow, literally making them a different kind of people than those who learn and internalize other values and beliefs. The third, which helps make the previous two possible, is a certain amount of interpersonal interaction. While members may never meet everyone else in the group, there must be some members with whom one interacts in an ongoing and intimate manner (at the very least, family). The more continuous and intense the personal interaction, the stronger the identity, although other indirect sources—newspapers, television, *etc.* — can have major impact on identity formation too. Finally, the group tends to have — and perhaps by necessity has — a shared sense of destiny, of the future and of facing that future together as an identity-group.

Identity necessarily separates one group from another. If we are the Xs, then you are not. The eminent psychologist Gordon Allport (1979) linked group identity to the pernicious phenomenon of prejudice. Prejudice is only possible when group confronts group or at least category confronts category: humans are distinguished into 'kinds' and often identify more or less strongly with their kind. There is an all-too-natural tendency, he allows, for people to overvalue the qualities of their own identity-group and to undervalue the qualities of out-groups. Identity and the prejudices that flow from it give us quick and easy generalizations and saturate all members — both in and out — with the same cognitive and emotional flavor. It also contributes to what he calls "re-fencing," that is, maintaining and strengthening group boundaries — keeping insiders in and outsiders out, by force if required.

Fourth Degree: Institutions

Beliefs and values and attitudes and identities cannot float in the air. They must be made substantial and concrete, and they must be routinized and standardized — and they will be, in the normal course of affairs as members of the group inevitably settle into patterns of behavior. These enduring and more or less large-scale patterns are institutions, and no social group can exist for long without them.

An institution is a constellation of social rules and roles in which humans participate. Marriage, for instance, is a social institution that establishes specific roles — husband and wife — and sets expectations for how those roles are to be played. Government is an institution, school is an institution, the workplace is an institution, and so on. Every one of us is situated in a particular crossroad of institutions, in which we are simultaneously a spouse, a son or daughter, an employee, a citizen, a student or teacher, and so on.

What is important about institutions is that they embody the beliefs and values of the group or society and that they regularize the behavior of members of the group or society. Institutions are the precipitate, the by-product, of the ways of thinking and feeling and acting in the group; when members do or think or say the same thing over time, it builds up the institution. Then, when new members (i.e. children) enter the group, they confront and are integrated into these institutions, learning how to be a proper member by participating in its institutions.

In a violent society, violence will and must be institutionalized, just like everything else. The family is often a violent institution; Deborah Prothrow-Stith, a researcher on family systems, has said straight out that "Violence is a problem that begins at home" (1991:145). Richard Gelles and Murray Straus maintain that "You are more likely to be physically assaulted, beaten, and killed in your own home at the hands of a loved one than anyplace else, or by anyone else in our society" (1988:18) — especially if 'you' are a woman or child. The reasons for this are partly practical: the family is where most people spend most of their time, where the interactions are the most intimate, and where the opportunities for competition and mutual annoyance are greatest. However, they are partly related to beliefs and values: not all societies demonstrate the same level of family violence, and those that have the highest levels are the ones with attitudes about gender roles and parental roles and violence in general that promote violence.

The family may be the first school of violence, but it is not the last. Organized sports, competitive workplaces, the military, and many others are institutions in which violence — symbolic or real — can be learned and practiced. Researchers have noted that one factor that correlates highly with violence is competitiveness, and most of our institutions are founded on it. On the other hand, groups and societies that devalue violence build other kinds of institutions, including a different kind of family, and children experience and internalize those models and roles. In other words, whatever a group institutionalizes, it is likely to get more of.

Fifth Degree: Interests

Groups live in the real world, where resources are often in short supply and almost always unevenly distributed. They therefore have not only identities but interests, and the two are often — indeed too often — entangled. By interests we mean the practical demands or goals of the group, such as wealth, power, land, jobs, education, and symbolic goals like prestige, self-respect, recognition, and such. Interests can also include imaginary ones like supernatural power, favors from the spirits, or places in heaven. Humans individually and groups collectively pursue their interests, and they are almost necessarily in competition for them.

Competition by itself can lead to violent clashes. However, when access to resources (real, symbolic, or imaginary) is or is perceived to be blocked by another group, conflict is most likely. Many individuals cannot help but notice that their opportunity to achieve their interests is affected or determined by their group membership: in the case of prejudice, they may find that their chance to get wealth or power or housing, *etc.* is shaped by their race or language or religion. The unequal and unfair distribution of resources, and the association of access with group membership, can turn identity into competition, competition into conflict, and conflict into deadly and prolonged — even genocidal — conflict.

Sixth Degree: Ideology

Finally, at least certain kinds of groups create and foster their own distinct ideas about how the world works and about what humans should do in response. A family or a sewing circle may not have an ideology, but a political party, a social movement, a nation, and a religion always do. An ideology is more than a set of ideas. We should think of it as more *inclusive* and more *idealistic* than the ordinary kind of ideas. In the extreme, it can be a totalistic and absolute vision of how things are — or how they ought to be.

The details of any particular ideology are less important than the general nature of ideology. Members do not even have to understand the details so much as be committed to them. As Hoffer puts it:

> The effectiveness of a doctrine does not come from its meaning but from its certitude. No doctrine however profound and sublime will be effective unless it is presented as the embodiment of the one and only truth.... It is obvious, therefore, that in order to be effective a doctrine must not be understood, but has to be believed in. We can be absolutely certain only about things we do not understand. A doctrine that is understood is shorn of its strength.... The devout are always urged to seek the absolute truth with their hearts and not their minds.... If a doctrine is not unintelligible, it has to be vague; and if neither unintelligible

nor vague, it has to be unverifiable.... To be in possession of an absolute truth is to have a net of familiarity spread over the whole of eternity (76–7).

In fact, he argues that it may be more effective to have a vague ideology, since members will not realize when it is contradicted or refuted nor when its goals have been reached.

Nevertheless, the details are far from irrelevant. Certain kinds of ideologies, certain models of the world, are more violence-inspiring than others. Ideologies, for instance, that regard the group as under threat can instill violence — but violence viewed as self-defense rather than as aggression. Ideologies that see evil afoot, with their own members as the good ones struggling against this evil, have the same effect. Ideologies that imagine the world or the entire cosmos as a battleground, such that violence or war is a (super)natural characteristic of existence, cannot help but valorize violence. And ideologies that aim at a perfect world, that envision the total eradication of imperfection (and any individuals or groups that represent imperfection) — that are idealistic in the extreme, in the sense of accepting no result other than the ideal result — are uniquely deadly, especially to non-members.

Hopefully it is clear how these six variables combine to enhance the scope (both extent and intensity) of violence. Circumstances that bring together all six will be more exquisitely violent — and less troubled about it — than ones that unite two or three or four of the variables. Accordingly, religion is not the only phenomenon that satisfies all six conditions. Political movements have done so with a vengeance. The French Revolution at the end of the eighteenth century was a total ideological re-creation of the world, in the mind of its more extreme agents, in the name of the 'people' of France. No wonder that it descended into terror and self-destructive bloodshed. The Bolshevik/Communist Revolution in Russia in the early twentieth century was an equally potent mix of identity, institutions, interests, and ideology in which counter-revolutionaries were deemed 'enemies of the people' to be liquidated. More recently, the Khmer Rouge regime under Pol Pot and the 'dirty war' in Argentina saw the same extremities of violence released on 'their own people' — although the perpetrators did not see the victims as their own people or even as people at all. Rather, the enemy was vermin, dirt, even disease. Argentine Minister of Foreign Affairs Admiral C. Guzetti is reputed to have said,

> When the social body of the country has been contaminated by disease which eats away at its entrails, it forms antibodies. These antibodies (death squads) can be considered in the same way as the microbes. As the government controls and destroys the guerrillas, the actions of the antibodies will disappear. This is already happening. It is only a reaction to a sick body (Suarez-Orozco 1992:239).

However, it is also evident that religion — or a certain kind of religion — is particularly well qualified to meet the conditions of extreme and 'legitimate' violence. Religion is a group phenomenon. It creates an identity among its members; it even amounts to a sort of large-scale family, with a shared name, face-to-face interaction, shared beliefs and values, and a common destiny. A religious group has its interests, practical and impractical. Finally, it has or is an ideology. Perhaps no other form of human organization and mobilization is so shaped by its ideology, since none — certainly no mere political or social group or movement — proposes its own cosmology (theory of how the universe functions) nor offers its *ultimate* rewards for success. Despite its posturing, a political party like the Republicans can imagine a day when they lose office; a religion like Christianity cannot imagine a day when it loses the struggle for reality with Satan or the struggle for truth with non-believers.

Believing in Harm:
The Diversity of Religion-Based Violence

As we said at the outset of this chapter, the in-depth analysis of religious violence has tended to focus almost exclusively on a few kinds of violence in a few kinds of religion. This is, again, not so much false as parochial: there are many other religions in the world, and many other forms of religion-related violence, than the ones we focus on. We will now explore these overlooked examples to gather a more complete picture of the connection between violence and religion.

We also highlighted above how discussions typically function either to accuse or excuse religion in its culpability for violence. Religion, in reality, is neither all good nor all bad —that is, all violent nor all non-violent. It would be more accurate to say that religion is diverse, even contradictory, on the issue of violence, just as humans are and just as nature itself is. Humans are altruistic and aggressive at the same time, caring and killing. Nature itself gives birth and death; it contains beauty and horror. Two things should thus be foreseeable. First, religion will take the existence of violence in the world seriously. No religion worth its salt would be able to deny or ignore the fact of violence; any religion that tried to maintain that violence did not exist, or that it was not important, would be cast aside as trivial. Religions must deal with violence. Second, the religious response to violence will be diverse, even ambiguous and contradictory. Any religion may and probably will condemn and condone violence simultaneously, of different forms and in different ways.

The two main or overarching responses of religion to violence entail *explaining* it and *justifying* it. Explanation is the process of accounting for it: why does violence occur in the world? Religions have come up with a number, but a limited number, of possibilities: human choice (what Christians typically call 'free will'), angry or offended spirits or gods, evil spirits or gods, violations of ritual obligations, punishments, tests, witchcraft and sorcery, impersonal forces like fate, or the flawed nature of existence itself (*e.g.* the Buddhist concept of *dukkha*). Some of these explanations suggest remedies, sometimes violent ones — like killing the witches — and some demand that we just accept it. But all help us make sense of it: the only thing humans apparently cannot do is suffer senselessly.

Justification is the process of making violence appropriate, legitimate, even virtuous. Religions have come up with a number of possibilities here too. Violence against witches may be acceptable: in the Judeo-Christian tradition, you should not "suffer a witch to live." Violence in the form of sacrifice is right and necessary in many religions. Forced conversion or persecution of non-members is a spiritual duty in some religions, even to the extent of holy wars. Violence against the self — either as a model of suffering, as a martyr to a higher cause, or as a purgation of the lower elements of the self — is valued and expected in some traditions. 'Defense of the faith' is justified frequently, as merely a special case of self-defense. And a certain kind of religion believes in and looks forward to a violent end of reality itself, in a final horrible, glorious cleansing of the cosmos of all evil and imperfection — a cleansing in which most human beings are the dirt.

So, any particular religion may embrace both loving and peaceful harmony and at the same time vengeful and righteous destruction. Neither pole is 'real' or 'authentic' religion. Authentic religion is as complex and self-contradictory as any other authentic phenomenon. Efforts to strip religion of its negative side are as futile as efforts to strip it of its positive side. Religion is both. In the most sensible statement on the subject, Lloyd concludes that religion is neither good nor evil but rather that it is *powerful* and *dangerous*, and that it is dangerous because it is powerful. "Religion is dangerous — and never not dangerous — because of the very thing that gives religion its distinctive power: its central and defining involvement with the 'that which' of ultimacy.... Ultimacy is an incendiary concept fraught with the potential for creating violence" (2003:23). Violent religion then is not "false religion or perverse religion or untrue religion" (118). It is just as real and just as religious as the friendly face of religion. It meets the spiritual needs of its members as much as nice religion does; it is even attractive to its members, who do not see their own religion as violent at all. And it is, he says, a real "live" option for religions and for religion as a concept. Violence gives meaning and motivation as much as — if not more than — non-violence.

Finally, since religion is not a thing but a system of modules, it would make sense that violence is one of the modular components that can be integrated in any religious system. This also implies that violence is not unique to religion but is itself a module or a set of modules that can be attached to other, including non-religious, phenomena. Contrary to those who think that religion is the *only* source or cause of violence, of course there are many other non-religious sources or causes as well. Rather, there are various forms or expressions of violence, which can be associated with religion or with non-religion. In every case that we consider, there is a secular version of the religious violence: people fight wars for religious and mundane reasons, they kill for both, they commit crimes for both, they persecute for both. The only exception to this rule may be sacrifice: while we use the word *sacrifice* in secular ways (like sacrificing restaurant lunches to save for a new car, or sacrificing one's life for one's country), these are not real sacrifices but metaphorical ones. Only crazy people believe that if they kill a chicken they will get a new car or that if they allow themselves to die that their country will automatically win the war.

Sacrifice

One neglected form of religious violence is *sacrifice*. The very word means 'to make sacred' (from the Latin *sacer* for 'holy' or 'sacred' and *facere* for 'to make or do'). Judeo-Christian religion has long since abandoned sacrifice as a ritual practice, although sacrifice was an essential — perhaps *the* essential — ritual practice in ancient Judaism, and Christianity is founded on the ultimate sacrifice, the god sacrificing himself.

Sacrifice entails the damage or destruction of some object, often a living being, for a supernatural purpose. Again, the early Judeo-Christian scriptures are replete with occasions of and descriptions of animal and plant sacrifice. Already in the second generation of humans, Cain and Abel were sacrificing (and their god certainly preferred animal sacrifice to plant, which was the cause of the first jealousy and the first murder). Noah sacrificed after the flood (although having only two of most kinds of animal, that seems like a bad idea — so divine providence caused him to take aboard *seven* of each type of animal suitable for sacrifice), and Abraham was asked to commit the epitome of sacrifice by killing his son. As the book progresses, the types and rules of sacrifice become more elaborate. There are "burnt offerings" and "peace offerings" (Exodus 20), "sin offerings" (Exodus 29), "wave offerings" and "heave offerings" (Exodus 29), and others such as "trespass

Religion and Violence

offerings" (Leviticus 5:19), "sacrifice of thanksgiving" (Leviticus 22:29), and "jealousy offerings" (Numbers 5:15). Leviticus lays out detailed instructions for various methods of sacrifice. Apparently the god enjoyed the smell of burnt flesh, which is described as "a sweet savor to the Lord."

Sacrifices were obviously still being conducted at the temple in Jerusalem in Jesus' time, since they are mentioned in the Christian gospels. And although Christianity does not demand blood sacrifice from followers, the religion is based on a blood sacrifice — of Jesus himself. Jesus is the "sacrificial lamb"; his blood washes away sin, the same way that actual lamb's blood did in olden times. Indeed, Christianity is not a repudiation of blood sacrifice but the ultimate expression of it. The fact that the suffering of Jesus provided a model for voluntary suffering in his followers (see below) cannot be overlooked.

Judeo-Christian tradition is hardly the only sacrificial one. Hinduism has also been a fundamentally sacrificial religion. Early Hindu texts like the Vedas consist principally of hymns and accounts of sacrifice. The god Agni, literally the deity of fire, is the object and the 'ruler' of sacrifice, and sacrifice is a critical if not *the* critical ritual act. Ancient Greece, which we celebrate as the cradle of rationality, practiced animal sacrifice, such as the *buphonia* or ox-sacrifice for Zeus. Dennis Hughes (1991), a scholar of Greek religion, mentions several purposes of sacrifice in their religion: for the gods of Olympus, for weddings and childbirths and funerals, in honor of heroes, in preparation for battle, as part of swearing oaths, and as purifications. In fact, the ritual of *pharmakos* may have involved human sacrifice or at the very least the scourging of human victims, who were whipped, cursed, and chased out of the city, carrying the ills of the group with them.

There is much more evidence of human sacrifice in prehistoric Europe. Miranda Green (2002) presents archaeological evidence from all around Europe, such as 'Lindow Man' who was found in a marsh where he had been left, strangled and with his skull fractured. A male at Hudremose had his right arm chopped off, while a male from Borremose had his face mutilated. A female unearthed at Danebury had a butchered pelvis, while a young boy was completely dismembered. Even more striking finds include an adolescent male in northern Germany who appears to have been drowned while blindfolded, with his head half-shaved, and made to sink with rocks and branches. A boy from a neighboring region was uncovered in a peat-bog where he had been left, ankles tied together, hands tied behind his back, and a rope tied around his neck that ran between his legs.

The compulsive human sacrifices of the Aztec and Mayan civilizations are particularly infamous. At least three major themes combine to produce these extensive religious killings. One was a belief that the sun was a tired and hungry god who needed a constant flow of blood to rejuvenate him and keep him returning every day. The second was the precedent of the gods themselves. According to one Aztec myth, the god Huitzilipochtli had been born fully grown and fully armed for battle from the womb of the goddess Coatlicue. A war god, Huitzilipochtli fought with his sister Coyolxauahqui and other gods and defeated them. His sister's broken body, beheaded and dismembered, landed at the bottom of the stairs of his temple (Matos Moctezuma 1984:136). Subsequent human sacrifices at the main temple at Tenochtitlan in what is Mexico City today re-enacted this victory: human victims were killed at the top of the temple, ideally by having their beating heart ripped out, then they were bled, and finally their bodies were tossed down the stairs to land where and as the vanquished goddess had fallen. In some particularly macabre rituals, priests would flay the skin off of the victims and wear it themselves, transforming themselves temporarily into gods. The third theme was a political one: the Mayan and Aztec emperors proclaimed their political and military prowess by leading vast sacrifices, often of defeated enemies, in a theater of absolute power over life and death.

Blood sacrifice is a global phenomenon. African cultures, from small pastoral ones to centralized kingdoms, practiced it. Pastoralists like the Nuer and the Dinka sacrificed cattle for rituals like male initiations or ancestral ceremonies. The kingdom of Dahomey offered the closest parallel to Mayan or Aztec practice. The living king and the spirits of dead kings demanded sacrifice, including human sacrifice. Melville Herskovits (1938), who conducted the pre-eminent study of Dahomey religion and politics, tells that occasions for human offerings were the death of a king, at the construction of a new

Religion and Violence

palace, before or after a war, at the opening of a new market, and on the occasion of ceremonies to feed his ancestors. Among the many other societies that performed sacrifices was the kingdom of Hawaii. Sacrifices were done for a plethora of social and religious purposes, including birth, marriage, and death, as well as in association with economic and artistic activities like building a house, setting fishing nets, cultivating crops, and learning dances and other skills. Making war or peace called for offerings, as did major ceremonies and dangerous voyages. Sickness, breaking of promises, and moral infractions; sorcery and divination; and propitiation to bring rain or fertility or to protect against sharks or volcanoes were all occasions for sacrifice. Finally, as elsewhere, the king was seen as the supreme sacrificer (Valeri 1985).

Despite the ubiquity of sacrifice as a mode or idiom of religions, it has been profoundly misunderstood among the scholars who have discussed it. Rene Girard, in his influential *Violence and the Sacred* (1977) claims that sacrifice is the essence of religion and that scapegoating or substitutive victimization is the essence of sacrifice. Walter Burkert concludes that "sacrificial killing is the basic experience of the 'sacred'" (1983:3). Both are wrong. Sacrifice is one practice commonly found in religions, but it is not universal; in fact, Burkert tries to link ritual sacrifice to the horrors of killing in prehistoric hunting, but it is precisely hunting and gathering societies that *do not* do sacrifice; nor are they horrified by killing. And even worse than taking one religious practice as the essence of all religion is taking one variety of that practice as the essence of the practice. In most religions and on most occasions, sacrifice has nothing do with scapegoats and substitute victims at all. What we find at the heart of sacrifice is a notion of power or energy or life-force that is contained in the blood or body of the victim and which can be transferred by removing and delivering that blood or body. It is another metaphor taken literally: blood is a physical substance required for life, but 'life' or 'energy' is construed as a (spiritual) substance in its own right that can be transmitted by and separated from the matter of the victim. This is why we see sacrifice so frequently associated with farming, construction (*e.g.* blood or body parts are placed on or buried under walls and buildings, *etc.*), difficult life-moments, and of course political leaders and often the gods themselves. In a kind of economy of life, the energy of the victim is spent for enriching the farmland, the structure, the event, the leader, or the god.

Self-Mortification and Self-Destructive Behavior

If there is a universal element in all religions, it is probably not sacrifice but self-mortification — any of the thousands of ways in which humans hurt or even kill themselves for supernatural reasons. This aspect of religious violence is more overlooked than sacrifice because it seems so pathological by modern standards (and of course it is) that we are inclined to deny that sane persons would harm themselves for any reason, let along a spiritual reason. Nevertheless, there are many spiritual reasons why humans mortify and destroy themselves, and some of the most familiar religions practice it as much as any.

The most total self-directed violence with a religious face is martyrdom, killing oneself or allowing oneself to die for a religious cause. In a way, it can be construed as self-sacrifice. Judaism to a certain extent and Christianity to a much greater extent have elevated martyrdom to a righteous act. By the time of the prophets like Isaiah, suffering had been valorized: the 'suffering servant' would accept oppression and affliction for his people or for all of humanity, a voluntary sacrifice who "poured out his soul unto death" (Isaiah 53:12). While Droge and Tabor in their aptly titled *A Noble Death* (1992) discover six cases of suicide in the Torah/Old Testament, the classic examples come later or elsewhere.

In the text known as *Testament of Moses*, a father urges his sons to "let us die rather than transgress the commandments of the lord of lords" (quoted in Droge and Tabor 1992:72). The Books of Maccabees give more models: Eleazar, for instance, refused to eat unclean food but instead "welcoming death with honor rather than life with pollution, went up to the rack of his own accord...as men ought to go who have the courage to refuse things that it is not right to taste" (2 Maccabees 6:18–20). In the next chapter, a mother and seven sons die happily rather than violate their religion, and in the fourteenth chapter a man named Razis resists arrest for his faith, "preferring to die nobly rather than fall into the hands of sinners and suffer outrages unworthy of his noble birth" (2 Maccabees 14:42). The book reports that "he tore out his entrails, took them with both hands and hurled them at the crowd, calling upon the Lord of life and spirit to give them back to him again" (2 Maccabees 14:46) — which, incidentally, the Lord did not do. Finally, the tale of the martyrs of Masada, who killed themselves rather than be taken prisoner by the Romans, is famous.

Martyrdom became a fixture of early Christianity, partly because it was seen to follow the model set by Jesus and partly because it was a way to ennoble the persecution that Christians were already experiencing. Even some non-Christians, like the Roman and anti-Christian polemicist Celsus, agreed that one should tolerate death rather than abandon religion: in his view, a believer "must remain firm in the face of all tortures and endure death rather than say or even think anything profane about God" (quoted in Frend 1967:54) — although the god(s) he had in mind included Helios and Athena. Others, like Tertullian, came to positively revel in the notion, seeing it as not just the only way to salvation but as a great and glorious choice: "condemnation gives us more pleasure than acquittal" (quoted in Droge and Tabor: 136). "I strongly maintain that martyrdom is good," he wrote, even using the medical analogy that we saw above: God "has chosen to contend with a disease and to do good by imitating the malady: to destroy death by death, to dissipate killing by killing, to dispel tortures by tortures, to disperse in a vapor punishments by punishments, to bestow life by withdrawing it, to aid the flesh by injuring it, to preserve the soul by snatching it away" (quoted in Droge and Tabor: 146). Only religion could develop such twisted logic.

Many others concurred. Origen regarded martyrdom as a kind of baptism that removed sins. Cyprian opined that "death makes life more complete, death rather leads to glory" (quoted in Smith 1997: 91). And many a martyr put this advice into action. Ordered to honor the Romans gods, Carpus and Papylus eagerly ran to their deaths (Droge and Tabor: 138). A woman named Vivia Perpetua actually assisted in her own death by steadying the executioner's sword against her neck, according to the book *The Passions of Saints Perpetua and Felicity*. Indeed a great number of 'acts of martyrs' or 'lives of martyrs' are collected in Christian literature.

Martyrdom is in no way limited to ancient Christianity or to Christianity at all, nor need it always be fatal. Islam has a tradition of martyrdom too, as evidenced by the verse in the Qur'an, "And whoever obeys Allah and the Apostle, these are with those upon whom Allah has bestowed favors from among the prophets and the truthful and the martyrs and the good, and a goodly company are they!" (Sura 4:69). Martyrdom in Islam is called *shahadat* and a martyr a *shahid*, from the Arabic root that means 'witness' (just like the Greek root of the word *martyr*). While most Muslims have not sought martyrdom the way that so many Christians have, it is still a noble destiny. As Ayatullah Sayyid Mahmud Taleqani (n.d.) puts it,

> The *shahid* is the one who has experienced the *shuhud* (vision) of truth. The sacrifice of his own life is not based on illusion or agitation of his emotions. He has seen the truth and the goal. That is why he has chosen to wallow in the blood and the dust. Such a person does so with the intention of intimacy with God, not on the basis of fantasies and personal desires. He is above these worldly matters. He has understood the value of truth in a deserved way. This is why he annihilates himself, like a drop in the ocean of truth.

For at least some Muslims, there is also an historical model of martyrdom in the figure of Husein (also spelled Husayn), who was killed in the early days of the religion. Members of the Shi'a Ali (the partisans of Ali) who believe that Ali should have been the next leader of the religion, better known today as the Shi'ites, often include self-mortifying behaviors in their rituals. In the festival of Asura, the devout flagellate themselves across the back with blades attached to whips to give themselves a small taste of martyrdom. Christianity has its share of such mini-martyrdoms. Self-flagellation appeared recently as a practice in parts of the Philippines (where a hardy few have even been known to crucify themselves), and 'penitential' self-flagellation has also been performed in European Christianity and its offshoots, such as the Penitente Brotherhood in New Mexico, which practiced it in the nineteenth and early twentieth centuries and in some areas may do so still (*e.g.* Carroll 2002).

Religion and Violence

There are numerous other forms of self-mortification in religions. Asceticism is a very common one, in which people intentionally hurt or deprive themselves. Ascetic behaviors can include extreme isolation, self-starvation, sleep deprivation, lack of sanitation, poverty, silence, and of course sexual chastity, or any other action that makes life difficult or uncomfortable (like wearing scratchy clothing, sleeping on hard surfaces, or exposing oneself to heat or cold). It can also include deliberate infliction of pain. The monastic tradition (secluding oneself off in a monastery) derived from individual feats of ascetic rigor. St. Anthony, the Egyptian Christian lone ascetic, set the model for what Harpham (1987) calls "heroic fanaticism" and experimentation in self-torment. Such self-treatment is often referred to as "discipline," as if the natural and pain-free body is undisciplined and unfocused, and nothing brings the body into focus like pain. In the extreme, Harpham suggests, the motto of the ascetic is "I am already dead" (26).

Buddhism presumes to minimize the pain of existence but often through the same ascetic, monastic practices as Christianity. Hinduism reserves a special life-stage for self-denial, the final stage of life (especially for men) when the duties of family and household have been satisfied. In late life, a man ideally was to become a *sanyasin*, abandoning home to renounce the world and its pleasures and wander as a poor spiritual athlete. The path was not as open or proper for women, although Lynn Denton (2002) found a community of female ascetics or *sanyasini* in contemporary India who engage in ritual fasting and sexual abstinence. And the most stringent form of self-denial was traditionally imposed on widows, who ideally were to kill themselves by joining their husbands on the funeral pyre to become *sati* or 'pure ones.'

The additional varieties of ritual self-abuse are too abundant to describe. Shamans in training often underwent painful ordeals, such as insect bites, food and sleep deprivation, drug ingestion, and physical operations. Participants in rituals frequently had to observe behavioral strictures on food or sleep or sex. Initiation rituals typically included direct or indirect infliction of pain, either in infancy (*e.g.* circumcision) or later childhood (scarification of the head or chest, 'female circumcision' or female genital mutilation, nasal septum piercing, tooth removal, and on and on and on). Interestingly, while religion is supposedly about the spirit, it cannot seem to leave the body unmolested.

Persecution

Religion not only turns its violence inward but outward as well. Every religion that creates a community of believers creates a community of non-believers as well — a *them* to our *us*. Sometimes their very existence offends us; sometimes, it directly threatens us. And, in virtually all cases, the peace and love and harmony that a religion offers is intended for co-religionists, not for the infidels and idolaters.

Persecution requires not only belief but power; the weak cannot persecute the strong. However, it is a tragic lesson of history that the persecuted tend to become the persecutors once they attain power. In Christianity's early years, it was the subject of persecution, although perhaps not as much as we tend (or they tended) to think: as Judith Perkins (1995) argues, Christianity was a small and ignored cult for most of its first two centuries, and the mentality of persecution was a useful one for mobilizing and enervating the faithful. Her assessment is that Christianity developed a "culture of suffering" long before and independent of persecution and that such persecution merely strengthened their culture. Early Christianity actually promoted the notion and virtue of suffering (see the discussion of martyrdom above), creating a role for itself as a ministry against suffering: the well do not need a doctor.

Nevertheless, there is no doubt that there was persecution of Christians by non-Christians in the Roman Empire. Mostly it came after the Christian refusal to conform to imperial religious conventions, like sacrificing to the emperor. (From Augustus Caesar on, the living emperors legally were gods and considered worthy of worship.) In other words, it was persecution of one religion by another religion. Once Christianity came to power in the Empire, it was more than willing to return the favor. When an orthodoxy was established by the Council of Nicaea in 325, all other dissenting views became *heresy*, from the Greek *hairesis* for 'a selection,' 'a choosing.' Such heresies included the belief that God was not a trinity or that Jesus was not divine or

Religion and Violence

that the sacraments of the Church were wrong or unnecessary. In 380 Theodosius set penalties for deviation from official belief, ranging from fines and loss of property to banishment, torture, and death; in 385 Spanish bishop Priscillian and six of his followers received the honor of being the first put to death under the new edicts, by decapitation.

Early Church authorities, while they did not take personal responsibility for the violence — they left that to the secular authority of government — were all the same often quite satisfied with it. Not at all sympathetic to his enemies, Tertullian wrote

> How shall I admire, how laugh, how rejoice, how exult, when I behold so many proud monarchs, and fancied gods, groaning in the lowest abyss of darkness; so many magistrates who persecuted the name of the Lord, liquefying in fiercer fires than they ever kindled against the Christians; so many sage philosophers blushing in red hot flames with their deluded scholars; so many celebrated poets trembling before the tribunal, not of Minos, but of Christ; so many tragedians, more tuneful in the expression of their sufferings (quoted in Freke and Gandy 1999:243).

The venerable Augustine and Aquinas agreed. In fact, Augustine asserted that it was actually doing heretics a favor to kill them: the Church killed "out of love...to reclaim from error to save souls." Accordingly, there was unjust persecution and just persecution, "an unjust persecution which the wicked inflict on the Church of Christ, and...a just persecution which the Church of Christ inflicts on the wicked." Aquinas, ever the legalist, argued that some crimes deserved capital punishment and that blasphemy and "unbelief" were the worst of crimes. Therefore, heretics "by right...can be put to death and despoiled of their possessions by the secular authorities, even if they do not corrupt others, for they are blasphemers against God, because they observe a false faith. Thus they can be justly punished more than those accused of high treason" (quoted in Levy, 52). He even imagined that saints were able to look down upon the suffering in hell for their pleasure.

Not surprisingly, persecution extended to three main constituents—non-believers or 'atheists,' heretics, and believers in other religions. The 'other religion' that was most at hand was Judaism, which was periodically persecuted throughout Christian history as late as Nazi Germany and, in some cases, beyond. The money and property of Jews were confiscated, their books and synagogues destroyed, their freedom of movement restrained (often forced to live in segregated ghettos), and more than occasionally their lives lost. Especially in Spain after the re-conquest from the Muslims, Jews were forced to convert to Christianity and were usually suspected of false conversion or back-sliding. Fortunately for the Faith, the Inquisition, which had been established back in the 1200s to deal with heresy, was available for this purpose as well.

The Inquisition had originally come into existence to combat break-away sects like the Free Spirits who claimed that they did not need the Church or the commandments to achieve salvation. Other figures like Peter Waldo, John Wycliffe, Jerome of Prague, and Jan Hus appeared with various dissenting beliefs and groups of followers, and most were 'inquired' and put to death. It was Martin Luther, beginning in 1517, who finally championed the reform and schism that survived to become the 'Protestant' movement — despite the fact that he was 'inquired into' and probably would have been executed if authorities could have arrested him. Luther, however, was no advocate of tolerance: in 1530 he called for imprisonment, torture, and death for *other* heretics like Anabaptists, and he was more than happy to continue the persecution of Jews.

In the American colonies, those bastions of religious freedom, persecution was practiced with equal fervor. Jews, Unitarians, and Quakers were run out of Massachusetts and other places. The model Maryland Toleration Act of 1649 stipulated that Christians — but only Christians who accepted the Trinity — were tolerated, but non-Christians and Christian blasphemers who denied the Trinity or said anything negative about God or Jesus "shall be punished with death and confiscation or forfeiture of all his or her lands and goods to the Lord Proprietary and his heirs." Naturally, those who were deemed to be doing evil, like witches, could be persecuted completely righteously. And we cannot even begin here to discuss the persecutions that native religions experienced for their presumed idolatry and devil worship.

As always, Christianity is not the only religion to bear blame for persecution, nor is religion the only source of it.

Religion and Violence

Contemporary Christians condemn persecution of co-religionists in places like China. Hindus and Muslims have persecuted each other, and continue to do so along the India-Pakistan border. Sikhs in Kashmir rightly feel persecuted. And religions of all kinds were persecuted by communist governments in the Soviet Union, China, Cambodia, and elsewhere. In the attempt to purge society of religion, priests of every faith were defrocked, sometimes forced to marry, publicly ridiculed and 're-educated,' and more than occasionally killed; religious properties were seized for secular uses or simply destroyed.

Persecution can come from religion or be directed at religion, or (ordinarily) both. It can also emerge from a combination of religious and other motivations, as in the case of the Ku Klux Klan and similar groups. The KKK was and is not just about religion, but religion is a crucial ingredient in its persecution of blacks and others, including Jews, Catholics, and immigrants of all sorts. As Imperial Wizard William Joseph Simmons wrote in letters of recommendation for Klan initiates in the early 1900s:

> Your best friends state you are a "Native Born" American citizen, having the best interest of your community, city, state, and nation at heart,... and you believe in —
> The Tenets of the Christian Religion
> White Supremacy...
> Upholding the Constitution of the United States of America
> The Sovereignty of our State Rights
> Promotion of Pure Americanism... (quoted in Wade 1987: 150).

As Wade's title reminds us, the symbol of the Klan is after all the burning cross.

Ethno-religious Conflict

Being a social and modular phenomenon, we should expect that religion can get wrapped up in other social and political issues and disputes as well. Many of the world's contemporary and historical ethnic conflicts have a religious component, or are in some cases primarily religious, but of course not all are. And even when religion plays a role in ethnic conflict, this conflict is almost never *about* religion.

ATHEISM ADVANCED

One can easily see the effects of religious identity in ethnic conflicts. Catholics fight Protestants in Northern Ireland, Hindu Tamils fight Buddhist Sinhalese in Sri Lanka, Jews fight Muslims in the Middle East, Christian Serbs fight Bosnian Muslims in (former) Yugoslavia, Muslims fight Hindus across the India-Pakistan border, Sikhs fight both Hindus and Muslims in Kashmir, Sunnis fight Shi'ites in Iraq — some of these disputes between religions and some between sects within the same religion. Religion often provides some of the grounds (quite literally) for the confrontations: Jews claim a tract of land based on religious beliefs and scriptures (a "Promised Land"), while Muslims claim at least part of it on the basis of their religion (Jerusalem being a holy city to them as well). Sinhalese insist that the Buddha himself bequeathed them the island of Sri Lanka and that Tamils are recent settlers if not invaders who have their own home (in India). Hindus in India accuse Muslims of being invaders and conquerors and not real Indians. Northern Irish Catholics remember their military defeat at the hand of conquering British and Scottish Protestants. Serbs seek to avenge the loss of their land and freedom to the invading Muslim Turks and their defeat some 600 years ago.

There is no doubt that members of one religious group have been willing to go to great extremes to battle or destroy other groups. Ante Pavelic, a Croat nationalist in Yugoslavia, is reputed to have advocated a "one-third, one-third, one-third" policy in regard to Serbs in his country: one-third would be killed, one-third would be pushed out of Croatia, and one-third would be converted to Catholicism (despite the fact that the Serbs were already Christians, albeit Eastern Orthodox Christians). As we discussed above, religion not only provides the claims for many of these disputes but also the stakes: as in the case of Israel and the Palestinians, some Israelis and non-Israelis alike (such as Pat Robertson) insist that their god wants Israel to have the land and that they will be punished if they do *not* fight to retain it. Muslims on the other hand can interpret the situation as a *jihad* in which Allah will reward them if they win (or even just struggle) and condemn them if they surrender.

Yet, despite the high profile of religion in some of these conflicts, the violence is not normally actually *about* religion.

186

Religion and Violence

That is to say, these are not doctrinal disagreements. Shi'ites in Iraq are not trying to convert Sunnis, nor are Catholics in Northern Ireland trying to prove that their religion is better or more true. The proof of this assertion is simple: Catholics and Protestants (and Sunnis and Shi'ites) co-exist in the United States but are not battling each other, despite the exact same doctrinal differences. Rather, equally or more important than the overtly religious aspects of these clashes are the identity aspects and the political or economic aspects, which are mortally intertwined.

To consider this more deeply, in Northern Ireland or Iraq, the violence has not really been between two religions (especially since, in both cases, the parties are denominations of the same religion) but between two *communities*. Granted, their communal identity is based on religious differences, but the religious differences are not the true issue. The aggravating issue is disparities in wealth, power, opportunity, and such. In Iraq in the immediate post-Saddam period, the Shi'ite majority threatens to monopolize the political power, which the Sunni minority monopolized previously. The threat, in other words, is not so much to their *religion* as to their *interests*, although it is religion that is coming to define their group identity and interests. To say it more clearly, *four different* dimensions are interacting here — religious ideology, yes, but also integration into groups, identity, and interests. The same can be said for Northern Ireland. Catholics and Protestants did not fight about transubstantiation or justification by faith; they fought about political unification with England or with Ireland, or about jobs, or about housing, or about civil rights. Catholics could not help but notice that they were not just a religion but a *class* and a lower class at that; religious identity affected their political and economic interests. In the U.S., where Catholics or Protestants are not distinguished as classes, the strife and violence does not materialize.

All of this is not to minimize the significance of religion is such competitions. Hindu authorities in Kashmir really did attack the Golden Temple of the Sikhs. Palestinians really do bomb Jews in Israel. But, in most cases, when people engage in ethno-religious struggle, they are not fighting so much for their religious beliefs as for their *religious group* and its interests. Having created an identity — and more critically, an identity distinction — on the foundation of religion, it is in most situations the religious community that is endangered, not the religion. If Protestants defeated Catholics in Northern Ireland, Catholicism would not vanish from the earth. However, the lives of fellow Catholics would be worsened — or lost. Religion, identity, and interest in these ethno-religious confrontations are so entangled that they really cannot be separated out again. But it is almost certain that, if the political or economic or social grievances could be removed, the religious differences (while still existing) would not be cause for continued or protracted violence. The fact that religion is added to the mix of identity and interest merely makes the conflicts much more absolute and intractable.

Holy War

Not all religions do or could have a notion of 'holy war.' Such an idea requires two components — a concept of 'holy' and an institution of 'war.' While all societies have their more or less violent tendencies, not all have practiced war in the sense of a prolonged, coordinated effort to conquer and sometimes occupy the land of another society and/or to vanquish or even exterminate the other society. As we explained in Chapter 3, most human societies, even if they engaged in war, would not have engaged in it for religious purposes, since their religions were local and not in competition with each other. It entails an attitude of absolutism — that one's religion is the only true one, or perhaps the only one at all — for religion to be a matter for war.

Holy war, then, is probably the only form of religious violence that is exclusive to the world religions, each of which sees itself as in sole possession of the truth and as in mortal competition with all other religions (local and world) for survival and expansion. Islam is the religion most closely associated in most people's minds with the doctrine of holy war or *jihad*, but of course Christianity had the doctrine long before (*crusade* or 'war of the cross'), and even before it, Judaism had developed the idea. The early Judeo-Christian writings are replete with god-ordered wars and conquests, beginning with the re-

Religion and Violence

occupation of Canaan by Moses' forces. As with later Islamic practice, ancient Hebrew war first required an offer of peace to the enemy, which was of course a demand for surrender and servitude; if the enemy refused the peace offer, though, the godly army could destroy them or use them righteously:

> When thou comest nigh unto a city to fight against it, then proclaim peace unto it.
>
> And it shall be, if it make thee answer of peace, and open unto thee, then it shall be, that all the people that is found therein shall be tributaries unto thee, and they shall serve thee.
>
> And if it will make no peace with thee, but will make war against thee, then thou shalt besiege it:
>
> And when the LORD thy God hath delivered it into thine hands, thou shalt smite every male thereof with the edge of the sword:
>
> But the women, and the little ones, and the cattle, and all that is in the city, even all the spoil thereof, shalt thou take unto thyself; and thou shalt eat the spoil of thine enemies, which the LORD thy God hath given thee.
>
> Thus shalt thou do unto all the cities which are very far off from thee, which are not of the cities of these nations.
>
> But of the cities of these people, which the LORD thy God doth give thee for an inheritance, thou shalt save alive nothing that breatheth:
>
> But thou shalt utterly destroy them; namely, the Hittites, and the Amorites, the Canaanites, and the Perizzites, the Hivites, and the Jebusites; as the LORD thy God hath commanded thee:
>
> That they teach you not to do after all their abominations, which they have done unto their gods; so should ye sin against the LORD your God (Deuteronomy 20: 10-18).

Compared to some later versions of holy war, the ancient Hebrew variety was not meant as a conversion tool, but it was clearly a tool to eliminate 'abomination' and to keep the religion integrated and pure against foreign influence.

Christianity, which launched its career as a religion of peace, succumbed to the lures and necessities of power and developed its own theory of holy war. This religion, like Islam and others such as Zoroastrianism, has a fundamentally dualist and war-like cosmology, with the forces of good and evil locked in a cosmic struggle for domination. Augustine was one of the first to articulate a view of two disparate and ultimately incompatible realities — the domain or city of God (*civitas dei*) versus the domain or city of the world (*civitas terranae*), the latter of which is inferior, full of strife, and essentially antagonistic toward the former. In the end, human violence could be and perhaps *should* be employed in this contest: humans are asked to become "warriors for God," "Christian soldiers," the army of God in a battle in which there is no neutrality.

Over time Christian scholars constructed a concept of *just war*, demonstrating that not all wars were ungodly or wrong. A just war had to meet certain conditions, such as being declared by a legitimate authority (including the Church), conducted with the right intention, prosecuted in proportion to the threat (no excessive force), and carried out in conformity with the rules of war (such as not killing non-combatants or prisoners, *etc.*). In practice, these standards were relative and often disregarded: it was up to the warriors to decide what was a legitimate authority and just cause, and protecting or even advancing the faith could qualify. Frequently, self-defense was asserted, if only defending the 'Holy Land' against infidels. So, the Crusades could fit the requirements, especially if, their promoters claimed, *Deus lo volt* — God wanted it. And it was easy to ignore the rules of war, as evidenced by the Crusader who famously ordered that all residents of a conquered city be executed, after which "God will know his own."

As Christian history proves, holy war can be conducted not only against other religions but also against sects within Christianity itself. The fratricidal wars of religion in the 1500s and 1600s, including the 30 Years War (1618–1648) pitted Christian against Christian, Catholic against Protestant — and not for the last time. It is estimated that as many as eight million Europeans lost their lives over religion during this period. Even earlier, Christian sects like the Cathars were wiped out.

Islam, of course, is most often held up as the model of holy war, if only because its doctrine is more formal and official. As in Christianity, the religion perceives the world as basically dualistic, with a domain of peace where true religion reigns (*dar al-islam*) and a domain of conflict and struggle where religion is absent (*dar al-harb*). The domain of peace is naturally where Islam is observed. The domain of strife is where it is not — but where it should and will be observed.

Religion and Violence

Jihad, the generally known word for holy war, actually does not mean war in Arabic; rather, *qital* is the Arabic word for violence or war. *Jihad* is 'struggle,' which includes the so-called 'greater *jihad*' of struggle against one's own immoral self and the 'lesser *jihad*' — the *jihad* of the sword — of struggle against the enemies of religion. Despite this distinction, however, the lesser *jihad* can and does employ real weapons and leaves real people dead. As the Qur'an unmistakably instructs: "Permission (to fight) is given to those upon whom war is made because they are oppressed, and most surely Allah is well able to assist them" (Sura 22:39), so "slay the idolaters wherever you find them, and take them captive and besiege them and lie in wait for them in every ambush, then if they repent and keep up prayer and pay the poor-rate, leave their way free to them; surely Allah is Forgiving, Merciful" (Sura 9.5). As in ancient Hebraic war, unbelievers are given the option to give up their irreligion and accept the truth, but if they fail to do so, war is authorized:

> Say to those who disbelieve, if they desist, that which is past shall be forgiven to them; and if they return, then what happened to the ancients has already passed.
> And fight with them until there is no more persecution and religion should be only for Allah; but if they desist, then surely Allah sees what they do. And if they turn back, then know that Allah is your Patron... (Sura 8: 38–40).

Notice that Islam also sees this violence as *defense*, namely defense against persecution:

> [P]ersecution is graver than slaughter; and they will not cease fighting with you until they turn you back from your religion, if they can; and whoever of you turns back from his religion, then he dies while an unbeliever — these it is whose works shall go for nothing in this world and the hereafter, and they are the inmates of the fire; therein they shall abide. (Sura 2.217)

Apparently this need not be direct persecution; it is enough that there are nonbelievers in the world to make the believers *feel* persecuted.

Although holy war has been widely exploited in the three Abrahamic religions, it is not limited to them. The Sikhs

191

of Kashmir and Punjab value war in the name of the faith. Sikhism (from the Hindi word for 'disciple') was born in struggle, specifically the struggle between Hindus and Muslims in the sixteenth century. A guru named Nanak proffered a new religious vision — literally a new religious movement — that accepted or rejected aspects of both. However, first the Muslim (Mughal) rulers and later the Hindu Indian ones opposed and suppressed the religion, martyring the guru Arjan in 1606. Thus, in 1699, the last human guru, Gobind Singh, instituted a military wing of religious purists, the Khalsa or 'company of the pure.' As a contemporary Sikh Web-site expresses it:

> The essential condition for entry into the Sikh fold is self-surrender and devotion to the Guru and God. Readiness for the supreme sacrifice or of offering one's head on the palm of one's hand to the Guru is an essential condition laid down by the Gurus for becoming a Khalsa Sikh. Seeking death, not for personal glory, winning reward or going to heaven, but for the purpose of protecting the weak and the oppressed is what made the Khalsa brave and invincible. This has become a traditional reputation of the Khalsa. Right from the times of the Gurus till the last India-Pakistan conflict (1971), the Sikhs have demonstrated that death in the service of truth, justice and country, is part of their character and their glorious tradition. They do not seek martyrdom, they attain it. Dying is the privilege of heroes. It should, however, be for an approved or noble cause.

It turns out they were lucky to have it, given that they experienced two 'holocausts' — in 1746 and 1762. The Khalsa are still a force today in the Sikh struggle for a homeland in Kashmir-Punjab, which they call Kalistan.

Lest one think that true religion cannot be warlike, it is well to remember that religions like Sikhism have established their own warrior organizations, like the various orders of knights in Christendom. Many of these orders were formed for or during the Crusades by order of the Church, such as the Order of St. John of Jerusalem, the Knights of Malta, the Teutonic Knights, and the famous Knights Templar. Article Three in the Constitution of the Teutonic Knights is blunt in saying:

> This order, signifying both the heavenly and the earthly knighthood, is the foremost for it has promised to avenge the

Religion and Violence

dishonoring of God and His Cross and to fight so that the Holy Land, which the infidels subjected to their rule, shall belong to the Christians. St. John also saw a new knighthood coming down out of heaven. This vision signifies to us that the Church now shall have knights sworn to drive out the enemies of the Church by force.

The same philosophy has appeared in other places and times, such as medieval Japan, where groups of fighting Buddhist monks (*sohei* or 'priest warriors') were created. Wars between monks and monasteries broke out in the tenth century, at which time the temple of Enryakuji established the first standing army of monks in the country. Perhaps the greatest of these Buddhist armies was the Ikko-Ikki (*Ikko* meaning 'single-minded' or 'devoted' and *Ikki* meaning 'league' or 'mob'), which conquered an area around Kyoto in the 1500s. As Dugdale Pointon (2005) describes it, "With their belief in a paradise waiting for them the warrior monks of the Ikko-Ikki were fearless and eager warriors proving very useful to whichever side they were aiding at the time. In battle they would often use mass chanting (*nembutsu*) to strike fear into their enemies and improve their own morale." They would not be the first or the last to excel on the battlefield with religion in their hearts.

Crime and Abuse

Finally, whether or not there is evidence that religion makes people more prone to violent crime and abuse, there is no evidence that it makes them less. This is a serious affront to the notion that religion is all about morality and that religious people are more moral than non-religious ones. The fact that the United States is the most religious industrialized nation and also the most violent one should give Christians pause. Whether or not religion increases crime, it is certainly the case that interpersonal violence and crime are more than occasionally committed in the name of their religious beliefs or by individuals who, because of their religious position or office, ought to know and be better.

Among the most lurid crimes are the murders of children by their mothers. Andrea Yates, the Texas woman who killed

193

her five children (named, significantly, Noah, John, Paul, Luke, and Mary) in 2001 was a troubled and religious person. There is no doubt, even if she was depressive and psychotic, that her immediate motivation for the killings was religious. She told doctors afterwards that "My children weren't righteous. They stumbled because I was evil. The way I was raising them they could never be saved... Better for someone else to tie a millstone around their neck and cast them into a river than to stumble. They were going to perish [in Hell]" (quoted in Baker 2002). This point of view (not inconsistent with Christian teaching) was apparently implanted in her by a fanatical preacher named Michael Woroniecki, whom she first met in 1992. According to an anonymous former follower (http://hometown.aol.com/niek0/scripts.html), Woroniecki taught that all humans are wicked from birth and that if they were not fixed and saved by the "age of accountability" (which is 12), they were bound for hell. Yates was accordingly worried that her children (the oldest of whom was 7) were reaching that age of irredeemability anyhow, so death now was preferable to eternal damnation later.

Unfortunately, this is not an isolated case. Two other women, Deanna Laney and Dena Schlosser (of Tyler and Dallas, Texas respectively — perhaps the problem is not religion but Texas!), also recently killed their children with a Christian flair. Laney, a Pentecostal, beat two of her children to death with stones ('stoned them') because God told her to. Schlosser, a member of the Way of Life Church, killed her 10-month-old because she wanted to give the child to God. And studies indicate that they are not alone: an item by Lisa Falkenberg cites two studies that link religiosity with child-directed violence. One found that of 39 women who killed their children, fifteen had religion-related motivations; the other concluded that one-fourth of its 56 child-killing mothers had religious delusions (Falkenberg 2004) — although at the time at least they did not consider them delusions at all.

In fact, in some instances the violent deaths of children or adults have been part of a more systematic belief. The infamous case of the Lafferty brothers was treated in Jon Krakauer's bestselling book *Under the Banner of Heaven*. On July 24, 1984, Ron and Dan Lafferty murdered the wife and daughter (Brenda and Erica) of their brother Allen because, once again, their god had told them to do it. Members of a fundamentalist sect of Mormonism, the Lafferty's are unrepentant to this day, reasoning that if their god orders an action, there is no way to disobey — which is precisely the problem. Similarly, when Jacques Robidoux starved his infant son to death in 1999, it was on his god's orders. Robidoux was a member of a group (an offshoot of the World Wide Church of God) known only as The Body, started by Roland Robidoux in 1978. Members believed that they received "leadings" or direct messages from God, one of which told Jacques to deprive his baby of solid food. Over 52 days, baby Samuel wasted and died.

Christianity is certainly not the only religion that has driven people to murder. Hinduism has a painful record of religion-inspired violence as well. A cult group known as Thuggee practiced ritual murders well into the nineteenth century. Members would infiltrate bands of travelers and assault them with ceremonial weapons like the magical pick-axe (*kussee*), a special scarf or cloth (*rumal*) for strangling victims, and a sacred dagger. Victims were dismembered and buried in collective graves, on top of which the successful killers would hold rituals. All of this was done at the behest of the goddess Kali, who demanded the dead as sacrifices to her. Religious models and values play at least partly into the too-common modern practice of bride-burning or 'dowry death,' in which husbands or their mothers injure or kill wives in staged 'kitchen accidents.' An abusive but not generally fatal biannual ceremony known as *Kuzhimattru Thiru Vizha* involves burying a child alive 'briefly' as a thanksgiving gesture; children are supposedly drugged into unconsciousness and then laid in a shallow grave and covered with dirt for up to a minute while priests pray over them.

In Muslim societies, as we have mentioned, girls are most often the objects of harm and abuse, as in honor killings for behaving inappropriately, including having sex before marriage, dating outside of the religion or ethnic group, or just 'acting too Western.' In more than a few cases, especially when living in Western countries, families have sent younger brothers to do the deed, since they know that Western law deals more leniently with minors. Females in these and many other societies are often married young and physically abused in their marriages, on the grounds that men have spiritual authority over women. And in a number of societies — at least eighteen, as surveyed by Dickeman (1975) — families kill one or both of twins, on the belief that twins are evil or unnatural or a bad omen of some sort.

Subcultures with a religious outlook and a self-defensive stance are apt to become dangerous to themselves or others. Members of TELAH, David Koresh's Branch Davidians, and Jim Jones' community in Guyana all turned suicidal, while Aum Shinrikyo turned homicidal. In 1984, the Rajneesh group settled in Oregon attempted to suppress resistance to their presence in The Dalles and take over the local government by poisoning the salad bars of local restaurants with *Salmonella*, sickening hundreds of people. And the contemporary militia movement in the United Staes has a dangerous strain of militant Christianity mixed into it. Many of its leaders are Protestant pastors, like James Bruggemann of Stone Kingdom Ministries in Asheville, North Carolina, who said, "No, folks, it is not a perverse joy I take in the impending doom of the enemy. It is a righteous joy!" (quoted in Dees 1996:21). With a volatile alloy of Christianity, rigid constitutionalism, racism, and conspiracy theory, they not only see themselves at war with evil forces but welcome the war. In fact, after the police raid on Randy Weaver's Ruby Ridge home in 1992, Pastor Pete Peters of the LaPorte Church of Christ called together leaders of many organizations at Estes Park, Colorado for what was dubbed the Rocky Mountain Rendezvous. The attendees drafted a letter to the Weavers, which read in part:

> Impelled by the spirit of our Heavenly Father, We, 160 Christian men assembled for three days of prayer and counsel, at Estes Park, Colorado.
>
> At our gathering the sad events of Ruby Creek [*sic*] were recounted....
>
> We have not the power to restore to you the loved ones who were cruelly stolen from you!
>
> But as Christian men, led by the word of our Heavenly Father, we are determined to never rest while you are in peril and distress!

We are determined to employ HIS strength and to work continually to insure that Vicki and Samuel's mortal sacrifices were not in vain!

We call for Divine Judgment upon the wicked and the guilty who shed the blood of Vicki and Samuel! (quoted in Dees: 65–6)

The movement has backed up its rhetoric with action. As far back as 1984, Richard Wayne Snell, of the Covenant, Sword, and Arm of the Lord organization, killed a black Arizona state trooper, and in 1985 David Tate killed a Missouri police officer on the way to the Covenant, Sword, and Arm of the Lord compound. Then too, the Oklahoma City bombing on April 19, 1995 had ties back to these groups and beliefs. Finally, many abortion clinics have been attacked and many abortion workers injured or killed in the name of religion; see the *Nuremburg Files* online for the evidence.

Not all religion-inspired deaths are intentional murders; some, like the Robidoux case, are more like religion-inspired neglect leading to death. But neglect is abuse too, and most modern people would consider depriving a sick person of medical care to be a form of neglect, but it is a fact that a variety of religious groups feel the right to decline medical care for themselves or their children in favor of spiritual cures. Not only do many religious groups such as the Christian Scientists reject scientific medicine, but American law often grants a religious exemption from safe and effective medical treatments. The result, as Seth Asser and others have noted, is a high rate of preventable death. In the study that he and Rita Swan conducted of religiously-motivated rejection of treatment, 172 child deaths occurred (from causes like diabetes, dehydration, trauma, infections, heart conditions, and tumors), of which 140 would have had a 90% survival rate with modern medical care (Asser and Swan 1998). The belief that parents were doing something effective, something ordained by their faith, led directly to the preventable deaths of their children. It is yet another case of people, thanks to religion, thinking they are doing good when they are really doing harm.

Chapter 6

The Atheism at the Heart of Science

In her book *A Jealous God* (2005) — which I do not recommend in any way — Pamela Winnick cries that science is on a "crusade" (a singularly religious notion) against religion. Actually, her book is relatively tame compared to the notes on the cover and jacket. Inside, the book is little more than a journalist's observations on a very few specific scientific areas such as abortion, stem cell research, and evolutionary theory, which merely suggests that "advances in reproductive technology and changing attitudes towards abortion spawned a radical, but shaky, redefinition of 'human life'" (*ii*). And she is at least half right: new facts, technologies, and attitudes *do* lead to "radical redefinitions," although there is no reason to believe that today's definitions are any more or less "shaky" than yesterday's. After almost three hundred pages of mild diatribe, she concludes: "The Galileo model of the scientist martyred by religion is now purely a myth," although she should have said "a thing of the past," since Christianity truly did martyr some scientists in the past, and might do so again if it had the power. "Science long ago won its war against religion, not just traditional religion, but any faith in a power outside the human mind. Now it wants more" (298).

Notwithstanding that science *depends on* the existence of 'powers' outside the human mind — like gravity and electromagnetism (it is only critical of 'powers' that merely exist *in* the human mind) — and that I have no idea what more she thinks science wants, the contents of the book are nothing compared to the comments on the outside, intended to attract the more feral critics of science. The jacket notes pronounce that "science has today become the world's most prominent, most dangerous religion — crusading against traditional morality and pushing its atheistic agendas beyond the laboratory, into the classroom, the judicial system, and the media." Why she objects to science extending into the classroom I cannot imagine, since that is where we learn it — unless she does not want people to learn it. On the back, the book is described as "an astounding exposé on science's crusade against religion and human values" (two different and perhaps diametrically opposed things!) in which "science has eroded human dignity and shielded itself from scrutiny by attacking religion — becoming itself an oppressive, narrow-minded system of faith that blindly pursues its own objectives, shirking off traditional values and moral responsibilities." It is amusing and ironic that the writer calls science a dangerous religion and an oppressive and narrow-minded faith system, as if to remind us that *religions* are dangerous and faith systems oppressive and narrow-minded.

I mention this otherwise histrionic and useless piece of work not because it represents the understanding of and attitude toward science of any significant portion of the population. Not all people, even all religionists, are hostile to science, and no person, not even the most religious, is hostile to all science (they still use automobiles and cell phones). Nevertheless, there is a definite contingent that has definite objections to it. And while Winnick and her ilk greatly exaggerate the hostility of science to religion, they are perhaps correct about the *threat* of science to religion.

If there is a war between science and religion, it would be well for partisans like Winnick to remember who started it. It was religion that in 1248 forbade the practice of surgery on the grounds that the Church "abhors the shedding of blood" (although apparently not the loss of life). It was religion that condemned vaccination in the eighteenth century, as in Reverend Edmund Massey's sermon in London entitled "The Dangerous and Sinful Practice of Inoculation," reasoning that disease was his god's righteous punishment. It was religion that led doctors in Boston to form the Anti-Vaccination Society to prevent inoculation as "bidding defiance to Heaven." It was religion that rejected the use of anesthesia for women during childbirth because it saved them from the "primeval curse on woman" imposed by the Christian god in Eden. It was religion that maintained an *Index of Banned Books*, including many scientific ones.

It was religion that arrested Galileo in 1633 for promoting teachings contrary to authority in works like *Dialogue on the*

Two Chief World Systems in which he defended the theory that the earth revolves around the sun. And it was religion that executed Giordano Bruno by burning at the stake on February 17, 1600 for publishing his ideas about the movement of planets, the relativity of space, and the possibility of multiple worlds (although according to the *Catholic Encyclopedia* he was not killed for his science but for "his theological errors, among which were the following: that Christ was not God but merely an unusually skilful magician, that the Holy Ghost is the soul of the world, that the Devil will be saved, *etc.*" Apparently execution is more justified for religious errors than for scientific truths. Church leaders refused even to look through Galileo's new telescope, arguing that it showed only illusion.

Martin Luther, that hero of anti-Church protest, was equally vitriolic about not just science but rationality. He called reason "the devil's bride," a "beautiful whore," "God's worst enemy," and claimed that "faith must trample under foot all reason, sense, and understanding." "There is," he opined, "on earth among all dangers no more dangerous thing than a richly endowed and adroit reason," which "must be deluded, blinded, and destroyed" (quoted in Kaufmann 1961:75). Religion has been trying to achieve this delusion, blindness, and destruction ever since.

The debate over the relation between science and religion is an old and checkered one, as I have already explored elsewhere (Eller 2004, Chapter 7), with not only scientists but religionists often arrayed against the "science is anti-religion" charge. In some cases, like the earnest but pathetic Francis Collins, both science and religion are represented, and pacified, in one person. Collins is a scientist of some renown, having led the public Human Genome Project. Yet he is also a religionist, a theist, and specifically a Christian. In his plea for tolerance and unity, *The Language of God*, he asserts that "the principles of faith are, in fact, complementary with the principles of science" (2006:3) — although he does not explain what the "principles" of faith are, nor can he, since faith has no principles, only doctrines. After a long, tortured, and futile quest in which he tries to marry Christianity *à la* C. S. Lewis to modern evolutionary genetics (which he admits satisfies neither science nor Christianity), he proposes that religion "provides another way of finding truth" in addition to science

(229), that "science can be a form of worship" (230), and that science "is not threatened by God; it is enhanced" (233). That religion has never in the history of humanity found one "truth"; that a scientist worshipping nature (or worshipping his slides and test tubes) would not be doing science; and that 'God' is not necessary, conducive, or beneficial to science seems to escape his awareness altogether.

In this chapter, I do not want to repeat my previous discussion or the whole tired, sordid debate. Rather, I want to apply the insights we have developed regarding the nature of religion to demonstrate, first, that the whole debate — both on the side of the religionists and the scientists — tends to be wrongly formulated and, second, that whatever science is, it is at heart atheistic. I am not suggesting that all scientists are or must be atheists (although it is well known that atheism is much more common among scientists than the general public). I am not even arguing that science is incompatible with religion, since the issue of compatibility is not so much right or wrong as meaningless. What I am arguing is that science is essentially and necessarily *a-theistic*: it knows no god(s), admits no god(s), and needs no god(s). As Laplace famously asserted, there is no place for that "hypothesis" in science. So, while not all scientists are atheists, all science is atheistic and cannot be otherwise.

Too Little Science, Too Little Religion

It is a frequently overlooked fact that the public clash between science and religion not only misrepresents science but equally misrepresents religion. It is easy to demonstrate the former. If one looks more closely at Winnick's complaints, it is plain to see that she is not rejecting all science but a few very specific scientific points or applications. Not surprisingly, her sole enemies are abortion, stem cell research, and evolutionary theory. It goes without saying that there is much more to science than these. And if one looks at Collins' treatise, it is plain to see that he is not talking about 'religion' at all but about his own particular and idiosyncratic version of religion, and that he does not understand science *or* religion.

There are few if any religion-defenders who dismiss science as a whole. Most religionists never even trouble with most science. I have never seen a serious religious attack on atomic theory or quantum theory or gravitational theory or on whole sciences like meteorology or botany or gemology (the study of gems). Religion is generally unconcerned with these sciences, *because these sciences are unconcerned with the questions that concern religion.* Nor do most religionists discard the 'scientific method': many think that experimentation is valuable (at least, say, when it comes to pharmaceuticals and car safety), and all, I think, accept the notion of cause and effect. Some actually build their case for their religion on the foundation of science, whether it is the 'Reasons to Believe' agenda or the more narrow and specious 'Intelligent Design' movement. Some of these are merely wrapping the mantle of science around religion, but others really do try to muster evidence for the age of the earth or other factual questions.

So, one of the main failures in the battle between science and religion is the tight focus on a very few bits of science and the generalization that they (mostly evolutionary theory and the sexual or reproductive sciences) *are* science. We scientific people, as we stressed in Chapter 2, tend to let ourselves get forced into defending ourselves on *their* terms, squabbling over and over about small territories of scientific activity — or, in the case of abortion or stem-cell research, policy questions made possible by scientific advances. We should, among other things, refuse to continue to contest these tiny scientific islands and shift the discussion to science more broadly. Love the science, love the results. Science: love it or leave it.

Thus, one arm of the unending and unprofitable brawl between science and religion is confusion of one or a few sciences or scientific interests or positions with science as such. There is, in other words, too little science in the science-*versus*-religion confrontation. Oddly, there is also too little religion. This may sound strange, coming from an avowed non-religionist, but the earlier chapters of this book should make my intention clear. When people — sadly, both pro-religion and anti-religion types — argue about science and religion, they are almost without exception talking not about religion, over even about theism, but about Christianity exclusively. One example will be illustrative. In the recent collection *Science and Religion: Are They Compatible?* (Kurtz 2003), among the thirty-nine articles there is exactly *one* that mentions any religion other than Christianity (Taner Edis' unique essay on Islam and science).

ATHEISM ADVANCED

As much fun as it is to hold this debate over and over again, it is utterly futile. Christianity is one religion in the pantheon of religions, not even the majority among theisms let alone among all religions. And as we showed conclusively, theism is only one but not the most common version of religion.

For starters, then, we should be more honest and admit that most of what religionists and scientists alike are fighting about is *science and Christianity*, not science and religion. Christianity is not 'religion,' any more than evolutionary theory is 'science.' Each is one type or variety of its larger whole (although evolutionary theory is more central to science than Christianity is to religion — religion has no center). In fact, it is probably worse than that: the religion in the science-*versus*-religion dispute is usually, in our corner of the world, Protestantism, or some species of Protestantism like Baptism or Pentecostalism — generally some literalist, evangelical form. As the reader may know, the Catholic Church has already accepted the principle of evolution, at least as far as the human body is concerned. So, having stepped out of the fray, the anti-evolutionist religionists are not *religion* or even *Christianity* but a *subset* of Christianity.

All of this means that the disagreements between science and religion, and the entire idea of compatibility, are hopelessly constricted. Let us consider, for instance, the argument about creation. Christianity cannot even completely agree with itself about this. Although all Christians do (or should) hold the position that there was a supernatural creator involved, the details of the position vary dramatically. Eugenie Scott, executive director of the National Council for Science Education, has done us a service by reminding us that "There is not one creationism, but many varieties, ranging from strict Biblical literalist young-earth creationism, through a variety of old-earth creationisms ('gap creation'; 'day-age creationism'), to progressive creationism, to continuous creationism, to theistic evolutionism" (1996:506). Some of these views are more compatible with science (*i.e.* evolutionary theory) than others — and more compatible with each other than others. So, it is not a meaningful question to ask whether religion is compatible with science; it depends on *which* religion, *which* science, and what one means by *compatible*.

Atheism Heart of Science

If the problem is inescapable within Christianity, it is even more so outside of it. Not all religions, for example, contain an account of creation (a cosmogony) at all. This will be a strange and disorienting notion to Christians, but so it is. In some religions, the earth or the universe is just there; the religious account begins *after* whatever kind of creation-event may have occurred. Such a religion will not pose the same difficulty for science, or *vice-versa*: it simply makes no claims about creation. Not all religions that contain a creation account place it in time the same way that Christianity does. The Hindu cosmogony, for one, would be more compatible with scientific knowledge of the age of the universe, since Hinduism posits a reality that is millions or billions of years old. (Note also that now Christianity's disagreement with *science* is augmented by a disagreement with *religion*, that is, another, non-Christian religion!)

The big question that separates the friends and foes of religion in the United States and Western civilization in general is the existence of a god. Friends of religion, like Huston Smith, stipulate that "Science can prove nothing about God, because God lies outside its province" (2001:137). Even champions of science like Scott take the easy way out, as when she writes that "Whether God created is therefore in fact not the main issue in the creation/evolution controversy, since 'God created' does not rule out the possibility that God created through the process of evolution" (506). Or, in a recorded speech she gave in 2000, she offered that evolution is about "what happened," not "whodunit" — which suggests that she thinks 'whodunit' is a legitimate question and that 'God' is a legitimate answer. However, both scientists like Scott and religionists like Smith (both of whom should really know better) assume two grossly illogical things: that a 'who' question is even necessary or possible in science, and that 'God' is the only possible or serious solution.

As we now know, not only are most theisms not Christianity, most religions are not theisms. If it is possible to insert a 'who' question into the scientific explanation of nature (and I will prove shortly that it is not), there are many possible culprits to this whodunit mystery. Even if nature required, say, a creator-god, there are many available candidates — Jehovah-god,

Allah, Zeus, Vishnu, Odin, and scores of others. On the other hand, recall that, cross-culturally, most gods have not been creator-gods at all but rather division-of-labor gods, with their particular tasks to perform; if Odin was a world-creator, Thor was not. And, most significantly, *the vast majority of religions have gotten along without any gods at all.*

Therefore, one approach to the dismissal of the question of god(s) as a serious scientific problem is that *the absence of god(s) is not a serious religious problem.* Most religions do not have god(s) and apparently do not need god(s). "The existence of god(s)" is not synonymous with religion, and it is absolutely, categorically impossible to insist on claiming that it is. The futility of a position like Huston Smith's becomes crystal clear. To begin, let us always keep in mind that there is no such thing as a generic god or god-in-general. So, when he says that science can prove nothing (and I assume, even more importantly, *dis*prove nothing) about his god, he is talking about one particular god (Christianity's god) or conception of god (monotheism). If we substitute any other god(s) in the statement, the absurdity emerges forcefully: "Science can prove nothing about Allah"; "Science can prove nothing about Vishnu"; "Science can prove nothing about Thor"; and so on *ad infinitum.*

But that is not the end of the troubles for religion. Science can also prove nothing about spirits in animals and plants and rocks and the sun and the moon and the wind and the rain. Science can also prove nothing about impersonal religious forces like *chi* or mana or *n/um.* Science can also prove nothing about dead ancestral spirits, not to mention the host of other beings like witches and ogres and leprechauns and fairies and elves. *And any of these, singly or in combination, make a perfectly acceptable answer to the putative whodunit question,* whether the event under consideration is the creation of the universe, a hurricane, the collapse of a building, the birth of a baby, or the sickness or death of a living human. Religion, in the conventional view, would demand that science defeat each of these supernatural claims; however, each religion would also find itself having to defeat the claims of the others. If, as one example, the dead ancestors made someone sick or well, then there is no need to refer to a god-answer to solve the problem of sickness.

It should be noted how very, very seldom religion in the modern American science-*versus*-religion debate raises the issue of animistic or animatistic or ancestral spirits or forces. No. Rather, religion — which, as we know, means Christianity and a very particular version of it — asks us to prove, disprove, or better yet accept *its* specific religious claims, with sheer indifference to and ignorance of other religious claims. To paraphrase Weinberg's famous quotation, not only is science indifferent to religion, but religions are indifferent to each other. Now the patent absurdity of the Hustonian position is clear. Huston Smith insists:

> If science cannot tell us what (if anything) is outside our universe, what can? Nothing *definitively*, but it would be foolish not to draw on every resource available. Inclusively, things are neither as science says they are nor as religion says they are. They are as science, and religion, and philosophy, and art, and common sense, and our deepest intuitions, and our practical imaginations say they are (43).

This statement is so muddled that I am ashamed that an intelligent scholar could utter it. Can science tell us what is outside the universe? How do we know there is anything outside — that there even *is* an 'outside' at all? What does 'outside the universe' mean? When he says, "nothing definitively" can tell us, he is dead on. But when he says it would be foolish not to draw on every available resource, he is talking double nonsense. It is not only foolish *to draw* on every possible resource but also *impossible* to do so. Shall we draw on every religion — overpopulating the spiritual world with a cacophony of gods, nature spirits, supernatural forces, and dead ancestors? Shall we also draw on non-scientific and non-religious 'resources' alike, including dreams and delusions, common sense and old wives' tales? How ridiculous.

Why Science is Spirit-less
— or Not Science at All

Readers will note that if they survey the contemporary works of science — from physics to mathematics to meteorology to psychology — they do not encounter any references to god(s).

ATHEISM ADVANCED

Of course, we can do a science of psychology of religion in which we discuss and explain religious psychological states like visions and trances, but general psychology does not appeal to god(s) *as an explanatory device,* in the sense of explaining experiences or dreams or neuroses in terms of god(s). Nor does meteorology mention god(s) in accounting for weather patterns, yet I have never heard any serious religionists condemn meteorology for its atheism, despite the fact that, formally speaking, meteorology is 'without god(s).' Mathematics is a science and a language of science free of god-talk, although some mathematicians (but usually amateurs) claim to see the "mind of god" in the elegance of numbers and numerical laws. In fact, of all the sciences, it is physics and biology where the inherent atheism of science bothers religionists most; these disciplines strive to describe and explain big questions — or at least the questions that Christianity pontificates on — without any reference to god(s).

It is true enough that science is a-theistic in the sense of making no mention of god(s) in its work; science is methodologically or operationally a-theistic. But then, that is not saying everything that needs to be said here. Most *religions* are also a-theistic, in that they do not include god(s) either. It would be false to say that most religions are therefore hostile to god(s). They are simply without the idea altogether. They get along fine with no god(s). But that does not mean that science is like some religions and unlike others. What we should say is that science, like most religions, is a-theistic, but, unlike all religions, it is a-religious. It is not anti-religious necessarily, but a-religious — without any of the claims that make religion distinctly religious.

Science does not include god(s) as explanatory devices in any of its fields or theories. But it also does not include nature spirits, or impersonal supernatural forces, or ancestor spirits. It excludes all of the cross-cultural forms of religious explanation, such as sin or heaven or salvation or *jukurrpa* or *nirvana* or *samsara.* And it also excludes non-religious potential explanations such as ESP, ether and phlogiston, UFOs, and invisible talking dogs. Let it never be said that science is uniquely resistant to religious explanations.

The perennial failure to understand why science eschews religious explanations for natural phenomena is rooted in the failure to understand the difference between science and religion. Some well-meaning and intelligent commentators, like Stephen Jay Gould, have suggested that the two differ in their "domain" or their area of concern. Gould referred to science and religion as "non-overlapping magisteria," kingdoms in possession of separate territories. But this is false: while there may be religious territory where science does not tread (because it is imaginary), there is no scientific territory that some religion has not left a footprint on. Both science and religion make factual assertions, about things like the age of the earth, the kinds of beings on it, and how those beings came to be. This simple and certain fact sheds light on the war between religion and science: when they agree on a factual issue, there is no animosity at all. It is only when they disagree that the trouble starts, and the more central the issue to religion, the more vociferous the struggle over the disagreement. Religion ceded meteorology to science without much complaint — although there were many bitter denunciations of Benjamin Franklin's "wicked iron points" — but the two sciences that touch most directly on questions of origins and life (physics and biology) draw most of its ire.

Another attempt to delineate the difference between science and religion boils down to their respective methods and philosophies. Science uses experimentation and the 'scientific method,' while religion purports to employ its own methods, although I argue elsewhere (Eller 2004) that religion has no methods at all. Eugenie Scott, for instance, is quick to point out that science starts from a position of "methodological naturalism," which she defines as "an attempt to explain the natural world in terms of *natural* processes, not supernatural ones" (2003:11). While that is undoubtedly true, it begs the question of why we would seek natural processes instead of supernatural ones, or why we would attempt to explain the natural world instead of the supernatural world. After all, most humans have explained at least some natural things in supernatural terms, and they have explained all supernatural things in those terms too. We could imagine a possible division of effort in which some researchers would explain (a) the natural in terms of the natural, (b) the natural in terms of the supernatural, (c) the supernatural in terms of the natural, and (d) the supernatural in terms of the supernatural. We would then have four different activities, only one of which — the first — would be science.

Why methodological naturalism as the foundation of science? Scott (at least sometimes) distinguishes the method of science from the philosophy of science, holding that "philosophical naturalism" is a second and separate matter from methodological naturalism. In her 2000 speech, she characterized philosophical naturalism, or philosophical materialism, as the position that nature or matter is "all there is," which is not, she maintains, a necessary corollary of science. "Science," she says, "is an equal opportunity methodology — you do not have to have any particular religious or non-religious belief as long as you are using the method of methodological materialism." But surely that is not quite right. You can have any belief you like, but you cannot *introduce any type of explanation* you like into your science and still have it be science. In other words, you might believe that a god makes hurricanes, but if you explain some actual hurricane with an appeal to god(s), you are no longer doing science.

Whatever reason people had for adopting methodological naturalism or materialism in the first place (and we will arrive at that reason below), it either requires or leads to philosophical naturalism/materialism. As Scott puts it elsewhere, "Science's concern... rules out supernatural causation" (2003:12). Let us restate the principle of methodological naturalism as this: *In doing science, we will seek only natural explanations as far as we can, until no natural explanations are possible, and only then will we consider non-natural ones.* The truth is, so far everything we have attempted to explain (at least everything that is a scientific matter) has availed itself of natural explanation; there is no remainder, no 'gap' for any other kind of explanation. As was the case with Laplace, so far we have had no need of the supernatural hypothesis, and there is no sign that we will soon. So, if everything that we study is natural and material, and if every natural or material thing we study seems to have a natural or material explanation, then philosophical naturalism or materialism is not a *philosophy* at all but rather an observational conclusion.

This takes us to our real point. *Why* does science methodologically and philosophically exclude religious explanations — and why are its method and philosophy inseparable? Why, we can ask, is science a-theistic to its core? Various thinkers, including myself, have offered various answers, basically listing the characteristics of science and of religion and noting the contrast. Despite the utility of these lists, they do not get to the heart of the matter, for it is not in their respective territories (especially facts versus morality) or in their contents or in their methods or even in their philosophies that they diverge most fundamentally. The key dimension along which science and religion separate, and along which they can never converge, is *agency.*

Let us step back and address the question of what precisely a religious or supernatural explanation is. Our previous discussion of the modular, by-product quality of religion offers the answer. A religious or supernatural explanation for some phenomenon is one that rests on the kinds of beings and/or forces that exist in the realm of religion, which are at least partly human-like agents. They are often but by no means always invisible, but then so are many natural phenomena (either absolutely invisible, like the wind, or invisible to the naked eye, like molecules). In many religions — and in probably all religions on some occasions — the invisible can become visible (or audible or sense-able in some way) — which is one of its uncanny qualities. However, when religious entities really are 'invisible' (to all of the senses), or to the extent that they really are outside the scope of nature (supernatural or trans-natural), *they are also undetectable.* But what can we possibly do with the undetectable? How can we study it? How can we know about it — or even know if it exists? We cannot. It is a null category as far as human knowledge is concerned. Science, therefore, limits itself to the detectable because that is the only thing we as humans have access to and can know.

But, a religionist can respond, gods or spirits or forces *are* detectable, in the design of nature, or the curing of illness, or the manifestation in oracles and divination, *etc.* The problem with such detections is that there are other possible interpretations of them. Sometimes illnesses respond to medical treatment, and sometimes the body fights them off. In other words, there are natural explanations too. The 'design' of nature can come about through natural processes, like natural selection —

and few religionists detect in the organization of a hurricane a divine hand at work (and certainly not a benevolent divine hand). The results of oracles and divination — say, tea leaves or tarot cards in a certain arrangement — can be explained statistically. That is to say, there are no clear and indisputable cases where non-natural causes are at work or are necessary to explain things.

Furthermore, if a religious explanation is due, then *any* religious explanation will potentially suffice. The mayor of New Orleans, Ray Nagin, recently said that the hurricane and flood that devastated his city was a result of (presumably) the Christian god's anger with America. That is one possibility. It might also be that god's anger with New Orleans or with Mr. Nagin personally. Or it might be Allah's anger at America, or Vishnu's, or Poseidon's or Neptune's or some other sea god's. Or it might not be their anger but their cruelty or whimsy. Or it might be the action of some other being like the animistic spirit of water, or of the Mississippi River, or of some local animal or plant. It might be a disruption in *chi*. It might be the ancestors of the local Native Americans or displaced French settlers seeking their revenge. There is simply no way to know, and no way to adjudicate between the possibilities.

Even worse, such a religious explanation is not really an explanation at all. If one decides, "God did it" or "Poseidon did it" or "the river spirit did it" or "*chi* did it" or "the Indian ancestors did it," how does that really *explain* anything? The arch-theist Alvin Plantinga (1997) was honest enough to admit that resorting to supernatural causes is a "science stopper" — which means for us a *knowledge-stopper*. To a person of scientific mind, that is reason enough to avoid such (non) explanations. However, for reasons that should be obvious to us now, this is not an objection for persons of religious mind, since they *expect* their phenomena to be inscrutable to begin with, and since *explanation is not the prime function of religion anyhow*, this is no objection for them. We rationalists greatly exaggerate the explanatory function of religion: religion does not so much explain anything as prevent members from seeking explanations. As Ian Barbour, a Templeton Prize winner for his work on science and religion, has found, and we agree, a religious notion like a god is not meant to be a hypothesis formulated to explain phenomena in the world in competition with scientific hypotheses. Belief in God in primarily a commitment to a way of life in response to distinctive kinds of religious experience in communities formed by historic traditions; it is not a substitute for scientific research. Religious beliefs offer a wider framework of meaning in which particular events can be contextualized (1997: 81–2).

Of course, when he says that religion and science are not *meant* to compete, he is being naïve or obtuse: since religion and science pronounce on the same issues, they cannot help but compete. But he is correct in two ways. First, religion is ultimately more about commitment than understanding, which is why religious people are happy to throw up their hands and conclude, "God works in mysterious ways," which is not an understanding at all. Second, religion is not so much a competing explanation of events as *a secondary layer of explanation of events.*

And that is the real issue at stake between science and religion. A good religionist, whether Christian, Muslim, or Azande, can say, "Sure, the warm ocean water stirred up a tropical storm, and prevailing winds drove it toward the southeast United States coast, which collapsed levees and flooded homes, killing people." What religion adds — *and science never can or will* — is *an agency-based component*, along the lines of "because God wanted it." The critical, and sometimes the only, distinction between religious and scientific explanations is that *religious explanations add a dimension of personality, of will, of agency* that scientific ones do not.

Our investigation of religion in Chapter 3 revealed that the central component of religion is *non-human agency*—that there are beings and/or forces in the world that are not (ordinary) persons but that have some of the qualities of persons, including physical qualities but most urgently psychological or personality qualities. That is, in the religious perspective, at least some and potentially all natural phenomena are *social* phenomena, in two senses — that spiritual persons are behind them and that the phenomena themselves are somehow relational, that they are about or directed toward us humans and our relationship with those spirits. Science fundamentally and essentially disagrees. Science does not include the component of agency in

213

its explanations. It does not posit minds behind events, and it does not consider those events to be social or about us in any meaningful way.

But why — why this dismissal of agency and meaning in natural events? The answer is simple but profound: science rejects or dismisses the element of agency in nature *because agency makes science impossible and paralyzes all human knowledge*. It has this unavoidable effect for two critical reasons. First, the entire project of science depends on the regularity and predictability of nature, and agency makes events irregular and unpredictable. By definition, agency or will is not completely determined by pre-existing conditions; it establishes a certain zone of freedom for the agents. They have their own desires or interests or wills (more or less) independent of conditions. Therefore, we never know quite what they will do. The exact same situation can lead to completely opposite results if the agents so choose; there is no connection between causes and effects. This frustrates and precludes the possibility of ever knowing with any degree of confidence what will happen next.

This problem might be overcome if we could know with some precision the mind of the agents. However, as the struggles of the human social sciences have shown, it is extremely difficult to do a science of intelligent agents, since they can act erratically and inconsistently. We can never know quite what is on their minds or how their minds will function in any particular circumstances. And what does it mean to 'know a mind'? It does not mean to know the causes antecedent to events. Agents do not act for causes. Science wants to explain natural phenomena in terms of cause, but agents act *in terms of reasons*. The difference is that causes refer to the *past*, to the conditions prior to the event, such that the event is an effect that follows the cause. Reasons, on the contrary, refer to the *future*, to the goals or purposes or ends of the agents, which may be and tend to be distinct from the prior conditions. Reasons are fundamentally teleological, aiming at future conditions: our reason for doing something is to attain some later outcome. This presents us with two unmovable barriers to knowledge: we cannot confidently know the agent's reasons, and we cannot know the future.

Atheism Heart of Science

We can say, then, that the crucial and incontrovertible difference between science and religion is the basic premise that each comes from and therefore the kind of answer that each is driven to offer. Religion functions on the *personal premise*, that some or all natural events are the results of the reasons of agents. Science functions on the *impersonal premise*, that (absolutely) all natural events are the effects of antecedent and non-agentive causes. In other words, when science explains a hurricane in terms of temperatures and winds, *etc.*, none of the components has any will or purpose or intelligence. They are completely determined by natural, non-personal factors. When religion explains something, one or more component has will or purpose or intelligence — sometimes an ultimate intelligence — and they are not determined by other factors. This realization that the vital difference between science and religion is impersonal *versus* personal explanations brings several persistent difficulties into focus.

1 The constellation of specific differences between science and religion makes sense. Scientists and religionists alike have tended to dwell on the details of the differences, rather than appreciate the core at the center of each constellation.

RELIGION	SCIENCE
The personal premise	The impersonal premise
Based on authority—Some people/sources have privileged access to agents or their minds	Based on questioning—No people/sources have privileged access to agents or their minds
Commitment—humans must put their "faith" in the agents	Skepticism—humans can and must test everything
Certainty—humans can (and must) be sure about their agents	Doubt—humans cannot be sure about their knowledge
Explanations are normative (based on what humans should do)	Explanations are inductive and deductive (based on experience, definitions, and generalizations)
Explanations take the form of narratives or stories	Explanations take the form of natural laws (mathematical if possible)

2 Science is harder to do than religion. Boyer, Atran, and others suggested that religion depends on counter-intuitive ideas about non-human agents. However, what is counter-intuitive about religious beings and forces is not that they are agents but they are *non-human* agents, with characteristics

that violate our experience of humans. It is entirely intuitive to expect agentive explanations, since that is what we do with each other. Science is, in this sense, much more counter-intuitive, since it asserts that there are no non-human agents. Science goes against our innate dualism, as Bloom called it, that everything is explainable in terms of minds.

3 In some profound and irreducible ways, it is impossible to disprove religious claims. The question of whether science can prove or disprove religion has preoccupied many religionists and scientists. Some religionists think that science can help prove the truth of religion, like the so-called intelligent design group. Some scientists argue that science can help disprove the truth of religion, like Victor Stenger. In his *Has Science Found God?* (2002), he proposes that religious claims should leave some testable traces and that those traces can be tested like any other empirical evidence. That much is true: if, say, prayer is claimed to have effects on health, then we can experiment on it just as we experiment on the effectiveness of drugs. However, the problem is that agents do not work like drugs: drugs should work the same way every time, while agents are, as we said, capricious and independent. The failure of any particular prayer experiment — or prophecy or oracle, *etc.* — can always be explained (away) by religionists in terms of the agency of the supernatural beings. It may be that the being chose not to answer those prayers, or that he/she/it/they knew he/she/it/they were being tested and tempted, or some such thing. Agents, especially super-human ones, simply will not let themselves be so pinned down. So, while we can falsify specific religious claims, we cannot falsify the basic supernatural, personal premise. We can only launch our inquiry from a different premise.

4 Religious belief is so resistant to disconfirmation. One of the truly vexing facts about religion is the impenetrability of contradictory evidence. Believers tend to continue believing whether reality supports their belief or not — and sometimes contradiction actually seems to strengthen their belief. The reason could be sheer stubbornness, but it is probably more. The root of belief persistence is that the 'personal premise' can

absorb disconfirmation in a way that science with its impersonal premise cannot. If science does the same experiment or makes the same observation and gets conflicting results, something is wrong: either our procedure was flawed, or we have drawn a faulty conclusion. Either way, identical causes should not lead to different effects. If religion gets an anomalous result — or no result at all — it can always be explained away by referring to the freedom of the agent. We do not know the plan of the divine being. He/she/it/they chose the outcome for his/her/its/their own reasons. You deserved it but I did not. And so on. Christians are quick to conclude that their god works in mysterious ways because if you and I both pray for health, you may get it while I do not. If, on the other hand, my car started on some days and not on others, I would not say that it is working mysteriously, I would say that it is not working at all. But my car is not an agent that wants to run some days and not others. The gods and spirits and ancestors do, in principle, have ways of their own, which may not be ours and may actually diverge from or conflict with ours. If we are in the hands of uncanny agents, we can never, in principle, know exactly what they will do — or if they have ever done anything.

In conclusion, the distinction between religion and science on the basis of agency settles the enduring question of the compatibility of the two — by making it a nonsense question. Religion can be added to science — and *any religion can be added to science, not just Christianity* — because religion makes a kind of claim that is irrelevant to and not even in the same dimension as science. Again, if science explains a hurricane in terms of natural causes, religion can always tack on, "and God did it." Or "and the animal spirits did it." Or "and the ancestors did it." In other words, religion not only allows for supernatural explanation but *for any supernatural explanation*. Richard Dawkins is correct when he says that "we cannot disprove these beliefs" but that "they are superfluous" and totally unneeded by science" (1986:316). All they do is paste an unwarranted and unnecessary addendum to natural explanation, as in the case of 'theistic evolution' which has a god somehow involved in the natural processes of evolution. So, when Scott opines that evolution or any science is about "what happened" but not "whodunit," she is right, but she is seriously wrong to think that this opens a door for religion. Science does not leave the question of *who* unanswered but rather rejects it outright as nonsensical and thoroughly anti-scientific. *There is no who, and if there was, it could be any who.* There is no agency or intention, and there cannot be, for the reasons just identified above. Personal agency is not another kind of explanation; it is an anti-explanation, the very impossibility of ever having an explanation.

How the Scientific Study of Religion Implodes Religion

Would you put your judgment above that of so many famous men and claim that you know more than they all? You have no right to call into question the most holy orthodox faith.

—Inquisitor Johann Eck to Martin Luther,
Diet of Worms, 1521

The alleged compatibility of science and religion, then, is a chimera. Surely one can glue one's religion onto a scientific explanation, but nothing is gained from it, and potentially much is lost, in the real intelligibility of nature (nature is *less* intelligible *with* non-human agents than without). The actual and deep incompatibility of science and religion emerges in one of the more recent forays of science, into the explanation of religion itself. When science arrogates to study religion scientifically, religion is demoted and demystified conclusively, which religion cannot survive. When the nineteenth century zoologist Ernst Haeckel allegedly asked, "Is the world friendly?" he highlighted the belief (or at least the concern) that the non-human and the natural was agentive and social — although of course not all social beings are friendly beings (some humans are quite unfriendly!). But Haeckel's is not a scientific question: the world is neither friendly nor unfriendly, since it has no feelings at all.

As we have seen, religion is essentially social, in both senses of the word. It is an activity that humans do together; it is created, maintained, and perpetuated by human group behavior (see Chapter 7). It is also social in the sense that it extends that sociality beyond the human world, to a (putative) realm of non-human agents who also interact with us socially. An essential characteristic, perhaps the defining characteristic, of social relationships is *order*. In our social human species, and most others similar to us, social order means well-defined social roles or parts to play in the group and a hierarchy or asymmetrical relation between these roles, with some possessing higher status or rank or prestige than others. In social systems, individuals or roles with high prestige have more rights and privileges — more social power — than those with lower prestige. High-prestige individuals and roles enjoy authority and the fruits of authority (more and better food, mates, *etc.*), while low-prestige individuals and roles defer to their superiors. In other words, social relationships tend to have built into them a quality of deference and respect: there are things that higher-ups can do that lower-downs cannot, and inferiors should submit to superiors.

Social relationships thus depend on boundaries, and it is no surprise that religion depends on boundaries too. And if lower humans defer to higher humans, it is only sensible that all humans would defer to beings and forces higher than they, especially the 'ultimately high' one(s). In thinking about religion, the most basic of all boundaries has often been regarded as the one between the sacred and the profane — between what humans must treat with respect and reverence and what they can treat casually or indifferently. As Durkheim wrote in *The Elementary Forms of the Religious Life*, "This division of the world into two domains, one containing all that is sacred and the other all that is profane — such is the distinctive trait of religious thought" (1965:52). Further, he thought that this distinction, this bifurcation of reality, is "absolute," and the sacred "is, *par excellence*, that which the profane must not and cannot touch with impunity." What happens when this most elemental of all boundaries is crossed? The sacred is corrupted, and the profane is endangered, and all of existence is put in jeopardy.

Science, not being of the sacred, must in this binary view be of the profane. But science does not stay on its side of the chasm; even worse, science does not recognize the presence of the chasm at all. Science goes wherever it will, asks whatever it will, finds whatever it will. Science even deigns to study religion — something for which religion never asked and which it does not welcome. *Religion*, from the religious perspective, is about acceptance, commitment, and respect — not poking and questioning. The breach of any boundary is a threat to the system that depends on the boundary. When the protective boundary of the skin is breached, harm usually ensues. Science breaches all boundaries, to bravely go, as the classic science fiction program put it, where no one has gone before. As such, science threatens religion in two ways (its methods and its findings) as it pursues two projects (the investigation of the natural world about which religion also makes claims and the investigation of religions themselves as objects of study). The potential, and actual, consequence of this process is a contraction and ultimately an implosion of religion, in Jean Baudrillard's sense of the disappearance of "any polarity between the one and the other.... This is what causes that vacuum and inwardly collapsing effect in all those systems which survive on the distinction of poles (good/bad, true/false, alive/dead, up/down, and especially left/right [in a political sense])" (1983:6). As when matter and antimatter collide, the collision of science and religion leaves belief shattered and ruined.

There are three particular manners in which science threatens to achieve — or has already long ago achieved — a radical implosion and disintegration of religion, making it little more than one profane object among other profane objects and therefore something impossible to believe. These include the practice and method of scientific study, the process of theoretical explanation, and the procedure of comparison (especially cross-cultural comparison). Like the crowd listening to Nietzsche's madman, most people have not heard and cannot hear the news of the implosion of religion, of the impossibility of belief. However, he predicted that a time would come when we could hear it, and understand it, and survive it, and perhaps even celebrate it, and that time has come.

Nothing is Sacred: Studying Religion

If nothing else, religion is respect; there are some things you can and cannot do, some things you can and cannot touch, some things bigger and more important than you. To disrespect the powers or truths of a religion is to risk wrath and retribution; however, to disrespect these powers or truths without consequence to render them powerless, irrelevant, and ultimately false: most modern Christians do not fear to talk about or enter the sacred places of the ancient Greek or Roman or Egyptian or Norse gods. However, no self-respecting ancient Greek or Roman or Egyptian or Norseman would have risked the sacrilege of approaching the gods in a less than worshipful and ritually pure state, and few if any self-respecting Christians would so risk blaspheming or disrespecting their god.

No religion asks — or quite frankly wants — humans to investigate it or the world it prescribes. As Augustine wrote in his *Confessions*, "There is another form of temptation, even more fraught with danger. This is the disease of curiosity.... It is this which drives us to try and discover the secrets of nature, those secrets which are beyond our understanding, which can avail us nothing and which man should not wish to learn." Clearly this is not the position of science; in fact, nothing could be more anathema to the position of science than this. If this were truly the scientific attitude, there would have been no research into the shape of the earth or the alignment of the planets. There would, in a word, be no science.

Science starts from two key premises that are not only foreign to religion but that actually transgress religion. One is that there are more things to be known, more research to be done, and that they are indeed knowable. The other is that the knowable can be known in terms of natural and not supernatural factors, which we now understand means *impersonal and not personal factors*. It is finally possible to define *supernatural* in a useful way, as *the realm of non-human agents*. As Lohman expresses it in his comparative discussion of the concept, "Supernaturalism is the extension of the volition schema to phenomena that do not in fact result from will and choice, like the origin of the world" (2003:176); it is "volition out of place" (184).

Science need not stipulate in advance that spiritual or supernatural beings or forces do not or cannot exist; what it does do, minimally and necessarily, is ignore them. In fact, terms and concepts like 'god,' 'spirit,' 'soul,' 'demon,' *etc.* are not even part of the scientific vocabulary. They tell us nothing, and the necessity to re-introduce them into our explanations would mark the utter failure of science and indeed of explanation. But ignoring such concepts is tantamount to rejecting them.

A scientific, or at least rationalistic or naturalistic, approach first began when ancient philosophers suspended traditional religious or supernatural explanations and attempted to find other answers, without reference to gods. It would not and could not be long before this inquisitive speculation turned on the gods themselves, as in the case of Xenophanes, who famously noted that different societies had different gods, relative to their own society. Still others were troubled by the fabled immorality of the gods themselves or by what we would come to call the 'problem of evil,' among them Theognis, who pondered:

> Dear Zeus, you baffle me. You are king of all; the highest honor and greatest power are yours, you discern what goes on in each man's secret heart, and your lordship is supreme. Yet you make no distinction between the sinner and the good man, between the man who devotes himself to temperate and responsible acts and the man who commits deeds of hubris. Tell me, son of Cronus, how can you deal such unfairness? (quoted in Wheelwright 1966:29–30).

Others expanded this line of natural or rational law. Parmenides wrote that "strong Necessity holds [Being] in its bonds of limit, which constrains it on all sides; Natural Law forbids that Being should be other than perfectly complete. It stands in need of nothing; for if it needed anything at all it would need everything" (quoted in *ibid*.: 98). Heraclitus went further still: "The universe, which is the same for all, has not been made by any god or man, but it always has been, is, and will be — an ever-living fire, kindling itself by regular measures and going out by regular measures" (quoted in *ibid*.: 71). Finally such men as Protagoras and Epicurus, as they watched both religion and society crumble around them, concluded that the gods may not even exist at all; as the former wrote, "As for the gods, I have no way of knowing either that they exist or that they do not exist; nor, if they exist, of what form they are" (quoted in *ibid*.: 240).

Atheism Heart of Science

Science in any serious sense was not born until centuries later, when scholars like Roger Bacon [1220–1292] and René Descartes [1596–1650] described the *method* for both asking and answering questions. Breaking with the ancient rationalist philosophy, the new 'natural philosophy' was to be empirical; instead of speculating or introspecting on things, we should observe, measure, even test. Of course, Descartes' method started from the premise of radical, virtually absolute doubt; he determined to take nothing for certain unless he could prove it to himself (whatever we might think of his proofs). But the point is that the first step of science is *doubt*, which is the contravention of tradition, authority, and even sacredness — all of the hedges that enclose religion. Observation, not authority and tradition, is to be the source of knowledge — a profoundly unreligious attitude.

The challenge of modern science to religion has come in a variety of forms. Some are indirect, such as the exploration of nature, for which religion already had its 'truths.' In the Western, Christian context, this came as a steady barrage of discovery and disproof of long-held factual positions. Columbus proved that the earth was round. Copernicus and Galileo proved that the sun was the center of the solar system. Medical science showed that microorganisms, not demons, cause illness. Geology suggested that the earth was much older than biblical literalists believed (and still believe). Astronomy concluded that there were many planets and galaxies out there, probably many capable of supporting life, and that all of them originated in a massive energy event in an unimaginably distant past. And perhaps most corrosively, biology demonstrated that life, including human life, could have appeared by purely natural, impersonal processes.

Other challenges were and are more direct, investigating questions that potentially confirm or refute aspects of religion itself. For instance, archaeological study illustrated that there were cities much older than any in the Judeo-Christian world and that many of the claims in that tradition do not conform to the evidence. History showed that some of the chronological claims of religion were unstable or wrong. Textual analysis of the scriptures themselves indicated problems with the 'divinity' of the Bible, pointing out multiple authors and sources, transcription and translation issues and errors, and rejected scriptures like the apocrypha and the Gnostic writings. Even worse, biographers like Strauss and Renan turned their tools on the very person of Jesus, treating him like any other human subject--and finding either subjective or contradictory material or no real material at all.

Finally, there was and is the head-on investigation of religion itself. It has taken such whimsical forms as attempting to weigh the soul. More seriously, scientists including medical practitioners have tested the efficacy of prayer, for example in its power to cure disease. (Given the suggestibility of humans, it is odd that no one to my knowledge has attempted to repair car engines with prayer.) Other investigators have examined various claims of miracles, from bleeding statues and stigmata to faith healing and spiritual apparitions. Some researchers (as we saw in Chapter 3) have poked around in the brain for a 'god spot,' while others practice and study various kinds of meditation and mysticism looking for an empirical manifestation of the sacred. Finally, still others have explored comparative religion and the relation between religious systems and society, as well as comparative ethics.

Is science actively trying to debunk religion? Occasionally. Even a sympathizer of religion like Joseph Campbell could assert that "it must, of course, be the task of the historian, archaeologist, and prehistorian to show that the myths are as facts untrue" (1972:11). But this is not always the case. The task of scientists is precisely to discover the truth and to separate correct conclusions from erroneous ones. Religion may have also come to that truth or not. Guessing may also come to that truth or not. That is not the point. The point is that science conducts its affairs with utter and complete disregard and indifference to religion; if religion agrees or disagrees, it is absolutely irrelevant to science.

Indifference is not hostility; in a way, it is the very absence of hostility. Nevertheless, indifference *is* hostile, because it means crossing boundaries carelessly and asking questions that appear and are disrespectful (not intentionally disrespectful, but void of respect, which is the same thing). It means peeking up gods' togas and pawing idols to see for oneself. It means probing sacred cows — and finding no gods, only guts. To a system like religion that depends for its existence on respect, this is quite hostile. Science, on the other hand, trespasses on the boundary of the sacred not because it is opposed to the sacred but because it has no concept of sacred at all. *Sacred* is a religious concept, not a scientific one and not a natural one. To science, nothing is sacred, because 'sacred' is not part of its vocabulary. So when science ignores religious boundaries, it handles religion roughly — like any pithed frog or pinned butterfly. And when science finds facts that refute religious claims — about man, about society, about the universe, or about god(s) — it comes as a tear of the skin that no religion welcomes or can withstand.

Religion is Not What You Believe: Explaining Religion

Science often only incidentally studies religion as it goes about studying the world. In areas where religion makes no claims or where religion has little at stake, science is free to do what it wants. Most scientists never study religion itself in any serious manner, confining their researches to butterflies and volcanoes and clouds. However, a contingent of scientists in a variety of disciplines makes religion their direct object of study.

When one studies religion, whether historically, sociologically, psychologically, anthropologically, and so on, one can do trivial things like count worshippers in church or evaluate their voting habits. This generates a certain amount and kind of information about religion, or at least religious behavior. But most influential students of religion have wanted to do much more, namely, provide a *theory* of religion, give an *explanation* of religion (see Chapter 3). What does it mean to 'explain religion'? The one thing it does not mean is to take it at face value — to respect its claims, its authority, its boundaries. If one were to explain scientifically some ritual or ritual in general, what one would *not* do would be to explain it as true: "Those people do that rain-making ritual because it really does make it rain."

Investigation of the sort discussed above — pulling down the statues and scriptures to give them a good look — is easily appreciated as a disrespectful (and entirely warranted and desirable) thing, but it is not always so easily grasped that explanation itself is a disrespectful thing as well. If a scientist asks a communion taker, "Why are you swallowing that wafer and wine?" and gets back the answer "Because it is the body and blood of Christ," he or she would not publish that as the *theory* of communion. That is a religious response, not a scientific analysis. The scientist is likely to 'translate' the behavior into some symbolic or psychological or social or perhaps biological idiom. That is, the scientist essentially concludes: "Well, that is what the believer says, but that is not what's really going on. Let me tell you what's really going on."

In other words, a scientific explanation or theory of religion can never be religious in nature — can never be in terms of religion. To explain something is to explain it *in terms of something else.* It is to give a reason for it, to propose *why it exists*, and the phenomenon cannot be the reason for itself. An illustration would be to contrast a *description* of a cat with an *explanation* of a cat: a description would list characteristics and basically answer the question, What is a cat? An explanation of a cat would be a reason for the existence, or perhaps the function, of the cat, basically answering the question, Why is a cat?

It should not be difficult to see that, whatever the specific explanation or theory of religion or any particular aspect of religion, the activity of explanation is once again fundamentally disrespectful to or dismissive of religion. Religion does not ask — or from its own perspective, need — to be explained. One goes to church and prays because 'God' says so and to get the attendant results. One believes the creation myth because it is true. One takes the communion in imitation of the Last Supper and at the order of Church law. Those are indeed reasons, but they are not explanations — let alone scientific explanations, let alone theories. They are the discourse of the believer, not the observer.

So scientific explanations transcend religious ones, and by doing so trump and cancel them; in an important sense, they neutralize the very religiousness of religion. They explain or theorize religion in terms of non-religion, explain and theorize the supernatural in terms of the natural and the human, *e.g.*

psychology, sociology, linguistics, politics, biology, *etc.* This is not necessarily to reduce religion to one or more of these things, but it is to transfer the explanatory — and real — power from the religious realm to some other realm.

Theories have ranged from the mildly respectful to the aggressively disrespectful, but none have taken religion at its word. All theories find the source or function of religion somewhere other than religion — in the brain, in the mind, in society, in politics, indeed *anywhere* but in religion. The important thing is that explaining and theorizing religion always takes the form, if not of *explaining away*, then of *explaining as* something other-than-religion. The effect of this *modus operandi* is dual.

First, it deprives religion of any privilege it might have as an intellectual and social phenomenon, let alone as a true phenomenon; religion is not a distinct phenomenon at all but an epi-phenomenon, an effect of other non-religious causes. If it is 'true' at all — as Durkheim and even Campbell assert — then it is true 'in a fashion,' that fashion being very much other than what the believer believes. And the scientist will tell the believer in just what fashion his or her beliefs are true.

Second, by depriving religion of privilege it once more wipes away any boundaries between religion and the mundane or profane domains of politics, kinship, and economics. Religion is just another domain of human culture, not a superhuman one and not even an independent one. Religion is the dependent variable to the independent variables of everyday social and physical reality.

Since religion cannot survive long at all without boundaries, some scholars have attempted to fill the vacuum with other boundaries that re-enclose religion but in a way foreign to religion. One of the most significant and appealing versions of this effort is the symbolic analysis of religion. Abandoning the truth-status and the uniqueness of religion (both of which are indefensible), these scholars have found a way to keep religion and debunk it too at the same time by means of the concept of 'symbol.' Now, no doubt religion uses symbols; the cross is a symbol of Christianity. However, to say that the cross is *only* a symbol, or that the wafer and wine are only symbols of Jesus or that religion as a whole is only a symbol, is to do rough justice to it.

ATHEISM ADVANCED

Of the symbolists, Clifford Geertz is probably the kindest to religion. However, in defining religion as a system of symbols, he too demotes religion to one among a set of "perspectives," including the aesthetic, scientific, and common-sense. It is different from them in detail but not in principle. Others have been even more corrosive; the founders of the symbolic movement, Ernst Cassirer and Suzanne Langer, can be seen this way. Cassirer, while establishing the profound and no doubt true fact that humans live in a "mediated" reality in which symbols are the medium, premises his analysis of religion on its self-evident falseness and contingency: "Religion claims to be in possession of an absolute truth; but its history is a history of errors and heresies. It gives us the promise and prospect of a transcendent world — far beyond the limits of human experience — and it remains human, all too human" (1954:97–8). Myth in particular is "fictitious"; in fact, it never claimed in the first place to be true but rather to be "dramatic." Myth, he says, is not about reason but about feeling, and feelings cannot be "wrong."

In her seminal *Philosophy in a New Key*, Langer ends up in the same place. Of myths she writes: "No sane human being, however simple, could really 'suppose' such events to occur; and clearly, in enjoying this sort of story nobody is trying to 'suppose' anything" (1942:140). Myth, "this remarkable form of nonsense," is not to be taken literally but to be interpreted symbolically. It is a kind of language emitted by a kind of mind, but a non-rational, non-discursive, and certainly not 'true' kind of language. Myth or religious language in general is metaphorical, metaphor being "the law of growth of every semantic" (119). She quotes Cailliet who called mythical thinking "vegetative thought," that overgrowth of image and meaning which she characterizes as "a rampant confusion of metaphorical meanings clinging to every symbol, sometimes to the complete obscurance of any reasonable literal meaning" (120–1).

As long as myth and religion are never approached in a literal way, everything stays fine. This, of course, introduces a new boundary, between the *symbolic* and the *literal* (*i.e.* true), or what Karen Armstrong calls the *mythos* and *logos* (see Chapter 10). Humans need both the mythos and the logos, she insists. Mythos is about being rich (in meaning), logos about being right. But if mythos is the realm where validity does not apply, then myths were never 'valid' (nor 'invalid') in the first place. Armstrong warns us that one of the greatest mistakes is to confuse mythos and logos — that is, in our present language, to cross the boundary between them, or to permit them to cross the boundary into each other's region — so that we take our mythos literally or take our logos metaphorically. The result of the former, she opines, is religious fundamentalism; the result of the latter, I presume, would be the inability to use a VCR or cell phone.

One last scientist who has offered to restore the boundary of religion is Stephen Jay Gould, whose *Rock of Ages* (1999) is an overt attempt to wall off the territories of religion and science. In the end, Gould tries to save religion by redefining it beyond all recognition; it is 'only' morality. But it is not even always morality; he admits that philosophy and anthropology — not to mention reason — can be sources of morality. So what subjects are left to rule in the kingdom of religion? He recreates a boundary, surely enough, but it is one that believers and scientists alike would reject. It is a hopeful good neighbor policy that does not work and cannot stand. And when he says that science "has no quarrel whatever with anyone's need of belief in such a personalized concept of divine power" he is wrong as we outlined above; he even goes on to say that his model of non-overlapping magisterial or NOMA "does preclude the additional claim that such a God must arrange the facts of nature in a certain set and predetermined way" (93–4). But if that is what the religion claims and the believers believe, then the religious reality precludes NOMA. Either a god exists or not, and either a god arranges facts or not. But questions of existence and of fact are *scientific* questions, and no boundary or amount of hopeful thinking will keep science away from them.

In conclusion, the project to theorize or explain religion proves two things. First, the act of theorizing is an act of deflation, of breaking boundaries and reducing or demoting religion to just one thing that humans do and just one consequence of what humans are — biological beings, psychological individuals, social and cultural collectivities. Second, attempting to redraw boundaries after they have been breached is an exercise in the betrayal and, quite honestly, in the further erosion of religion. Religion, because it cannot begin to hope to hold the ground it formerly did (having been studied and repudiated — the sun does not revolve around the earth, *etc.*) — is redefined as holding only the ground that momentarily seems unbreachable; but that ground is unstable and does not constitute what the religion and its believers claim it constitutes.

1 Religion + 1 Religion = 0 Religion: Comparing Religions

As we have established, much of the debate about religion occurred, and still occurs, in a vacuum of understanding about religion. Not only do people not know enough about their religion, they do not know enough about *religion* — which means *religions*. That is, most believers do not understand that there are other beliefs and other believers who believe those other things just as firmly as they do. Or, when they did notice other religions, the typical response was persecution, forced conversion, holy war, and other religiously-motivated hostility.

Humans have always known that other groups had other gods or no gods at all. This has not always or often led to scientific curiosity about, much less open acceptance of, such diversity. The other-believers were *non*-believers, infidels, heretics, atheists. Pascal Boyer tells of an encounter with a prominent Catholic theologian who praised anthropology thus: "This is what makes anthropology so fascinating and so difficult too. You have to explain how people can believe in such nonsense" (2001:297). Indeed, science often involves explaining somebody's nonsense; but for science it is *all* nonsense.

This myopia is not limited by any means to theologians. Even scientists have felt the need to distance themselves from the beliefs that they study. Lewis Henry Morgan, one of the founders of anthropology, opined that "all primitive religions are grotesque and to some extent unintelligible" (1978:5–6). Evans-Pritchard, the highly regarded anthropologist of Azande witchcraft, qualified his enthusiasm by stating that, "Witches, as the Azande conceive them, cannot exist" (1937:63). Finally,

Atheism Heart of Science

Suzanne Langer quotes Grace De Laguna who refers to primitive religions as "elaborate and monstrous systems of belief" as well as Andrew Lang who holds that the belief in magic "requires for its existence an almost boundless credulity" (1942:37–8). Attitudes like these, as judgmental as they are, make sense and are nearly inevitable based on the assumption that *our* religion is right and *theirs* is wrong. In fact, attitudes like these basically made the comparative study of religion impossible since there were not even different religions to compare, only 'true religion' and false belief. All of the opinions expressed above evince a disdain for the belief-systems that they encounter and describe: it may be possible and interesting to study them, but they are certainly not true and hardly even religions but just ludicrous and monstrous ideas. This constitutes a profound commentary on the very definition of religion — what counts as religion and what does not.

We take it in stride today that we can study religions comparatively. The modern comparative study of religion starts from the premise that other religions at the very least have value and may, to some extent, have truth. This is not only a different perspective on religions but a perspective that is shared with (at least some) religions. The effect of this kind of open-minded toleration on religious value and religious truth is not widely understood. It was understood by the Puritan settlers of Massachusetts, who in no way practiced or respected toleration. Nathaniel Ward, for instance, criticized the idea of toleration by asserting that anyone who tolerated another religion "besides his own, unless it be in matters merely indifferent, either doubts his own, or is not sincere in it" (quoted in Levy 1993:240). We tend to condemn this opinion today, yet its implications are inescapable.

These implications come in two forms. The first relates to the issue of value. If one stoops to compare (other than as an exercise in which is best) one's religion and some other religion, one is honoring and elevating that other religion in the process; if it is not as good as one's own, it is still good enough to receive consideration. At least one is gracing it with the label of religion. But that is implicitly to declare that one's own religion is not the standard of all value, which is what most (at least world) religions explicitly claim. It is to assert that one's own religion is comparable to if not equal to the other(s). This is to disrespect — and often to disobey (since one is not supposed to respect 'idols') — one's own religion.

The second implication relates to the issue of truth. Scientists do not compare round-earth and flat-earth views of geography, except as a historical and cultural oddity. We must ask ourselves, "What is the *point* in comparing religions — what are comparative religionists trying to accomplish?" If a religion is true, then the only possible result of comparison is to show the lies and mistakes in the others; comparative religion becomes apologetics. But the scientific comparison of religion is not apologetics; it does not start from a demand that *any* particular religion is true — and often finds that *every* particular religion is false.

One does not have to go far, or even be very scientific, to discover contradictions between religions. An obvious one concerns the divinity of Jesus: Christianity teaches that he was the son of God, Islam that he was not. Both of these positions cannot be true simultaneously. Somebody is wrong. If we linger on the surface of comparative religion, we can accept, even smile at, such contradictions, but if we penetrate at all, we find that we must resolve these mutual exclusions. The result tends to be one or both of the outcomes discussed in previous sections: we set about to find the empirical (*i.e.* scientific) answer to the problem, taking neither tradition or scripture as our authority, or we abolish the contradiction by transferring it from the realm of truth to the realm of symbol or allegory or *mythos* or illusion.

Truth pays a heavy price. The comparative study of religion throws doubt on the specific truth-claims that any particular religion makes; at the very best, it puts religion on the defensive, making it prove what it had always simply preached. At worst, it forces such religion to abandon falsified truths and retreat to unfalsified or unfalsifiable ones. In that way, it ends up being something like Gould's truncated rump religion. One possible and common and popular outcome is to affirm that all religions are 'true in their own way,' which represents a second cost. Our very concept of truth becomes vague and flabby and inoffensive: we would not want to hurt anyone's feelings or seem intolerant by telling someone they are wrong. This is the modern condition of toleration, which either ends up saying that we are all true or that truth does not matter or does not exist. All of these positions are equally foreign and hostile to religion *qua* religion.

In the final analysis, there were not even supposed to be 'religions.' There was only supposed to be *religion* — one true, and therefore compulsory, factual statement about the spiritual world and moral imperative flowing from those facts. Here, most purely and profoundly, religion implodes — not because religion and anti-religion (*i.e.,* science or symbology) meet but because *religion and religion meet.* Nothing is more destructive to religion than other religions; it is like meeting one's own anti-matter twin.

First, other religions represent *alternatives to* one's own religion: other people believe in them just as fervently as we do, and they live their lives just as successfully as we do. Then, the diversity of religions forces us to see religion as a culturally relative phenomenon; different groups have different religions that appear adapted to their unique social and even environmental conditions. But if *their* religion is relative, then why is *ours* not? Finally, awareness of other religions reduces the truth-probability of one's own. Assuming that there are, say, 1,000 religions in the world, each with an equal chance of being true and all at least to some degree mutually exclusive, then each religion has a 1/1,000 chance of being true and a 999/1,000 chance of being false. In other words, whatever you believed before the comparison, there is only a 0.1% chance of being correct and a 99.9% chance of being incorrect. If that is not upsetting to religious credulity, I do not know what is.

Out of the Scientific Study of Religion: Incipit Atheism

Nietzsche announced that god was dead and that we humans had killed him/her/it/them. How had we done this? We now know the answer: by studying god(s), by explaining god(s), and by comparing gods.

To study god(s) or religion(s) is to demystify them, to bring them within human reach and human knowledge, to cross any boundary between them and us, in fact to dispel the very boundary. It is to knock them off their pedestal, pull them down from heaven, and put them under our microscope. It is to lose fear and respect

To explain god(s) or religion(s) is to reduce them, to no longer take them for granted or at face value, to trespass against the boundary between religion and other human characteristics or activities. It is to see them not as causes but as effects, not as creators but creations. It is to deprive them of all uniqueness, to liken them to dreams, metaphors, or political ploys.

To compare god(s) or religion(s) is to wound them most mortally, to demonstrate their very mortality, to erase the boundary between religion and religion, between beatific and blasphemous, between heavenly and heretical. It is to question almost without care or thought the value and truth of religion — and at the same time the value and truth of value and truth. It is to see religion as a colorful, fascinating, important, but all-too-human construction — and therefore as culturally relative and not true at all.

Some who study religion scientifically may love or even believe religion, but scientific study is neither loving nor believing. Science is detachment, objectivity, perhaps cold, hard disinterest. It cannot stop at any boundaries, bow to any masters, spare any feelings. If false is false, it must go. Science is unrelenting and unforgiving, not because it is cruel but because it has no such concept as 'relent' or 'forgive.' The hammer does not hate the nail, and the telescope does not hate the stars; it does not have any emotions on the subject at all — it is, remember, impersonal — and things are immeasurably better that way. In fact, the hammer is a potent metaphor here. Nietzsche attempted to "philosophize with a hammer" and destroyed idols along the way. Science often literally employs a hammer — or a scalpel, or a lens, or a light, or other invasive and destructive device — to plumb the depths of the unknown. This why Stephen Jay Gould took such pleasure in the motto *Frango ut patefaciam*, translating to "I break in order to reveal." Science breaks to reveal truth — and it breaks religion in order to reveal the truth about religion.

The scientific study of religion rebukes religion, whether it sets out to or not. In its methods as well as its assumptions and its goals, it erodes religion at every step. Even those who hope to support religion with science only highlight the authority of science over religion; why else would religion need support? What is left to religion is often the gaps in human knowledge, but this 'god of the gaps' is a weakened and trivial god — one that will be weakened and trivialized still more as knowledge advances. Science reduces the scope, and therefore the power, and therefore the significance of the supernatural or spiritual, not only in the sense of pushing back their province but in radically and virtually completely removing them from the discourse.

The consequence of the scientific study of religion is stripping religion of many of its claims, evacuating it out of much of the *magisterium* of science (*i.e.*, fact), and diminishing it in many fatal ways. The likelihood is that this process will continue, until the god of the gaps has few if any gaps left to hide in; then there will no place for gods at all. Science, without malice but equally without mercy, makes religion, perhaps more than anything else, *smaller*, and a small religion appeals to no one. The further religion retreats, the less its truth or falseness concerns us, the less *it* concerns us; religion shrinks not so much in rightness as in relevance. Already today, as Richard Dawkins has written, it is intellectually respectable to be without god(s), to be an a-theist. Tomorrow, following current trends, it will be intellectually necessary.

Chapter 7

Atheism in Solitude:
Reason and the (Religious) Madness of Crowds

In his *The Varieties of Religious Experience*, William James defined religion as "the feelings, acts, and experiences of individual men in their solitude, so far as they apprehend themselves to stand in relation to whatever they may consider the divine" (1958:42). He was wrong.

James is wrong because religion is not solitary but rather fundamentally and thoroughly social and collective. You never see a religion of one, unless it is a prophet or founder of what will become a new religion — but then such a person is always a member of some pre-existing religion which he or she is changing, and he or she also always aspires to build that new religious movement into a larger, potentially mainstream, and maybe even universal, religion.

Beyond that, no individual ever invents a private religion out of thin air. A religion is a tradition, a culture, and so is by definition shared; the individual is not the first, nor will he or she be the last, to hold it. It is acquired from a believing community, which instructs the individual on what the 'true' beliefs and values of the community and the religion are. So, in direct contradiction to James' evaluation, the sociologist Emile Durkheim famously characterized religion as "a unified system of beliefs and practices relative to sacred things, that is to say, things set aside and forbidden — beliefs and practices which unite into one single moral community called a Church, all those who adhere to them" (1965:62). The key to religion for Durkheim, in addition to the notion of the sacred, is the existence of a believing community, which is integrated into a moral community by sharing common ideas, values, and worldviews.

In a way, James' individualist perspective on religion is a product of his particular discipline, namely psychology (see Chapter 9 below), which tends to emphasize the personal, even the interior and mental, over the social and collective. In another way, the privatist approach to religion is neither factual nor philosophical but *political*. Martin Luther had necessarily to perform this trick to extricate Christianity from the Catholic Church: religion had to be, he argued, a matter of "conscience" which was essentially individual. This step was incumbent upon him, since Catholicism was an established church but Luther's view was a new religious movement with no members; therefore, all members of the Lutheran church would need to be (individually) plucked from the (collective) Catholic congregation. But when all was said and done, Lutheranism would be constituted as a new church and community (at which point, not surprisingly, the call to conscience would quiet down considerably and settle into a new orthodoxy).

In the modern Christian and American context, religion has been privatized largely as a matter of political politeness. Believers are left free to believe whatever they want, as a personal choice and commitment, as long as they do not act on it so as to injure others who may and do believe something different. It is a political compromise: keep your religion, but keep your religion to yourself, and we can all get along. The opposite experience — of people brandishing their religion in public like a banner or a weapon — has been and can be observed for its dangerous consequences.

Religion is a group phenomenon; a person is either born into an authentic, traditional religious community (like a tribal religion) or, in the voluntarist style of Christianity and other world religions (Islam, Buddhism, and many newer ones), joins the religion. Conversely, atheism has typically resisted group formation. Atheists are notorious non-joiners; it has been bemoaned over and over that atheists are not group-oriented and tend to be somewhere between individualists and loners. Atheists are infamously difficult to corral into organizations and to lead once they have been corralled (not that religionists are any less prone to disagreement and schism). Atheist groups have a tendency to be volatile, fractious, and transient. I discussed this problem myself in my previous book, where I came to the conclusion that atheist individualism is not a principle of atheism so much as a personality trait of atheists. But I wonder if it is more.

Atheism In Solitude

I still hold that there is nothing inherent in atheism as a philosophy or worldview or whatever it is that is contrary to groups and grouping. However, the fact that *there is something — and something critically essential — in religion that is dependent on groups* makes me a bit suspicious. One can be atheistic in a group, but one can *only* be religious in a group. Therefore, perhaps there is something about groups that is antithetical to being atheistic and something about being atheistic that is antithetical to groups. In order to evaluate this hypothesis, we must learn more about groups and their proclivities. We will find, as others have found before us, that groups have a recurrent set of features that are more compatible with religious than with irreligious thought and behavior. In fact, human groups, as we discovered briefly in Chapter 5 on violence, have a number of quite undesirable characteristics that seem to bring out the worst in humans and are certainly not conducive to cool-headed logic. In a word, it appears that *when you believe, you believe together, but when you think, you think alone.*

Groups Behaving Badly: On the Psychology and Sociology of Collectivities

Madness is something rare in individuals — but in groups, parties, peoples, ages it is the rule.

—Nietzsche, *Beyond Good and Evil*

Irrational, even violent, thinking and behavior is one present danger that humans face. Of course, individual human beings are subject to odd, obsessive, or psychotic behavior, although in fairly small numbers. But all observers concur that the chances increase dramatically for humans in groups (as we mentioned in Chapter 5).

Extreme, bizarre, and destructive group activity can find many motivations and take many forms. Charles Mackay, in his 1841 study *Extraordinary Delusions and the Madness of Crowds*, focuses primarily on political and especially economic fantasies and delusions, showing how, in certain moments and circumstances, otherwise basically intelligent people can act stupidly. The cases that Mackay describes include a variety of investment crazes like the tulip mania of the 1600s and the South-Sea bubble and Mississippi scheme of the 1700s. He cannot fail to mention some religious crazes too like the Crusades, alchemy, witch hunts, and prophecies, although he intentionally limits his indulgence in such cases because "a mere list of them would alone be sufficient to occupy a volume" (1958:*xvii*).

Mackay makes two key points which will inform the rest of our discussion of group insanity. First, he notes that there are certain conditions and motivations which seem to trigger it. Among these are "the love of gain, the necessity of excitement, or the mere force of imitation [or] political or religious causes, or both combined" (354). He notes in particular that group agitation "is always greatest in times of calamity" (258), driven by fear, uncertainty, and a little bit of opportunism. Not surprisingly, any doctrine or worldview that emphasizes or invents calamity has the potential to spark strange behavior.

His other point is that larger-scale collectivities — societies, ages, or entire civilizations — have the same capacity to go nuts as regular small-scale groups and parties. As we discuss in Chapter 9, these large-scale collective phenomena have typical ways of thinking and acting just as individuals do. Thus,

> In reading the history of nations, we find that, like individuals, they have their whims and their peculiarities; their seasons of excitement and recklessness, when they care not what they do. We find that whole communities suddenly fix their minds upon one object, and go mad in its pursuit; that millions of people become simultaneously impressed with one delusion, and run after it, till their attention is caught by some new folly more captivating than the first (*xix*).

Every nation or historical period, he concludes, "has its peculiar folly; some scheme, project, or fantasy into which it plunges" (354) and from which it extricates itself only slowly, if at all.

Gustave Le Bon:
On the Religiousness of Groups

Religion is therefore hardly the only kind of group delusion that humans are susceptible to, but it is one of the worst. Even more, the earliest major study of crowd behavior, Gustave Le Bon's *The Crowd: A Study of the Popular Mind* (1896), suggested that there is a definite affinity between group processes (what we would call *group-think* today) and religion.

Le Bon, like all commentators, would acknowledge that humans have crazy and dangerous capacities as individuals. However, two anomalous things seem to happen in groups: the worst of individual human psychology gets expressed, and the group evinces its own unique (and mostly negative) emergent qualities. As he says, whenever more than a few individuals "are gathered together in a crowd for purposes of action...from the mere fact of their being assembled, there result certain new psychological characteristics, which are added to the [individual] characteristics and differ from them at times to a considerable degree" (*v*).

Le Bon stresses this latter development as what he calls "the law of the mental unity of crowds" (2). By this he means that

> the fact that they have been transformed into a crowd puts them in possession of a sort of collective mind which makes them feel, think, and act in a manner quite different from that in which each individual of them would feel, think, and act were he in a state of isolation. There are certain ideas and feelings which do not come into being, or do not transform themselves into acts except in the case of individuals forming a crowd. The psychological crowd is a provisional being formed of heterogeneous elements, which for a moment are combined, exactly as the cells which constitute a living body form by their reunion a new being which displays characteristics very different from those possessed by each of the cells singly (6).

We mentioned a few of these traits in Chapter 5 in our examination of religious violence. Primary among them is the inability to reason: "crowds display a singularly inferior mentality" (*ix*), as if humans in groups revert to their lowest level of intelligence. A group also experiences a sense of "invincible power which allows [the individual] to yield to instincts" which would otherwise be restrained (10). In fact, he suggests that the crowd acts virtually unconsciously, demonstrating poor qualities like "impulsiveness, irritability, incapacity to reason, the absence of judgment and of the critical spirit, the exaggeration of the sentiments," and other such undesirable traits (17). In short, individually the person may be rational but "in a crowd, he is a barbarian" (13).

Le Bon proceeds to explain that the behavior of crowds is not only more irrational but more emotionally intense. In their frenzies of passion and desire, they allow nothing to stand in their way. Combined with the observed "suggestibility and credulity" of crowds, these emotions have the potential to become quite dangerous. "The first suggestion formulated which arises implants itself immediately by a process of contagion in the brains of all assembled, and the identical bent of the sentiments of the crowd is immediately an accomplished fact" (22). Operating on this collective belief and goal, the individuals lose the ability to appreciate the facts around them and to adjust their behavior in light of the facts. Their "collective observations are as erroneous as possible," and Le Bon urges "the most utter mistrust of the evidence of crowds" (31). Still worse, individuals in crowds lose "all sense of responsibility" (35), giving themselves over to the crowd as their mental and moral motor.

Three final qualities that Le Bon finds in crowds, resulting from their low level of functioning, are "intolerance, dictatorialness, and conservatism" (39). He writes that

the opinions, ideas, and beliefs suggested to them are accepted or rejected as a whole, and considered as absolute truths or as not less absolute errors. This is always the case with beliefs induced by a process of suggestion instead of engendered by reasoning. Every one is aware of the intolerance that accompanies religious beliefs, and of the despotic empire they exercise on men's minds.

Being in doubt as to what constitutes truth or error, and having, on the other hand, a clear notion of its strength, a crowd is as disposed to give authoritative effect to its inspirations as it is intolerant. An individual may accept contradiction and discussion; a crowd will never do so. At public meetings the slightest contradiction on the part of an orator is immediately received with howls of fury and violent invective, soon followed by blows, and expulsion should the orator stick to his point. Without the restraining presence of the representatives of authority the contradictor, indeed, would often be done to death.

Dictatorialness and intolerance are common to all categories of crowds (39).

To cut short a very extensive analysis by Le Bon, we may note that he determines that all human crowds and their beliefs and behaviors assume "a religious shape." He employs an appropriately wide definition of religion, not merely belief in or worship of a god but any circumstance in which a person "puts all the resources of his mind, the complete submission of his will, and the whole-souled ardor of fanaticism at the service of a cause or an individual who becomes the goal and guide of his thoughts and actions" (64). In any such case, the member of the group is experiencing the "religious sentiment" (an interesting contrast to the "religious experiences" that James welcomes in his discussion; see Chapter 9 below), which include "worship of a being supposed superior, fear of the power with which the being is credited, blind submission to its commands, inability to discuss its dogmas, the desire to spread them, and a tendency to consider as enemies all by whom they are not accepted"(63). Not surprisingly, "Intolerance and fanaticism are the necessary accompaniments of the religious sentiment," and "blind submission, fierce intolerance, and the need of violent propaganda which are inherent in the religious sentiment" (64). Finally, history shows too clearly that religion depends on these very characteristics: "All founders of religious or political creeds have established them solely because they were successful in inspiring crowds with those fanatical sentiments which have as result that men find their happiness in worship and obedience and are ready to lay down their lives for their idol" (65).

Sigmund Freud: Groups, Love, and Leaders

Freud may be the best-known early psychologist of group behavior, despite the fact that his psychoanalytic theory was very much an individual-psychology approach. In his 1921 *Group Psychology and the Analysis of the Ego* he confronts the problem that, regardless of all individual ego-centered psychological processes his research has uncovered, there is still a challenge "to explain the surprising fact that under a certain condition this individual...thought, felt, and acted in quite a different way from what would have been expected. And this condition is his insertion into a collection of people which has acquired the characteristics of a 'psychological group'" (1960:6).

Freud begins his investigation by extensively citing Le Bon on the features of psychological groups. He then suggests that a straight-forward psychoanalytic interpretation would have it that within the group, the individual is allowed "to throw off the repressions of his unconscious instinctual impulses," such that the supposedly unique nature of the group would be nothing more than "manifestations of this unconscious, in which all that is evil in the human mind is contained as a predisposition" (9). However, he quickly finds this solution inadequate; something must be added to the individual, interior view of behavior.

His solution is a wily combination of a familiar psychoanalytic idea and a new one. Freud's theory in all its permutations is a theory of drives and energy, in particular the energy he called *libido*. In his early formulations this was merely sexual energy, but in later versions it became a more general life force or integrative energy — the energy that binds or *cathects* one part of the self to another and subsequently the self to its 'objects' (including other people). It is, in a certain real sense, 'love' (and so he uses the term *eros* to describe it, as opposed to the disintegrative or death instinct he calls *thanatos*). Libido, eros, or love being such a powerful force, Freud ventures to "try our fortune, then, with the supposition that love relationships (or, to use a more neutral expression, emotional ties) also constitute the essence of the group mind" (31).

Two specific processes function in the Freudian love relationship — identification and idealization. In identification, the individual not only attaches emotionally to an object but literally internalizes the object as part of the self "by means of introjection of the object into the ego" (49). At an extreme, the object takes the place of the ego: "a considerable amount of narcissistic libido flows onto the object" (56). One consequence of this high valuation of the loved object is idealization. "We love it on account of the perfections which we have striven to reach for our own ego, and which we should now like to procure in this roundabout way as a means of satisfying our narcissism" (56).

These are the mechanisms that Freud uses to explain group psychology. The bond between the individual and the group is a variation or substitution for the bond between one individual and another. The group serves as a surrogate object, and the individual 'loves' the group and its members. Even more, an idealization takes place, in which the group is conferred with wonderful qualities, perhaps perfection itself, and absorbed as the ideal and identity of the self; however, since this is done collectively and mutually, it is stronger than any ordinary love. Freud concludes, "A primary group of this kind is a number of individuals who have put one and the same object in place of their ego ideal and have consequently identified themselves with one another in their ego" (61). In a way, the members are in a mutual hypnotic state, for in both there is "the same humble subjection, the same compliance, the same absence of criticism" (58). The group is the hypnotic relationship writ large, and "the hypnotic relation is...a group formation with two members" (59).

But there is one additional crucial piece, for the group has a feature that no love relationship or hypnotic trance has — a leader. The leader not only practically speaking directs the group but represents it, personifying it and its perfections. The group member is bound emotionally and energetically to each other member (perhaps only conceptually, since he or she may never meet all of the members) but is bound to the leader with especial intensity. Reciprocally, the leader is bound to or loves the member and all members equally — or so the illusion of the group suggests. It may be and probably is an illusion (since the leader cannot know all members either), but Freud maintains that "Everything depends on this illusion" (33).

Thus, of all identifications and idealizations, the leader is the object of the greatest identification and idealization. The leader evinces the perfection that the group and its members seek, often giving rise to a cult of personality. In the extreme case, the leader supplants both the individual's self and the group as the ego-ideal of the members. One interesting effect of this idealization and idolization of the group and its leader is the outward direction of any negative feelings. Freud always admits that humans have ambivalent emotions (love/hate) in all relationships, but the negative or critical feelings are particularly inappropriate and unwelcome here. Within groups, negative attitudes toward other members are minimized or denied, resulting in narcissism toward the group and aversion or hostility toward outsiders. Such groups tend to overlook the failings of their own while being intolerant or "hard and unloving to those who do not belong to it.... [C]ruelty and intolerance toward those who do not belong to it are natural" (39).

One other phenomenon follows from this analysis. If the individual is not only tied to but identified with this group and its leader, then it makes sense that the loss of the group or leader would be a difficult and devastating development. It would be like losing a lover — or like losing a self. Without the leader the group could unravel, and without the group the individual could unravel. This is why, Freud asserts, "A panic arises if a group of that kind becomes disintegrated" (35). This is perhaps also why it is so difficult to detach a member from such a group — in the case of religion to 'deconvert' him or her. Leaving a group that one has identified with and idealized is much more than changing one's opinions; it is like — *it is* — breaking an emotional bond and tearing out a piece of oneself.

Elias Canetti: Crowds of Power, Power of Crowds

If there is anything that has surfaced from the previous portrayals of groups and crowds, it is that such collectivities are less about truth than about power. In fact, all of our authors agree either that groups are prone to error or that correctness is beside the point to them. Groups and crowds are about feeling and doing, not thinking.

Elias Canetti, in his *Crowds and Power*, elaborates on the types of crowds and on their desires and goals. In his opinion, such multi-person structures have two main aspirations, which are intimately related: to be dense and compact and to grow. Density means that body is pressed against body and mind against mind in a solid and impermeable front; within the group's collective body, the individual cannot be touched. And once a group or crowd comes into existence, "it wants to consist of *more* people: the urge to grow is the first and supreme attribute of the crowd. It wants to seize everyone within reach; anything shaped like a human being can join it" (1963:16). He refers to such a grouping as an "open crowd," which, in its aggressive growth stage, accepts no limits or boundaries: everyone can (and should?) belong.

An open crowd can reverse, diminish, and disintegrate, and arguably most do. However, if it survives and reaches a certain stage of growth, it can transform into a 'closed crowd.' The closed crowd has achieved 'maturity' or stability; it "renounces growth and puts the stress on permanence. The first thing to be noticed about it is that it has a boundary. It establishes itself by accepting its limitation. It creates a space for itself which it will fill" (17). It has become, as we noted in Chapter 4, a new establishment, a new orthodoxy. Preservation and institutionalization replace expansion.

The key to crowd formation, Canetti writes, is "discharge." Before discharge, "the crowd does not actually exist; it is the discharge which creates it. This is the moment when all who belong to the crowd get rid of their differences and feel equal" (17). Within the group, social distinctions disappear: every member is an equal, all "brothers and sisters," a true "family." But of course this liminal undifferentiated state cannot last forever. Rules will eventually settle, institutions will form, orthodoxies will appear, and then the seeds of a new order — what Canetti calls "crowd crystals" — form.

One factor that Canetti emphasizes as holding the group together is its destructiveness. Groups particularly enjoy breaking fragile objects and boundary objects (like windows, doors, walls, and such). However, they will happily destroy more permanent things—buildings, statues, entire cities (think of the Taliban destruction of the enormous Buddhas sculpted into the mountains of Afghanistan), precisely because these materials represent permanence and the old order. The new must smash the old, as well as any boundaries that threaten to hem it in.

ATHEISM ADVANCED

Eric Hoffer, who wrote specifically about mass movements, stated that a dynamic popular movement "can rise and spread without belief in a God, but never without belief in a devil" (1966:86). By this he did not mean an actual religious conception of a devil but rather an *enemy*. Canetti agrees when he claims that one of the central features of a crowd "is the feeling of being persecuted, a peculiar angry sensitiveness and irritability directed against those it has once and forever nominated as enemies" (22). Unfortunately, the group can find enemies on the outside as well as the inside, the internal ones — the traitors, the apostates, even the merely mildly interested — being the most threatening. The group feels and acts "like a besieged city and, as in many sieges, it has enemies before its walls and enemies within them" (23). *Defensiveness* is a crucial attribute of, and excuse for, aggressive group behavior, and nothing that is done out of self-defense is altogether wrong.

Canetti stresses the role of opposition in creating and maintaining the group: "The surest, and often the only, way by which a crowd can preserve itself lies in the existence of a second crowd to which it is related" — and of course opposed (63). The sheer knowledge — indeed, the sheer imagination — that there is an opposing group can secure the group's boundaries and enflame its passions. Specific ideas or prejudices about the other can enhance the process. Direct conflict, rather than a failure of or threat to the group, can be its greatest success and strength. In fact, Canetti suggests that war "is primarily the eruption of two crowds" (72). At this point, everyone *in* the group must be *for* the group; it can tolerate no dissension, for to dissent is to abet the enemy. Inside the group is safety, happiness, and truth; outside "everything [is] death," evil, inhumanity, un-civilization (72).

There are two other qualities that a successful long-lasting group needs. One is a core of dedicated, even fanatical members. This is what Canetti called the "crowd crystals," the men and women around whom the group forms, its leaders or inspirational figures (of course, such crystallizing figures need not be alive, as in Jesus and Paul or Muhammad or the Buddha). Crowd crystals are "the small, rigid groups of men, strictly delimited and of great constancy, which serve to precipitate crowds" (73). It is the inner circle, the elite, the avant-garde (in Lenin's terms) who mobilize and direct the group. Its composition changes slightly and slowly if at all, and its members "are trained in both action and faith" (73); they are the true believers. They must show absolute confidence in the truth and goodness of their group, in their own ability and knowledge, and in the ultimate success of the group.

The second mandatory quality of a winning group is a *goal.* What exactly does it want, what is its reason for being? If having no goal is death to a group, having too easy or accessible a goal is little better. As Hoffer once again realized, a movement "with a concrete, limited objective is likely to have a shorter active phase than a movement with a nebulous, indefinite objective" because it will attain its goal and have no further reason to aggregate. However, when the objective is indefinite, remote, or even impossible — like "an ideal society of perfect unity and selflessness" or of course something like "heaven" or the "kingdom of god" — "the active phase is without an automatic end" (142). With what Canetti calls such "invisible goals," the movement and the group will never end, will never achieve satisfaction or success, but will be kept striving eternally.

Finally, the leadership and the objective unite in the *command.* This is why groups of the sort identified by Mackay and Le Bon and Freud and Hoffer require a rule and a rule-giver, and the people await one — in fact, they are not a people at all until they receive one.

A command addressed to a large number of people thus has a very special character. It is intended to make a crowd of them and, as far as it succeeds in this, it does not arouse fear. The slogan of a demagogue, impelling people in a certain direction, has exactly the same function; it can be regarded as a command addressed to large numbers. From the point of view of the crowd, which wants to come into existence quickly and to maintain itself as a unit, such slogans are useful and indeed indispensable. The art of a speaker consists in compressing all his aims into slogans. By hammering them home he then engenders a crowd and helps to keep it in existence. He creates the crowd and keeps it alive by a comprehensive command from above. Once he has achieved this it scarcely matters what he demands. A speaker can insult and threaten an assemblage of people in the most terrible way and they will still love him if, by doing so, he succeeds in forming them into a crowd (311).

ATHEISM ADVANCED

The implications of this discovery for the discussion of language in Chapter 2 should be apparent; the implications for morality will be explored in Chapter 10, and the implications for atheism will be the final topic in this chapter.

Gordon Allport: The Prejudice of Groups

It has been by now securely established that groups are unusually prone to exclusionary, rigid, intolerant, even hostile us-*versus*-them thinking and acting. According to the highly-regarded psychologist Gordon Allport, the common phenomenon of prejudice — negative opinions or behavior toward others unlike ourselves — is essentially a group occurrence. It is based on false generalization and antagonism, which admittedly "are natural and common capacities of the human mind" (1979:17). But the specific shape and direction, and ferocity, of prejudices is rooted in groups; he defines prejudice as "an avertive or hostile attitude toward a person who belongs to a group, simply because he belongs to that group, and is therefore presumed to have the objective qualities ascribed to the group" (7).

The most natural thing for humans is to organize into collectivities, social assemblages or factions of some kind or another (families, clubs, parties, congregations, societies, nations, *etc.*); it is also natural for human groups to avoid each other. "Everywhere on earth," Allport writes, "we find a condition of separateness of groups" (17). From this separateness follow erroneous opinions about members of other groups and, often enough, genuine conflicts of interest with them (as well as, more than occasionally, imaginary conflicts too). But groups have more than interest; they also have identity. The group to which an individual belongs has been dubbed by psychologists and sociologists the individual's "in-group," and Allport explains that "in-groups are psychologically primary. We live in them, by them, and, sometimes, for them. Hostility toward out-groups helps strengthen our sense of belonging" (42).

In other words, the role of rivalry and animosity for groups is not accidental or peripheral but critical and central. It clearly marks the group (*versus* other groups), sets its boundaries, defends those boundaries, and mobilizes its members in that defense. It is, in short, good for group solidarity:

Allport reminds us that "A nation is never so cohesive as in wartime" (148). In such times, the perfection of the group is emphasized, and loyalty to the group is demanded; disloyalty or acknowledgement of imperfection tends to weaken the "war effort." Scapegoating and demonization of the other — a type of rationalization — escalates. It is not surprising that a group that can keep its members at such a high level of alertness is particularly effective; inter-group prejudice and hostility has "survival value" (293).

Allport makes two other observations that are worth our attention. The first is that the degree of antagonism between groups is not directly related to the degree of *difference* between them. Rather, in what he calls the "narcissism of small differences" (371), it may be little things that separate yet irritate the groups, and it is usually nearby instead of remote groups that raise their ire (this might explain why religious sects tend to spew more venom on other sects of the same religion than on foreign religions or even atheists). The second is his description of the prejudiced personality, which is in a word and by definition intolerant. He finds that the prejudiced mind is also characterized by ambivalence toward parents, moralism, dichotomization or dualistic thinking (see Chapter 9), a need for certainty, externalization of conflict, institutionalism, and authoritarianism (397). He pronounces:

> Prejudiced people demand clear-cut structure in their world, even if it is a narrow and inadequate structure. Where there is no order, they impose it. When new solutions are called for they cling to tried and tested habits. Wherever possible they latch onto what is familiar, safe, simple, definite (403).

In other words, they are conservative and traditionalist.

The Religiosity of Groups, the Groupness of Religions

It is plain to see that our scholars of human collective behavior have little good to say about it. People in groups — even more so than the same people individually — are prone to irrationality, emotionality, irritability, intolerance, and hostility. Some observers, like Le Bon, have explicitly noted the similarity between group psychology and behavior in general and religion in particular: all serious groups, he assessed, have something of a religious nature. What is important for us to realize now is that all religions, contrary to what James believes, have something of a group nature. It is important for us to realize that this is not a good thing for humanity.

Religion is eminently and irredeemably social and collective, and to insist otherwise is stubborn and/or political. Yes, religions are composed of individuals, but so are all groups, so the point is trivially true. But a religion is no more merely individuals than a group or crowd is; it is not nothing more than the sum of the individual strengths and weaknesses, capacities and incapacities, of the members. (This is one area where the psychologistic theories of Boyer and Atran fall short). The religious group, like all groups, has its own unpredicted emergent qualities, and even more; the group not only brings out but *puts in* many of the mental and social characteristics of the member. Religion instills beliefs, values, and behaviors in individuals; it turns them into particular kinds of individuals, it is *formative* of them, to a greater or lesser extent, *as* individuals.

Religion is unquestioningly group-oriented in a number of interlocking ways. First, to follow Durkheim, religion is communal, it is a property of a community (in both senses of the word 'property': as a possession and as a trait). The theme of *The Elementary Forms of the Religious Life* is posited early in the book, where he states that "religion is something eminently social. Religious representations are collective representations which express collective realities" (1965:22). Later he reminds us that individuals do not make religions; groups do. Religious beliefs

> are always common to a determined group, which makes profession of adhering to them and of practicing the rites connected with them.... [T]hey are something belonging to the group, and they make its unity. The individuals which compose it feel themselves united to each other by the simple fact that they have a common faith (59).

Such a united group he refers to as a "church."

Atheism In Solitude

For most of the religions that ever existed in the history of humanity, religion and the community were one, and the "church" (an unfortunate choice of term) was the entire society. The Yanomamo society had its religion, the Warlpiri society had its religion, the Ainu society had its religion, and so on. The community or society was more or less natural or authentic rather than voluntary, and so was its religion. That is to say, the collectivity was a 'moral community' in the Durkheimian sense even without the religion — they were bound together by ties of blood and marriage and neighborhood and exchange and history — but the religion added a further dimension to that bond. Community and identity became not just natural and moral (in the sense of sentimental) but supernatural and *moral* (in the sense of rules and obligations).

Second, every religion that has ever existed has been, if not hierarchical, then at least *organized* (accordingly, the common distinction between 'organized religion' and something else — whatever that might be — is false). The organization of a religion may vary from a few specialist roles, like the shaman or diviner, to an ordained priesthood with an international papacy at the top, but there are always social differentiations within it. That the social organization of a religion mirrors the social organization of the mundane society is easy to see: societies that are egalitarian and uncentralized have egalitarian and uncentralized religions, while societies with stratified classes and central governments have stratified and centralized religions (including layers of formal and politically-powerful priests and a god who is like a king or dictator). If society is organized into clans, then there are clan spirits. If society is organized into villages, then there are village spirits. As Durkheim appreciated, religion is thus a reflection, a symbolic representation, of the structure of society; in a sense, religion is the group's symbolic awareness of its social existence.

Third and maybe most critically, religion is something that must be learned by the individual and transmitted by the group. As we have stressed here and elsewhere, human beings are not born with a religion. If they were, we would either expect to find all humans having the same religion or baby Buddhists popping up in Christian countries and baby Christians popping up in Buddhist countries. We see neither. Rather, people tend quite predictably to acquire the religion that is available to them in their social environment.

Now, as you will recall, our modular approach to religion held that humans are born with a set of mental and social modules that lead to or produce religion, but this is not the same thing as saying that humans are born with religion. Similarly, humans may be born with a set of linguistic and cognitive modules that lead to language, but that is not the same thing as being born with language. We have the capacity to acquire or produce language, but we can acquire or produce any actual or potential language. Likewise with religion: if we have a 'religion-acquisition device' in our brain, we can still acquire or conceive any actual or potential religion.

But the alleged "animist" inclinations that Boyer and Atran and Bloom mention — the inclinations to attribute agency to the non-human world — do not lead smoothly and inevitably to religion. As Graham Harvey (2006) finds, in his recent study of animism, young humans have a proclivity to attribute thought and feeling to nature but it is adult humans who carefully and thoroughly groom that proclivity in certain directions to cultivate it into religion. Thus, religious adults are *more* animistic than children, who might either grow out of it or grow it into something other than an orthodox religion, like perhaps 'deep environmentalism.'

Therefore, religion is absolutely, undeniably about training individuals to adopt a group's beliefs and doctrines. It is inculcation, indoctrination, initiation into a believing community and a belief tradition. It must and does exist prior to the individual and will exist after the individual is gone. Religious individuals believe what they are taught to believe, do what they are taught to do, feel what they are taught to feel. The preposterousness of James' argument that religion is solitary is illustrated strenuously in the gargantuan effort that a religious community has to make to recruit and retain members. They do not leave it to chance or to the whims and private musings of the individual. Why else church schools, catechisms, incessant retellings of the myths, and incessant re-enactings of the rituals of the group? Why else obligatory regular (weekly or more often) gatherings and obligatory annual holidays? The religious group cannot even stop at indoctrination of youths but must continually refresh the inculcation and internalization of religious identity throughout life — sending them on missions, requiring them to confess or otherwise perform, and forcing them to accept religion in many or all of their major life events (like marriage or death), to name just a few.

Fourth, religion gives members things to do together. It is extremely important for us to remember that religion, or any other group identity or ideology, is not exclusively about doctrines but actions. People must do something, and they must do something *together*, as a congregation. An obvious component of religious action is ritual, but it is hardly the only component (we will return to ritual below). Religious groups ask much more of the member, in both formal and informal ways. Everyone knows that one of the attractions of a religion is friendship, camaraderie, community. 'Fellowship' is an explicit key to Christian practice — and frankly it does not matter what they are fellowshipping about. As we will investigate in Chapter 9, and as we are all familiar, religious groups provide much more than simply religious functions; they are places to eat, talk, sing, dance (depending on the sect), sew, bowl, play bingo, as well as to get childcare, healthcare, and counseling. They are opportunities, in other words, to socialize.

Fifth and finally, it is vital for us to understand, as we said in Chapter 3, that religion is fundamentally social in the sense that it posits a social relationship between humans and the non-human entities of religion. The whole point of religion in all its guises, we determined, was the socialization of the non-human world, such that humans are in relationships of exchange, dependence, and kinship with non-human beings and/or forces. (This is why Christians often say that their religion is not a religion at all but a "relationship with Jesus." Of course that's true: every religion is a relationship with its putative beings and/or forces, and 'religion' is always what some other group is doing.) The problem is that humans do not spontaneously discover these putative beings and/or forces. As in our third point above, they must be instructed as to which beings and/or forces exist and what their particular qualities are; that is the content of religious instruction. Once the individual has been so in-*structed* (*i.e.*, had the religious structures internalized through training), it is safe to leave the member in solitude, *but not before*. Once the individual is transformed into the-kind-of-individual-who-believes-this, then the individual is predetermined to have certain kinds of experiences or to interpret experiences in certain ways ("if I hear a voice, it must be God").

The power of religious predetermination cannot be overemphasized. We tend to see the process at its end, when people believe things and have experiences that confirm their beliefs. However, these beliefs must be implanted by energetic efforts over years or decades. Until that is accomplished, religions do not want people spending too much time alone, and for heaven's sake do not want them improvising. As Pink Floyd sang in their ominous "Welcome to the Machine," "What did you dream? It's alright, we told you what to dream." And this is literally so, even in the cases of individualistic religious practices like the 'vision quest.' Surely, the person is expected to go alone and have a private vision, but the person has been so thoroughly prepared by growing up in a society that has vision quests and talks about vision quests and interprets vision quests that *he ultimately has a completely conventional private vision*. As we will say in Chapter 9, he and everyone in his society has a typical experience that is repeated again and again as 'personal experience.'

There is one other remarkable implication of the internalization of communal, conventional religious concepts. In a serious sense, *the religious person is never alone, even when he or she is apart from the crowd*. Since the religious world is peopled with beings and/or forces, the human who lives in a religious world is in constant, or at least potentially constant, communion with them.

So, James' opinion about religion in solitude is not only false in that religion is always corporate and traditional and predetermined but in that the situation he describes — where the religious individual is alone and free to experience whatever he or she might experience — never actually happens. All religious persons take their religion with them into that solitude; why would it be a surprise that they find it there?

Ritual: Group Behavior, Individual Transformation

Even mere marching can serve as a unifier.
—Eric Hoffer, *The True Believer*

In this section we want to focus briefly on a religious behavior *par excellence* — ritual. Much has been said and written about it, and everyone seems to agree on its importance. But few seem to understand where its importance lies. Some say in the doctrines and beliefs that it enacts; others in the meaning or symbolism it deploys. But a rare and recent few suggest that the significance of ritual is not what the ritualist is doing but simply *that he or she is doing it*. What follows then is a reconsideration of this central religious concept, as part of our reconsideration of such religious concepts as myth and morality (Chapter 10), belief (Chapter 11), and previously of theism (Chapter 1), religious language (Chapter 2), and religion itself (Chapter 3).

Ritual seems like a self-evident term: it is religious activity, usually formulaic and repetitive and almost necessarily communal. Religious people gather to do rituals. Thomas Barfield defines it as "prescribed, formal acts that take place in the context of religious worship" (1997:410), although 'worship' is a religious term that we should be careful about.

Roy Rappaport thinks of it as "the performance of more or less invariant sequences of formal acts and utterances not encoded by the performers" (1992:249). That ritual is prescribed and not encoded by the individuals who do it indicates that it is prescribed or encoded *by somebody or something else* and therefore that it is not a completely voluntary or private act. Furthermore, it is *interaction*, whether that interaction takes place between humans, between humans and objects, and between humans and non-human beings and/or forces.

Victor Turner, one of the great anthropologists of ritual, suggested that ritual is nothing less than "a periodic statement of the terms in which men of a particular culture must interact if there is to be any kind of a coherent social life" (1981:6). Ritual then may constitute the very possibility of a social group of humans.

ATHEISM ADVANCED

Despite the obvious importance and near-universality of religious ritual, Western culture and Christianity — especially Protestant Christianity — have shown a propensity to disparage and trivialize ritual. Catherine Bell, in her major study of ritual, reminds us that "theoretical descriptions of ritual" — and not only theoretical but often theological and popular descriptions —

> generally regard it as action and thus automatically distinguish it from the conceptual aspects of religion, such as beliefs, symbols, and myths.... Ritual is then described as particularly *thoughtless* action — routinized, habitual, obsessive, or mimetic — and therefore the purely formal, secondary, and mere physical expression of logically prior ideas (1992:19).

That would be on a good day. On a bad day, observers have been inclined to regard ritual as action without ideas or beliefs at all. People can engage in behavior, they might say, without any understanding of, agreement with, or commitment to the ideas and concepts behind it whatsoever. Action is empty and rote; only belief counts. That is of course a wonderfully Western and Christian (and especially Protestant) notion but not one that is shared with all religions, even with Catholic Christianity. Even Protestants themselves have not eliminated ritual; they just demand more, much more.

At any rate, let us establish immediately that ritual is neither unique nor universal to religions. There are religions (like Protestant Christianity) that are less ritualistic, and religions that are more ritualistic. More crucially, like violence and other religious behaviors, there is religious ritual and there is non-religious ritual. Religious ritual is a subset of the much larger set of rituals: there are rituals for high school graduation, for the inauguration of presidents or the coronation of kings, for initiation into clubs and fraternities, or for washing one's hands (which we usually discredit as obsessive or compulsive behavior, but where is the real difference between lighting candles or praying fervently and washing your hands fervently?). In fact, unlike most of the other aspects of religion, ritual is not even a uniquely *human* phenomenon. All manner of animals engage in ritualistic behavior, especially in the areas of fighting, feeding, and mating. 'Ritualization,' as it is sometimes more generally termed, is a style of behavior, not any particular action, let alone a necessarily religious action.

A ritual — religious or mundane, human or animal — stands out from other behavior through its stereotyped, exaggerated, repetitive quality; it is precisely *not* individualistic activity. Ritual behavior is behavior that the individual produces *because he or she has to*, whether that compulsion comes from instinct (in animals) or instruction (in humans). In both cases, the common element is the desire, first, to communicate something and, second, to elicit some response. Without getting too graphic, when an animal exhibits ritual surrendering behavior, it wants the rival to stop the fight; when a male animal exhibits ritual mating behavior, he wants the female to submit to sexual contact and literally assume the position. So there is communication after a fashion, but it is not so much communication of facts or concepts as of desires and desired responses.

When humans perform rituals, the same is true. Ritual communication is ordinarily not about factual states of affairs like 'Today is Wednesday' or 'The earth is round.' Rather it is communication — if that word even serves any longer — about human intentions and hoped-for outcomes. In secular rituals we can fairly guarantee the outcomes, since the rituals are mostly 'performatives' like the linguistic performatives we discussed in Chapter 2. That is, if we want to get married, or if we want to conduct a marriage, the ritual does the trick; the marriage ritual *is* conducting a marriage. Similarly, a graduation ceremony really does graduate people, and an initiation ceremony really does initiate people. Ritual action, in such cases, is *effective*.

Religious ritual is no different, with the disclaimer that we humans cannot quite guarantee its successful outcome. In other words, religious ritual is communicative interaction with religious partners, by which we typically mean the entities (beings and/or forces) of religion. But we are not telling these entities anything that they do not already know, nor are we communicating particularly clearly. If I wanted the entities to know that the earth is round, I could say it plainly, and if I wanted the entities to give me health and long life, I could ask it straight out. Instead, humans employ all sorts of 'symbolic' (by which we mean 'obscure' or 'false') means to state their business. But what is their business? It is to express their desire for some state of affairs (long life, health, fertility, relief of sins and what not) and to incline the entities to do their part to bring this state of affairs into reality. It is, to be indelicate, exactly like rolling over on the ground to expose one's belly or displaying one's plumage and hoping that the partner will turn around (one way or the other!). If religious ritual is yet more stereotyped, exaggerated, and repetitive than mundane ritual, it is only because the stakes of the communication are higher and the differences between the partners (human and non-human) are greater.

So, three things have emerged as true: (1) ritual is *performance*, which means that it is thoroughly social, (2) ritual is *communication* but not in the ordinary propositional sense of transmitting data, and (3) ritual is *effective*, or ideally so, since its purpose is to realize certain desired conditions. The one thing it is *not* is private or individual, and it cannot be solitary without being pointless and ineffective: somebody has to witness or receive it, and this other party must know and understand it too. Now, to say that ritual is effective is not to say that one gets everything that one expresses in a ritual wish. However, even 'false' ritual can have and regularly does have two other, equally significant kinds of effect. They are *personal* (*i.e.*, on the individual) and *collective* (*i.e.*, on the group or its institutions, that is to say *political*).

The political efficacy of rituals is too vast a topic to consider here, and it is probably secondary to the individual, psychological efficacy, so let us focus on that. Sensitive students of religious ritual have agreed that ritual is not so much an *expression* of inner individual qualities as an *impression* upon or into the individual of outer collective qualities. Thus, rituals *in-form* or *in-struct* the individual, but not in the sense of information or data but in the sense of *form* or shape — literally introducing form or structure into individuals, making them into a particular kind of person, a person who believes and feels and behaves in particular ways, a person who has certain Geertzian "moods and motivations," and thereby a person who is a good member of the collective.

Durkheim was the most ardent advocate of the psychological power of ritual. For him, again, religious notions are collective notions; no individual comes up with his or her own 'in solitude.' Rather, religion is activated for the individual in the gathering of the group; in religious assemblies we are "animated by a common passion, we become susceptible of acts and sentiments of which we are incapable when reduced to our own forces" (240). And for him, the key to the efficacy of religion and religious gathering is ritual activity; during ritual,

> everything changes.... The very fact of concentration acts as an exceptionally powerful stimulant. When they are once come together, a sort of electricity is formed by their collecting which quickly transports them to an extraordinary degree of exaltation. Every sentiment expressed finds a place without resistance in all the minds, which are very open to outside impressions; each re-echoes the others, and is re-echoed by the others. The impulse thus proceeds, growing as it goes, as an avalanche grows in its advance (247).

This collective emotional experience Durkheim dubbed "effervescence," and it is the psychological condition in which human beings are open to suggestion and to internalizing that suggestion most deeply. So, almost a decade before Freud wrote his study of group psychology, Durkheim had likened the relation between the individual and the religious group as a "hypnotic" one.

Durkheim is undoubtedly correct, with two important warnings. First, not all rituals are equally ecstatic, and, as we will see in a moment, ecstasy and intense emotionality are not critical to the ritual function. Second, he overestimates the efficacy of the *specific* ritual moment; his theory of ritual is, as my graduate advisor used to say, too "muscular." The moment of performance of ritual cannot achieve all of these ends by itself; in fact, if you were to set a person down at a ritual in a foreign culture or religion, he or she would either have the 'wrong' experience or no experience at all. Rather, as we mentioned above, the ritual moment must be prepared and predetermined. That is to say, long before and many times outside the ritual, people talk about the ritual, remember the ritual, interpret the ritual, sometimes even rehearse the ritual. Members are given plenty of opportunity to prepare themselves for the ritual and are specifically prepared to expect certain events and certain experiences in the ritual. When the ritual moment comes, all of that preparation leads, not inevitably but ordinarily, to the 'correct' individual/psychological outcome.

From this view, rituals (and religions in general) are not so much meaningful or informative as *creative or transformative*; Victor Turner says as much when he notes that the central function of ritual

> is its creative function — it actually creates, or re-creates, the categories through which men perceive reality — the axioms underlying the structure of society and the laws of the natural and moral order. It is not here a case of life being an imitation of art, but of social life being an attempted imitation of models portrayed and animated by ritual (1981:7).

In fact, as we all know well, there may be little or no information transmitted by ritual or religion and even less received by the individual members. Most religious individuals have only a passing and fragmentary notion of the beliefs or doctrines of their religion; in many religions, it is not even the job of the average member to know much or do much about religion, which is left to the experts. This is why Frits Staal, in his influential and aptly-named essay "The Meaninglessness of Ritual," argued that ritual (and arguably all of religion) is not about information or belief or meaning but about *rules* or even more about sheer *doing*: the rule is 'Do this' As he asserts, "Ritual, then, is primarily activity. It is an activity governed by explicit rules. The important thing is what you do, not what you think, believe, or say" (1979:4).

That ritual is "pure activity" which "is performed for its own sake" (10) makes it sound trivial, even contemptible, to us. However, as Hoffer and others have discovered, action-for-action's-sake can be very important and effective. Action, especially collective action, of any kind is "a unifier" (1966:120). The behavior need not be profound or even meaningful to the performers; the key components of such behavior are that *they are doing it, they are doing it together, and they are doing it because they were told to do it.* Thus, whether it is marching in the streets (as Hoffer mentioned in the quotation to introduce this section), collecting toys for tots, or fighting a war against an enemy, the point of collective action is *collectivity* and *activity*.

Additionally, people who are brought into unity are brought into *uniformity*, often literally with uniforms, and uniformity entails the loss of individuality and the susceptibility to group sentiments and group doctrines that all groups — religious and otherwise — depend upon. As Hoffer puts it, collective action of any sort at all has the ability "to strip its followers of their distinct individuality and render them more soluble in the collective medium" (121). "There is," he finds, "less individual distinctness in the genuine man of action... than in the thinker or in one whose creativeness flows from communion with the self... An active people thus tends toward uniformity" (120). The Nazis discovered the power of mindless corporate activity, including the aforementioned marching; as Hoffer quotes Hermann Rauschning, "Marching diverts men's thoughts. Marching kills thoughts. Marching makes an end of individuality" (121). So we should be rightly suspicious of any organization that holds too many marches.

Why, then, ritual or any other corporate behavior? Ask religionists why they do it and they will answer, "Because it works." Ask non-religionists why the religionists do it and they will answer, "Because that's what religionists are supposed to do." Both would agree deep down that people do rituals because they have been told to do them, either by a leader like a priest or by their supernatural authority, their god. Ritual, other than obsessive-compulsive disorder or a personal superstition, is never an individual thing — individual in motivation or individual in meaning. If no one ever told Christians to celebrate Christmas, they never would.

The fact that ritual is meaningless, concludes Staal, is not its weakness but its strength. Things that are done meaningfully can be understood, analyzed, and criticized. Things that are done meaninglessly can only be technical, even mechanical, even obsessive: since we are not sure what we are doing, why we are doing it, or whether it is successful, we must attend to the minutiae of it, make sure we are conforming to the correct traditional or authoritative details of it, and usually do it over and over again. As Staal comically puts it,

> If I detect a mistake in cooking or calculating, I perceive the result and understand the reason. But if I make a ritual mistake, I don't notice any difference and don't see any reason. I am not even sure whether I made a mistake or not, and there is no way to determine it. It is like being in a foreign culture where strange things happen and it is not clear whether one has made a *faux pas* (12).

263

Indeed and quite literally, if one is doing a ritual that involves uttering chants in an arcane ritual language or performing weird inexplicable actions, then one cannot understand the ritual; one can only attend carefully to the mechanics of it to assure that one is doing it 'right' (that is, *how one was taught to do it*). Or to be blunter, the point of the ritual is doing the ritual. The action is its own reason; it is a necessity, even a command. No wonder the Nike slogan is "Just do it."

Groups without Reason, Reason without Groups

"[I]t remains a fact, indeed, that great decisions in the realm of thought and momentous discoveries and solutions of problems are only possible to an individual working in solitude"
—Freud, *Group Psychology and the Analysis of the Ego*

If groups tend to be irrational, then rational people might tend to be averse to groups. And if religions are fundamentally groups, then non-religious people might be fundamentally anti-group or at least not joiners. Is this merely a recurring personality trait, or is there something more going on here?

As we suggested at the top of the chapter, there is nothing about atheism that prevents it from founding groups; it is not misanthropy or anarchy. In fact, two things are true: there *are* atheist groups out there, and atheists are human beings. Human beings are social creatures, and they cannot help but seek and enjoy the company of others like themselves. Atheists gather in atheist groups and in non-atheist groups — bowling leagues, book clubs, and concert audiences.

All the same, that atheists are congenitally a bit suspicious of groups may be a logical, even unfortunately necessary or salutary, thing. Atheism does not force or command atheist individuals to be solitary. *But solitude may be a contributing condition to being an atheist.* Our entire analysis in this chapter has led us to conclude that groups are not conducive to thinking, let alone to thinking rationally and, even more so, thinking *originally*, thinking non-conventionally. Groups seem quickly to progress (or regress) to convention, to structure, to leadership and orthodoxy. Atheists are if anything, certainly in the present world, unconventional and unorthodox in their thinking; maybe they must also be somewhat unstructured and leaderless. Whether this is just a learned response and aversion to *religious* structure and leadership, or whether it is a real and essential freedom from structures and leaders, I have not determined. The one thing I know is that there is no such thing — conceptually there *can be no such thing* — as a 'free believer' but there can be no other kind of thinker than a 'free thinker.'

Personally, I get pleasure from the association with other human beings — well, certain human beings and in relatively small doses — but I would describe myself as "not a group kind of guy." More importantly, I find that I do most of my best thinking not only when I am alone but when I am quiet. Indeed, thinking is not just a private but a serene activity. To reformulate James' opening definition, thought or reason may be the acts and experiences of individual humans in their solitude, so far as they apprehend themselves to stand in relation to the facts of reality.

Believing inescapably involves and requires the group; beliefs are things learned and inherited by the individual, not created by the individual. Believing depends for its very existence on the group: its source and their sustenance is the group. But through this dependence, it exposes itself to all of the vices of the group — the irrationality, the irritability, the intolerance and rigidity, the excess and violence. Beliefs, even religions, do not of necessity have these qualities, but too frequently — and the more formal the group and the doctrine, the more likely — they do.

Atheists may be irritable at times (and not without reason), perhaps even a little rigid and excessive and malicious. These are qualities that abide in humans, and we are humans. However, as we have seen, groups accentuate the negative in humans and offer comparatively little positive. Presumably, irritable, rigid, excessive individual atheists would be even more so in groups, plus all of the undesirable emergent properties of the groups themselves — the 'group psychology' that is added to whatever individual psychology already exists.

ATHEISM ADVANCED

So we atheists may have to reconcile ourselves to the reality that we are not the group type and that atheism is not a thing to group around. If groups are as counterproductive to human rationality and decency, and as productive of conventionality and extremism, as we have surveyed, individual atheists and the philosophy of atheism may be safer without them. Thus, the possibility or identity of atheism may actually be an obstacle to group formation and group action, yet without corporate organization, we are threatened to remain a peripheral and puny force in contemporary culture. It is a paradox: our greatest strength — our ability to bear or to seek solitude, to think alone, to reason our way through the veils of irrationality, delusion, and belief that groups produce and perpetuate — is also our greatest weakness. Perhaps the best we can hope is to organize our groups and to function through them, but, paradoxically, never identify with or idealize them too much, and definitely never 'believe in' them.

Chapter 8

Religion and the
Colonization of Experience

When Christian missionaries penetrated the South African kingdom of Tshidi in the early nineteenth century, they did not convert the natives by debate and theological teaching. In fact, as John and Jean Comaroff describe in their historical studies of missionization in Africa, the missionaries were disturbed by the "widespread indifference that met their theological disquisitions" (1991:8). Other historians of conversion echo the same message: non-Christians hearing the Christian message for the first time often found the new religion uninteresting or incomprehensible. And why not? The native society always had its own religion, and at least initially the native society was frequently strong and well-integrated. The missionaries were usually few, weak, and strange. And above all else, as we introduced in Chapter 2, the new religion spoke a language — not just English but 'Christian' — that made no sense to the people and did not serve their social or emotional needs.

In many cases, missionaries claimed native minds and souls long before those natives expressed any commitment to or understanding of the new doctrine. Christopher Vecsey (1996), for instance, tells that Catholic priests typically baptized South American Indians *before* the locals understood, or often even received, religious training. By doing so, the priests asserted their control over, virtually their ownership of, Indian souls prior to and independent of any native belief in the supposed truths of Christianity. Having been baptized, the natives were only at the beginning of their journey to Christian identity and belief.

This journey, as Vecsey recounts, was not left to chance but was rather "a strategy well conceived, consciously planned, taught in their seminaries, and refined over time" (1996:18). In the first step, the priests "either insinuated themselves into Indian towns or established villages of evangelization where the populations could be concentrated to increase the efficiency of instruction." After giving gifts to the locals and "winning confidence," the missionaries proceeded

> to place themselves at the center of Indian social life, persuading the natives to build them a friary and church. From these parish centers (*cabeceras*) the missionaries set up *visitas* around the periphery of their territory, which in time might become missions with their own resident priests. Within each village the Franciscans attempted to win the loyalty of native leaders and make the children "their own," thus undermining the social order by being both authorities and sources of goods (18).

Naturally, within these novel religious communities "the mendicants ruled, and they seized control of the Indians' lives... and friars enforced their rules with whips and stockades" (19). And equally naturally, the priests applied their most intense efforts on the weakest and most impressionable members of the native groups, "the youths — especially the sons of the native aristocracy — as a means of building a future Church, but also of influencing the adults" (20).

The situation of these non-Western peoples may seem remote from the situation of the familiar American Christian or other modern world-religion member. However, it is not. It is critical to remember two things. First, as we have repeatedly stressed, no one is born with any religious belief. Second, even in the case and explicit doctrine of world religions like Christianity, no one is born a member; membership must be *actively and voluntarily sought* (even if there is extreme pressure on the individual to seek it). In other words, every member of a religion like Christianity, including in the United States, *is essentially a convert*, which means that each one has undergone — and perhaps is continuously undergoing — the same processes that are only more conspicuous in these exotic circumstances.

The most important lesson in these examples is that the conversion process *is not primarily about ideas, let alone about beliefs*. At a certain point, the missionaries in Latin America or Africa did not care whether or not you as a native *believed* Christianity, for with baptism you were now a Christian and you would continue to grow as a Christian under their steady and heavy influence. As this Christian influence solidified,

Colonization of Experience

you would be surrounded and eventually outnumbered by Christianity. In the end, so they hoped, you would have no choice but to speak Christian, think Christian, and therefore *be* Christian.

Not Belief but Experience

Peter Berger famously portrayed religion as a "sacred canopy" (1967) that embraces everything and everyone beneath it. The fabric of this canopy consists of many threads, *only a few and maybe the least significant of which are beliefs*. We rationalists, who again stress and sometimes overestimate ideas and facts and propositions and argument, tend to fail to appreciate this, much to our own detriment. Why, as we perennially ask ourselves, do the plain facts of things and our logical arguments continue to have so little effect on religious people? How can they cling to their demonstrably false or irrational beliefs when the evidence is so clearly against them? Why don't they abandon their beliefs and get real?

We gave part of the answer in Chapter 2: religion — any religion — is much more than a way of believing but also a way of talking and therefore also of thinking. This is true and essential to understand. As long as religious people continue to talk about and think about the world in religious terms, those religious terms will have life and effect. But language, as crucial as it is, is only part of the story. As Ninian Smart wrote in *Dimensions of the Sacred* (1996), religion has many dimensions, only one of which is doctrinal or philosophical or what we might call belief. Beyond this, there are the mythical-narrative, the ethical-legal, the organizational-social, the material-artistic, the political-economic, and the ritual-practical dimensions. To over-emphasize the significance of only one of these is to misunderstand religion completely and to waste our efforts on one-eighth — and potentially the least important one-eighth — of the problem. We will return to this matter of belief in our ultimate chapter.

Our concern in this chapter is the other seven-eighths of religion, its neglected and underestimated but critically powerful non-belief aspects. Quite frankly, members of a religion often have only a fuzzy or partial notion of the beliefs of their faith; in some cases, they may actually dismiss some of the purportedly official beliefs. Not all Christians, for instance, believe in a hell, and those who do have a wide variety of beliefs about it. Looking to the authorities (the Pope or Jerry Falwell) to settle such disagreement and diversity is futile; even worse would be consulting the scriptures or other sources, since history has proved that this only invites more disagreement and divergence. Of course, this situation is not unique to Christianity; any large and widely-distributed religion (or other thought-system) is going to have its doctrinal disputes, its rivalries and schisms. Michael Gilsenan finds the same in Islam: belief is diverse and arguably the least important way to comprehend the religion. When it comes to conversion or the struggle between religions or sects of religions,

> Furniture, ways of sitting, modes of dress, politeness, photography, table manners, and gestures overturn societies too. Such conventions, techniques, and ways of acting in and on the world are as important as any religion, and changes in them may be as dislocating as changes in belief.... We do not have to accept or impose the primacy of religion over social, economic, or political factors (2000:20).

He is of course correct, but with one caveat: these "conventions, techniques, and ways of acting in and on the world" are not as important as religion, *they are religion.*

Once more, we rationalists and non-believers are obsessed with reason and belief to the exclusion of the non-rational and non-belief elements of the religion and the society around us. Our discussion of language in Chapter 2 was intended to illustrate how we take our language — which is largely *their* language — for granted. To purge ourselves of religion is to purge ourselves of religious language. Our discussion in this chapter in intended to illustrate how our entire way of life is largely *their* way of life, a taken-for-granted, almost invisible religious way of life. We are surrounded, occupied, permeated, literally *colonized* by religion just as surely as the natives of Latin America or Africa were. If anything, we are more colonized, since it all seems so normal and self-evident to us. So, whether or not we *believe* religion, we *experience* religion constantly and everywhere, in every facet of our existence. Some we as

Colonization of Experience

atheists actively root out, like crèches and commandments displays. Some we do not even recognize as religious because it has become so incredibly ubiquitous and routine. Therefore, to purge ourselves of religion is to purge ourselves of religious influences in many or all aspects of ordinary life. Becoming aware of the falseness or irrationality of religious beliefs is the first step in freeing oneself from them. Becoming aware of the colonization of language by religion is the first step of freeing oneself from it. But the greatest and most challenging task of all is to become aware of the colonization of experience (everyday life, space, habits, and the like) by religion — how religion has insinuated itself into every nook and cranny of individual and collective existence and made itself essential or natural or inevitable. This awareness is the first step of freeing oneself from its gravitational pull, its almost absolute and largely unquestioned grip.

Recasting Experience in Religion's Image

The Comaroffs mentioned above directed our attention away from belief and doctrine in the cases of African conversion to Christianity. Theology was quite beyond the grasp of the native — and of most modern believers today. Learning the lesson quickly that total comprehension of doctrine is neither possible nor necessary, missionaries and religious teachers discovered that controlling lives was more important than convincing minds, and that the former basically leads to the latter. The goal became — and remains — to make religion omnipresent yet invisible: "Like the water in which fish swim, it is the amorphous, largely unremarked medium of life itself.... This, we believe, is why recasting mundane, routine practices has been so vital to all manner of social reformers, colonial missionaries among them" (30–1). In fact, what customarily seems to us like a vast doctrinal, theological project becomes what the Comaroffs call a "revolution in habits" (8), an effort to "refurbish the mundane" (9), an "epic of the ordinary" (29), "the everyday as epiphany" (29), and ultimately a condition in which the religion becomes "naturalized habit" (31).

They chronicle an arsenal of means by which religion achieved these ends. One of the key methods has been to take command of the economy and of work and to reshape it in Western, colonial, Christian ways. As in so many other regions of the world, the evangelists "tried hard to persuade [the natives] to use intensive farming techniques — techniques that bore within them an unspoken agrarian aesthetic, a gendered sociology of production, and a set of practical dispositions all attuned to the promise of profit" (8–9). In simpler terms, the missionaries wanted the natives to give up traditional practices and to produce the 'modern' way. By doing so, the intent was manifold. The people would learn the virtue of hard work and discipline — good Protestant values. They would begin to work for profit, not merely sustenance, and thereby acquire the wealth to indulge in modern Western desires like consumption. Central to the plan was to reverse native gender roles, in which women had been the primary producers; this traditional economy seemed not only backward but sinful to the colonialists.

The colonization or Christianization of farming, which might appear to us either trivial or contradictory, was crucial. Even in Barbara Kingsolver's novel *The Poisonwood Bible*, the American missionary was keen to get the people of the Congo to plant and work on the modern Western model, as destructive as that was. In real life, the 'mission garden' often served as the model of proper, modern Christian activity, just as the mission and the missionary served in multiple ways. The evangelists referred to the "civilizing role of cultivation" (123) which, among other things, "expressed itself in squares and straight lines" (27). Enclosure, including fences, introduced notions of private property. Labor was promoted as an end in itself, idle hands being after all the devil's workshop. Of course, missionaries also wanted to integrate the natives into the market; trade was viewed as a civilizing force, and money was celebrated as a means to create a new life of industry, thrift, saving, and happiness.

The Christianization of the natives went far beyond their economic affairs to their very bodies. Pagans and primitives were notable for two physical qualities, dirt and nakedness. Cleanliness being next to godliness, the locals were encouraged

Colonization of Experience

to adopt colonial standards of hygiene; I recall stories from Australia of missionaries literally hosing Aboriginals off, to strip away the "filth" literally and symbolically. "Savages" who previously went about naked or nearly so were taught to wear Western (and of course gender-appropriate) clothing. The English even imported used clothes from home to dress the natives, resulting in some odd and unintended fashion statements. Perhaps more importantly, traditional native dress seemed from the European perspective to lack the social differentiation and status (in other words, 'class') markings that the colonialists felt were good and necessary. To become Christian was also to become class-conscious.

The Comaroffs mention a number of other arenas in which Christianity expressed itself. A proper Christian woman was not only supposed to be clothed modestly but to be consigned to the home; hence, women who had formerly been independent and productive citizens now became house-bound wives who cooked and sewed. Houses themselves had to be constructed and furnished to promote good Christian values and attitudes — rectangular, private (with doors and locks), functionally specialized (with separate rooms for eating, sleeping, *etc.*), and stocked with tables, chairs, cupboards, and all the accouterments of Christian living. The society as a whole finally took on Western, Christian qualities: settled into permanent villages with straight roads and square blocks, public spaces, and specialized buildings like schools, stores, administrative centers, and naturally churches.

Other researchers have observed how missionaries alternately destroyed, modified, or monopolized other facets of life. Unchristian marriage practices were forbidden, such as polygamy or child marriage. In other cases, missionaries simply interjected themselves into traditional cultural practices; Maia Green (2003) explains that priests in Tanzania appropriated the custom of secluding young girls before marriage, taking charge of the daughters of Christian tribe members so as to make themselves necessary in traditional marriage and to control the marriage choice itself (so that the girls would get proper Christian husbands). The church even participated in the tradition of bridewealth, collecting money or gifts from the husband's family and distributing them to the bride's family.

ATHEISM ADVANCED

In Tanzania as many other locations, religious authorities acquired access to if not monopoly over every component of life from food to medicine to education to employment to transportation. Natives came to the missionaries for supplies and often stayed for, or were detained for, preaching and singing. The tribal people understood the power of the church, even if not its doctrines, and they appreciated the wealth of the church, even if they also perceived its greed and self-interest. In Green's case, the locals sometimes insultingly called Catholicism *dini ya biashara* or 'the religion of business' (49). Finally and predictably, missionaries interjected themselves in critical moments of life like birth and death. That the churches would impose their particular brand of morality goes without saying.

The Religious
Colonization of Our Lives

This is only a small sample of the ways that a religion can take up residence in a society, referring only to a few unfamiliar peoples. But now that we are alert to how religion can permeate the mundane details of other people's lives, it is incumbent on us to examine how religion has permeated and colonized the everyday life and ordinary habits of our own society and virtually every human society that exists or has ever existed. It will not be difficult to find it. If anything, it will be surprising and alarming just how pervasive and subtle religion is. As non-believers we are not immune to their influence. In many if not most of these examples, religion has not invented the phenomenon but has conquered, dominated, and possessed it just as surely as if it had.

Critical Life Events

In every life there are certain critical events, individual and collective, that humans cannot help but notice. Some of these events are natural in the sense that they would occur with or without culture and religion, while others are artificial in the sense that they only exist because culture and/or religion say they exist. Among the natural life-events are two of the biggest, namely birth and death. These events are full of both power and significance, so it is no surprise that humans attend to them, celebrate them, interpret them, speculate about them, and finally ritualize them (see Chapter 10 for more on myth and ritual). Something so powerful, important, mysterious, and anxiety-provoking is fertile soil for religion.

Religion hardly creates birth or death, yet it often claims that it does. Despite their naturalness, religion rushes in to supernaturalize them. In conventional Christian thinking, birth, or even conception, is a divine phenomenon, with a spiritual being (the Christian god) implanting a spiritual substance (soul) in the new human. Exactly when or how this happens is unclear; the belief is vague, but that appears to make little difference to its force. At death, this spiritual substance supposedly separates from its fleshy shell and progresses on to its next, and final, destination, also spiritual. The timing of the death has potential religious significance: death has a reason, and the superior spiritual being ends a life when it sees fit to do so (even when the death is a child, a newborn, or merely a fetus).

Therefore, birth and even more so death call for religious intervention. An entire class of religious specialists (priests, ministers, rabbis, and so on) is tasked to preside over death (and to a much lesser extent birth, in the Christian tradition) so as to facilitate a proper or successful outcome. In the Catholic tradition, this would include 'last rites' or the sacrament of extreme unction. Without it, the soul might not attain its final spiritual destination, ideally near the spiritual being. And even when there is not a functionary actually present at the death, there is traditionally a religion-laced ritual or funeral following the death, again traditionally presided over by a religious official taking the occasion to make religious references.

Obviously, Christianity is not the only religion to demand a seat for itself at the table of life and death; rather, life and death are the stock in trade of religion. Among many Buddhists in the world, the main occasion on which monks might interact with laypeople is at death — in this case, not to facilitate a final destination but the next and hopefully better rebirth. Buddhism is as sure as Christianity that there is something next; it is

ATHEISM ADVANCED

just sure that it is something other than what Christianity is sure of. In many ancient systems, including Tibetan Buddhism and Egyptian religion, death was circumscribed by belief and ritual, presided over by specialists, codified in scriptures, and memorialized in architecture.

In addition to these basic life events, there are other unpredictable crises for humans, which are also invaded and occupied with religion. Sickness is a likely candidate: think about how clergymen visit the ill in hospitals. Religion of course also purports to be able to alleviate or cure many such illnesses as well as to explain them in the first place. Other life situations in which religion is likely to make an appearance include infertility, perceived bad luck, and any other manifestation of misfortune; religion is quick to chase the ambulance of human suffering.

Besides clearly natural crises or changes, other more properly social ones have been colonized by religion too. Marriage is the most obvious instance: a married person is not physically different from an unmarried person, and marriage is not a natural state but a cultural one, albeit a nearly-universal cultural one. Religion did not invent marriage, let alone sexual mating; two humans can be emotionally and socially committed to each other and can produce children without the sanction of religion or any other authority. However, as with birth and death, religion often intrudes and seeks a role in the relationship and institution and even insists that marriage is a holy or god-given institution and not a simple secular or social one. The religious specialists again demand the right — perhaps the sole right — to direct the event, and the entire proceedings may be moved into the space of the religion (the church, temple, *etc.*; see below), soaked with religious language and symbols.

Many more examples could be produced, depending on the society and religion. Some regard occasions like embarking on or returning from a voyage or starting a new venture or business as times for ritual or religious activity. A common but not entirely natural moment for religious intervention is at 'maturity' or the entrance into adulthood (often especially for males). There is no objective or physical difference between the minor who exists one day and the adult who exists the

276

next. Yet from the bar mitzvah of Judaism to the confirmation of Catholicism to the initiation ceremony of the Warlpiri Aboriginals, religious leaders may participate in transforming the youth not only into an adult but into the correct kind of adult — a full-fledged member of the religious community. This may include some teaching, but also some experiences and even some bodily operations, like circumcision, scarification, nose-piercing, or tooth removal. Sometimes a new name is given, and with it a new identity — an identity as an adult with rights and responsibilities in the social and religious life of the group. In other cases, religious performances may accompany events in youth, like christening ('making Christian' or introducing to Christ and Christianity) and infant baptism, all of which are ways to lay claim to humans in the name of the religion. This notion of christening can even be extended to inanimate objects, so that ships and other objects are christened and hence Christianized.

Finally, there are also critical events in the life of the group or society, separate from the lives of individuals. These might include wars, disasters, famines, outbreaks of disease, and such. Religion is just as likely to show up at these moments with its ministrations, offering what anthropologists call *rites of intensification* to strengthen and re-integrate the group. Americans will remember how the Congress gathered on the steps of the Capitol to sing immediately after the disaster of 9/11. Preachers gave their interpretations of the meaning of the event and their recommendations for preventing future catastrophes. Likewise, after the tsunami in Southeast Asia or hurricane Katrina religious specialists appeared to share their unique brand of assistance.

Space

Religions generally tend to maintain that they are spiritual or supernatural, although, as we considered in Chapter 2, such concepts are not universal to religions. Nevertheless, even the most otherworldly religions also exist in the real material world. More, they will and must take up residence in the material world, marking geography and space the way that a dog marks its territory. Truly, by filling physical space with these reminders of the non-physical, religion literally does lay claim to the territory. Religious space does not convey any data or belief; instead, it proclaims, "You are in Christian (or whatever religion) country." Religious occupation of space is not an opportunity to think or believe or even to meditate; it is an opportunity for religion to soak into the pores of society, to colonize the very body of the earth.

All religions have their sacred spaces, locations which are more religious than others, for whatever reason. Sometimes these are symbolic places but probably more often they are sites where, according to the religion, *something supernatural happened* or where *something supernatural is today*. The historian of religion Mircea Eliade called them "hierophanies," physical manifestations of the super-physical. For Judaism and Christianity, the city of Jerusalem is a holy place, for concrete historical reasons. Within the city, some sites are especially sacred; for Christians, the locations where Jesus is believed to have walked, suffered, and been buried were *consecrated* ('with-sacred-made'). Modern-day Christian pilgrims still perambulate along the Via Dolorosa, the path their savior supposedly trod on his way to crucifixion. Modern-day Jews still perform prayers and leave prayer-messages at the Western or 'wailing' wall on which the Temple of Yahweh once stood. Islam too sees Jerusalem as a holy place, with its Dome of the Rock atop the old Jewish Temple Mount; in addition it has its own unique places, in particular Mecca, the city of the prophet Muhammad. Accordingly, a key pillar of the Muslim faith is the pilgrimage or *haj* to Mecca at least once in a lifetime. Within the borders of Mecca, some sites are yet more sacred or holy, especially the structure called the Ka'aba, regarded as the center of the Muslim world.

In other societies and religions, places may demand religious attention because spirits lived or live there. Among Australian Aboriginals, the land was criss-crossed with tracks of the creator-ancestors, the Dreamtime beings. These beings literally gave the land its current form through their adventures there; the land is the living product, the hierophany, of their doings. All of Aboriginal space was in a sense sacred space, because it was formed in sacred time by sacred beings. Mount Fuji is a center of power for Japanese, as is Mount Meru for

Colonization of Experience

Hindus. Rivers are often sacred sites, like the Ganges in India. Of course, wherever a spirit is believed to reside — potentially any body of water, any mountain or hill, any tree, any cave — is a candidate for sacredness or at least spiritual concentration.

It is also possible for humans to create a sacred space, and probably all societies do. Groups and their religions need ceremonial spaces where they can perform their rituals, sacrifices, dances, *etc.* Australian Aboriginals painted designs of ancestral spirits on caves and rock faces. A place can become sacred because a religious personage lived there or died there; tombs of Muslim saints are often sites of worship or religious activity. Religions with advanced construction technologies can erect their own holy structures, from pyramids to temples to stupas to ashrams to cathedrals. Occasionally the ground may already be holy on account of some event that supposedly occurred there, like the cathedral of St. Peter, the site of the Catholic Vatican. This was the spot where the Apostle Peter was reportedly killed. When no historical hierophany consecrates the ground, humans can import sacredness by incorporating an object — in particular a relic or body part of a saint — to plant sacredness there. While cathedrals no longer loom over human space the way they did in medieval times (although some modern megachurches come close), contemporary religion compensates in the sheer quantity of churches: in some locations, a church stands on every corner, an inescapable presence in and intrusion into everyday life.

But the religious colonization of space goes far beyond these large-scale and official uses. Religions like to carve their initials into otherwise unremarkable spaces. The vast statue of Jesus overlooking Rio de Janeiro is only the most dramatic example: there, Jesus, and with him Christianity, basically shout their ownership and hegemony over Brazil's land and people. Lesser Christian sculptures adorn other Christian lands, and other religions equally built their gods into the landscape in ancient Greece and so on. The large or lighted crosses on American hillsides convey the same message; as the Christian scriptures assert, the very rocks and stones are made to sing the religion.

Not content to invade the public spaces, religions also squeeze themselves into private domestic spaces. Many homes around the world contain family altars with religious objects and images, used as centers of religious observance. Christian homes are likely to feature pictures of Jesus (contrary to the biblical injunction against making "any likeness of any thing that is in heaven above, or that is in the earth beneath, or that is in the water under the earth" [Exodus 20:4], the conveniently-forgotten clause of the Second Commandment), crosses, scriptural verses, and other paraphernalia. Many people also introduce their religion into semi-private spaces like the workplace, not to mention schools and government buildings. Such people cannot walk around their own homes or offices or schools without constant reminders of their religion — which is precisely the point. Of course, each religion does this differently: orthodox Jewish and Muslim residences cannot have images of people or anything else, but they might have sacred objects or writings. Jewish homes may feature a *mezuzah* or small case containing a scroll with scriptural verses (especially Deuteronomy 6:4–9 and 11:13–21) attached to the doorpost. Chinese traditional religious ideas may dictate the very arrangement of the furniture in the house, on the principle of *feng shui* or the flow of animatistic forces in the space.

Finally, a commonly underappreciated method of colonizing space is by *naming* it; indeed by acquiring or asserting naming rights the religion, like the corporation that owns the rights to a sports venue, displays its power and achieves name recognition. The number of religion-inspired place-names that exist in the United States is truly astounding yet generally unremarked: Corpus Christi (Texas), St. Louis (Missouri), New Canaan (Connecticut), Rome (New York), Bethlehem (Pennsylvania), San Francisco (California), and St. Augustine (Florida) are only a few examples. It is almost as though people are living inside the religion.

Time

Just as religion conquers and organizes space, it also conquers and organizes time, structuring the yearly, weekly, and often daily course of private and public events. Some of these means of time-colonization exploit real natural happenings, while others are occasions invented entirely by religion.

Colonization of Experience

For instance, the annual cycle of seasons is a natural process, but religions often abuse it to generate an annual religious cycle. With or without religion, late December would provide the shortest day of the year in the northern hemisphere, and planting time would be in the spring and harvest time in the fall. Is it a mere accident that Christianity has claimed for itself a date in late December for the birth of 'the Son' when other cultures and religions have noted roughly the same date (the winter solstice) for the birth of the sun? Furthermore, Sir James Frazer in his epic comparative study of mythology, *The Golden Bough*, observed that farming societies only naturally celebrate the early spring (around the spring equinox, in late March or early April) as a time for planting as well as a time for ritual: the earth, in the north, is after all coming back to life after the long death of winter. Is it a coincidence that Christianity's rebirth ritual, Easter, superimposes on the traditional ancient equinox occasion? In fact, we know that the very name *Easter* derives from a pre-Christian Germanic nature goddess (Astare or Oestre) and that the date of the ceremony is determined by wildly non-Christian means (the first Sunday after the first 'Paschal' full moon after the spring equinox).

Many if not all religions populate the annual cycle with sacred days, rituals, festivals, and the like. We refer to such rituals as calendrical since they occur with yearly regularity. Of course, religion is not the only source of calendrical events; after all, July Fourth and Thanksgiving and Veterans Day are annual observances too although they are not distinctly religious (notice even here though that religion may find a way to creep into these ceremonies as well). Christianity is by no means the only religion to insert itself into the yearly round. Judaism has its Yom Kippur and Rosh Hashanah and Hanukkah, Islam has its Ramadan and Eid, Hinduism its Diwali and many others, Buddhism its Buddha's Tooth Day, and on and on. Catholicism was particularly effective at filling the year with religious events — saint's days, feast days, and all manner of occasions like Lent and Assumption. Probably the majority of days of the year had some religious connotation; time was literally marked in terms of religion.

The very practice of calendrical dating — counting the years — is frequently appropriated by religion. Most readers will unproblematically assume that the present year is 2007 (the year in which this book was written) or 2008 or 2009, *etc.*, depending on when the reader reads it. However, it is not 'really' 2007 (in other words, the world is not really 2,007 years old), and it is not 2007 according to all calendars. It is 2007 *according to the Christian calendar*, which calculates time from an imagined event of interest to Christianity. Other religions figure their time differently. Islam counts time from the *hijra* or flight of Muhammad from Mecca (622 in the Christian calendar), when 'Muslim time' begins; therefore, most of the Christian year 2007 coincides with the Muslim year 1427. (Because the Muslim lunar calendar does not use intercalary months to synchronize it with the solar year, Muslim years are shorter than Christian years and more Muslim years have elapsed since Christian 622 than simple arithmetic would lead one to expect.) Judaism counts time from its supposed "beginning" of the world, so most of the Christian year 2007 falls in the Jewish year of 5767. Chinese civilization keeps its own calendar, as does Hinduism (actually, more than one calendar), ancient Mayan culture, and a number of others.

The weekly cycle also provided an opportunity for religious permeation. The week is certainly not a natural phenomenon; there are not really seven days in a week (a week could be any length we want, and 'week' is a cultural concept that many societies lack altogether); one day is not objectively, empirically different from another. Nor did Christianity invent the seven-day week; in fact, the Hebrews did not even invent the seven-day week but borrowed it from the ancient Babylonians and put their own supernatural sanction on it. Having acquired the concept of the week, Judaism proceeded to structure it with the weekly observance of a *sabbath* or god's-day. Christianity then inherited this tradition (a disputed one, since some Christians celebrate their sabbath on Saturday and some on Sunday). Even those of us who do not go to church or have any other religious interests on Sunday still live within the system provided by religion. Interestingly, when the French revolutionaries in the late 1700s tried to purge their society of religion, one thing they did was institute a new week composed of ten days (and no sabbath). And of course, religion may go beyond claiming one day a week for itself: many Christian congregations offer or compel services throughout the week.

Colonization of Experience

Not to leave any opportunity unexploited, religions may demand daily activities or cycles. Islam is the best example, with its pattern of five compulsory prayers distributed throughout the day; thus, a Muslim is never more than a few hours away from a religious observance, and religion is constantly reinforced during the day. Virtually every activity one engages in must be mindful of religion, since one must find a time and place not only for the prayers but the necessary ablutions and rituals. Most Christians do not accept such a daily burden of religion, although in a sense the ringing of church bells every hour reminds Christians even more frequently than Muslims that religion is in charge of their time.

Lastly, some religions lay down standards and expectations that may occur only once in a lifetime or even less often. For Muslims, the pilgrimage to Mecca is a duty for some time in one's life, and no doubt many lives are lived in anticipation, preparation, and remembrance of the grand event. For Australian Aboriginals, an initiation ritual might occur every few years. Indonesians practice a ritual called Eka Desa Rudra which is performed only once every century to renew the world. The Mayans and Hindus function in even greater cycles of time, to thousands or millions of years. Many Christians live in expectation of the end of time itself.

The Arts

In my earlier book I pondered what "atheist arts" might look like. So far, the world has never seen such a thing, since all the arts of humanity have been so very drenched in religion. In form, in function, and in content, our arts have been almost completely loaded with and commandeered by religion.

Humans are the kinds of beings who express themselves, objectify and, in a sense, make themselves in their products. Birds make nests and beavers make dams, but it is not quite the case that these animals are expressing some inner nature or exploring their own life and identity in the process. Perhaps the evidence of this is that, anywhere in the world, a robin makes essentially the same nest and a beaver makes essentially the same dam. Humans, however, display their creativity and their diversity in their arts; it might be fair to say that human nature actually is creativity and diversity.

ATHEISM ADVANCED

Humans produce a variety of artifacts, if by this we include not only material objects but immaterial ones like stories and songs. In fact, story-telling and singing are likely the two oldest and most universal art-forms in our species. We tell stories about many things — our own lives, our history, our society, anything that is important and interesting to us — and we sing about many things. Religion did not invent story and song. It has, however, colonized them just as surely as our space and our time. It is not surprising that, religion being so important to many people and cultures, religion would be the subject of song and story. What is surprising is how much religion has monopolized both.

Any religion comes largely in the form of a literature which we usually speak of as its mythology. Myth, which will be one of the main subjects of Chapter 10, is the narrative accounts of the actions of ancestral, usually powerful and creative and often supernatural beings. Humans tell stories, and they tell stories about the doings of their spiritual entities. These myths frequently provide the material for rituals and songs; rituals may be enactments of mythical events, and songs may be the myth performed (myths are usually not stories in the form of "This happened, then that happened" but rather a sequence of verses or chants or other song-like utterances).

It is then unremarkable that religious 'facts' and themes would comprise much of the narrative and music of a society. What is remarkable is how these facts and themes reverberate throughout its culture in realms that are not mainly or particularly religious. That a society like the United States would portray its religious myths in newer media like movies and television is unspectacular; a movie like *The Ten Commandments* or *The Passion of the Christ* is completely predictable, since societies like to tell their stories over and over. In India, tales like the *Mahabharata* are made into soap operas. Repetition is an important component of colonization; why else tell the Christmas story dozens of times every year? Not for educational purposes; surely no one in American society is unfamiliar with it. It is part of the inundation of society with religion.

The most interesting, and seductive, reproduction of religion in everyday life is the ways in which its images and themes underlie other, apparently secular artistic products.

Colonization of Experience

Movies like *The Matrix* or the most recent *Superman* film are not overtly religious, yet the plots and characters and symbols embedded in them are obviously and overtly drawn from religion. The notion of a savior, a 'chosen one,' is so commonplace and compelling that we remake it even outside of religion. Images of the cross and ideas of resurrection resonate with us in ways that, say, images and ideas from the *Mahabharata* or the *Qur'an* would not. These themes make sense to us, they feel right to us. They are already in our heads, whether we are Christians or not. No doubt the Warlpiri and the Ainu and all the world's peoples reproduce their own religious themes throughout their experience.

Religion shows up in other facets of art as well. The history of Western painting and sculpture is largely the history of Christian painting and sculpture; both have regularly depicted biblical or mythical events or individuals, from Michelangelo's 'David' to DaVinci's 'The Last Supper.' Partly this is because religious patrons often commissioned the work: what else would Michelangelo paint on the ceiling of the Sistine Chapel but scripture-inspired scenes? But partly this is because these events and individuals were the ones kept alive and re-produced by language and art alike.

Music was rapidly put to use by religion. In fact, at one time in Western history, church music was probably the only available form other than folk music (much of which itself was steeped in religion). Gregorian chants and choral and organ music were part of religious services. Even Baroque composers like Bach often either worked explicitly as church musicians or intentionally wrote on religious subjects (*e.g.* Handel's *Messiah*). The same is true in other religious traditions: the cantor in Judaism sings religious utterances, and the Muslim muezzin essentially sings the call to prayer. In popular culture, church hymns have morphed into gospel music, Christian rock, and other styles without sacramental functions but with the same message. Hardly a public occasion can occur without hearing "Amazing Grace," and we routinely sing the lines "God bless America" or "God shed his grace on thee."

Architecture in the West is unmistakably beholden to religion, as in many other parts of the world. The most dramatic structures in ancient Egypt were its pyramids and temples, and the Acropolis in Athens was a shrine to the city god Athena. Ancient Rome built great temple complexes, and in the Dark Ages when Europeans could hardly stack one stone on top of another, their creative energies went almost exclusively into cathedral building. Still most of the grandest edifices in Europe are its churches — consciously designed to be grand to represent or better yet to *embody* the experience of the majesty of the god worshipped therein and humanity's dependence upon him. That churches were often laid out literally in the shape of a cross was a double-dose of religion: a religious space modeled after a religious myth. Literature, dance, and all other arts were in their own ways equally influenced by and filled with religion.

Language

We have already had the occasion to say a fair amount about language, but it is worthwhile to remind ourselves how completely religion determines how we speak and what we speak about. Inadvertently, even against our will, we continuously refer to and reproduce religion in our speech.

That we literally talk about religion is the least of our worries. Everyday English is filled with sayings, proverbs, metaphors, and images derived from Christianity. Whenever we say "Damn it" or "Go to hell" or "For God's sake" or "Jesus H. Christ," we are invoking religion, and a particular religion at that; notice that we seldom say "Go to Valhalla" or "For Vishnu's sake" or "Muhammad H. Prophet." "Bless you" after a sneeze is almost as reflexive as holding a door for someone. Of course, one can say these things without any belief in them, as most atheists do: just because you say "Holy cow" does not mean that you think that bovines are divine. All the same, these and a multitude of other utterances keep religion in the air.

Part of any actual language is a set of scripts and metaphors, drawn from various sources. English has some from Shakespeare ("A rose by any other name..."), from Nietzsche ("What doesn't kill you makes you stronger"), and many others. For better or for worse, a great number of common English phrases and images come from Judeo-Christian scriptures. When we say that something is our "cross to bear," or we ask if we are our "brother's keeper," or we refer to "forbidden fruit"; whenever we talk about "speaking truth to power" or "seeing through a glass darkly"; whenever we call a woman a "Jezebel" or compare someone to "David" as opposed to "Goliath," we are speaking Christian.

As we can see, many of these specifically religious phrases and images have diffused into vernacular, secular language. Every English speaker knows terms like *original sin* or *transubstantiation* or predestination, even if they do not know more technical terms like *kerygma* or *agape*. (There is a whole theological language which is mysterious and incomprehensible to most Christians.) When French-speaking or Spanish-speaking people say goodbye, they refer to god — *adieu* or *adios. Vaya con dios*, 'go with God.' 'God willing' is the English equivalent of the commonplace Arabic saying, *enshallah*. Whenever Muslims mention Muhammad's name, they add *salal lahu alaihe wa salam*, 'Peace be upon him.' *Allahu akbar* — 'God is great.'

We have already raised the issue of stories and myths. We will return to this question, and the power of myth and narrative, in the penultimate chapter.

Everyday Habits

As a true epiphany of the everyday we should expect to find religion distributed throughout our mundane activities, and certainly we do. Religions, for instance, tend to affect eating habits: one of the prominent components of Judeo-Christian tradition (interestingly ignored by most contemporary Christians but still followed by many more orthodox Jews) is dietary restriction. Particular foods (*e.g.* shellfish or pork) cannot be eaten at all, while edible foods must be prepared in religiously appropriate ways (*kosher*). Muslims have their own rules against pork, while at least some Hindus refuse to eat beef. Buddhists are enjoined not to eat meat of any kind, and Jains should ideally not eat anything that is alive or has senses, which would include the leaves of living lettuce, fruit on the vine, or insects that might dwell in such substances.

Perhaps the most extensive system of food regulations is found in the religion of the Hua people of New Guinea. This worldview depended on their concept of *nu,* a semi-spiritual but also quite concrete substance carried by matter, including human matter such as "blood, breath, hair, sweat, fingernails, feces, urine, footprints, and shadows" (Meigs 1984:20). Food conveyed *nu* as well and was "in some sense congealed *nu*" (20). It also shared in the *nu* of those who acquired or prepared it, leading to an elaborate system of dietary and other restrictions. Some foods were more associated with female qualities — soft, juicy, fertile, fast-growing and cool. Others were more masculine — hard, dry, infertile, slow-growing, and hot. Males needed to avoid feminine foods or foods prepared by women, but more so at certain times of life than others: they were especially vulnerable in late childhood and adolescence, when their maleness was building, but in adulthood there were fewer limitations and by old age almost none. Women, with their surplus of *nu,* were fertile, and possessed the special ability to feed others.

Other traditions penetrate eating habits in other ways. Islam prohibits alcohol, although Christianity often uses is as a sacrament; however, some Protestant sects are as anti-alcohol as Islam, substituting grape juice for wine (in denial that their founder Jesus reportedly drank wine routinely). Mormons abstain from coffee.

The methods and occasions for consuming food and drink are also influenced by religion. Jews believe that they should not consume meat and milk together; they also ceremonially eat *matzo* (unleavened bread) at Passover. Hindus as well as others may set aside a portion of food as an offering to the gods. And many Christians cannot even start a meal without a religious invocation, that is, saying grace and thanking their god for the food. Feasting and fasting may equally be religious commandments; Muslims are ordered to fast for a month during Ramadan.

Eating is hardly the only moment for religion to ingratiate itself into everyday life, but it is a particularly effective moment, since it presents itself several times a day. As we mentioned, Muslims are instructed to interrupt their day five times for prayers, and many Christians practice minimally a daily bedtime prayer, in one common form of which they are called to remind themselves of their own mortality ("if I should die before I wake").

Colonization of Experience

In systematic and unsystematic ways, religion is omnipresent in mundane existence. The Catholic church developed a systematic practice of regular confession of one's alleged spiritual and moral failings, a semi-public admission of one's badness and therefore of one's need of the 'cure' that only religion can provide. Religion even finds its place in the most trivial aspects of life, like sneezing: why one needs to say "Bless you" after a sneeze — and not, for instance, after a cough or burp — is beyond me.

One of the overlooked means of reproducing religion in the lives of individuals takes the form of personal naming practices. It is astonishing to think of the number of common personal names (sometimes even referred to as 'Christian names') that derive from religion. Adam, Joseph, Mark, Matthew, Luke, John, Paul, Peter, Michael, Jacob, Timothy, and my own David are only a few for men; for women, Judeo-Christianity gives us Eve, Rachel, Rebecca, Ruth, Esther, Leah, and of course the ever-popular Mary. Few English speakers give the name Jesus to their sons, but Spanish speakers often do; some names, like Abraham or Ezekiel or Jedediah or Moses, were commonly used in the past but have fallen out of favor.

Not surprisingly, other religions draw from their own stock of religious names. Many Muslim men are named Muhammad or Ali or Hussein after early figures in their tradition. Hindu men may be named Rama or Krishna. Even tribal societies followed the practice: Lienhardt (1961) reports that the Dinka pastoralists of east Africa frequently gave the names of their divinities Deng, Garang, and Macardit to men and that women were most commonly named after the spirit Abuk.

Finally, religion naturally tries to insinuate itself into the secular aspects of life. One prime example is education. In most traditional societies, including pre-modern Europe, education and religion were not formally separated at all; children, if they attended school at all, attended one owned and operated by a religion. Even today, many religious groups operate their own schools, and the education they offer may differ more or less in curriculum from public and secular schools. (Many Christian families opt for home schooling.) Islam has its *madrasa* where often the entire curriculum is religion and the textbook is the *Qur'an*. Judaism has its *yeshiva*, and other religions have various institutions for perpetuating themselves. The other main example is government, which may absorb religious notions and terms ("One nation under God"), religious practices (oaths and invocations), religious images, and other religious references ("So help me God"). Of course, each local religion refers to its own particular local beliefs and behaviors. Even lesser and arguably thoroughly secular activities like sports competitions may find religion creeping in, whether in the form of team prayers or spectator invocations.

Religions may not stop at the big activities and institutions. Many attempt to be 'full-service providers' of everything from child care to entertainment. In her revealing book *Bible Believers* Nancy Ammerman depicts a fundamentalist church that strives to be "the center of the world" for its congregation (1987:48), providing not only belief and order but a full slate of life to substitute for the secular alternatives. At the extreme or ideal, "almost every spare minute is spent on activities related to church. The church *is* their leisure activity. If they bowl or play softball, they join the church team," (106), not to mention church book groups (reading Christian literature, of course), church arts and craft clubs, and so on. At the recently discredited New Life Church in Colorado Springs (where founder and leader Ted Haggard had been found guilty of gay "sexual immorality"), the *Denver Post* reports that there were "800-plus small groups, including ones dedicated to fly-fishing, quilting, scrap-booking — even hula dancing" (Gorski 2006).

Bodily Habits

A special case of everyday habits includes actions taken on or to the body; here, religion is literally *embodied* in the physical being of members, just as religion is embodied in the land and space of the society. The colonization of the human body by religion is probably one of its most unappreciated powers yet probably one of the most profound.

Most religions ordain some standard of decoration and comportment for the body. Christians dangle crosses from their necks or, more recently, don WWJD ('What Would Jesus Do?') bracelets. Orthodox Jews, at least at prayer, may fasten the phylactery (a small wooden box containing scripture, tied on with leather straps) to the forehead and arm. Individuals may wear or handle beads and other objects.

Colonization of Experience

Hair, for some reason, is of great interest to many religions. Christians do not seem to observe many dramatic practices regarding hair (although more traditionalist women may be encouraged to wear their hair simply), but other religions have firm and recognizable norms. Orthodox Jewish men are known for the earlocks or long curled strands of hair hanging from the side of their head. Muslim men are often expected to grow a beard. Sikh men are not supposed to cut their hair at all, leading them to wear a turban that gathers it on top of their head. In Hinduism, hair may be worn long and matted or shaved off the top of the head in the form of a tonsure, such as we associate with friars from the medieval period in Europe.

Clothing is another overt influence of religion on the body. As the colonial regime discussed above indicated, wearing clothing at all ("covering one's nakedness") is not a universal human practice, and Judeo-Christian and other traditions enforce the habit at least partly for mythical and doctrinal reasons. Regulations of dress are particularly although not exclusively applied to women. In Muslim countries, women may be expected to cover themselves with anything from a modest headdress or scarf to a completely body-disguising veil.

Jewish men may wear the small covering on the crown of their head, the *yarmulke*. Sikh men are commanded to wear a more elaborate set of adornments, known as the five K's: unshorn hair (*kesh*), a ritual undergarment (*katcha*), a comb (*kanga*), a bracelet or bangle (*kara*), and their sword (*kirpan*). Mormon men and women are also supposed to wear a special kind of underwear known as the "temple garment" which Elder Carlos Asay describes as an "armor of God" (although it is made of cotton) which serves three purposes: "it is a reminder of the sacred covenants made with the Lord in His holy house, a protective covering for the body, and a symbol of the modesty of dress and living that should characterize the lives of all the humble followers of Christ" (2006). The Amish are renowned for their standard dress style of hats and suspenders for men and long skirts and bonnets for women.

It is not merely the clothing draped from the body that may display the marks of religion; the body itself may be and frequently is marked. Religion is literally *inscribed* in or on the body, making the very body a record and witness of religion. Jewish tradition, followed un-self-consciously by most Christians, entails a genital operation for males called circumcision; Judeo-Christianity is not unique in this regard, as Australian Aboriginals and other groups also practiced male circumcision. Some Muslim and African societies perform genital operations on females. Various cultures consider tattooing to be an important ritual statement, whereas Judeo-Christianity has tended to see it as a sacrilege. There are cultures that practice different types and degrees of scarification, nose-piercing, tooth removal or filing, skin painting, ear and lip piercing and/or stretching, and virtually any other body manipulation one can imagine. The human becomes, in the process, essentially a walking work of cultural and religious art.

Care and maintenance of the body may have religious or ritual ramifications. Cleanliness is a major concern in some traditions, with ritual baths and the like. Washing is not, however, always for practical hygienic purposes. Many religions require ablutions that do not particularly make one physically clean but spiritually clean; Muslims for instance should perform ablutions before their scheduled prayers. Many religions are profoundly concerned with pollution of the body, which may come from extraordinary circumstances like handling a dead body, from social circumstances like killing, or from ordinary natural circumstances like childbirth. When I was traveling in Nepal, signs posted at Hindu temples asked women who were menstruating not to enter, lest they pollute the premises.

Religion teaches people particular ways to carry the body, gestures to make, proper ways to sit and stand, *etc.* The gesture of the cross over one's head and chest in Catholicism is a good example. Buddhism and Hinduism involve various hand gestures felicitous of meditation, as well as breathing techniques and manners of sitting (cross-legged); in fact, the entire discipline of yoga is designed to instill habits in the body suitable to religious states of mind, just as meditation is designed to instill habits of the mind through control of the body.

Not surprisingly, many religions have something to say about sexual uses of the body. Some, like Christianity, would really prefer if sexuality did not exist at all, but given its reality, they lay down guidelines for how, when, and with whom to engage in it. Christianity and colonialism gave us the famous 'missionary position' for proper Christian intercourse. Different religions establish different taboos around it. In other traditions, sex may be acceptable (although still regulated) for laypeople but proscribed for full-time religious specialists, like monks and priests. In yet other cases, sexuality may be ritualized and even integrated into religious practice, as with temple prostitutes and the entire sect or discipline of Tantrism.

Unsurprisingly, the final disposition of the body at death is fraught with religious implications and, as we noted, is generally hijacked by religion. This may involve burial, burning, preservation, or any of a number of other methods. Parts of bodies may be saved as family or ritual objects, and the names, likenesses, and stories of the dead may be remembered and celebrated or tabooed and never mentioned again. No matter what, death is not left to chance — or to secular means.

Decolonizing Everyday Life:
How to Make a Non-Religious World

The previous discussion, as extensive as it is, is almost certainly not exhaustive. There are details and examples, and perhaps entire categories, that have not been included. Readers are invited to interrogate their surroundings and experience for traces of religion. What the previous discussion *does* accomplish is to solve the greatest mystery confronting atheists: why don't our arguments sway religious people away from religion? The answer, we can see plainly now and in conjunction with Chapter 2, is that mostly and usually religious people are not *argued* into religion in the first place. They are *colonized* into it. They see it everywhere, they live and breath it, and (if the religion is really good at its colonial project) they are not given the chance to experience or imagine a world without it.

In the last chapter of *Natural Atheism* I posed the question of what an atheistic world would look like. Unquestionably there are many possible forms it might take, just as there are many possible forms for a religious world to take. But we know now at least what must be done. The recovery of the world from religion will demand more than arguments, and even more than reclamation of the language. It will demand the decolonization of everyday life — nothing more, but nothing less, than a new revolution in habits, a new epic of the ordinary, a new refurbishment of the mundane. We cannot argue and debate while leaving all of the institutions and infrastructure of religion in place. They must be rooted out and vanquished, and new institutions and infrastructure — a new experience — raised in their place.

A simple and conventional word for this project is *secularization*. We all have some sense of what this means; scholars of the past century or so expected it to be an inevitable and successful process: religion would shrivel in front of the advance of science, industry, urbanization, and the general rationalization and modernization of contemporary life. The prediction was that religion did not need to be directly attacked; rather, its everyday underpinnings would be eroded, and it would topple or evaporate on its own. The prediction, as at least the short-term trends have suggested, is far from correct; the death of religion has been greatly exaggerated.

Yet, the process of secularization continued and continues. Some see fundamentalism as a rear-guard action, a violent death-throe of a losing cause. I think this judgment is premature. The institutions of religion remain, and in some cases they gain strength. The battle for the mind and even more so for the body and for the time and space in which it lives is not over nor is its outcome clear at this point.

Even more, secularization is a vague and complex concept and process. Some — including many atheists — imagine it as an absence of religion or as an actual antipathy toward religion. This is probably yet another occasion of 'speaking Christian,' in which the secular has been seen as in opposition to the religious or the spiritual in a sort of zero-sum game: more secularism means less religion. But as recent observers have begun to explain, there is more than one kind of secularization.

One of the most articulate commentaries on secularization comes from Peter Glasner (1977), who describes not one but ten senses of the term and process in three different domains, cognitive, normative/behavioral, and institutional. Under cognitive varieties he mentions what he calls *secularization* in contrast to *segmentation*. By 'secularization' he means all the

Colonization of Experience

conventional cultural shifts — industrialization, urbanization, and modernization — that cause people to live and think in new, non-religious ways. Work especially becomes regimented, efficient, practical, and competitive, and people have all of the choices and distractions of present-day life, with football games and malls to visit instead of churches and shrines. 'Segmentation' refers rather to the development of a mental separation between 'religious matters' and 'other matters,' in which *other* eventually comes to outnumber or outweigh *religious*. One may pray and expect miracles in church, but at work or at home one does not take those particular concepts — what Glasner calls those "plausibility structures" — along. One does not pray at work; one gets down to business. Religion and its beliefs and practices become ultimately one specialized thing to do at one special place (church) on one special day (Sunday).

In the normative category he puts *transformation, generalization, desacralization,* and also *secularism.* 'Transformation' is a change within religion over time, particularly to accommodate new social and cultural realities. Protestantism was a transformation from Catholicism (in Max Weber's analysis, an adjustment to the new regime of capitalism and a growing independent middle class). Televangelists and Christian rock music are newer transformations, more secular but hardly less religious. 'Generalization' in a certain way might actually result in *more* religion; by becoming less specific or demanding, or more abstract and inclusive, religion may increase its appeal and membership. For instance, when early Christianity waived the circumcision or dietary requirements, more people were attracted to it. As modern American Christianity becomes more liberal and tolerant, sometimes not even preaching hell or Jesus, fewer people are offended or driven away (interestingly, this generalization of religion is precisely what the early fundamentalists railed against). 'Desacralization' means that "no special esoteric-supernatural forces operate within the world, and that life can be lived in accordance with human rationality" (42); the sacred ceases to be compelling or real. 'Secularism' goes further and "denies the existence of a sacred order" (46) at all — a position essentially identical to atheism.

Under the third category (*institutional*) Glasner identifies *decline, routinization, differentiation,* and *disengagement.*

'Decline' entails certain quantitative measures of loss of importance of religion in people's lives; these could include decreases in church attendance or membership or in the number of churches or congregations. It could also take the form of diminished "religious identification" or acceptance of particular religious beliefs.

'Routinization' is a kind of settling down of religion, as when a religion becomes mainstream and evolves a hierarchy, a set doctrine and practice, and an organized (perhaps international) structure. This especially applies to new religions: Mormonism (or Scientology) was once an idea in one man's head, then a small enthusiastic movement, but gradually grew into a routine, 'normal' religion. Christianity itself started as a small charismatic movement and eventually settled into the structure of the Catholic church — although new small charismatic movements continuously emerge.

'Differentiation' refers to the relationship between the religion and the rest of society. In many small tribal societies, and even perhaps in medieval Western society, religion was simply a part of every aspect of life. When society becomes more differentiated, religion becomes a distinct and separate institution along with government, work, home, *etc.* Religion may actually get stronger, and it certainly is not destroyed, but it is specialized.

Finally, at the end of this road is 'disengagement,' where religion is detached from some or all key dimensions of life; over there we do religion, over here we do something else, and religion has nothing to do with what we do here (*e.g.* home, work, sports, family).

It is apparent that not all of these developments are antireligious and that many if not all of them are taking place within American society simultaneously. For most religious Americans, religion is more or less routine, differentiated, and disengaged, but they are clearly not hostile to religion. They merely bend religion to their needs and ignore it when they do not need it or find it inconvenient. Religion may be intensified for them in its specialized instances (like church services) but weak or irrelevant at other times. Hence, religion

Colonization of Experience

is transformed (and always will be) and generalized. Empirical 'counters' of religion may even decline — say, fewer people attending church — without meaning that religion is in danger; people may just get their religion other ways, like television, books, or the Internet. Religion may, in the end, become a more private affair, partly because Americans tend to privatize or individualize everything and partly because of the unavoidable diversity and pluralism of religion: in a society where your sect or denomination is not the only or even majority one (which is the case with all sects and denominations in America), publicizing your religion can be nothing but divisive and disruptive.

A Case of Decolonization

So secularization, while it is a kind of cutting back of religion, is hardly antithetical to religion. Like a tree that gets pruned, religion can actually emerge stronger and healthier for having been trimmed and secluded safely behind the doors of churches and homes. And all religion is secular to a certain extent: it exists in the real physical world and it manifests itself in myriad real physical ways. A purely spiritual religion would be an abstract intellectual affair, not a way of life, and as such it would probably actually be unthinkable since it would be unlivable.

The sort of secularization we see in contemporary America is important and a good first step. However, as we can plainly see, it is not doing any harm to religion. What would a really serious, sustained, and successful decolonization of everyday life look like? There have been perhaps two prominent examples in history. One is the communist attempt in the Soviet Union, the People's Republic of China, and their satellites. The problem with these cases, besides the fact that atheism has been negatively associated with communism already, is that they were not as successful as they hoped, since they did not last very long — about eighty years in Russia and less than sixty years so far in China. The fall of the Soviet Union revived religion more or less completely.

The other and lesser known model of decolonization comes from early modern England, with and after Henry VIII. It lasted longer and was considerably more effective, although religion still persists even in England. Still, the processes and actions in sixteenth-century England provide some guidance for what a major decolonization effort might be.

Thankfully, John Sommerville, whom we mentioned in Chapter 2, has given us a valuable, and for our purposes hopeful, study of this process. He notes, significantly, our assumption

> that the fading of religious significance from common activities must have been a very gradual process and clearly visible only at a late stage. One of the surprises of this study will be how early this process began and how sudden and dramatic are parts of the story. Secularization often proves to have been a matter of conscious debate, promoted theologically and decided politically. The rapidity of the change was commented on by English and foreign writers at the time (1992:11–2).

Interestingly in this case, decolonizing secularization came before real industrialization and urbanization; so, while these conditions may promote irreligion, they are not essential to it.

What Sommerville calls "English society's visceral rejection of its religious culture" (16) is intimately related to Henry's struggle against Catholic authority. It is important to remember that Christianity had arrived late on the British isle and had triumphed still later; the King Arthur legend basically involves the victory of Christianity over older local religions. So England had been briefly and superficially Catholic for a few centuries when Henry's battle with the church began in the early 1500s over his right to divorce. Sommerville argues that "some secularization had already taken place before the 1530s" (12), but after that date the process accelerated greatly. By the 1700s English religion "was no longer the basis of that culture" (16) — in other words, while Christianity continued and continues to exist in the country, it did and does not permeate and dominate it.

His account of this progression follows our own discussion above. Physical space was freed from religious hegemony; in fact, "No aspect of secularization could have been more obvious and dramatic than this activity" (20). Church property and wealth was seized; and church artifacts and resources (not only

Colonization of Experience

valuables like gold and silver but the very doors and windows) were sold. Metals from bells and such objects were melted down for ammunition. Monasteries were razed or converted to other uses, and hundreds of local churches were destroyed or abandoned. Crosses in public places and icons of saints were dismantled. In 1538 all shrines of saints were closed, and by the 1570s religious landmarks were deleted from maps. Science eventually provided a new model of space itself in Newton's theory of a uniform, grid-like universe without sacred or supernatural spaces or forces, what Sommerville calls an "empty, neutral world" (18).

Time was also liberated. In 1532 the number and excessive celebration of holidays was limited; in 1539 the number of saints commemorated during the year was cut by almost half. Perhaps more importantly than the change in quantity was the change in attitude toward holy days: they were now seen as human-made and in fact determined and authorized by the government. The throne could set as many or few religious days, on whatever date they chose, as they liked. Mundane inventions like clocks and watches had the effect of introducing and popularizing "an undifferentiated and secular time" (41), and the growing disciplines of wage-labor reinforced this experience of time not as a sacred thing but a commodity.

This relates to the decolonization of work. For instance, medieval work had had a semi-religious component: serfdom and peasantry were virtually religious (albeit low) statuses, not unlike the Hindu caste system, and many labor guilds had a religious character of symbols, ceremonies, and such (think of the Masons). At a grander scale, work itself had a penitential nature; it was thought to build morality or serve as punishment. In the new regime, work was mere industriousness, undertaken for profit and demonstrating human mastery of the non-human world.

Having already mentioned language in Chapter 2, let us note here that the arts too were gradually freed from religion. In fact, Sommerville comments that "the English Reformation destroyed more religious art than it produced" (82). Music was one conspicuous arena of secularization: nonreligious music appeared, old religious forms like chants and choirs declined, and new, non-traditional instruments were introduced. With these changes "it seemed like the music existed for its own sake and not as an aid to devotion" (91). A secular literature emerged, not the least the plays of Shakespeare, which explored human themes and not religious ones.

Finally, scholarship began to emancipate itself, turning its attention to questions of nature and — most shockingly all — taking a naturalistic, scholarly approach to religion itself. By the mid-1500s writers began to develop economic and political theories, leading eventually to the works of Thomas Hobbes, Adam Smith, and John Locke. Francis Bacon wrote on the new science itself, and advances were made through naturalistic views of the body and disease. Religion either fell out of favor — Sommerville reports that the Society of Antiquaries prohibited the very discussion of religion in 1614 (147) — or under the scrutiny of the naturalists. David Hume was only the most famous debunker of miracles and other aspects of revealed religion.

Ultimately, education itself was removed from church control and its curriculum updated with humanities and liberal arts. The overall effect can rightly be called a secularization of thought, which Sommerville suggests "was not a cause of the secularization of other aspects of English life" — in fact, probably an effect of them — but "it is the fullest expression of that process. For it marks the full consciousness of secularization" (167).

Last but by no means least, government and the concept and experience of power were disengaged from religion. The state asserted its primacy over the church: Henry was head of both church and state, and his leadership of the church came from his leadership of the state. He claimed the right to approve or disapprove all religious decisions emanating from Canterbury and to appoint non-clergy to important offices. He established secular courts and a secular monarchy; he was not king 'by divine right.' Parliament expanded as a secular counterbalance to church councils, and he even knighted new secular noblemen to rule secular estates under his charge. The clergy were brought under his authority, becoming paid professionals of the state. Marriage, family, oaths, and other institutions formerly dominated by religion were converted into civic matters; some of the more Puritan groups apparently

Colonization of Experience

"objected to any clerical intrusion into the rite [of marriage]"
(139). Cumulatively, religious attention and fervor were
redirected to the state; nationalism replaced supernaturalism.

The Lesson for Contemporary Non-Religionists

Twenty-first-century American society has been colonized
by religion just as surely and just as thoroughly as the peoples
of Latin America and Africa in an earlier era (and, honestly,
continuously today). The colonizers did not debate with
the natives; they built a world around them in which they
experienced religion moment by moment and could not *not*
experience it. Only Henry and his English successors mounted
a response against the pervasive power of religion that
achieved any degree of success — if only by containing religion
to religious institutions while purging everyday society of much
of its influence.

Contemporary American atheism is what atheism has
been for most of its history: a series of *arguments* about and
against religion. Its strictly limited successes should be an
indication of the misdirection of its efforts. Those who know
how to win know not to debate but to dominate, to invade,
to undermine, and ultimately to institutionalize and to
naturalize. Argumentative atheism must transform itself into
a decolonizing atheism, and then a recolonizing atheism, and
ultimately to an institutionalizing and naturalizing atheism.

In practice, this means that atheism — or the more inclusive
worldview and movement which it will and must become (see
Chapter 11) — must first root religion out of its penetration
of society and everyday life. This must include public and
private space and time. Public crosses and all other displays
must come down. Religious holidays must be eliminated; in
fact, the entire idea of 'holiday' or 'holy day' must disappear.
The sabbath must be overthrown. In an ideal world, churches,
mosques, synagogues, temples, stupas, ashrams, and all other
religious properties would be de-commissioned and converted
into secular public facilities. Religious images and displays
in homes would be discouraged, and in schools, government
buildings, and other public locations absolutely forbidden.
At the extreme, cities and other geographic sites would be
renamed.

ATHEISM ADVANCED

Language must be cleansed of religious terms, metaphors, and references. The arts must be freed from religious influence — thankfully, a project that is well under way. Habits of food and dress and comportment and sexuality must be purged of religion; the body itself — *especially* the body — must be freed if the mind is to be free. We can and perhaps should even discard biblical or Christian personal names and take advantage of the many names that have other sources (even if they have been used in previous Christian history); instead of David or Mary or John or Rachel, name your atheist boys Richard or Robert or Edward or Howard or Alexander and your atheist girls Jennifer or Victoria or Susan or Diana, to suggest but a few from the variety of the world's cultures and traditions. And finally, our institutions must be thoroughly secularized. Education, medicine, science, and above all government must be separated from religion.

A decolonized space, time, language, art, body, and politics cannot be left vacant. Atheists will need to offer something in their place. This need not be, it should not be, a mindless aping of religion. We do not need to organize our own Sunday services, nor are we compelled to invent atheist churches or holidays. Some atheists have already begun this process, recolonizing time with solstice celebrations or recolonizing the life-cycle with nonreligious weddings or funerals. We might go further to create new events or observances or to abandon old ones.

We must not be afraid or reluctant to create a new life and society. We need not even hesitate from crawling into the shells left behind by religion, just as religions have crawled into each other's old shells. If Americans are committed to gift-giving in late December, we can take over this habit, just as Christianity took it over long ago. We must remember that religion has invented very little, more often seizing and taking credit for what was already there. And we must not flinch from, indeed I think we must energetically engage in, marginalizing and stigmatizing religion — in the same way that religions have stigmatized and demonized each other. What religion remains, like ancient Greek religion in a Christian society, will be a curiosity, art, mythology, but not something to be taken seriously.

Colonization of Experience

How likely is all of this? I would submit, not very likely. At best, it is a very long-term project; therefore, the sooner we start, the better. It is also a project that will meet a great deal of resistance; even Henry's secularization efforts encountered resistance. Frankly, atheists have not shown much interest in or capacity for this kind of creativity in the past; we tend to like to argue, or else we want to be left alone. We cannot expect that we can predict or dictate where this path will lead; like any culture, it is organic and will grow in its own way — in fact, in multiple and contentious ways. Not all atheists will agree on the institutions, practices, symbols, and terms that we use, anymore than all religionists do. And I fear that none of this is possible without the sponsorship of government.

All of the great colonizations of religion have come when political authority embraced the religion, from Constantine and Christianity to Asoka and Buddhism to Muhammad and Islam. All of the great decolonizations have come when political authority embraced the secular, from Henry VIII to Mustafa Kemal (in Turkey) to Lenin. In America, not only with its religious society but its democratic political system, this will be particularly difficult, since the government cannot dictate institutions and practices, and atheists as a minority are singularly unlikely to win a mandate to introduce such changes.

Against all these odds, we stand here without religion. We know what we think is true. Now we must begin to think about how we would live and how we would promote this vision of a religion-free existence. The point is that a purely argumentative atheism cannot achieve the goals we seek, any more than an argumentative religion could or did. Atheism has to grow beyond its arguments and become a fully-realized civilization. It has thousands of years of civilization and habit to struggle against, and not all of that history must or can go. But, as Marx said, we have spent enough time describing the world; the duty now is to change it. We have a world to win.

Chapter 9

My Impossible Ones:
The Thoughts and Thinkers
Behind Western Religion

In the last chapter we advanced our understanding of
religion, initiated in the first three chapters, as much
more than a belief system, more than a way of thinking
and speaking, but rather a more-or-less complete and
institutionalized way of life or comprehensive and pervasive
interlocking set of embodied experiences. Every group of people,
every society, has its particular way of thinking, speaking,
and living, manifested in its particular institutions and
concepts; in anthropology, we call this their *culture*. A culture
is a roughly consistent — but never completely consistent —
constellation of concepts and relationships and the actions
that real human beings individually and collectively engage in.
These real individual human beings are subsequently shaped
and in-formed by their culture — again never completely but
sufficiently so that we can distinguish American individuals
from, say, Japanese or Warlpiri ones. Just as there cannot be a
religion-in-general or a language-in-general, there cannot be a
human-in-general but only a specific kind of human, influenced
by social surroundings.

A culture can be (and historically has been) as few as some
hundreds of people or as many as hundreds of millions. Cultures
may and do also share features as still larger cultural families
or what Samuel Huntington (1996) calls "civilizations" such
as "Western civilization" or "Islamic civilization" or "Hindu
civilization" or "Chinese civilization." Cultures, and more so
civilizations, despite their diversity are distinguished by a
core of prevalent and immensely powerful ideas. Furthermore,
these key ideas are usually articulated or represented by a few
key figures, often artists or philosophers or religious leaders.
However, two absolutely essential points must be stressed.
First, these towering historical figures are always backed up by
an entire population in which the ideas are present, whether
in active or dormant form; the famous men who get credit for

world-changing contributions are less prophets and founders of new ideas than spokesmen and carriers of ambient ideas. If their thoughts were not at least somewhat familiar to their audiences, the thoughts would make no sense and have no appeal.

The second essential point is that while religion seems to be central to many if not all cultures and civilizations, this religion always rests firmly on a broader and deeper cultural, intellectual, and aesthetic foundation. In other words, Islamic civilization is obviously defined by Islam, but there are older and wider cultural roots of which Islam is not so much a cause as an effect. Likewise, Western civilization is generally defined by Christianity, but there was an established tradition of civilization in the West long before Christianity appeared, based on Greek and Roman patterns, which is critical to Western Christianity: it provided the soil for Christianity to implant and flourish, and it shaped and influenced Christianity into a 'Western' religion. That is to say, Christianity was as much determined by Western culture as determining of it.

The significance of this realization is that, as much as Christianity is a problem for our culture, it is not *the root problem of our culture*. There were and are bigger yet largely taken-for-granted, even invisible, qualities of Western culture that make Christianity possible in the first place and that make it the kind of religion it is today. So, even if we were to root Christianity out of our culture, there would still be persistent tendencies in our society to adopt or establish another religion like it, or if not a religion then something else as irrational and pernicious. In fact, the deep-seated characteristics of Western culture do not only express themselves in religious terms but in myriad ways which seem natural to us. It is only in contrast to other cultures, other lived realities, other views of the world, that we can perceive our own clearly.

Our first order of business in this chapter will be to examine the core concepts of Western civilization which have predisposed it to adopt a religion like Christianity and which have modified Christianity into the sort of religion it can adopt. These concepts are not in themselves especially religious, but they have tremendous implications for religion. Next, we will see how this lens of Western thinking handicaps our perceptions and understandings in a variety of ways, not only religious. Finally, we will explore the main thinkers who have helped create and maintain this crippled Western worldview and brought us to where we are today.

The Core Errors of Western Civilization

> If one has character one also has one's typical experience which recurs again and again.
>
> —Nietzsche, *Beyond Good and Evil*

As character or personality is to the individual, culture is to the society. Actually, as anthropologists insist, character and culture are intimately related: individuals are 'enculturated' into the concepts and values of their society so that public qualities become personal ones, and individuals then act in such ways as to reproduce the sociocultural qualities that produced them in the first place. Therefore, an individual with character has his or her recurring experiences, and a society has its collective recurring experiences. Mutually reinforcing each other (as we will discuss in the next chapter), the experiences and the bases for them seem uniquely real.

Every group, society, and civilization views the world in a particular way, none of which is natural in the sense of genetically determined or of just-the-way-it-is. As philosophers like Suzanne Langer (1942) and Ernst Cassirer (1954) have suggested, all humans perceive reality indirectly, through a lens of cultural symbols that mediate between us and reality (see Chapters 2 and 10). No culture or civilization is entirely wrong about its worldview, but each presents unique problems for itself in terms of its expectations, assumptions, or preferences about reality and the actual reality it confronts. Sometimes, those expectations, assumptions, and preferences seem to override the reality in front of their faces.

In *Twilight of the Idols* Nietzsche discusses what he calls "the four great errors," including misconceptions about causality and free will. In this section, I present certain errors or blindnesses or resistances in Western culture that I think are more basic and problematic even than Nietzsche's subjects.

ATHEISM ADVANCED

Our notions about cause and will are probably derivative of these more basic ideas and concepts, and of course the ancients were debating cause and will long before Christianity was dreamed up. The four deeply embedded concepts discussed next form a complex but integrated network with overlapping and mutually supporting properties. My claim is not that any or all of the four are utterly unique to Western thinking but that in concert they constitute the bedrock of Western civilization.

Dualism

Perhaps the single most persistent characteristic of Western thinking is its unregenerate *dualism*, the view that there are two distinct kinds or substances of things in reality, in particular *body* or *mass* or *matter* on the one hand and *mind* or *spirit* or *ideas* (immaterial substance) on the other. Even more fundamentally and recurrently, dualism takes the form of a tendency to see the world in binary pairs, often if not always in opposition in some way. Thus, we Westerners tend to break reality down into life/death, male/female, good/evil, nature/nurture, one/many, conservative/liberal, us/them, and other such either/or dualities.

It is fascinating to consider just how powerful and apparently inescapable this habit is for us. The anthropologist Claude Levi-Strauss went so far as to posit that all human cognition is binary in nature and that much of our mental energy is spent trying to resolve the irresolvable contrasts or contradictions between the poles of the pair. Myth and ritual themselves, he opined, are attempts to straddle or unite the opposites of life and death or male and female or nature and culture — always and necessarily unsuccessful because the two cannot become one.

Dualism and the notion of binary pairs is not a necessarily religious idea, but the implications for religion are imminent. Greeks like Plato (see below) were separating body from intellect, or ideal from actual, or true from illusory, centuries before Christianity — and not only separating but devaluing. For Plato and his school, the intellectual and 'ideal' were not only different from but superior to or truer than the physical and actual; in fact, we could quite literally build a set of synonyms (*e.g.*, intellectual = ideal = true = good). A religion like Christianity that also seemed to make a distinction between body and spirit, between good and evil, between heaven and hell, would consequently make sense to and appeal to habitual dualists.

That strong dualism can lead into conceptual traps and mistakes should not be hard to see. A dualist attitude can quickly evolve into a polar one, in which only two extreme and mutually exclusive positions exist. Perhaps the key to ancient Greek philosophy is the Law of Exclusion, explained by Aristotle as the principle that something cannot be itself and something else at the same time and in the same way. Of course, it could be itself and something else symbolically —as with the communion wafer that is literally a wafer but symbolically the body of Jesus — but *literally* and *symbolically* are different (*binarily* different) ways. At an extreme, binary/dualist thinking ends in the logical fallacy of the false dilemma or the excluded middle, demanding that only two positions or conclusions are possible and that the falsity of one is the proof of the other.

Essentialism

Closely related to dualism is the notion of *essentialism*; it might be possible to have one without the other, but their compatibility and virtual interdependency make it unlikely. The idea behind essentialism is that every thing, every type or species, has some inherent quality — some *essence* — that makes it what it is and not something else. In other words, there is some essence to humanity that makes a being a human as opposed to an animal (another crucial binary pair). Presumably, there is some essence to a male that makes him a male instead of a female. Further presumably, there is some essence to me that makes me *me* instead of you.

The sheer reductive absurdity of essentialism is a sufficient objection to it: do I, David Eller, have one essence (the 'David Eller essence') or three (human, male, and David Eller)? Of course, I am also a mammal, an animal, and a material being. What then is my essence? Essentialism further relates to and supports dualism by pushing us to distinguish between the authentic and the fake on the basis of essences: is, for instance, a post-operative male-to-female transsexual a real woman or a false woman? If being a woman means possessing the 'essence of womanhood,' then it is hard to see how a medical operation might grant that essence — unless the essence of womanhood is breasts or some such feature. But if so, then a woman who lost her breasts to cancer would lose the essence of womanhood and be something other than or less than a woman. It is not only a false line of thought, it is offensive as well.

Essentialism supports dualism in another way, in terms of attempting to identify the one quality or feature — the *sine qua non* or 'without that, not' — that makes a thing what it is. This has two important implications. The first is a drive to locate that one quality — the necessary and sufficient condition — that makes *definition* and *classification* possible. Aristotle's and other Greek philosophers' — and since them almost every scholar's — attempts to define terms in unambiguous ways is an exercise in linguistic essentialism: 'by truth I mean X' or 'let us use the term *religion* to mean Y.' Anyone who studies non-Western philosophy and literature will notice the comparative absence of such efforts. Once so defined, entities can be organized into categories that share the essence (say, warm blood or walking upright) so that we can cleanly and unambiguously group entities into classes with like qualities.

The second implication is a strange and dangerous tendency not only to identify but to reify essences. *Reify* means to perceive or understand something as real or concrete. Reification leads in two opposite but equally significant directions. One is the treatment of qualities as things. As Richard Nisbett (2003), whom we will meet again below, points out, ancient and modern Western languages have a capacity and habit of turning adjectives and verbs into nouns, which are attributed with a kind of independent reality apart from the objects that have the qualities or perform the action. Thus, a big tree has the attribute of 'bigness,' and a good act has the quality of 'goodness.' Emotional states, like being happy or sad, become things ('happiness' and 'sadness'). And drinking too much becomes a thing called 'alcoholism.'

All of these reifications are achieved through grammar — by adding –ness or –icity or –ism to words. Accordingly, the behavior of believing can be transformed into a belief (see Chapter 11). The other and often simultaneous form of reification is treating categories as things, in other words taking the general for the real. I, David Eller, am a human mammal animal, but only I, David Eller, am a real entity. However, we tend to reify 'human' into a thing as well as 'mammal' and 'animal,' *etc.*, when they are only generalizations and classes. Likewise, 'religion' is not a thing, nor is 'theism' nor even 'Christianity'; the *thing* is probably a particular denomination or sect like the Southern Baptists. Sometimes, as in Plato below, the class or type or generalization is actually seen as *more real* than the particular entity. In other words, bigness is real, and humanness is real, but I, a big human, am less-than-real. In the case of religion, each denomination or sect of Christianity, say, claims that Christianity is a real thing and that there is only one Christianity, a 'Mere Christianity' — usually *its* version, that is.

One last effect of essentialism that has consequences for the next errors is the tendency thereby to see an individual as a collection of qualities or essences. To say this another way, Western culture has the habit of attributing a nature to each individual or entity and of holding that individual's or entity's nature as responsible for, indeed as the explanation of, his/her/its actions. For instance, asked to explain violence, the essentialist answer is that it is "human nature" or some particular individual human's nature or personality to be violent. Asked to explain altruism, the essentialist answer is that it is "human nature" or some particular individual human's nature or personality to be helpful. (Notice that we have two contradictory natures!) In these and other cases, the explanation for whatever phenomenon is sought *internally* to the individual or entity, in its supposedly inherent qualities, rather than in his/her/its circumstances and situation. The implications for law and psychology (especially the mental-illness industry) are clear.

Immutability

It is a direct consequence of dualistic and essentialist thinking that immutability would find a home in Western culture, and long before Christianity came along. *Immutability* is simply the idea that things do not or cannot change, at least not in *essential* ways. Most fundamentally, one kind of thing cannot come from or have its source in another kind of thing, nor become or turn into another kind of thing.

This problem vexed the ancient Greeks to no end. How could *Being* come from *Non-being* (these constituting the only two dualistic options)? How is change possible at all? Or is change an illusion? For many Greek philosophers, the idea of something coming into being, of something *becoming*, was somewhere between confusion and contradiction. Parmenides wrote, "How could What Is be something of the future? How could it come-to-be? For if it were coming-to-be, or if it were going to be in the future, in either case there would be a time when it is not. Thus coming-to-be is quenched, and destruction is unthinkable" (quoted in Wheelwright 1966:97–8). For Zeno, even motion was an unthinkable kind of change: "If anything is moving, it must be moving either in the place in which it is or in a place in which it is not. However, it cannot move in the place in which it is, and it cannot move in the place in which it is not. Therefore movement is impossible" (108).

In terms of the history of life, immutability as a principle basically asserts that there *is* no history of life. Rather, each type of thing (cat, dog, horse, human) is a species which could not come from anything other than a previous member of its own species. Beings could certainly be classified, and even ordered or ranked (in terms of their 'perfection' or conformity to some ideal type), resulting in the classic 'Great Chain of Being' with a place for every kind of being and each being in its proper place. But the suggestion that beings could change their place by changing their type threatened to make classification itself impossible.

Immutability then is entirely opposed to and incompatible with the notion of evolution, that life-forms could alter from one generation to the next, let alone that a completely original life-form could emerge. Like begets like, or so everyday observations indicate. Cats do not have puppies, and dogs do not have kittens. And again, something could not come from nothing: there would have to be a something from which all things came. And not surprisingly, this 'something' would also have to have the quality of immutability. It must be eternal, unchanging, unmoving, uncaused, something whose very essence is Being — something like the Christian god.

My Impossible Ones

It should be obvious how immutability flows necessarily from essentialism. If each type or species is defined by its essence, then it could not change type without changing essence, which is nonsensical, nor can it give rise to a different essence. Since essence itself is unchanging and basic, then the products of essence (species) would also have to be unchanging and basic. *Human* is a thing and *ape* is a thing, and one thing cannot become another thing.

Absolutism

It follows from the three previous principles that things — whatever kinds of things under scrutiny — must be absolutely and universally the way they are. In fact, it was the Greeks who also gave us the notion of 'universal law' or 'natural law.' According to Heraclitus, the universe "is the same for all... it always has been, and will be" (71). This natural law, as Parmenides expressly calls it, is "perfectly complete. It stands in need of nothing; for if it needed anything at all it would need everything" (98).

One of the corollaries of absolutism is precisely universalism. What is true here and now must be true there and then. What is good here and now must be good there and then. The same facts, definitions, relations, and values obtain everywhere and everywhen. There is not merely truth and good but *Truth* and *Good*. Furthermore, the essential absolute truth and good cannot be alloyed with falseness or bad; true must be all-true, good must be all-good. This leads to another corollary, which is simplicity or unity, or we might call it 'purity.' There can be pure true or pure good without any admixture or blemish of false or bad. In fact, given essentialism, there *must* be: there is an essence of truth, an essence of goodness, which cannot co-exist with, come from, or become false or bad.

A critical consequence of the essentialist/absolutist/simplistic view is the tendency, even the compulsion, to overlook details, since details only serve to muddy the situation. If there is, for example, an essence of cat-ness, then one not only can but should ignore the differences between particular cats — their color, size, shape, and so on. As Nisbett notices, Westerners tend to consider few factors when making observations or drawing conclusions (2003:129): there are the central or key or *necessary* factors, and then there are the trivial or peripheral or *contingent* ones. In fact, classification itself requires attention to a finite set of defining traits and the exclusion of other secondary ones. Whether this crab is smaller than that one, they are both crabs. We literally learn to 'not-see' the little differences in favor of the (to our minds) essential similarities. This habit of course has implications for every phase of life, including politics, economics, gender, and all others: issues are seen in simple terms and call for simple solutions.

Finally, it is likely that a worldview given to dualist, essentialist, immutable thinking will seek universal and unchanging rules or laws of reality — probably if not necessarily quantifiable. The universe should be *ruly* and those rules should apply universally (otherwise we arrive at contradiction). The rules or laws of nature more than likely would pertain to the natures or essences of things, such as that objects are naturally attracted to each other (*i.e.* gravity) or that objects are naturally at rest. And the universe would be composed of essential unchanging absolute substances, be they earth, air, fire, and water, or modern chemical elements. We might say that science itself is born out of such an absolutist approach to universal law-abidingness, and science would certainly be undoable if there did not appear to be some regularity in the world. (It is amusing to ponder how Christianity often takes credit for giving birth to science, since science originated in Christian societies; but we can now see not only that science was coming along anyhow before Christianity but that Christianity did not even quite give birth to itself: both are products of a pre-Christian worldview.)

Implications of the Western Worldview

We might ask ourselves, are we Westerners really all that different, and what difference does it really make? After all, not all Western cultures are identically committed to the above conceptions, and some non-Western cultures demonstrate some degree of some of them. Now, every anthropologist, and everyone who has spent extended periods in radically different

My Impossible Ones

cultures or even read extensively about them, has anecdotal evidence of variations in thought-processes and experience. Is there, however, concrete evidence of important differences between Western and non-Western worldviews, and what are the ramifications if there are?

Fortunately, the aforementioned Richard Nisbett has done a significant study of the divergence between Western and Chinese thought and worldview, which can be traced back to cultural practices and observed in experimental settings. It really is true, he finds, that Westerners attend more to objects — in particular, to objects *in isolation from each other* — than Chinese and other Asians, who attend to relationships and contexts. For the Chinese, "nothing exists in an isolated and independent way, but is connected to a multitude of different things. To really know a thing, we have to know all its relations, like individual musical notes embedded in a melody" (2003:175).

Increasingly of late, Western culture, including Western science, has stressed the importance of integration and holism and context. However, these are more difficult for Westerners to grasp and take seriously, given our habitual training. Nisbett notes that Western parents very early on draw children's attention to objects and their properties: we ask them questions like "What is this thing?" and "What is it like (long, short, big, small)?" Asians, research indicates, are less inclined to focus on things and more inclined to focus on substances. In one study, American and Japanese subjects were shown a pyramid made of cork and then asked to select another object that was similar; Americans usually chose another pyramid, while Japanese usually chose another piece of cork (81). Nisbett's conclusion is that Westerners learn to see "a world of objects — discrete and unconnected *things*," while Asians "are inclined to see a world of substances — continuous masses of *matter*" (82).

The two civilizations apply their principles to people as well. Western culture tends to see humans as individuals, with qualities or properties or personalities that are internal, while Asian cultures tend to see humans as nodes in a social network, whose qualities are not entirely determined personally but by the relationships they are in. Thus, while we Westerners expect individuals to be consistent, Eastern cultures expect and virtually demand that individuals be different in different situations and relations. This view carries over into other animate beings: an experiment demonstrated "that Chinese tend to attribute the behavior of fish shown in video scenes to external factors and Americans to internal factors" (116).

As interesting as these results are, what serious consequences flow from them? If other experimental data be correct, Westerners with their essentialist and absolutist worldview literally miss or minimize details of our world. Yet another study asked American and Korean subjects to analyze facts provided to them about a real-life murder; the Americans paid attention to less than half of the information, while the Koreans paid attention to two-thirds (129). A follow-up questionnaire found that Koreans were generally more holistic in their perceptions than Americans and that "the more holistic the individual... the more reluctant to assume that a particular item of information might be irrelevant" (130). It makes you wonder whether you would want Americans on your jury.

The differences do not only concern the evaluation of information. Westerners actually seem to perceive less information in the first place. A final pair of clever experiments suggested that Easterners take in more details of the context and background of events than Westerners. In both setups subjects were shown images (of fish in one case, airplanes in another) with a strong foreground object against a detailed background. When asked to describe the scene, Americans and Japanese equally referred to the foreground, but Japanese were 60% more likely to mention information in the background. In the case of the fish scene, Japanese subjects tended to start with a reference to the environment ("It looked like a pond") while Americans tended to pick out the one key object ("There was a big fish, maybe a trout, moving off to the left") (90). Naturally, the Asians were better at noticing changes in the background, since the Westerners did not really see it in the first place.

The differences continue in the realm of consistency and change. Eastern worldviews, Nisbett argues, do not expect or even desire immutability or non-contradiction. For them, "The world is not static but dynamic and changeable. Being in a given state is just a sign that the state is about to change. Because reality is in constant flux, the concepts that reflect reality are fluid and subjective rather than being fixed and objective" (174). And because the world is complex and changing, "oppositions, paradoxes, and anomalies are continuously being created. Old and new, good and bad, strong and weak exist in everything" (175). Objects, events, and human beings are not expected to be all good or all bad, etc. Opposites inhere in each other, as in the famous and indicative Taoist symbol of *yin* intermixing with *yang*. The idea of purifying things of their mixed or even contrary qualities would simply never occur, and classifying things in terms of one key or essential quality would not seem natural. To Westerners like us, tolerating unresolved inconsistencies feels particularly foreign (recall Levi-Strauss' alleged human need to resolve binary oppositions), but as one Japanese anthropologist quoted in Nisbett's book stated, from the Eastern perspective "To argue with logical consistency... may not only be resented but also be regarded as immature" (106).

The worldview of a culture or civilization can manifest itself not only in what those people see or consider but what they will accept if they see it. Frans de Waal, the Dutch primatologist, has noticed that Eastern and Western cultures have different ability and willingness to perceive intelligence, emotion, and cultural behavior in non-human animals. De Waal relates this attitude to "the pervasive human-animal dualism of the Judeo-Christian tradition [which] has no parallel in other religions or cultures" (2001:69). Although this is indeed a fact of the Judeo-Christian tradition, re-introduced by Descartes (see below), it is of course not original to these religions. Western cultures have a long tradition of denying mind and feeling to animals, as well as dualistically cutting off mind from feeling in the first place. Animals were and are often believed to have neither mind nor emotion; some modern folks even insist that they do not experience pain (despite their obvious howls or thrashes of agony). Christianity only intensified these preconceptions with its radical separation of humans from the 'natural' world.

Even worse, until very recently it was assumed that *human* thoughts and emotions could not (and perhaps should not) be studied naturalistically. Psychology as a science began only a little over a century ago, and scientists just a couple of decades ago believed that emotions were too subtle, too immaterial, to be studied at all. The idea of non-human animals possessing intelligence, let alone consciousness, and human-like emotions and other behaviors still fits poorly with traditional Western conceptions, never mind that the facts suggest strongly that animals do. De Waal informs us that as recently as 1980 there was an (unsuccessful) attempt to ban research on animal language in Western science — presumably on the basis that it would be too upsetting to find that humans are not so different from animals after all (32). It has simply not been acceptable, he concludes, to "acknowledge continuity between humans and animals" (64).

Not surprisingly, some of the earliest and most important primate and animal behavior work came out of the East, where "human self-definition doesn't hinge on a Freudian defeat of basic impulses or a denial of the connection with nature" (32) — although the struggle of "man against nature" hardly started with Freud, or even with Christianity, and again has ancient cultural roots in the West, where something (here, humanity) can only be itself in absolute contrast to everything else. Japanese scientists do not carry all of this limiting cultural baggage: "Inasmuch as a sharp dividing line between humans and animals is not part of Oriental philosophy, and anthropomorphism was never seen as a problem, there were fewer impediments in place than in the West to conceive culture as applicable to other animals" (88). So, whether or not science was invented in Christian societies, it appears that there are characteristics of such societies that do not always qualify them to do the best and most objective science. Particularly when it comes to evolution and human descent from non-human primates, non-Christian cultures may be much less encumbered.

> To the Buddhist and Confucian mind, both ideas are eminently plausible, even likely, and there is nothing insulting about them. The smooth reception of this part of evolutionary theory — the continuity among all life forms — meant that questions about animal behavior were from the start uncontaminated by feelings of superiority and aversion to the attribution of emotions and intentions that paralyzed Western science (116).

Despite Western science's many accomplishments and its emerging holism, perhaps there are areas in which it is still restricted and blinded by its cultural roots and where it could learn from, or defer to, other practitioners. Perhaps this emerging holistic approach will eventually mature and displace dualistic, essentialist, immutabilist, and absolutist notions with other more useful and more accurate ones. De Waal makes his own contribution to this project with his concept of "cultural naturals," behaviors like language that are neither nature nor nurture but a complex dialectical interplay of both.

The Men and Ideas That Shaped and Perpetuated Western-Christian Thought

In Nietzsche's 1888 book *Twilight of the Idols* (one of the greatest and most hopeful book titles in the history of writing), under a section called "Skirmishes of an Untimely Man," he discussed what he called "My Impossible Ones." His discussion has provided the title and the idea for the current chapter. Nietzsche's intention was to select key historical figures who had led — or misled — culture and thought, and such is my intention as well. What I want to provide is a double service to my readers: first, to familiarize them with the great names and ideas with which they may or may not be familiar but with which any contemporary rationalist must be basically fluent, and second, to demonstrate how these ideas which are typically credited to Christianity have a pre-Christian and non-Christian pedigree.

Christianity, as important as it is, is not as important as we or they think it is — and definitely not as original. As we stated at the outset of the chapter, Christianity as we know it found hospitable soil in places that already had Christian-compatible concepts and attitudes, and even more, Christianity as we know it is a product of Christian doctrine and the pre- and non-Christian concepts and attitudes that it met and incorporated. In other words, Christianity was as shaped by Western culture as it was shaping of the culture; the Christianity we know was *made compatible with* the pre-existing culture.

Ultimately, the men (historically they have been almost exclusively men) who have contributed most to Western-Christian civilization are not so much the authors as the spokesmen of core ideas; humans, even the greatest thinkers

among us, do not invent out of thin air but imbibe and represent — perhaps in a clearer or more authoritative way —
the concepts and views available in their societies. They are
the voices of an age or culture, not its creators.

Many of the great minds of Western history have wrestled
with religious questions and have made their mark with
religious contributions. This is partly because, for much of
Western history, religious (that is, Christian) questions were
the only kind that were asked — or were permitted to be
asked. Another part of the reason is that religious questions
have tended to coalesce the central and foundational aspects
of the civilization. In other words, as much as Christianity has
attempted, quite consciously, to eject pagan (Greco-Roman)
elements from Western civilization (for instance, Plato's
Academy, which had existed for almost a thousand years, was
shut down by the Christian emperor Justinian in 529 CE), it
has also absorbed and been transformed by them such that
the two are inseparable. It is fair to say that Christianity is
historically equal amounts of ancient Jewish cult, ancient
Greek philosophy, ancient Roman hierarchy, and late ancient/
early pre-modern European/Germanic warrior culture. Notice
that, of these influences, only one is religious.

Plato (c. 427 BCE–c. 347 BCE)

There is no single more influential figure in all of Western
intellectual history than Plato. He wrote on such a wide
variety of subjects, and with such authority, that he essentially
invented much of Western culture as we know it. His influence
reverberates through Western thought until today and can be
perceived in virtually every philosopher and theologian who
ever wrote in the Western tradition. He is more significant to
the cultural history of the West than any Christian personage
or writer, including Paul and Jesus, because he embedded
dualism and essentialism in the Western psyche centuries
before Christianity was imagined. He was certainly not a
Christian, but Nietzsche described Plato as "pre-existently
Christian" and Christianity as fundamentally Platonic: "how
much Plato there still is in the concept of 'church,'" he wrote in
Twilight of the Idols ("What I Owe to the Ancients," section 2).

My Impossible Ones

It is stunning to discover how much Christianity owes to this particular ancient. Plato is a complicated figure, since his opinions and style changed over time, and because he often demurred from solving problems, only raising them instead. For instance, in his famous *Euthyphro* he did not settle the question of what makes for pious or moral behavior; he merely pointed out the contradiction between behavior that is pious/moral because the gods say so (and thus arbitrary) and behavior that is pious/moral in itself (and therefore independent of the gods). However, certain key or bedrock themes are identifiable from his work.

Plato is best remembered, and has his deepest impact, for his notion of a realm of Forms. Repeatedly he voices the dualistic message that the 'apparent world' or the world of phenomena is apart from, and inferior to, the 'real world' or the world of ideas or form. In the apparent world, which is the world we live in — the world of objects, events, and the human perception of them — things are imperfect, partly because they vary and partly because they change and decay. Any particular table, for example, is not a perfect table but a mere manifestation of the concept or idea of 'table'; any tree is not a perfect tree but a mere manifestation of the concept or idea of 'tree'; any human is a manifestation of the idea of 'human'; and any good action is a manifestation of the idea of 'good.'

Plato's claim seems to be that we can experience tables and trees and humans and good actions with our senses — they are *sensible* or perceptible phenomena — but that we cannot experience the forms of which they are instances. These forms are only intelligible to our mind: we can know them with the proper training and preparation, but they are not available to the senses or to the untrained (read, 'un-philosophical') mind. They are supra-sensible, then, but not beyond our knowledge; in fact, they are *only* accessible through 'knowledge,' by which Plato means something other than the accumulation of sense-data. We can, then, never experience our way to these forms; we can only think our way to them.

In typical Greek style, the forms were held to be truer than the phenomena *via* which they were experienced, since the forms were more 'perfect,' and perfection was seen as a quality in itself. Apparently, they were not *mere* ideas but *real*

321

ATHEISM ADVANCED

for Plato, existing as entities or things, perhaps even in a place or dimension like a world or *realm* of forms. This represents precisely the kind of essentialism and reification we discussed above: thus, something is a tree because it possesses the quality of 'tree-ness,' and something is good because it possesses the quality of 'good-ness.' Tree-ness and good-ness are more real and more perfect than any actual tree or good and reside in their own (higher) dimension of reality. This world of forms is not heaven in the Christian sense, but it surely seems to anticipate it.

The person who acquires the ability to know forms or ideas is the philosopher, who knows (and presumably lives) the truth. Plato's most well-known and colorful portrayal of this process comes in *The Republic* and his 'parable of the cave.' Most humans, he insists, live in the shadows, mistaking the apparent for the real and taking it seriously. The philosopher, the truth-knower, not only sees in the light but *sees the light itself* and cannot go back to chasing or arguing about shadows. He may be viewed as a madman, certainly unconventional, but he was seen reality and will not exchange it for mere material things. He has experienced a *metanoia*, literally a 'change of mind,' a turning-away and a turning-toward — what we might call, and Christianity *will* call, a *conversion*.

Plato even makes an argument for an immortal soul based on the concept of forms, in various ways. First, the soul or mind (*psyche*) is the part of us that can comprehend forms and is therefore necessary for our advancement into higher awareness and being. The soul is itself *the human* form, which participates in the form of Life and therefore is perfectly alive, meaning that it cannot be other than alive (*i.e.*, dead). The soul is also necessary for morality, which is supra-physical (often involving doing what is difficult or unpleasant, not what our physical being might choose); in fact, having a soul may be the very condition of moral behavior.

In conclusion, Plato obviously did not inherit his opinions from Christianity, since Christianity was still over three hundred years from being born. Rather, we might justifiably say that Christianity inherited many of its opinions from Plato, who had planted them firmly in Western soil by then. In Roman times, there was even a philosophical school known as Neo-Platonism which revived many of the master's ideas. So when Christianity arrived with its foreign, Middle Eastern traits, it met pre-existing concepts like a realm of perfect being, an eternal soul, the individual pursuit of perfection, and the conversion of the individual to truth. We might in earnest say that Christianity is post-Platonic rather than that Plato was pre-Christian. Remember that Paul himself is supposed to have been a Hellenized Jew, which means that he had been exposed to Greek thinking before he was exposed to Christianity. As we proceed below, we will see Western thought continually struggle with and under the influence of Plato — raising the same questions and largely coming to the same answers.

Tertullian (c. 155–c. 230)

It is good for Christians to remember that their religion was not born fully mature with Jesus or the Gospels or even the teaching of Paul; in fact, in a very real sense, Christianity or any other religion is not mature today and never will or can be. Any religion continues to grow and change — to *evolve* — from the day it starts until the day when it is forgotten. No single moment in that evolution is the 'real' or 'mature' religion.

Most Christians of course have little or no knowledge of the evolution of their religion; they assume that Christianity as they know it has always been, which is wholly incorrect. It took minimally three centuries for Christianity to settle on an orthodoxy, and it has never actually achieved the orthodoxy it has greedily sought. Throughout its history there have been disagreements and schisms, and any alleged orthodoxy has only been and could only be the triumph or authorization of one *version* of the religion versus all the other competing versions. Many people contributed to the early crystallization of Christianity, and Jesus and Paul are debatably not among the most significant. Here we choose one particularly prominent figure to highlight, who, without much modern credit, helped shape the Christian belief and style that we consider normal today but that was an innovation at the time.

Tertullian came to Christianity late, around age forty according to historian of Christianity Justo Gonzalez (1984).

ATHEISM ADVANCED

Up to and past this time, every detail of Christian doctrine and practice was in dispute — whether Jesus was man or god or both, whether the end was soon or distant, whether the bishops were equal or the bishop of Rome was dominant, what the correct date for Easter was, and so on. No one position had emerged as authoritative, and Christianity was full of diverse opinions, which condemned each other as heresy. If the literary style of writing texts "Against Heretics" predated Tertullian, he gave it a lawyer's flair, since he was apparently trained in law or rhetoric and, as Gonzalez puts it, "his entire literary output bears the stamp of a legal mind" (74). In fact, his most famous and influential document (and he wrote a huge number of short books or treatises) was *The Prescription against Heretics*, incorporating the Latin legal term *praescriptio* "as if it were a case of a suit between orthodox Christian and the heretics" (74) — anticipating by almost two thousand years such books as *The Case for Christ* (Strobel 1998) or for that matter *Atheism: The Case against God* (Smith 1989). We still speak his Christian legalese today.

The most oft-quoted passage in Tertullian's work comes from *The Prescription against Heretics*, in which he argues for the absolute sufficiency of Christianity as opposed to any other ideas or even questions, particularly scholarly and philosophical ones and what would today be scientific ones. In it, he says:

> What indeed has Athens to do with Jerusalem? What concord is there between the Academy and the Church? What between heretics and Christians? Our instruction comes from 'the porch of Solomon,' who had himself taught that "the Lord should be sought in simplicity of heart." Away with all attempts to produce a mottled Christianity of Stoic, Platonic, and dialectic composition! We want no curious disputation after possessing Christ Jesus, no inquisition after enjoying the gospel! With our faith, we desire no further belief. For this is our palmary faith, that there is nothing which we ought to believe besides.

Tertullian sees Christians as on a search, not unlike Plato's search for the Truth, the Forms, the Light. And perhaps like Plato, he thinks he knows where people should search and what they should find. He writes, "As for us, although we must still seek, and *that* always, yet where ought our search to be made?... Let our 'seeking,' therefore be in that which is our own, and from those who are our own: and concerning that which is our own,—that, and only that, which can become an object of inquiry without impairing the rule of faith." By this advice, he is virtually assuring the outcome of the process, since the process can only take a certain course and consider a certain source — the Christian source, that is, which can never threaten Christian belief.

This is what he calls his "rule of faith": that a Christian should never ask questions other than the standard Christian questions, accept answers other than standard Christian answers, or consult sources other than the standard Christian sources. It guarantees that Christians will think and speak 'inside the box' of Christian orthodoxy. And what is that orthodoxy?

> ...the belief that there is one only God, and that He is none other than the Creator of the world, who produced all things out of nothing through His own Word, first of all sent forth; that this Word is called His Son, *and*, under the name of God, was seen "in diverse manners" by the patriarchs, heard at all times in the prophets, at last brought down by the Spirit and Power of the Father into the Virgin Mary, was made flesh in her womb, and, being born of her, went forth as Jesus Christ; thenceforth He preached the new law and the new promise of the kingdom of heaven, worked miracles; having been crucified, He rose again the third day; (then) having ascended into the heavens, He sat at the right hand of the Father; sent instead of Himself the Power of the Holy Ghost to lead such as believe; will come with glory to take the saints to the enjoyment of everlasting life and of the heavenly promises, and to condemn the wicked to everlasting fire, after the resurrection of both these classes shall have happened, together with the restoration of their flesh.

As long as the Christian accepts these truths without question, "you may seek and discuss as much as you please, and give full rein to your curiosity, in whatever seems to you to hang in doubt, or to be shrouded in obscurity." However, speculation beyond established orthodoxy — and questions about or criticisms of that orthodoxy — should cease. "Let such curious art give place to faith; let such glory yield to salvation. At any rate, let them either relinquish their noisiness or else be quiet. To know nothing in opposition to the rule (of faith), is to know all things." In other words, shut up, don't think, and believe. Indeed, "all doctrine must be prejudged as false which savours of contrariety to the truth of the churches and apostles of Christ and God."

Another of Tertullian's accomplishments was a contribution to the doctrine of the Trinity and of Jesus' status. In a late writing, *Against Praexas*, he offered the notion of "one substance and three persons" to describe God. As for the issue of Jesus' humanity or divinity, he referred to "one person" with "two substances" (humanity and divinity taken as dualist essences). Thus, according to Gonzalez, "Tertullian coined the formulas that would eventually become the hallmark of orthodoxy" (77).

Tertullian was also a major advocate of martyrdom, based on the model of Jesus' suffering, the vileness of the world, and the beauty and power of dying for one's belief. He called the world "a prison" and all of humanity "criminals" who not only deserved to die but who should be happy to die, for God had granted them a "supply of comfort" which was "the fight of martyrdom and baptism…of blood" (quoted in Droge and Tabor 1992:145). Life is a disease, and death is a cure, but the price of recovery is one's own blood, with which the martyr "may purchase for himself the whole grace of God, that he may win full pardon from God by paying his own blood for it" (quoted in *ibid.*: 128). "The only key that unlocks the gates of Paradise is your own blood," and "those whose victory is slower and with greater difficulty, those receive the more glorious crown…. [Therefore] seek to die a martyr" (quoted in Smith 1997:92). And in his *De Spectaculis* he reveled in the torment of the nonbelievers in hell.

The irony of anti-heretics like Tertullian is that one man's heresy is another man's orthodoxy. In his thirties Tertullian joined what was considered a heresy by the church, the Montanist movement, and even attacked the official church — for which his writings were proscribed in the sixth century.

My Impossible Ones

René Descartes (1596–1650)

"I think, therefore I am" — even people with minimal knowledge of philosophy have heard of this phrase, expressed originally in the Latin form *cogito ergo sum* and sometimes known simply as 'the *cogito*.' Descartes was a polymath who made two invaluable contributions to the world. One was his analytic geometry, which we all remember fondly from the high school graphing exercises we did, plotting equations on X, Y coordinates. The other was his 'method,' basically a radical kind of skepticism, which involved *doubt*, the suspension or setting-aside of that which we cannot know with certainty. The method promised to allow back in only that which we could demonstrate to know. Unfortunately, it allowed much back in besides.

Descartes' first great work was *Discourse on the Method of Rightly Conducting the Reason, and Seeking Truth in the Sciences* (1637), usually referred to simply as *Discourse on Method*. It was written around the same time as Francis Bacon's seminal works on science, *Novum Organum* (1620) and *The New Atlantis* (1627), and so they share credit for formulating modern science. In this section, we focus on his second and maybe more famous work, *Meditations on First Philosophy* (1641), in which he penned his renowned quotation. By the end, however, he had restated the case for dualism in such a forceful way that we have not escaped it today — although some are trying.

Descartes opens his meditations by commenting on the many "false beliefs" he found in himself and others throughout his life, in particular "facts" that he had learned through his senses (echoing Plato's distrust of sense-data). How could he ever trust again? How can humans ever know anything with confidence, let alone certainty? His novel approach is to take this lack of confidence and certainty as far as possible, even to the point of rejecting his belief in 'God,' at least as a good being; perhaps God is an 'evil genius' who falsifies everything that Descartes and all other humans sense and experience.

Having presumed that all is false or illusion, he then tries, cautiously in his own view, to accept only that which he can know without doubt. He finds that there is, in actuality, one thing which he cannot doubt — his own existence. Even if he doubts everything including his god, he exists as a doubter. And even if he is deceived, he exists as a victim of deception. God himself "can never cause me to be nothing so long as I think that I am something." "So," Descartes concludes, "that after having reflected well and carefully examined all things, we must come to the definite conclusion that this proposition: I am, I exist, is necessarily true each time that I pronounce it, or that I mentally conceive it."

The problem is, *what* exactly *am* I? Here Descartes' dualism comes to the fore. It always appeared (but appearances can be deceiving!) that a human being is a body; what could be more certain than one's own body? But a human is not his or her body in a simple sense: the body can change, the body can decay, the body can lose parts, and I am still me.

Descartes can even imagine (or can he really?) that his body ceases to exist altogether, but when it does, he exists to imagine it. Therefore, he must *not* be his body but rather something else, something separate: "But what then am I? A thing which thinks. What is a thing which thinks? It is a thing which doubts, understands, [conceives], affirms, denies, wills, refuses, which also imagines and feels." In other words, I can conceive of myself without a body, but never without a mind, since then I could not conceive of anything.

> I possess a body with which I am very intimately conjoined, yet because, on the one side, I have a clear and distinct idea of myself inasmuch as I am only a thinking and unextended thing, and as, on the other, I possess a distinct idea of body, inasmuch as it is only an extended and unthinking thing, it is certain that this *I* [that is to say, my soul by which I am what I am], is entirely and absolutely distinct from my body, and can exist without it.

Descartes thus arrives at the dualist division between body and mind/spirit/soul, which yet co-reside in some essential way. The body is nothing but matter and is in a sense dead; it is the mind/spirit/soul that animates it and gives it life. The mind/spirit/soul *is* its life (taking the metaphor of life-force literally, as I discussed in my previous book). Matter is clearly a substance, but mind/spirit/soul is a different substance, a real and independent thing — in fact a *more* real and independent thing than matter, since it can exist after and apart from matter. Further, unlike the body (which has parts and can be divided into parts), mind/spirit/soul is indivisible; one cannot have half of a mind, which makes mind also more perfect than body. Of course, Descartes is wrong in this analysis: the works of neurologists and psychologists prove today that mind *is* a composite phenomenon and that persons can lose parts of their mind (think of Alzheimer's disease) or literally parts of their brain while retaining others.

At any rate, Descartes has achieved, in his own mind, one of his two main purposes: to prove that there are two fundamentally distinct substances or essences in reality — matter and mind — and that humans are really or essentially mind, not matter. His second purpose is to rescue the God-concept. This was conventional and obligatory in philosophical writing in the Christian regime. He admits that humans get most of their knowledge, their ideas, from sensory experience, and about these we can be wrong. But he finds that he also has an idea of 'God,' which no sensory experience could give. Where else could such an idea come from? Notice that he never considers the possibility of *learning it from his society*. He assumes that the idea of God is simple and universal, but we know that this is not so: some religions and societies have never had such an idea, and others have had very diverse ideas about it.

Having started down the wrong path, he is doomed to walk it to the end. What precise idea of this god does he have? "By the name God I understand a substance that is infinite [eternal, immutable], independent, all-knowing, all-powerful, and by which I myself and everything else, if anything else does exist, have been created." This is a nice Christian idea of God but is by no means the only possible one; it is also far from simple but made of many elements which might be separable. Nevertheless, in his thinking, such a grand idea could not come from perception of material things, since they lack these qualities, nor could it come from himself, since he is too small to conceive it himself. There is only one possible source of this idea of God: God. *God* put the idea there, which proves that God exists. And — in his most unjustified twist — since there is no mention of an evil genius in this idea, and no reason to presume that his god is a deceiver out to fool him about His nature, he can rest assured that his idea of 'God' is true.

ATHEISM ADVANCED

Armed with two unassailable truths — his own existence as disembodied mind and the existence of a good god — Descartes ultimately manages to re-import all of this doubted knowledge. For, if He exists, is good, and is not a deceiver, then this god serves as guarantor of the rest of reality. The reality of this god means that there is a reality out there; a non-deceitful god means that my perceptions are guaranteed to match reality; and a good god means that "He has not permitted any falsity to exist in my opinion which He has not likewise given me the faculty of correcting" — presumably the faculty of reason. Given these conclusions, we confront two puzzles: why did Descartes ever doubt his senses in the first place, and how does he explain real errors that his god seems to permit?

Immanuel Kant (1724–1804)

Religion can find allies in strange places, and no one has offered Christianity more succor in an unexpected way than Immanuel Kant, who stands at the transition between classical and modern philosophy. In attempting to solve certain urgent problems in philosophy, Kant thought he had found a way to drop religion and keep it too, all outside the reach of scientific and philosophical criticism. He did so by a new twist on the oldest trick in the Western book — dualism.

Kant wrote during the period of the rise and potential exhaustion of *empiricism*, the school of thought which maintains that all human knowledge comes from sensory (empirical) experience. John Locke (1632–1704) was its greatest proponent, denying that there is any such thing as an innate idea, but rather that the mind is like a blank slate (a *tabula rasa*) filled in by experience. From our senses we acquire simple ideas, and we advance to more complex ideas (including the idea of a god) by combining or processing these simple ideas.

David Hume (1711–76), however, had discovered a problem for this theory: we have many ideas which cannot seem to be discovered in experience, like *cause*. The only thing that empirical observation gives us, he asserted, is sequential action: this ball hits that one, then that one moves. But we cannot 'experience' cause, nor can we experience generalizations (only specific things) or natural rules or laws (only specific events), *etc.* For instance, I see this dog and that dog and another dog, but I cannot see the 'category of dog' or 'dog in general,' and I see objects fall but I do not see the 'law of gravity.' What Hume calls "inductive knowledge," knowledge that proceeds from the specific to the general, seems either impossible or untrustworthy from the empiricist perspective.

Kant's crucial achievement was to try to solve the innate-*versus*-empirical debate (another dualism) by giving a little credit to both. To simplify tremendously what is likely the most difficult argument in all of philosophy, Kant theorized that sensory experience is the start of all knowledge but not the end of it. "That all our knowledge begins with experience there can be no doubt" is the first sentence of his great book, *Critique of Pure Reason,* first published in 1781. But, he goes on to say, "it by no means follows that all arises from experience"; rather, "it is quite possible that our empirical knowledge is a compound of that which we receive through impressions, and that which the faculty of cognition supplies from itself" (Kant 1990:1). With these words, he commences to bridge the dualism between experience and "pure thought."

To make a dense, 500-page story short: while the mind does not have any knowledge at birth, it does have certain qualities or "faculties" to it. It is not exactly a *tabula rasa,* but then even a blank slate has its properties (two-dimensional, black, adhesive to chalk, *etc.*). The innate-idea-*versus*-empiricism, nature-*versus*-nurture dichotomy was always a false one. At any rate, Kant gives the name "pure reason" to this faculty "which furnishes us with the principles of knowledge" (15), which make experience and knowledge possible in the first place. In other words, we are born with a set of "pure representations" which cannot come *from* experience but which we apply *to* experience to generate knowledge; among these are *space* and *time,* each being "not a conception which has been derived from outward experiences" (23). He goes on to develop a table of mental "categories," the "pure Conceptions of the Understanding," including notions like substance, cause, unity, reality, and the like — the precise things that Hume remained skeptical about. There is no need for skepticism, Kant decides, because "these rules of the understanding are not only *a priori* [*i.e.,* before experience] true, but the very source of all truth, that is, of the accordance of our cognition with objects" (157).

ATHEISM ADVANCED

To call these mental furnishings 'true' is problematic; at least, according to him, they are present. But at any rate, Kant concludes that some things are objects of "a possible experience" and other things are not. Some things we can have sensory or empirical contact with, which he calls *phenomena* and are the proper subject of science and speculative, theoretical philosophy. However, some things are beyond sensation and cannot be experienced directly in any way; these so-called *noumena* include the famous "things-in-themselves" which may be behind objects of experience but cannot themselves be experienced. They are roughly Plato's forms. In other words, I have an experience of a cat (small, furry, warm) but I cannot possibly know what a cat is *really* like — I can have no knowledge of the cat-in-itself, only of the cat-as-I-experience-it.

So we are given a new dichotomy, and an absolute one. If there are things-in-themselves (and apparently Kant thinks there are), they are beyond knowledge and beyond pure reason. He proceeds to prove this by showing how reason alone cannot settle certain "transcendental" problems, like whether the universe is finite or infinite, whether freedom exists or not, and of course whether 'God' exists or not. These "transcendental ideas" (infinity, substance/essence, freedom, and God) are "beyond the region of possible experience," and reason is helpless before them; literally, Kant gives both sides of the rational argument over these "antinomies of reason," showing that both sides can be argued rationally. In fact, he indicates that, on the basis of empiricism alone, the negative seems to win. But — and here is the key movement — there are other considerations besides empirical fact and pure reason. Among them are "practical interest," "speculative interest," and "popularity."

Popularity is obvious enough: if many people believe it, "this constitutes no small part of its claim to favor" (265) — which we know is a logical fallacy. Speculative interest refers to the additional questions it promises to answer: *if* freedom exists, then certain other things become true or important (like, say, individual legal responsibility). But the primary point for Kant is *practical* interest — that the idea or belief may be useful or "good for something." With this turn, 'God' is re-introduced. God — by which he means of course the Christian god — is not

My Impossible Ones

an object of any possible experience, but that is no objection against it; it is almost an argument for it. God is not a sensory object but an "intelligible object" that we can confidently posit.

Kant performs this trick by erecting what I call the "Kantian wall." This is the wall between possible experience — the things we can know from evidence — and everything else. All of our familiar knowledge, acquired by senses and instruments (like microscopes), is on this side of the wall, where reason rules absolutely. However, on the other side of the wall is who-knows-what. We cannot see over it, actually or potentially. It is beyond any sense or instrument. We can literally know nothing about it. Over there, Kant simply places 'God' and anything else he desires and says, "It exists." The two problems are that we, as he asserted, cannot *know* if something is over there or not. Even worse, we cannot even know if there *is* an 'over there' over there. It is possible — in fact, quite conceivable — that there is nothing on the other side of the wall and truly no 'other side' and no wall at all. But it is a brilliant way to rescue anything you want to rescue and to place it absolutely beyond analysis or criticism. He apparently knew what he was doing too, since he wrote in the Preface to the second edition of the *Critique of Pure Reason*, "I had to deny knowledge in order to make room for faith." Actually, he had to create a whole irrational dimension to make room for faith.

Interestingly, Kant explicitly undertakes to destroy the rational 'proofs of God.' He argues firmly against the ontological, cosmological, and what he calls physicotheological proofs of the theologians' god. "I maintain," he concludes," that all attempts of reason to establish a theology by the aid of speculation alone are fruitless, that the principles of reason as applied to nature do not conduct us to any theological truths, and, consequently, that a rational theology can have no existence" (356). So much for Aquinas and his "systematic theology," Descartes and his case for a god, and all the rest before and after. What is truly odd is that Christian apologists today continue to trot out the discredited arguments that were demolished once and for all over two hundred years ago.

Without a rational leg to stand on, where is the support for religion? Kant's answer was novel at the time but familiar today: *morality*. Until Kant, Christians had used the truth of religion

333

to sustain their morality, but Kant used the truth of morality to sustain religion. As he described in his 1793 follow-up, *Religion within the Boundaries of Pure Reason* (an oxymoron if there ever was one), morality is not about happiness or pleasure, since many demands of our morality deprive us of pleasure or make us unhappy. Morality is not about any practical ends at all. Rather, morality is about *duty* (which is why his moral theory is called *deontology* or the theory of duty), about that which we must do simply as an end in itself. The details of his moral argument are not necessary here, because they are so flimsy, but the point is that humans are supposed to use their reason to will the "highest good," a noumenal concept which we cannot grasp with our pure reason but which is intelligible in the same way 'God' is (*i.e.*, we deposit it behind the wall). Even more, the pursuit of the highest good by finite and limited creatures like ourselves seems to demand a perfect will (like a god) and an infinite amount of time to pursue it (like an immortal soul). Thus, Kant's god and the soul, while not proven, are accepted as postulates to enable and authorize our struggle for moral perfection — the Platonic notion of perfection haunting Kant two thousand years later.

Even with this grossly simplified treatment, it should be apparent how Kant has effectively, in his mind, salvaged religion — conventional Christian religion — from the threats of reason and empiricism. As he grants, "intelligible objects" like his god are "a mere product of the mind alone" (318). No wonder Nietzsche expressed such continuous disdain for the old philosopher. In *The Anti-Christ*, section 10, Nietzsche says this of Kant:

> A backstairs leading to the old ideal stood open; the concept of the "true world," the concept of morality as the essence of the world (—the two most vicious errors that ever existed!), were once more, thanks to a subtle and wily skepticism, if not actually demonstrable, then *at least* no longer *refutable... Reason*, the prerogative of reason, does not go so far. . . Out of reality there had been made "appearance"; an absolutely false world, that of being, had been turned into reality. . . . The success of Kant is merely a theological success; he was, like Luther and Leibnitz, but one more impediment to German integrity, already far from steady.

My Impossible Ones

Nietzsche further ridiculed Kant's dependence on the notion of a 'faculty' to explain human cognition, as if that adds any understanding at all: how do we know space? By a faculty of space in the mind. It is simply explaining old beliefs by refusing to explain them and rather turning them into mental facts. It is a classic case of Western transformation of processes into properties of things, in this case a quality of the thinking person.

So Nietzsche, justifiably, regards Kant's philosophy as "pious," as a restatement of otherworldly Christian cosmology (the best things in this world are not in 'this world') and of imperative Christian morality ('thou shalt'). Kant even refers to this moral duty as an imperative (the "categorical imperative") which further must be universal or universalizable (you should be able to will the maxim of your actions to be a universal imperative, like 'One should never steal'). This is why Nietzsche judges Kant to be "in the end, an underhanded Christian."

Søren Kierkegaard (1813–55)

In *Beyond Good and Evil* ("On the Prejudice of Philosophers," section 6), Nietzsche says, "Gradually it has become clear to me what every great philosophy so far has been — namely, the personal confession of its author and a kind of involuntary and unconscious memoir." And, since we are concerned in this chapter with the collective or civilizational aspect of thought, it can rightly be added that every great philosophy is the collective confession of its age. This characterization might be more aptly applied to the work of Kierkegaard than almost any philosophical writer.

To recognize, as Patrick Gardiner does in his brief synopsis of Kierkegaard's brief career (he lived for only forty-two years and wrote for about twenty), that the philosopher grew up in an "atmosphere of gloom and religious guilt" (1988:3) and suffered in his adulthood from an "almost paranoiac feeling of isolation" (13) is not to engage in *ad hominem* attacks but rather to understand one of the sources of his ideas. To further recognize that he lived in an era of rapid intellectual and social change — of the apparent triumph of reason and science but the perceived impoverishment or trivialization of human existence — is to appreciate the 'existential' problem which his contemporaries faced but which he perhaps before all others keenly felt. As Gardiner puts it, Kierkegaard believed that humans of his time had virtually "forgotten how to exist" and "had succumbed to an impersonal and anonymous mode of consciousness which precluded spontaneous feeling and was devoid of a secure sense of self-identity" (39). In this, many of us moderns can recognize ourselves.

Kierkegaard was a Christian. However, he was in particular a post-Kantian Christian, which means that rational proofs of Christian doctrine or God's reality were unavailable. Kant had obliterated them (yet it is funny to think about how they have revived in our time). Kierkegaard was not interested in proof; he was interested in *choice*, which gives us his one great contribution to modern Christianity — the notion of the "leap of faith." Here too, he was reacting to an earlier idea. Gotthold Lessing (1729–81) had already struggled with Christianity in the way that Hume and Kant compelled him to: in his *On the Proof of the Spirit and of Power* he had concluded that empirical facts like the life of Jesus could never be adequate to arrive at absolute eternal conclusions like the divinity of Jesus. Between the particular/factual and the general/supernatural was a divide across which he could not make himself leap. Kierkegaard was familiar with and referred to Lessing in his own *Concluding Unscientific Postscript*, arguing that we not only can but must make the leap.

Kierkegaard fundamentally held that humans could not live — or at least live meaningfully — in mere objectivity, for this was "general" and abstract and disinterested. Humans were the kind of beings who had to choose — pick a way of life that was specific, concrete, and personally interested, even passionate. A person could not live on the "spear point" of indecision, doing or being neither this nor that. Rather, a person had to decide, and some decisions presented a sharp either/or alternative with nothing in between; hence the title of his book, *Either/Or*, where he states that without choice there is no humanity but that the "choice itself is crucial for the content of the personality: through the choice the personality submerges itself in that which is being chosen."

My Impossible Ones

The implication for Christianity is profound. Kant and Lessing seem to have established that Christianity cannot be proven, yet Kierkegaard not only wants Christianity but wants a deeply and seriously lived Christianity. The only way to reconcile the rational situation with the ardent wish is to choose it *in spite of, to an extent because of,* its rational unacceptability. In *Fear and Trembling* he uses the biblical story of Abraham's near-sacrifice of Isaac to demonstrate that there is something higher than the rational or the universal, which is the irrational and the personal — in a word, *faith.* Faith like that of Abraham "is namely this paradox that the single individual is higher than the universal" and that on occasion one must "transgress" reason and morality for a higher *telos* ('end,' 'goal,' 'purpose') that suspends human knowledge and value.

The notion of paradox plays a large role in Kierkegaard's thinking, and it would be wrong to expect a system or theory in his work. Systems and theories are bloodless and inhuman; only life lived in full passion is important or real. We might agree with this to an extent. However, he proceeds to argue, in his *Concluding Unscientific Postscript*, that truth is therefore subjective or that subjectivity *is* truth. Christianity is a paradox, he explains; the greatest paradox of all is that a god could become a human, that the eternal could appear in the world of time, in other words that 'God' could be incarnated in Jesus. There can be no proving it; there must be a "leap of faith" to believing it. How does one make this leap? By choosing to do it, by an act of will. Religion, in this construction, is more about what one wants than what one knows. But what one wants *is true*, he asserts.

A more vexing question is *why* make the leap, why will to believe? The answer is reminiscent of, in fact essentially repetitive of, Father Tertullian's famous dictum, "I believe because it is absurd; it is certain because it is impossible." Kierkegaard agrees that Christianity is at best uncertain, at worst patently absurd: it contradicts everything that experience and reason (Kant's two sources of knowledge) provide. In a convoluted and unsatisfactory argument, Kierkegaard claims that this is a support for Christianity: truth is that "objective uncertainty" to which we personally hold fast through our "passionate inwardness," and truth is this sense *is* faith. If we could know, if we could even establish probability, there would be no faith: "If I am able to apprehend God objectively, I do not have faith; but because I cannot do this, I must have faith. If I want to keep myself in faith, I must continually see to that I hold fast the objective uncertainty." Presumably then, if someone could demonstrate to Kierkegaard the existence of a god, he would not want to hear it, since it would ruin his faith.

That this position is patently ridiculous is obvious. It makes a virtue out what would be, in any other area of life, a vice. It mocks the very idea of knowledge and reason, and it threatens to make anything you want or feel qualify as your truth. But by this standard, Christianity is true but also Islam is true, Buddhism is true, Hinduism is true, and all of the thousands of ancient and tribal religions are true. Is this where Kierkegaard wants to take us? (I presume that he was either only aware of or only interested in his own Christian religion.) Finally, if absurdity is the measure of the desirability of faith, what other things should we have faith in? There is an infinite variety of absurd things to believe: how about a god with a human body and a cat's head that only exists on Tuesdays? Kierkegaard's will to believe is ultimately a stubborn and pathetic refusal to let go of what has been shown to be false; it is a case of taking the admonition of being "a fool for Christ" only too seriously.

William James (1842–1910)

By the mid-1800s it was inevitable that scientific investigations would turn to religion itself (as we discussed in Chapter 6). David Hume had already examined the concept of miracles, and later scholars studied the history of the Christian canon (*i.e.* how the Bible came to be written) and the 'biography' of Jesus. The newly emerging science of psychology would naturally inspect religion in its unique way — or ways, since psychology could be dismissive and hostile (like Sigmund Freud) or friendly and protective toward religion.

William James, the eminent late-nineteenth-century psychologist, should be counted among the friends and protectors of religion. He made two significant contributions, one more pious (and unoriginal) than the other. His first and pious work was his 1897 essay "The Will to Believe," which

explicitly defends "the lawfulness of voluntarily adopted faith."
In this regard, he is simply giving more nuanced form to the
problem raised by Kierkegaard, but in allegedly more scientific
garb. Religion, he suggests, is a "hypothesis," just like any other
scientific proposition. And like scientific hypotheses, he thinks,
religious ones present us with a dualistic, binary option — true
or false, this or that, "either/or."

This so far is utterly unoriginal. The original spin is James'
formulation of the three kinds of options which one might
meet. Each of these options reduces to yet another binary
pair: living or dead, forced or avoidable, and momentous or
trivial. "A living option is one in which both hypotheses are
live ones," he writes in one of the great tautologies of Western
history. As an example he offers the choice "Be a theosophist
or be a Mohammedan," neither of which choices "is likely to
be alive." This would be a big surprise to the theosophists and
Mohammedans (that is, Muslims) of the world. A forced option
is one where we must make a choice and cannot sidestep the
decision (cannot, I suppose, remain on Kierkegaard's spear
tip). As examples he contrasts the choice between carrying
an umbrella or not with accepting some truth or not; he finds
the former to be avoidable and the latter forced since there is
no middle ground to it. However, this fails, since there is no
middle ground between having an umbrella or not, and there
may be a middle ground between accepting a truth or not,
like for instance waiting to hear more about it or demanding
some evidence for it. Finally, a momentous option appears to
be one that a person only encounters rarely, a kind of 'once
in a lifetime opportunity' which is further irreversible and
high-stakes; presumably religion in one of these, although the
Christian god seems to make his offer of forgiveness ongoing,
and identification with any religion certainly seems to be
reversible (you can deconvert).

At any rate, without the philosophical analysis of
Kierkegaard, James understands that there are some options
which cannot be decided on the evidence (in fact the evidence
may indicate that there is no decision to make at all: should
I use this magical amulet to protect against leprechauns or
not?). In situations where evidence and reason fail to settle the
question, James concludes with his famous thesis which could
have come (and did come) from Kierkegaard:

> Our passional nature not only lawfully may, but must, decide an
> option between propositions, whenever it is a genuine option that
> cannot by its nature be decided on intellectual grounds; for to say,
> under such circumstances, "Do not decide, but leave the question
> open," is itself a passional decision — just like deciding yes or no
> — and is attended with the same risk of losing the truth.

Of course he is wrong here: leaving the question open is not
a passional decision but a rational one. If scientists do not have
conclusive evidence that, say, a medicine is safe and effective,
they declare it neither safe and effective nor unsafe and
ineffective; they postpone a declaration and do more research.
Even worse, as with Kierkegaard, our subjective passions are
no guarantor of truth whatsoever, which may actually be more
critical in medicine than religion: believe a false religion and
no harm is done, but swallow a false medicine and great harm
may result. James' subsequent assertion that "faith may bring
forth its own verification" is frighteningly true, in two ways:
the faith you have will prejudice what counts as verification
in the first place (in other words, if you believe in miracles,
you are likely to describe certain events as miraculous), and
every religion or faith-system happily finds its own verification
(in other words, if you are a Christian, then the Bible justifies
your beliefs, but if you are a Muslim, the Qur'an justifies *your*
belief). It is all wonderfully, disturbingly circular.

James' other important work on religion is his 1902 *The
Varieties of Religious Experience*. It is ostensibly an objective,
scientific, psychological study of religious experiences and
behaviors; it is really just this side of a work of Christian
apologetics, since the particular 'experiences' it purports
to study are distinctly Christian, such as 'the sick soul,'
'conversion,' 'saintliness,' and 'mysticism.' He begins with the
false definition of religion that we encountered at the opening
of Chapter 7 above: feelings, acts, and experiences of the
individual in solitude. He admittedly refers to this as "personal
religion" which he sees as "more fundamental than either
theology or ecclesiasticism" (1958:42). Written more recently,
he might have called this a phenomenology of religion, trying
to get at the original, pure religious experiences which give rise
to doctrines and churches and religions. The "institutions" of

religion he dismisses as "second-hand religious life" (24). The original religious experiences, he claims, "we can only find in individuals for whom religion exists not as a dull habit, but as an acute fever" — what he calls the "geniuses" of religion (24).

The book is a curious blend of useful and useless opinions. James is most helpful when he acknowledges that there seems to be "no one elementary religious emotion, but only a common storehouse of emotions upon which religious objects may draw," just as there is "no one specific and essential kind of religious object, and no one specific and essential kind of religious act" (40). Rather, as we have maintained in this work, there is no essence to religion, it being rather a composite phenomenon. Even more, there is nothing unique or essential about religious feelings, objects, and acts: "These are each and all of them special cases of kinds of human experience of much wider scope. Religious melancholy, whatever peculiarities it may have *qua* religious, is at any rate melancholy. Religious happiness is happiness. Religious trance is trance" (37). In other words, religion is only a derivative phenomenon of more basic, more general, *more human* tendencies and abilities.

The disappointing aspect of James' discussion is what he overlooks or simply gets wrong. Individual religious experience is his supposedly fundamental subject, but he admits that there are "other things in religion chronologically more primordial than personal devoutness in the moral sense. Fetishism and magic seem to have preceded inward piety historically" (42). Perhaps they merit a chapter too. And once he has carefully selected the religious experiences he will treat, what do such religious experiences have in common that separates them from mundane ones? His first answer is that they are more "serious" to the experiencer: "There must be something solemn, serious, and tender about any attitude which we denominate religious.... It is precisely as being solemn experiences that I wish to interest you in religious experiences" (47). Of course, even he notices that solemnity is neither a uniquely religious state nor a pure and absolute one:

> Things are more or less divine, states of mind are more or less religious, reactions are more or less total, but the boundaries are always misty, and it is everywhere a question of amount and degree. Nevertheless, at their extreme of development, there can never be any question as to what experiences are religious (47).

ATHEISM ADVANCED

Now, any rational person knows that "extreme" cases are not the only or the real cases, so the whole project is suspect from the beginning.

The last thing we will say about James and his religious experiences is that they are, and must be, coming near the end of an intellectual tradition which has long since destroyed the rational or empirical foundations of religion, which is now distinguished by its *emotional* quality. The ideas of religion are less important and less authentic (and more likely to be demonstrably false) than the *feelings*: "If religion is to mean anything definite for us, it seems to me that we ought to take it as meaning this added dimension of emotion, this enthusiastic temper of espousal, in regions where morality strictly so called can at best but bow its head and acquiesce" (54). It is Kierkegaard's subjective truth and passionate commitment; it is Kant's non-rational, unknowable, but all the same confidently known reality. James not only resembles Kant when he speaks of "the belief that there is an unseen order, and that our supreme good lies in harmoniously adjusting ourselves thereto" (58), but he explicitly invokes Kant in his insistence that, despite the lack of any possible knowledge or experience of God,

> We can act as if there were a God; feel as if we were free; consider Nature as if she were full of special designs; lay plans as if we were to be immortal; and we find then that these words do make a genuine difference in our moral life. Our faith that these unintelligible objects actually exist proves thus to be a full equivalent in *praktische Hinsicht*, as Kant calls it, or from the point of view of our action, for a knowledge of what they might be, in case we were permitted positively to conceive them. So we have the strange phenomenon, as Kant assures us, of a mind believing with all its strength in the real presence of a set of things of no one of which it can form any notion whatsoever (61).

That, despite Descartes' claim that he and everyone else had a clear idea of God.

My Impossible Ones

C. S. Lewis (1898–1963)

Wrong from the very title, *Mere Christianity* has ruined more modern minds than perhaps any piece of literature in the twentieth century (although other writers like Lee Strobel have certainly vied for the honor). Even Francis Collins, the director of the public Human Genome Project and presumably a man of some scientific acumen, fell into the trap: in his sadly-named *The Language of God*, he recounts how he abandoned his natural atheism after reading *Mere Christianity* (2006:23). If he could be misled, what chance do the scientifically-uninformed have?

Lewis himself was a former atheist, he testifies, who became a lay Christian, in particular an Anglican. So starts the running fallacy in his book. As we have established incontrovertibly, and as anyone with eyes can see, there is no such thing as 'mere Christianity'; there is rather a whole collection — literally *thousands* — of different Christian churches, sects, and denominations. Lewis is not and cannot be a mere Christian, anymore than he can speak mere language or even mere English. That he admits as much makes his project particularly futile, and I am amazed that anyone has ever read his book past page six, where he explains, "The reader shall be warned that I offer no help to anyone who is hesitating between two Christian 'denominations'" (1960:6). At least he is aware of the internal divisions within Christianity and that he is no help.

Moreover, he seems to realize that these real divisions threaten to undo his efforts, and so he avoids them but not before he admits them: "I think we must admit that the discussion of these disputed points has no tendency at all to bring an outsider into the Christian fold" (6). These are the truest words in his little tome. Worse yet, which *particular* fold would the outsider join? Again, one cannot be a Christian in general; I can virtually picture a crowd of Christian proselytizers, like the *paparazzi* — some standing in their papal robes, others in their Protestant black suits, others in their Mormon underwear — all shouting to you, trying to get your attention, holding out pamphlets for you to read, and competing to get you to come their way. No, Lewis says (violating his own code), "Our divisions should

343

never be discussed except in the presence of those who have already come to believe that there is one God and that Jesus Christ is His only Son." Like Tertullian, don't discuss it until you believe it, and after you believe it, don't discuss anything else. "To say more [*on any of these controversial topics*] would take me at once into highly controversial regions, and such talk would "wreck a book about 'mere' Christianity" (7). Right again, Mr. Lewis: your book is a wreck.

So, Lewis' project runs aground before it starts. But what is his project? Interestingly, now that we understand some Western intellectual history, it is a complete derivative, or just a restatement, of Kant's moral faith argument. Lewis asserts that there is a Moral Law that all humans experience. This was the notion that swung Collins, who describes it as "very peculiar," this "concept of right and wrong [which] appears to be universal among all members of the human species (though its application may result in wildly different outcomes)" (2006:23). Imagine a universal law that results in wildly different outcomes, and you see the problem. Lewis too acknowledges the "differences between moralities" but discounts them as less than "total" (1960:19). This allows him to conclude that there is "a real Right and Wrong" (20); it's just that we keep getting mistaken ideas about it.

What Lewis finds fascinating about this Moral Law is that humans cannot actually obey it. It is not an instinct, since we follow instincts fairly automatically. It is not a sheer social convention, but it is not a natural law either, since natural laws describe what *is* rather than what *should* be (the law of gravity is not a norm but a mathematical statement of regularity). The Moral Law must, in an astounding *non sequitur*, "somehow or other be a real thing — a thing that is really there, not made up by ourselves" (30).

Now commences a series of *non sequiturs* which are so mind-bending that the only interest they hold for us is the grandeur of their absurdity. A materialist view of the universe, he opines, cannot account for morality, since the Moral Law seems to demand something "behind the universe" (a noumenon, an intelligible object?) which is "more like a mind than it is like anything else we know" (32). We recognized this as the familiar animist or agency dimension of religion from Chapter 3. Lewis admits that "I am not yet within a hundred miles of the God of Christian theology" (34), but he closes the distance fast. If there is a Someone behind the Moral Law, then this Someone must be "intensely interested in right conduct" (37). If this Someone is morally interested, it must be a being who "takes sides" on moral questions (44) — that is, a theistic being rather than a pantheistic or deistic one. It must be a being who provides "free will," despite the fact that this can lead to immorality. Even so, this being "thought it worth the risk" (52)!

Somehow or another we get from this minimal god to the Christian god and even to Jesus. Here we get Lewis' famous justification for Jesus in terms of three alternatives: either he was a madman, a liar, or the real son of God, and "it seems to me obvious that He was neither a lunatic nor a fiend" (56). But that is not at all obvious: there are many people who have claimed to be divine who *are* lunatics or fiends. Or some of them are just wrong. And — a possibility Lewis does not consider — maybe this Jesus is just a fairy tale; maybe he never existed at all. Nevertheless, proving to himself that Jesus was the genuine Son of God, Lewis arrives at the death and resurrection, which is the real point. "We are told that Christ was killed for us, that His death has washed out our sins, and that by dying He disabled death itself. That is the formula. That is Christianity. That is what has to be believed" (58). How this might work, or what it might mean, are not only unclear but should not be asked; like Tertullian before, Lewis says that we cannot know and must not speculate, since this leads to division of opinion and, presumably, also would not attract skeptics.

As we can see, Lewis has constructed an elaborate — yet in his mind, a barebones — system of belief on the fragile foundation of 'Moral Law.' If we can refute the concept of Moral Law, the whole structure comes crashing down, and we will do just that in the next chapter. Actually, it is a self-refuting if not vacuous notion to begin with. What is really fascinating is how Lewis moves from Moral Law to "mere Christianity" to conventional, mainstream (especially Anglican) Christianity so easily and rapidly and yet seldom gets called on his trick. By the final sections of the book, too insipid to discuss further here, he has restored not only a personal god but the Christian Trinity — which, by the way, is *not* a feature of 'mere Christianity' since many Christians do not accept it. He also says some remarkable things about "Christian behavior" which I assume we can take to mean morality. For instance, in discussing sex, he explains to us how the sexual impulse in humans is wrong. Sex outside of marriage he calls "a monstrosity" (96). Any women who have ever been wooed by Lewis' siren should read his discourse on male domination of the household. Any group, you see, must have a head; apparently, equal partnership is unthinkable. And the man must be the head because, "Well, firstly, is there any very serious wish that it should be the woman?" (102). (Interestingly, Lewis confesses that he is not married, so why should we take his advice?) "There must be something unnatural about the rule of wives over husbands, because the wives themselves are half ashamed of it" (103). Men of course are the ones who interact with the public world outside the family; women's interests are entirely domestic, but they are lionesses about their home, looking out exclusively for their own. "The function of the husband is to see that this natural preference of hers is not given its head." He ends his treatise with this hypothetical:

> if you are a married woman, let me ask you this question: Much as you admire your husband, would you not say that his chief failing is his tendency not to stick up for his rights and yours against the neighbors as vigorously as you would like? A bit of an Appeaser? (103)

And this is the man from whom we are learning about the Moral Law?

New Minds, Same Old Thoughts

There is any number of other, more contemporary figures who might be included in this list of shame, but most or all of them are derivative of the ideas long active in Christian and Western civilization. Paul Tillich comes to mind, whose *The Courage to Be* (1952) is little more than recycled Kierkegaard with a liberal-Christian bent; in good essentialist form he even encourages us to enhance "the most essential part of our being [over] the less essential" (5). The popularizers of comparative religion, like Huston Smith and Joseph Campbell, have done more to promote a lukewarm religiosity or spirituality and thus to make religion more tolerable by being less religious. I am always amazed when these men are read and praised by Christians, since both reduce Christianity and all other religions to some 'perennial philosophy' which is conspicuously *not* Christianity — or any other actual religion either, for that matter.

Even among us, the rationalists, the non-theists, the irreligious, the non-believers, the inescapable gravity of not only Christian language but Western language shows its force. One of the worst examples is the otherwise estimable scientist Stephen Jay Gould, whose *Rock of Ages* (1999) tries to save religion from science (and why he would care to do that, I don't know) by truncating religion and assigning it to its own safe Kantian kingdom — the "non-overlapping magisterium" of morality. That religion also inevitably and necessarily makes factual claims, and that morality is neither essential nor unique to religion, does not deter him. The rationalists we have lost, more or less completely, to religion are only the most obvious casualties; Antony Flew and his recent conversion to some sort of watered-down deism is the prime example.

Amusingly but disappointingly, reminiscent of Nietzsche's madman announcing the death of God, apparently the news has not yet arrived — both that god(s) are dead and that the rational or scientific proving of god(s) is dead. On the other hand, Kant has clearly arrived, because the moral argument has effectively displaced the logical argument in much modern Christian practice; as Kierkegaard, Lewis, Tillich, and Gould illustrate, Kant has established that you cannot get there from here in terms of knowledge and faith. Yet many still try: not only do theists continue to offer 'proofs of God,' but atheists continue to offer counterproofs. It is too late for that. We know better. It is well established that one can neither prove nor disprove supra-empirical, supra-logical claims. It would be like trying to prove that *glorb* exists or has this or that quality. We don't need to disprove it. We need to invoke the burden-of-proof standard — that if you cannot muster some evidence for it, or even meaningfully define it, we have no obligation to even honor it with our attention. We further need to dismiss out of

ATHEISM ADVANCED

court any argument for religion *other than* evidence. We finally need to be wary of the words, ideas, and concepts that are so deeply embedded in our language, our thought, or institutions, and our civilization that we, atheists and freethinkers that we are, can hardly avoid thinking about them — and thinking them, subjectively, into 'truth' again.

Chapter 10

Of Myths and Morals:
Religion, Stories, and the Practice of Living

Many years ago, I began to notice that news items, including those in major news magazines, were increasingly opening their reports with personal anecdotes. To choose a random day not long ago, the *Denver Post* of Christmas Eve 2006 featured five stories on the front page, of which three started as follows:

- Article about homebuyers and risky lending practices: "Carmen Pedrego said the builder assured her she could own a brand-new home for no more than her monthly rent."
- Article about workers returning from Iraq: "Mark Mondello dropped his bag 5 feet away and knelt quickly to meet the outstretched arms of his 3-year-old daughter, Regan. He closed his eyes and wrapped his arms around her, cradling her face against his in a lingering embrace."
- Article about the recent snowstorm in Denver: "Denver's public works department said that by noon Saturday, the city had sent a snowplow down all city streets, even residential ones. Tell that to Earthel Ware. She said that she watched crews go down Gaylord Street in the Five Points area Friday night, but they never visited the street she lives on, Vine Street."

The two remaining articles actually featured a personal name within the first five words — Israeli Prime Minister Ehud Olmert in one, Charles Dickens in the other.

Compelling journalism? No doubt. But I cannot help but notice two important facts about such writing. First, a few decades ago it was much less common. Second, atheistic writings almost never take this form. We dwell on ideas, not individuals. When I was a child, my mother used to say, "Small minds talk about people, average minds talk about events, and great minds talk about ideas." I wonder if it is as simple as that.

There is no dispute that personalizing an event or an idea is an effective — but even more, an emotive — way of getting a point across. We do not know Carmen Pedrego or Mark Mondello or Earthel Ware, but when we hear of their tragedies or triumphs, it somehow packs more of a load than if we were to hear that no-money-down loans were ruining the housing market or that there was a blizzard somewhere. After all, the accounts of housing markets and natural disasters are only interesting and important because they affect real people. A news item about a snowstorm at the South Pole would be irrelevant to most readers.

Beyond this journalistic and arguably at least mildly manipulative strategy, it is true that humans are story-telling beings. No one would want to read a newspaper or a book that was a mere list of facts, happenings, or rules. That is why dictionaries and cookbooks make for comparatively un-thrilling reading. Stories 'make it hang together'; they provide not just a sequence but a narrative, a plot, and more than occasionally a theme. In many cases, they also provide a purpose, a goal, a *telos* (in the sense of 'teleology'), that is, an experience that the events and actors were heading toward some climax or conclusion the whole time — almost as if the events were destined or fated in some way. In a word, turning a series of episodes into a story gives them *continuity and meaning*. And turning a series of episodes into *someone's* story gives them *personal* continuity and meaning.

If humanity is a story-telling species, and if stories are the coherent meaningful narratives of the lives of persons, *and if religious or supernatural beings are extra-human persons,* it makes perfect sense that humanity would also tell stories about these extra-human beings. They too have adventures, have not only sequential but meaningful existences, and often enough move toward some historical destination or fate. It is natural, in other words, that humans would tell myths. Humans have religion, humans have stories, therefore humans have religious stories.

Myths and Morals

Humans also have one other impulse or concern or perhaps need. Humans wonder what they should do, what is good to do, what is important and worthwhile to do. They choose their behavior and judge and respond to the behavior of others. Humans are, for lack of a better word, *moral* beings — not that they always act morally but that they make moral considerations.

Both myth and morality are, in most people's minds, religious matters, although in Western and Christian societies, morals generally receive more attention than myths. In fact, many Western, Christian people would insist that morals are real concerns (even that morals are 'real') while myths are not real concerns (even that myths are 'false'). After all, no members of a religion ever call their own stories myths, although they are often happy and proud to call their behavioral rules morality — even or usually *the* morality. Furthermore, we tend to fail to see the relationship between myths and morals. Again, this is partly a result of the disparaging of myth: since myths are false, they could not possibly be related to *our* morality.

Yet, there is little disagreement among theists that morality is intimately related to religion, that morality is perhaps impossible without religion. "How can you be good without god(s)?" they regularly ask (or rather, without their *particular* god). Too often atheists get sucked into this theistic mindset, either conceding morality to religion (like Stephen Jay Gould did) or attempting to defend atheist morality. When atheists engage in this activity, I fear that they are once again speaking Christian in a way that does not advance atheism at all.

In this chapter, we will explore these two concepts, myth and morality, which are chronically misunderstood by theists and atheists alike. We will see, as we have become accustomed to seeing, that neither is unique nor universal to religion. We will find, more urgently, that religion has usurped morality in ways that are partly understandable and partly strategically important. Most urgently of all, we will discover that morals *are* in fact frequently connected to myths in ways that we overlook, much to our own detriment: we atheists, we rationalists, we literalists often fail to appreciate — and take advantage of — the power of stories.

ATHEISM ADVANCED

Myth and Religion

"In the beginning," god(s) did this or that. The Judeo-Christian scriptures begin as a story, and they continue as a story through to the end. If Judeo-Christianity is correct, we are all living in this (unfinished) story even now.

A religious story is commonly and technically called a *myth*. English speakers ordinarily use the word 'myth' with two different but related meanings: as a religious story and as a false claim, a misunderstanding, or a lie of any sort. For instance, we may hear of "the ten myths about cancer" or, as Thomas Szasz entitled one of his books, *The Myth of Mental Illness*. Consequently, 'myth' often means false religious stories. One's own religion is never a myth; myth is someone else's (false) religion. Accordingly, Christians do not say that they have myths. The ancient Greeks or Norse or Egyptians had myths. Traditional societies had or have myths. But Christians, they maintain, have history and truth.

Despite the fact that even some scholars have used 'myth' in the pejorative sense, we use the term here merely to refer without prejudice to any religious narrative. Let us define *myth* simply as a story about one or more non-human, superhuman, or religious characters, which the possessors of the story take to be true. ('Mythology' we will reserve for the collective myths of a particular society or religion, such as Greek mythology, and for the academic study of myths.) This definition will distinguish between myth and other kinds of narrative genres like legend, folk tale, fairy tale, and so on. These other styles may involve non-humans, like the Three Bears or the Big Bad Wolf, or super-humans (or at least extraordinary humans), like Paul Bunyon. The difference is that, I presume, no one who tells these sorts of tales thinks that they are *true*. They are clearly and overtly fictional, even if they are culturally important and instructive in some way (*e.g.*, children might be told the Hansel and Gretel story to prevent them from wandering off in the woods).

There are also, of course, stories that people tell that they take to be true but which have no non-human, super-human, or religious characters or significance. Some such stories qualify as history: if we recount the story of Julius Caesar crossing the Rubicon to conquer Rome, we are retelling history. Other stories are of questionable historical validity: did George Washington really chop down a cherry tree, or did Abraham Lincoln really walk miles to repay a debt? Still other stories are of only personal historical interest or validity; *my* story, the story of what happened to me in my life, is biography or autobiography.

Obviously then, myths are a subset of the much larger and more diverse category and phenomenon of *narrative* or *story*. As with violence and so many other issues, there are religious narratives (myths) and there are non-religious narratives (all the other genres). Myths need not even have *exclusively* supernatural characters: often if not usually, there are religious characters interacting with human and other natural beings.

We might profitably place 'narrative' under an even more inclusive heading of 'folklore' or 'literature' — often but not always 'oral literature.' There are many things humans do with words (see Chapter 2), inside religion and outside, beyond telling stories. One of the great students of folklore, Alan Dundes, suggested this arguably still incomplete inventory:

> myths, legends, folktales, jokes, proverbs, riddles, chants, charms, blessings, curses, oaths, insults, retorts, taunts, teases, toasts, tongue-twisters, and greeting and leave-taking formulas.... It also includes folk costume, folk dance, folk drama, folk instrumental music..., folksongs..., folk speech..., folk similes..., folk metaphors..., and names. Folk poetry ranges from oral epics to autograph-book verse, epitaphs, latrinalia (writings on the walls of public bathrooms), limericks, ball-bouncing rhymes, jump-rope rhymes, finger and toe rhymes, dandling rhymes (to bounce children on the knee), counting-out rhymes..., and nursery rhymes. The list of folklore forms also contains games; gestures; symbols; prayers (*e.g.*, graces); practical jokes; folk etymologies; food recipes; quilt and embroidery designs; house, barn, and fence types; street vendor's cries; and even the traditional conventional sounds used to summon animals or to give them commands (1965:3).

Therefore, while myth is found in religion, it is by no means the only kind of verbal behavior found in religion. The Judeo-Christian scriptures are a good illustration of this point. Those writings include myth (like narratives about the creation of the universe or the birth of Jesus) but also songs, proverbs, prayers, genealogies, sermons, ritual instructions, and behavioral injunctions (like the Ten Commandments and the 600-plus additional rules or laws). Over the centuries, the religion has accumulated other oral or written additions like church history, lives of the saints, martyr tales, masses and liturgies, interpretations and commentaries, and popular literature.

So, not all story-telling is religious, and not all of religion is story-telling. To focus momentarily on religious story-telling or myth, we note that most people associate myth with origin stories, the accounts of events that caused or started some aspect of current existence. For instance, the first book of the Judeo-Christian writings contains an origin story (actually two contradictory origin stories) of the earth, plants and animals, and humans. It proceeds to give the origins of death, shame, sin, women's suffering in childbirth, languages, circumcision, the kingdom of Israel, and many, many more things. However, not all myths are origin stories: the tale of Samson, for example, does not particularly explain how or why anything began, nor do many of the other incidents reported in the texts. They are just things that happened. They may have, again, instructive value (if you are like Samson, trust in your god but not in women), but they are not etiological accounts.

The same is true in other of the world's mythologies. Greek myths might tell of how humans acquired fire (Prometheus) or why there are ills and misfortunes in the world (Pandora), but other stories, like the trials of Hercules, do not appear to establish or explain anything. So, some myths appear to provide explanations, while others do not. Explanation is not the essence of myth. As we will see below, Bronislaw Malinowski will argue that explanation is not really the point of myth at all.

Surprisingly, many of the qualities of existence that those of us raised in a Western Christian atmosphere would regard as desperately in need of explanation are not included in other religions' mythologies at all. Evans-Pritchard notes that the Nuer appear to have no creation myth; things have just always been this way as far as they know. Likewise, the Kaguru of East Africa did not know the story of the creation of their world nor care very much about it (Beidelman 1971). Among the islanders of Ulithi in Micronesia, none of their gods were creators, and their religion thus contained no creation story (Lessa 1966).

When religions do contain origin or explanation stories, they naturally have very different things to explain. For example, Kaguru society had a system of unequal kinship groups or clans; so, while they were uninterested in the origin of the universe, they were, quite reasonably, interested in the origin of the clans. As Beidelman reports,

> While there is a general legend common to all Kaguru, this varies in detail from clan to clan. Kaguru may cite this legend to prove their common origin and thus explain their common culture, but they also use it as a means to account for the differences in Kaguru society, differences which provide the most basic feature of Kaguru social organization. That feature is clanship: Kaguru are divided into about one-hundred exogamous, matrilineal clans (*ikolo* or *kolo* or *ikungugo*). Clan size varies from a few hundred to several thousand members.... Kaguru say that although they may have left their original homeland without such social distinctions (no one stresses this point, however), somewhere en route clans came into being. Most clans derive their names from a series of events said to have occurred during the migration to present-day Kaguruland. Some clans are also said to be related to one another, and this too is explained through such legends (1971:32–3).

Cubeo society in the Brazilian Amazon included the role of shaman, which was ripe for an origin story. Goldman gives this brief account of the first Cubeo shaman or *paye*:

> Once there were no *payes*. A youth named Djuri wishing to become a *paye* went to the forest...and sat in a small clearing and thought about how he should go about making thunder. While he was deep in thought, Onponbu [Thunder Man], the owner of *dupa* appeared. He knew the thoughts of the youth and he could see that he had a clean body. He decided to make him *yavi* and set down beside the boy three objects — a fragment of *dupa*, a small container of beeswax, and a tray of eagle down. The youth prepared the *dupa* and beeswax for inhaling and he also inserted the eagle down up his nostrils from where it moved to lodge in his head.

ATHEISM ADVANCED

That night he had visions, and he then understood how to make thunder. In his visions, he saw the houses where the *payes* gathered and saw that there were very many in them. He slept and when he awoke before dawn, he heard the first thundering in the East where the rivers fall off the earth. He fell asleep again and dreamt that Onponbu was asking him if he was satisfied with what he had been given and if he believed he had learned how to make thunder. Onponbu advised him how to live. He cautioned him not to sleep with a woman. "You must guard the conduct of your life," he told him. "You must not eat what others eat. You are to eat only farinha of starch.... You should not eat anything hot or take food directly from the hand of a woman. Set hot food aside until it turns cold, and it will cause you no harm" (2004:303–10).

Onponbu proceeded to give the boy many gifts, including thunder and lightning. He also taught him to seek out specific powerful plants. And he transformed the boy into a shaman by literally changing his body, inserting spines into his forearms and put a stick in his mouth. Finally, the new shaman received ritual objects like the ones used by contemporary *payes*.

And so on. The point we are making here is that different things exist for and are interesting to different societies, and their religions reflect these cultural realities. And it goes without saying that the same human reality (say, death or disease) can receive quite different, even diametrically opposed, mythical treatment in different religions. The common factor in all myth, though, is the (putatively historical or true) recounting of the exploits and adventures of specific religious entities or *agents*. The significance for us is that *human* agents live historical or meaningful or narrative lives, so it is only natural for humans to attribute these same qualities to *non-human* agents. If, as we asserted in Chapter 3, religion is basically the assignment of human-like qualities to non-human beings and/or forces, then two things become transparently true which explain myth: first, these non-human agents would behave much as human agents do, and second, humans would talk about these non-human agents — including telling stories about them — much as humans talk about each other.

Is There a Mythical Mentality?

Observers of myth have inevitably noticed that these stories are often, to be kind, *fantastic* (that is, having the quality of fantasy) or, to be less kind, ridiculous and *false*. On a good day, the myths of one religion are incompatible with the myths of another: each, for instance, that has a creation myth has a *different and contradictory* creation myth. Why, many wise analysts have pondered, do humans engage in such patently absurd behavior? Why do humans make myths at all?

One of the dominant approaches to myth, given the predilections of Western culture toward dualism and psychologization (see Chapter 9), is to see it as a product of a distinct and inferior mental process. In other words, myth is viewed as an outcome of a separate mythical way of thinking which shares little or none of the quality of normal or rational thinking. Perhaps the firmest statement of this position comes from Lucien Levy-Bruhl (1857–1939), who posited two modes of thought, 'logical' and 'pre-logical,' which operate on two utterly incompatible principles. Logical thought, he opined, rests on the so-called Law of Exclusion, the claim that a thing cannot be itself and something else at the same time and in the same fashion. The logical mind knows that a tree cannot be a tree and a human at the same time, or that a wafer cannot be a wafer and the body of Christ at the same time. Myths that tell of impossible events like an animal becoming a human, or a human becoming an animal, or a god becoming a human, are rejected by the logical mentality, which is the modern mentality, which is, in Levy-Bruhl's thought, *our* mentality. The modern, logical, Western mind produces facts and knowledge, not myth. It is the pre-logical process that generates myth, symbolism, and all of religion. This mode of thought suspends the Law of Exclusion and operates on the Law of Participation: one thing can be itself and something else simultaneously. Thus, there can be animal-humans and plant-humans and animal-plants and living-dead and god-humans. Contradictions do not trouble the pre-logical mind, which is a 'primitive' mind, which is a 'religious' mind.

Levy-Bruhl eventually disavowed the most extreme interpretation of his own theory, realizing that there is not

ATHEISM ADVANCED

an unbridgeable gulf between the so-called primitive and the modern person; in fact, many modern Western people accept some pre-logical, 'participatory' notions — for example, that the communion wine is the blood of Jesus or that Jesus was man and god in one — and all primitive or traditional peoples have plenty of logical ideas and understandings. No humans ever walked around with their heads full of nothing but myth. Nevertheless, this dualistic-psychological approach has survived and reappeared in many forms.

Sigmund Freud adopted it in most of its Levy-Bruhlian glory. According to Freud, there are two modes of mind, a "primary process" and a "secondary process." The latter involves effective, rational action on reality whereas the former is not in touch with or even particularly interested in reality. The primary process works in the isolated unconscious mind, where drives and instincts and wishes are not distinguished from reality. These drives and instincts and wishes — many of them painful or unacceptable and most of them sexual in nature — must and will be expressed. This expression, however, is often indirect, marked by creative and imaginative substitution, of which dreams are the most conspicuous instance. Dreams, then, are a symbolic 'language' for the primary mental process, but not dreams alone: neuroses and other mental illnesses are symbolic (*e.g.* hysterical blindness might be a symbol of seeing something terrible and painful), as well as slips of the tongue (so-called *Freudian slips*). Significantly, higher cultural achievements — like art, ritual, and myth — belong to this same symbolic process, as well as children's thinking and primitive culture in general.

Freud's student Carl Jung followed the master's approach. In his famous essay "Concerning the Two Kinds of Thinking," he argues that while dreams are "apparently contradictory and nonsensical," they arise from a distinct and important mental process, which is a symbolic one (1949:9). Why, he wonders, are dreams symbolic, and *how* are they symbolic? The purpose of symbolic thought is to *prevent* our understanding of dreams by obscuring their meaning. The reason is a different mode of thinking than the everyday rational mode.

Ordinary thought, what he refers to as "thinking with directed attention" or simply "directed thinking," is "reality thinking" — logical, adjusted to external conditions, effective, clear, and certain. However, the source of symbolic thinking is a separate mode, undirected or "dream" or "fantasy" thinking. Dream/fantasy thinking "turns away from reality, sets free subjective wishes, and is, in regard to adaptation, wholly unproductive" (22). Jung locates this same dream-mentality in ancient history and "primitive society," in particular religion. In ancient and primitive settings, logic was never followed, and everything "was considered according to its anthropomorphic or theriomorphic attributes, as human being or animal" (25). Thus, he draws "a parallel between the phantastical [sic], mythological thinking of antiquity and the similar thinking of children, between the lower human races and dreams" (27–8).

This dualism persists to today, particularly in the work of Karen Armstrong, who puts her dichotomy in terms of *mythos* and *logos*. *Mythos* is a way of thinking that is not directed toward or concerned with practical matters and is not meant to be taken literally. It is, she says, an ancient form of psychology, bringing into the light obscure and otherwise inaccessible regions of the unconscious. It is not and does not attempt to be factual or rational, and so it cannot be demonstrated or verified. It speaks of history, or casts itself in historical terms, but it is not historical: its 'historical events' are not actual specific and unique occurrences in the past but rather "external manifestations of constant, timeless realities" (2000:*xv*). *Logos*, on the other hand, is the logical, the rational, the pragmatic, the literal and, in our time, the scientific. It is propositional, that is, makes claims that are either true or false and can be verified or falsified as such. It is functional rather than expressive, goal-oriented rather than contemplative or playful.

All of these theories suggest a radical break between the kind of thinking that produces myth and the kind of thinking that produces facts or knowledge or science. However, in the mid-twentieth century, a new perspective was introduced by philosophers like Suzanne Langer, Ernst Cassirer, and Gilbert Ryle that was very influential on social-scientific studies of myth and religion like those of Victor Turner and Clifford Geertz. Langer opens the door for us by hypothesizing that there is one basic quality of all thought — and not the one we might expect. It is not reason but *symbolism* that is essential and foundational to thought. All human mental activity, from the processing of raw sense-data to the highest reaches of philosophical and scientific analysis, is "primarily symbolic" (1942:16). Symbolization, the process of making and using symbols, then is "the starting point of all intellection in the human sense, and is more general than thinking, fancying, or taking action" (33). Her argument is that all thinking starts with concepts and that all concepts are symbolic in that they refer to types or classes of things, not individual things: a name like 'David' refers to a specific person, but 'person' refers to a general kind of being, and the abstraction from individual person to type or category or concept is symbolic.

Identifying a single core mental process, she proposes that there are different kinds of symbols, some "precise" or "discursive" like language (in which each symbol has a single definite meaning) and others imprecise and non-discursive like art or music or myth. Linguistic symbols, she argues, constitute a vocabulary with a grammar for combining the symbols. Further, it is possible to construct a dictionary of meanings (*i.e.*, each word can be defined or explained in terms of other words) and to translate symbols or words from one language to another. Non-linguistic, artistic or expressive symbols, on the other hand, have no vocabulary or grammar: there is no 'definition' of a note in a symphony or a spot of color in a painting. Therefore, you cannot create a 'dictionary' of artistic symbols, to the effect that a B-sharp in music means this or a certain line in a sculpture means that. Finally, you cannot translate the 'message' of one artistic form into another: how would you express Beethoven's Fifth Symphony in clay?

Myths come in words, but they are not to be taken as scientific or factual or literal statements. They are rather manifestations of this non-discursive, expressive language which operates primarily through *metaphor*, as we discussed in Chapter 2. Metaphor, or the process of analogy on which it is built, is still thinking, she insists, but it is not "rational" or fact-related thinking and is not to be taken literally. It is not trying to denote or explain anything. In fact, she proposes that much of it is image-based and driven, and images quickly lead to other images, forging more associative links. The result is a journey along metaphoric chains that go where no one can predict: "Metaphor is the law of growth of every semantic" (119), as people make more and more analogies and associations and play with the ones they have. The end-product is a tangled and virtually impenetrable forest of meaning and metaphor which she calls "vegetative thought," in which "the very use of language exhibits a rampant confusion of metaphorical meanings clinging to every symbol, sometimes to the complete obscurance of any reasonable literal meaning" (120–1).

Ernst Cassirer pushed further the scope and importance of the symbolic/metaphorical function. In his *An Essay on Man* he accepts that as history or as explanation, myth and symbol fail, being full of "errors and heresies" (1954:97), "a logic of absurdity" (29), but only if we approach them logically or take them literally. However, he urges us to see symbols, myths, and all metaphors not as *what we think* (*i.e.*, not a truth-claims) but as *how we think* — that symbols permeate and mediate our perceptions and thoughts utterly:

> man lives in a symbolic universe. Language, myth, art, and religion are parts of this universe.... No longer can man confront reality immediately; he cannot see it, as it were, face to face. Physical reality seems to recede in proportion as man's symbolic activity advances. Instead of dealing with the things themselves man is in a sense constantly conversing with himself.... His situation is the same in the theoretical as in the practical sphere. Even here man does not live in a world of hard facts, or according to his immediate needs and desires (43).

The same perspective leads Gilbert Ryle to suggest that mind and meaning are fundamentally public or external and social, since these symbolic/metaphorical resources of thought and experience are shared by and acquired from society. That is to say, a group's or religion's symbols and metaphors, including but not limited to its myths, are the shared lenses through which the members perceive and understand their world. Mythical and other symbols are the depository of a people's memories and experiences.

Myths, from this angle, are one facet in the lens of a religion and, more generally, of a culture. Hence, Geertz in particular came to see all of culture as symbols, by which he means "any object, act, events, quality, or relation which serves as a vehicle for a conception" (1973:91). Public, cultural symbols thus "are tangible formulations of notions, abstractions from experience fixed in perceptible forms, concrete embodiments of ideas, attitudes, judgments, longings, or beliefs" (91). Rational or irrational, logical or pre-logical, they are available to members of the group and prior to members of the group (that is, the symbols exist before any particular individual is born) and are "ingredient" to the thinking, feeling, and *behaving* of the individuals. To paraphrase Turner, we are all creations in a forest of symbols.

Myth as Proposition and Performance

We will return to the question of myth, meaning, and action — which is the central question of this chapter — below. For the moment, this appreciation of myth as a symbolic resource for human thought and action leads us to regard myth in a new light. If myths (and other symbolic expressions) are not be taken literally as if they were trying to say something, then perhaps *what* myths say is less important than *how* they say it. To be more direct, it is an empirical fact that myths are not always, maybe seldom, told in the way that we would tell the story of the Three Bears. In other words, myth-tellers may not say, "Then Goldilocks did this, and then the Papa Bear did this, and then the Baby Bear did that" — but then, neither do fairy-tale tellers.

We can summarize the point by saying that myths are not so much told as *performed*. This performance can take many shapes and demonstrate many properties. Most importantly, myths are often incorporated into or are part of rituals. During the ritual, some or all of a myth may be spoken. But even when it is, it is not always or often narrated the way we narrate a story. It may be sung or chanted, for instance: one incident or episode may be extracted from the body of the myth and repeated over and over again. It may be acted out, mimed or danced. It may have to be accompanied by sacred objects and performed by actors with particular qualities (in certain social groups, holding certain religious offices roles, or decorated in certain ways) in particular states of ritual preparation ('purified,' having fasted or abstained from sex, *etc.*). As a Cubeo informant told Goldman, he could not simply recite a myth: asked to recite a myth, the informant said, "'It cannot be done this way, I cannot sing without dancing.' Then after a long pause, he added, 'I cannot dance without wearing the mask'" (2004:5).

There are often clear and crucial standards for how, where, and when a myth can be performed. In some societies, story-telling, or the telling of particular kinds of stories, may be a gender prerogative; as Douglas Parks (1996) describes the oral traditions of the Arikara people, it is males who tell the main myths. Myths may also have a seasonal or other temporal component: the Arikara only recite their stories during the winter, and other cultures may have select times of day for story-telling, like evening. They might also be repeated only before certain audiences (say, fully initiated men) or, as in the case of many Australian Aboriginal societies, different and less esoteric or sacred versions might be told in front of general audiences, the inside or esoteric versions reserved for initiated men. Finally, there may be specialists with the right or duty to tell myths — priests, shamans, designated story-keepers, or owners of the myths.

Beyond the proper occasions and persons to perform myths, there are also often specialized speech styles in which to perform them. That is, performing a myth is not just telling the story, let alone merely listing the events in the tale. But then, telling a fairy tale or folk tale is often more than the details or the action of the story. Imagine, for instance, telling the story of the Three Little Pigs without doing the voices of the pigs and the wolf and without the sound effects (the 'huff and puff').

Richard Bauman (2001:171), an expert in oral performance, has derived a set of common keys to performance which distinguish the telling of a myth from other, ordinary kinds of speech. One of the most prominent keys is what he calls "special codes, *e.g.* archaic or esoteric language, reserved for and diagnostic of performance." One familiar example from Christianity is the use of Latin for religious services; other religions often have formal and even secret terms for use specifically and solely in mythical contexts. Another stylistic option is "special formulae that signal performance, such as conventional openings and closings, or explicit statements announcing or asserting performance." These formulae vary by type of speech event, so that English speakers might say, "Once upon a time" to introduce a fairy tale but not a myth: picture someone saying, "Once upon a time, God created the heavens and the earth" and you get the point.

A frequent if not universal tactic in good myth- and story-telling is the use of metaphor and other figures of speech. There are also many distinctive "formal stylistic devices, such as rhyme, vowel harmony, [and] other forms of parallelism," including repetition, not to mention special "patterns of tempo, stress, pitch" and "patterns of voice quality and vocalization." These qualities in particular are generally lost when myths are committed to writing (how do you indicate in writing that the little pigs spoke in a high-pitched, squealing voice?), yet they are often essential to a good performance of the narrative. Finally, Bauman mentions "appeal to tradition" and "disclaimer of performance" as important oral properties. A disclaimer may include something like an assertion that one is about to tell a story or has just finished. And if anything, the appeal to tradition is the fundamental property of myth: one is not inventing a story, probably not even much embellishing it, but telling it either 'as it really happened' or 'as it has always been told.'

The upshot of this discussion is that myths — like much of religion as we now understand it but contrary to common opinion — are not so much something to know as *something to do*. In fact, many members of the group may not know the myths at all, or only fragments of them, and/or only less-sacred versions of them. Myths may never be told in a straight-forward narrative fashion, and they are hardly ever, in most religious traditions, explained and analyzed. The point of the myth is not to impart any information but simply *to do* the myth in the right way at the right time. We are, habitually, overemphasizing the meaning or the cognitive or intellectual aspect of myth and religion in general by focusing on the content rather than on the form, the style, and the performance. If you asked most members of any religious group what their myth means, they would sincerely not know and probably not care — as long as they do it or have it done for them. 'Myth,' in short, is *verbal action*, and it often does not exist at all except as background knowledge *until it is enacted*. To be honest, scholars and fieldworkers often attribute myth where there is actually mostly or only performance: *myth* is *our* explanation for what they are saying and doing, *our* product of summarizing and codifying their practices.

Morality and Religion

There is no doubt much more stress in Western, Christian cultures on morality than on myth. Again, Christians would insist that they do not have myth but that they definitely have morality, or even that their religion *is* morality above all else. Atheists, often taking their lead from Christianity and literally speaking Christian, tend to allow themselves to be swept along with Christian thinking on this subject. We atheists do not much trouble ourselves with myths (for us, all myths are false by definition, since myths refer to supernatural, religious beings and we reject the very notion of such beings). But we trouble ourselves very much with morality, down to trying to prove that we have morality too or that we can be good without god(s).

Given the amount of time and energy that Christians and atheists alike — and not just them but philosophers, politicians, lawyers, and social scientists — have devoted to the problem of morality, it is remarkable that so little progress has been made. As the famous early twentieth-century moral philosopher G. E. Moore wrote almost one hundred years ago, morality or ethics "is a subject about which there has been and still is an immense amount of difference of opinion.... Actions which some philosophers hold to be generally wrong, others hold to be generally right, and occurrences which some hold to be evils, others hold to be goods" (1963:7). Surely any topic that has resisted progress and agreement for so long must be being approached in the wrong way.

In this section, we are not going to try to adjudicate all of the various and diverse theories of morality. That is a fool's errand, and the failure to settle the question over the past 2,400 years probably indicates that it is a question that is not going to be settled — one that *cannot* be settled. Nor are we going to defend any particular morality. Rather, we are going to interrogate the very concept of morality and its relation to religion. We will find that there is a core of misunderstanding about morality — roughly the same core as in the misunderstanding of myth, ritual, belief (see Chapter 11), and religion as a whole. But we will also find some guidance from our earlier discovery that religion and all its elements are more about *doing* than *knowing*, and this will be particularly relevant since morality is fundamentally about human *action*, not human *knowledge*. This will ultimately bring us back to the question of myth and morality and finally to the lesson for atheism about both.

What is Morality?

One of the basic reasons why humans have made so little headway on the matter of morality is that hardly anyone attempts, and no one as far as I have determined has ever succeeded, to define what is meant by *morality*. Scholars and theorists of morality either seem to jump directly to their discussions without explaining exactly what they are talking about — presumably on the assumption that we all already know — or give some unhelpful definition such the painfully circular one I find in my Webster's dictionary: "a moral discourse, statement, or lesson; a doctrine of system of moral conduct; particular moral principles or rules of conduct." Turning to philosophers for assistance, we find the *Stanford Encyclopedia of Philosophy* offering this handy meaning: "a code of conduct put forward by a society or, some other group, such as a religion, or accepted by an individual for her own behavior." The *Dictionary of Philosophy* and the *Internet Encyclopedia of Philosophy* do not even contain entries for it, deferring to "morals" or "moral philosophy."

We all — at least 'we all' in the Western, Christian tradition — do have a thumbnail sense of what we mean by morality, perhaps encapsulated by Michael Shermer's definition of "right and wrong thoughts and behaviors in the context of the rules of a social group" (2004:7). But this and the other above definitions do not get us anywhere, since they merely substitute one unknown ('morality') with another unknown ('right and wrong thoughts and behaviors') or by the very same term ('morality is about morals').

Myths and Morals

Let us at the outset clarify one bit of language: let us not use the words *right* and *wrong* in the context of morality at all. These are words that belong to the context of propositions or fact-claims, where 'right' means *correct*, and 'wrong' means *incorrect*. Thus, it is right to assert 'The earth is round' or 'Two plus two equals four,' and it is wrong to assert 'The earth is flat' or 'Two plus two equals five.' Only a proposition can be right or wrong; a single word or concept cannot be. It makes no sense to say "Polygamy is wrong" or "Abortion is right." It would be equivalent to asserting that polygamy is false or that abortion is true, which is meaningless. The proper distinction for moral discourse is 'good-*versus*-bad' or 'proper-*versus*-improper' or 'moral-*versus*-immoral.'

As we encounter it, 'morality' is a singularly vague and profitless concept. It does not tell us *what* is moral, since different societies, religions, and other groups seem to disagree profoundly and loudly about it. It does not even tell us what a 'moral concern' is. In the United States, for instance, as the debacle with Janet Jackson at a past Super Bowl showed, a woman's bare breast is a huge moral problem; in other societies, where perhaps women walk around topless or totally naked, it would not be. It would not be accurate to say that it is 'moral' in this other society; rather, it is not even on their list of moral concerns. For many Americans, premarital sex is a big moral issue, while in some societies it is not on their 'moral radar' at all.

So, morality as a concept does not convey much meaning. Worse yet, at the same time that it does not mean enough, it threatens to mean too much. What I am suggesting is that there are many behavioral concerns or norms or rules for humans that would not fall within the range of someone's (or maybe anyone's) morality. For instance, men in the United States are not supposed to wear dresses or make-up; that is not right or good or normal, but it is not quite 'immoral.' Eating with your hands is not good, but it is not immoral either. Showing up on time for work is good behavior, but no one would call it "moral." As the atheist philosopher Kai Nielsen, author of *Why Be Moral?* explains, "Not all practical discourse is moral discourse. Not all conduct is moral conduct and not all advice or appraisal of conduct is moral advice or moral appraisal. Nor are all attitudes or dispositions to action moral advice or moral dispositions to act" (1989:40).

In other words, there is apparently a spectrum of behavioral concerns, and behavioral standards, and somewhere on the spectrum are the moral concerns and the moral standards. One is tempted to claim that the moral ones are the really serious ones; but do Americans really think that Janet Jackson's or any other woman's breasts are among the greatest concerns in the country? If so, they need to get their priorities straight. Likewise with gambling or smoking or drinking or swearing: these are often regarded as moral issues although they are not on the same level as murder, nor do all societies and religions fret about them.

Having found no essence to morality, let us acknowledge that, like language and religion before, there is probably no such thing as 'morality.' Rather — just as there is no such thing as 'language' but only languages and no such thing as 'religion' but only religions — so there are morali-*ties* but no morality. As Nietzsche rightly put it in *Beyond Good and Evil,* (section 18),

> Strange as it may sound, in all "science of morals" hitherto the problem of morality itself has been *lacking*: the suspicion was lacking that there was anything problematic here. What philosophers called "the rational ground of morality" and sought to furnish us was, viewed in the proper light, only a scholarly form of *faith* in the prevailing morality, a new way of *expressing* it, and thus itself a fact within a certain morality, indeed even in the last resort a kind of denial that this morality *ought* to be conceived as a problem — in any event the opposite of a testing, analysis, doubting, and vivisection of this faith…. [I]t is precisely because they were ill informed and not even very inquisitive about other peoples, ages, and former times, that they did not so much as catch sight of the real problem of morality — for these come into view only if we compare many moralities.

In other words, when people — including professional philosophers — have talked about morality they have generally and un-self-consciously meant *their* morality (usually *Christian morality*) as if it were the only one on earth or the only one of any interest. The other moralities have either escaped their grasp completely or have simply been filed away under 'false morality' in the same way that religions have dismissed other religions as false religion.

It might be more useful, therefore, to talk about 'moral system' than 'morality.' There are many moral systems, which collectively we can refer to as 'morality' (just as there are many religious systems which collectively we can refer to as religion), which vary dramatically from each other but presumably have some thing(s) in common to belong to the same category. What a future *theory* of morality will be, then, is not advocacy or exegesis of any one particular moral system, much less the invention of yet another moral system, but a description of what actual moral systems have in common and the range of variation between them, as well as an explanation of what makes moral systems possible or why humans have such things.

We can suggest that there are three dead-ends down which a future theory of morality should not go. One is an appeal to the 'goodness' of acts and/or actors. Besides being hopelessly circular (moral = good?), such an approach falls into the familiar Western habit of reifying an adjective into a noun. As an adjective, 'good' is a judgment made by *somebody* for some *purpose*: candy is good to eat but bad to build houses out of. And sugar is bad to eat if you are a diabetic. But to transform the *judgment* of 'good' into the *quality* of 'goodness' is to commit a tragic fallacy. There is no more such a thing as goodness than there is such a thing as tallness or coldness.

A second path to avoid is the issue of pleasure and pain. Some moral theories (which are nothing but disguised moral systems) maintain that morality is all about maximizing pleasure and minimizing pain. But that is frivolous, first since a moral system often explicitly *interferes* with pleasure (*i.e.*, it may be very pleasurable to have premarital sex or for homosexuals to have gay sex) and second because a moral theory or system like utilitarianism mires us in the relative and cumulative pleasures and pains of actions in nonsensical ways: in other words, if my action causes me one unit of pain but gives two other people one unit of pleasure each, is it thereby moral? The whole approach is off base and not the way that real people make their moral decisions.

The third path to avoid is the question of 'universalizability.' Many philosophers, from Kant to Nielsen, insist that a moral principle must be a universal or at least universalizable principle. Kant was the first to make this urgent: the basis of his moral philosophy was what he called the "categorical imperative," that one should act in such a way that the principle or maxim of one's action could be universalized. So, if I do not kill, I am saying, "It is always and everywhere bad to kill." Nielsen offers an updated version of the central claim: "For an act to be moral or for an attitude to be moral, it must be *universalizable*. By this is meant the following. If *A* is morally right for *X*, it is similarly morally right for anyone else in like circumstances" (63). But the qualification "in like circumstances" is the death of universal morality since it is no longer universal, or merely trivially so: in other words, if I say, "You should never kill, except if you are a soldier in the line of duty facing enemy combatants," we are no longer talking about *universals* but *situationals*. Otherwise the universal moral claim is that it is bad to kill *unless* you are a soldier and *unless* you are at war and *unless* your victim is an enemy combatant, *etc.* But that is a mockery of universalization.

Even worse, universalizability is much easier to achieve and therefore much less useful than these moral theorists think. A Muslim father who kills his daughter for having sex before marriage (a so-called honor killing) would presumably have no trouble universalizing that action. 'It is good for a father to kill a daughter who has dishonored her family' is not just a possible universalization but the actual maxim of his action. Therefore, people can and easily do universalize all kinds of things that we might find morally reprehensible. It is no help at all.

Finally, many people, especially religionists, hold that there is an essential dependence of morality on religion; that is the claim that gets atheists scrambling to defend their morality. However, if morality is a vague and contradictory term, and if there is no essence to morality — and, as we have seen, if there is no essence to religion either — then the morality-needs-religion or the morality-equals-religion position is exposed as the nonsense that it is. Like ritual and myth and belief, morality is neither unique to nor universal to religion. This is what makes attempts like Stephen Jay Gould's "non-overlapping magisteria" (1999) so mind-boggling. His basic assumption is that science is about facts and that religion is about morality; then he admits that there are other kinds of — and foundations for — morality than religion, including reason, culture, philosophy, and nature. So not all morality is religious, and not all religion is moral.

As any informed person knows, the Judeo-Christian scriptures never use the words 'morality' or 'moral' once, at least in the King James translation. Of course, there is a preoccupation with 'correct' behavior, but much of this behavior is ritual rather than moral. For instance, the well-known (and generally ignored by Christians) dietary laws in the early books of the Hebrew bible do not say that certain foods are immoral but rather that they are "unclean" or "abominable." Even 'sin' is often not a matter of immorality but of impurity which one can eliminate with a blood-sacrifice (although how *that* works is never explained) or with the simple passage of time, *i.e.*, impurity wears off. And hardly ever does the Israelite god *explain* why certain acts are forbidden or demanded; there is no little or no informational content and a lot of imperative command.

It may prove, on closer inspection, to be the case that morality is not only a Christian preoccupation but a relatively late Christian preoccupation. It is not found in all religions. In fact, the nineteenth-century ethnologist E. B. Tylor wrote in his classic 1871 *Primitive Culture* that the "moral element which among the higher nations forms a most vital part, is indeed little represented in the religion of the lower races," such that morality or ethics was most often *not* a central part of religion. There is empirical evidence to support this claim. Nadel (1954) explicitly states that the Nupe religion was "altogether silent" on ethical matters, that it offered no portrayal of the "ideal person," that it contained no myths of good and evil, and that it promised no supernatural rewards for good behavior.

Similarly, Nuer religion diverges from our popular expectation of morality: Evans-Pritchard finds that "the ethical content of what the Nuer regard as grave faults may appear highly variable, and even altogether absent" (1956:188). The author continues: "It is difficult also for the European observer to understand why Nuer regard as grave faults, or even as faults at all, what seem to him rather trivial actions" (189). No doubt the feeling would be mutual: the Nuer might find it hard to understand why American Christians get so exercised about women's breasts or smoking, *etc.*, just as the Christians would be surprised to learn that the Nuer think that such things as "a man milking his cow and drinking the milk, or a man eating with persons with whom his kin are at a blood-feud" are seriously bad. It shows again that what is a moral priority in one culture might not even be a moral issue in another, including the highest moral priorities in one culture: "Homicide is not forbidden, and Nuer do not think it wrong to kill a man in a fair fight. On the contrary, a man who slays another in combat is admired for his courage and skill" (195).

The Evolution of Morality

The impenetrability of morality in the modern philosophical and religious analysis seems like sufficient evidence that we have been barking up the wrong tree. Morality is not a thing at all but rather a category under which many and various moral systems are classified. There appears to be no essence to morality, such that we could say unequivocally that this action or even this issue is a moral one. Most assuredly, morality does not begin and end with religion.

I submit that everyone — theists and atheists alike — has been asking the wrong question about morality until recently. The questions that have been asked perennially have included 'What is the moral thing to do?' and, as Nielsen asks in the title of his book, 'Why be moral?' But the first question resists answer because it is simply an appeal to some particular moral system: 'What is a moral thing to do *for a Christian,*' for instance — and even on this they cannot agree. The second question resists answer because it is a nonsense question. As Shermer has aptly expressed it, "asking 'Why should we be moral?' is like asking 'Why should we be hungry?' or 'Why should we be horny.' For that matter, we could ask, 'Why should we be jealous?' or 'Why should we fall in love?'" (2004:57). In other words, we have been looking for the wrong thing in the wrong place.

The question that we should ask, the only question that makes sense and is important, is 'What is it about humans that makes them a 'moral' species?' Even this one is not quite right, since we do not even know what 'moral' means nor do we find it in every human group. Let us reformulate the whole investigation along lines that Nielsen suggests (without accepting his conclusion). Let us describe 'morality' as a generalization of *moral systems*, each of which is distinguished by a certain kind of talk, which he and we will call *moral language*:

> Moral language is the language we use in verbalizing a choice or decision; it is the language we use in appraising human conduct and in giving advice about courses of action; it is the language we use in ascribing or excusing responsibility; and finally, it is the language we use in committing ourselves to a principle of action. Moral language is a *practical* kind of discourse that is concerned to answer the questions: "What should be done?" or "What attitude should be taken toward what has been done, is being done, or will be done?" Moral language is most particularly concerned with guiding choices as to what to do when we are faced with alternative courses of action.
>
> As a form of practical discourse, morality functions to *guide* conduct and *alter* behavior and attitudes (1989:39).

Now the questions that seem important to pose and to answer are 'Why are humans concerned about appraising and advising conduct?' and most profoundly 'Why do humans need to guide and alter their behavior?' and 'Why do humans need external, *principled* guidance for their behavior?' In short, why are we the kind of beings for whom moral concerns are possible and necessary?

Until very recently, there was only one conceivable answer — the Kant/Lewis answer. Humans have 'free will' to choose between courses of action — this free will having been installed by a god but constrained (though not very effectively) by divine rules and divine rewards and punishments. In a word, morality was a *supernatural* phenomenon. But atheists obviously cannot accept this position, partly because we do not accept god(s) and the supernatural at all and partly because then it would be true that atheists could not have morality. Fortunately, recent research has suggested that morality has a perfectly *natural* basis and is a perfectly *natural* phenomenon.

A great deal of literature has accumulated over the last couple of decades to support this claim, although Darwin predicted it more than 130 years ago. In his *The Descent of Man*, first published in 1871, he mused that morality was not really such a mystery at all but rather that "any animal whatever, endowed with well marked social instincts, the parental and filial affections being here included, would inevitably acquire a moral sense or conscience" (1882:98). If this is so, then we should expect to find rudiments, evolutionary traces, or 'building blocks' of morality in the non-human natural world. And of course we do.

The details of the research into the evolution of morality are too vast and too varied to explore in depth here, and we do not need to. What we need to illustrate is that it is *possible* to give a natural, evolutionary explanation, so that non-natural, supernatural, and creationist explanations are not necessary or welcome. Since Darwin, an accelerating line of investigation has developed, starting at least with Edward Westermarck's 1908 *The Origin and Development of the Moral Ideas* and reaching critical mass with E. O. Wilson's 1975 *Sociobiology: The New Synthesis*. Since then, the field has provided conceptual and empirical studies like Peter Singer's 1981 *The Expanding Circle*; Robert Wright's 1994 *The Moral Animal: The New Science of Evolutionary Psychology*; Marc Hauser's 2000 *Wild Minds: What Animals Really Think* and his 2006 *Moral Minds: How Nature Designed Our Universal Sense of Right and Wrong*; Michael Shermer's aforementioned *The Science of Good and Evil*; Richard Joyce's 2006 *The Evolution of Morality*; and the many works of primatologist Frans de Waal, including *Primates and Philosophers: How Morality Evolved*.

These scientists and philosophers disagree on a variety of issues, but there is a consistent core to their messages. The core of the core is that morality is not utterly unique to humans but has its historical, evolutionary antecedents and (therefore) its biological bases. In other words, morality does not appear suddenly out of nowhere in humans but emerges gradually with the emergence of certain kinds of beings living certain kinds of lives. This is not to assert that animals have full-blown morality any more than they have full-blown language. It is to assert that morality, like language, is not an all-or-nothing thing but rather the kind of phenomenon that a being can exhibit more-or-less of until we cross a threshold into a full human version.

Myths and Morals

The key to the evolutionary theory of morality is that particular sorts of beings — especially *social* beings who live for long periods of time in groups of their own kind — tend reasonably to develop interests in the behavior of others and capacities to determine and to influence that behavior. This might start most obviously with offspring: parents of many species, from birds to apes, show concern for their offspring, disadvantage themselves for their offspring (for instance, by spending time feeding them), and even put their own lives at risk for their offspring (the notorious problem of 'altruism'). Other species may show these same behaviors toward adult members of the family, or toward adult members of the larger social group, or ultimately, in humans, to all members of the species and perhaps to other species as well. In this regard, human morality is an extension of more short-range helping behaviors.

While Western culture and philosophy have been focused on competition and selfishness (for interesting reasons beyond the scope of this book), scientists have discovered lately that nature does not always operate on the principle of selfishness. Lynn Margulis' 1987 *Microcosmos: Four Billion Years of Microbial Evolution* was one of the first biology texts to suggest that cooperation and symbiosis might be equally important processes in the natural world and may have even formed the first complex animal cells. We know today that humans have 'good bacteria' in our digestive tract without which we could not survive. Cooperative or helping (that is, 'un-selfish') and eventually reciprocal behavior now being seen as possible and valuable, it becomes easier to see. As de Waal writes,

> Evolution forms animals that assist each other if by doing so they achieve long-term benefits of greater value than the benefits derived from going it alone and competing with others. Unlike cooperation resting on simultaneous benefits to all parties involved (known as mutualism), reciprocity involves exchanged acts that, while beneficial to the recipient, are costly to the performer (2006:13).

With such costly but pro-social behaviors, we have taken a long step toward morality. Or, as Shermer puts it, human morality or the capacity and tendency to have moral sentiments or moral concerns evolved out of the premoral feelings and tendencies of pre-human species. De Waal and other animal-watchers have gathered an enormous amount of data on pre-human morality, including sharing, signs of fairness, gratitude, self-sacrifice, sympathy and comforting, and many more. Sufficient data have built up that O'Connell (1995) has catalogued hundreds of reported cases of 'empathy' and 'moral' behavior in chimps. Moreover, this has been observed in an extraordinary variety of species, from birds to elephants to primates.

The link between social living and morality — or at least 'premoral behavior' — can be appreciated readily enough. As de Waal reminds us, social living depends on social *regularity*, which he characterizes as a "set of expectations about the way in which oneself (or others) should be treated and how resources should be divided" (2006:44). Individuals without some sense of what to expect from others — and of what others expect of him or her — would not be properly 'social.' And this social regularity entails some method for handling exceptions and deviations: "Whenever reality deviates from these expectations to one's (or the other's) disadvantage, a negative reaction ensues, most commonly protest by subordinate individuals and punishment by dominant individuals" (44–5).

Thus, a certain amount of regularity and predictability in behavior is a requisite for social co-existence and for the eventual formation of morality. However, it is only one component. In fact, in keeping with our analysis of religion itself, let us regard morality not as a single monolithic skill or interest but a composite phenomenon of multiple skills and interests, all evolved, and many evolved for other non- or pre-moral purposes. Behavioral regularity is one building block, but ants and bees achieve this goal without morality or even learning; it appears to be instinctual.

To reach premoral behavior, and ultimately human morality, a variety of other pieces must be in place. One of the essential ones is a certain degree of 'intersubjectivity,' the ability to understand (and therefore hopefully predict) the thoughts and feelings of others. We might call this, at least at a fairly high level of development, the notion of *agency* that we introduced in Chapter 3. I am an agent, and the other members of my family or group or species are agents — with thoughts and feelings similar to mine. Beyond the mere awareness of others' thoughts and feelings is the capacity to *share* them in some way, what de Waal calls "emotional contagion."

Borrowing the term from Hatfield, Cacioppo, and Rapson (1993), de Waal proposes that, as beings approach moral status, they develop the capacity to experience the experiences of others. Fortunately, some of the most fascinating recent work has identified a basis for this phenomenon in so-called 'mirror neurons' in the brain. Discovered in the 1990s in monkey brains, mirror neurons, as the name suggests, imitate or mimic the activity of other parts of the brain — or of other brains. Experiments have shown that "neurons in the same area of the brain were activated whether the animals were performing a particular movement...or simply observing another monkey — or a researcher — perform the same action" (May 2006:3).

What is truly remarkable, as the last words indicate, is that this process operates across species. If this work is correct, and it is very promising, then it provides a literal biological explanation for empathy: individuals with mirror neurons, including humans and other primates, can actually feel what others feel. This research gives the old saying, 'It hurts (or pleases) me more than it does you' some new seriousness.

In addition to the above-mentioned premoral competences, Hauser names a few others. One is the ability to inhibit one's own actions. Most species have difficulty preventing themselves from acting, but humans and some primates can do so, although not perfectly. Another is memory, which is crucial for preserving and learning from previous interactions with the same individuals: can this other individual be trusted, and has he or she reciprocated before? A third is the ability to detect and respond to cheaters or those who violate expectations. A fourth is symbolic thought, ultimately in the form of language and even quite abstract thought about rules and principles.

Hauser admits that few if any animals meet all of these qualifications, but then neither do very young human children — proving that morality must be developmentally achieved by each human individual. However, many or most of these talents exist in non-human species, and by the time these talents all appear together in one species, namely humans, we have a patently un-mysterious and un-supernatural moral sensibility.

The fact that non-humans do not have human morality, de Waal reminds us, is no reason to discount the natural, prehuman roots of morality:

> To neglect the common ground of primates, and to deny the evolutionary roots of human morality, would be like arriving at the top of a tower to declare that the rest of the building is irrelevant, that the precious concept of "tower" ought to be reserved for its summit.
>
> Are animals moral? Let us simply conclude that they occupy several floors of the tower of morality. Rejection of even this modest proposal can only result in an impoverished view of the structure as a whole (2006:181).

Morality and the Interaction Code

Morality is not supernatural; neither is there a 'moral law' that all humans share. Rather, there are interpersonal, social, behavioral regularities and concerns and the biological bases for them which add up in humans to a moral sense. Since there is no moral law but rather moral habits or moral interests or moral concerns, the foundation on which C. S. Lewis built his elaborate argument for Christianity comes crashing down: no moral law, no need for a moral law-giver, and no need for his god. 'Morality' is little more than what the premoral tendencies and capacities feel like to an incorrigibly social and painfully self-aware species like humanity.

In a way, our initial question has been answered. Why do humans have morality? Because all social species have morality-like traits, and humans simply have more of them. But there is another dimension to this question. Why do humans *need* morality in ways that other social species seem not to? In other words, what is morality doing for us that *something else* accomplishes for them?

It appears that, in the course of evolution, humans have gained some abilities and lost some abilities. We have gained self-awareness and language and formal abstract thought, but we have lost many instincts that, for most species, make these wonderful qualities unnecessary. Most species are born

Myths and Morals

knowing more or less what to do. Of course, there are species, including non-primates like lions and dolphins and birds of prey, that must learn some of the critical skills (like hunting) without which they would not survive; this is why such animals raised in captivity must be "taught" by humans *how to be wild animals.* So, humans are hardly the only species that needs to learn to be itself. *But no other species needs to learn so much nor needs to learn it so badly.*

In the words of American anthropologist Clifford Geertz, humans are very "incomplete" beings. They require non-biological, "extra-somatic" resources to complete their inadequate biological and instinctual birthright. The encompassing term for these resources is *culture.* Hence Geertz describes culture as "a set of control mechanisms — plans, recipes, rules, instructions (what computer engineers call 'programs') — for the governing of behavior" (1973:44). Because we are not born with innate control mechanisms, humanity "is precisely the animal most desperately dependent upon such extragenetic, outside-the-skin control mechanisms, such cultural programs, for ordering his behavior." Culture is how humanity settles its potentially rich but actually quite indefinite nature into specific plans of meaning and plans of action. Even Nielsen agrees that morality exists because we humans "need some social mechanism" to guide our behavior, although he still thinks that morality is a matter of "curbing personal desires" rather than informing those desires in the first place (1989:70).

Given the relative and quite real inadequacy of human inborn guidance, it is no surprise that humans have had to invent their own nor that humans have invented such a diversity of them; the source of cultural diversity is multiple solutions to the same general challenges. Humans have had to invent solutions to many problems other than the so-called moral ones. Everything from what foods to eat and how to prepare them, what clothes (if any) to wear, what name to call things, and of course what values and rule to adopt in relation to each other are problems to solve, offering an endless opportunity for creativity and an almost endless variety of answers. But let us focus on the interpersonal behavioral area.

There are arguably three relevant facts about humans: they must behave, they must behave in relation to each other (that is, they must interact), and they must behave within some shared standard or norm or code of action. As we considered in Chapter 7, many species handle their interaction problem through *ritualization*, a more or less instinctive and therefore universal (within the species) set of behaviors that are intended not so much to communicate as to elicit responses. Humans also ritualize, although, as with language and moral behavior, they do so relatively more self-consciously than other species. Humans have to invent — and have invented many times — what John Skorupski (1976) has characterized as an "interaction code" that will govern their interpersonal behavior, that will tell them what to do and what to expect others to do, that will create and maintain regularity in their interactions.

According to Skorupski, the interaction code provides individuals in social situations with more or less clear and definite (and often *quite* clear and definite) behavioral guidelines: it amounts to directing individuals that such a person in such a situation should perform such an action. By this process, relations — and not always *equal* relations, debunking the assertion that equality or fairness or justice is central to morality — are formed and perpetuated. As Skorupski explains, social interaction demands "that people should use the code to establish the relationship which ought — in accordance with other norms — to hold between them, to maintain it, to re-establish it if it is thrown out of equilibrium and to terminate it properly" (83–4). The interaction code thus specifies how "the people involved in an interaction [depending on] their relative standing or roles, and their reciprocal commitments and obligations," should comport themselves in order to achieve mutual understanding, acceptance, and ongoing successful interaction (77).

The interaction code of a society takes many forms, from small and trivial to grand and momentous. At the low end of the interactional spectrum are little, mundane social forms and scripts, the minutia of daily life; some examples would be greetings ('How are you?' 'Fine, thanks, how are you?'), thanks, apologies, hand-shakings, and such familiar yet meaningful gestures. All competent members of society know how and when to perform them.

At a slightly higher level, for slightly more formal situations, are matters of *etiquette*. These include writing thank-you notes, using the correct fork, wearing the appropriate clothing, and so on. Certain situations or social contexts have their own specialized interaction-code requirements, such as the workplace, the court room, the class room, a wedding or funeral, and many more.

On occasions of greater seriousness, such as the meeting of two heads of state, a yet more formal level of interaction like *protocol* appears. Protocol specifies exactly where individuals should stand, where and when they should sit, what they should say or do regarding each and every detail of their interaction. The point, obviously, of protocol is to minimize the possibility of misunderstanding (and perhaps war) by controlling and predetermining as much of the interaction as possible.

Religious ritual is a particular version of protocol for religious occasions and purposes, in which the behavior is more or less completely specified. Some religions, like ancient Hinduism, codify ritual behavior to an extreme extent, specifying each hand gesture and spoken word. When religious ritual becomes totally frozen and unchangeable, we might speak of *liturgy*.

Somewhere within this continuum of interaction-code behaviors is what we commonly think of as morality or moral behavior. It is not necessarily at the 'high end' and it is not necessarily restricted to only one position on the continuum; it may be spread throughout the possible range of human actions. Whatever else moral behaviors share with each other (and there seems to be very little), they are actions felt to be important and must be done lest the person be perceived as a bad person or wants the society to be shocked, offended, or damaged.

Comprehending morality as only one aspect of a much more inclusive interaction-concerned system of behavior solves many problems for us. First, it illustrates why some kind of interest in correct behavior (whether or not that interest is moral in the familiar Western-Christian sense) is universal among humans. As Nielsen put it earlier, humans face multiple behavioral options and, as social beings, are constantly advising and appraising their own and each others' behavior: why did that other person do that, and what should I do now? The interaction code provides ready-made, prefabricated solutions to most important social dilemmas, and it provides a way to function effectively in the group. If individuals perform the proper interaction-code behavior, others will know that they understand their situation and will be understood in turn. Even more, since human social interactions are very frequently hierarchical, performing your expected interaction-code behavior indicates that you *accept* your place in the system: for example, if a Japanese inferior bows deeply to his superior, or if a peasant prostrates himself before the king, then both have submitted themselves to the authority of their better. When my students call me Dr. Eller and I call them by their first name, we have demonstrated our unequally-ranked relationship.

Second, as we suggested, some parts of the interaction code are more formal and elaborate than others: the clothing you wear to a friend's party is less rigidly determined than what you would wear to a wedding, which is less rigidly determined than what you would wear to a dinner at the White House, and so on. The specificity and restrictiveness of the behavior is a sign of the gravity of the situation and the inequality of the participants. Part of this formality and elaboration is insuring that the interaction is done correctly, but another part is self-referential, that is, a way "of marking out, emphasizing, underlining the fact of code behavior" (87). In other words, in insignificant social situations, one can improvise more freely, but in very serious ones, it is better and safer to do what everyone else does and what has always been done before. Also, the more formal and elaborate the behavior, the more apparent it is that something special is going on — that this is not everyday, voluntary behavior but an enactment of a code that we have all bought into.

This, further, explains why religious rituals are decidedly repetitive, formal, and compulsory. All interactions are social, that is, performed with or to agents who advise and appraise us and who, hopefully, respond to us. Religious rituals are interactions too, only *with non-human and super-human agents* whose advice, appraisal, and response are singularly important to us. As Skorupski asserts, "to a large extent religious rites *are* social interactions with authoritative or powerful beings within the actor's social field, and ... their special characteristics are in large part due to the special characteristics these beings are thought to have" (165).

Myths and Morals

Since the stakes of the interaction are often great — we are hoping to receive some major benefit from it, such as health or long life or good fortune or something — we are particularly concerned to do it right. Also, since the inequality between the participants is so great — teachers are higher than students, and kings are higher than peasants, but gods are higher than anyone — the pressures to perform the interaction precisely in conformity with the interaction code are maximized. My students may praise me for my wonderful teaching, but when one talks to one's ancestor spirits or god(s) or whatever, one may really pour on the superlatives.

Finally, it is worth noting that the interaction code, because it is so ubiquitous and so essential to human social life, is often invisible or opaque to participants and, even when it is perceived, not much understood. In fact, humans can often perform the prescribed actions with little comprehension of what they are doing or why. People who choose the correct fork at a formal dinner need not know the history of forks or of formal dinners nor why this particular fork is good to use. It might actually be detrimental if individuals had to reason out which fork, which suit, which words to use in every situation. Rather, performing the interaction code is more like mastering a skill than learning a body of knowledge. We do not *know* the code; we *do* the code. It is about *acting* rather than *thinking*, which is one reason why it is often disparaged as 'empty ritual.' But as we have seen, and as it is easy and important to see, action and ritual are not empty. They are full, if not of *meaning*, then of *consequence*: if one of my students walks up to me and shouts, "Give me your book!" I know precisely what he or she means, but they are unlikely to get their wishes fulfilled.

On Morality, Myth, and Imperative

> And everything that you like you should first let yourself be commanded to do.
>
> —Nietzsche, *Thus Spoke Zarathustra*

It might seem like we are a long way from our earlier discussion of myth, but when we consider what all this morality talk has to do with religion, the connection between the two sections of this chapter suddenly becomes clear. As we all know and have admitted, many people — perhaps most people — continue to think that there is an essential dependence, even an identity, between morality and religion. We have exposed the errors in this position: morality is not exclusive to religion or universal to religion. Morality is a vague and diverse concept, and it appears to have perfectly natural and social sources. It does not even seem to be a thing at all but a composite of more basic psychological and social skills and abilities that humans share with their non-human ancestors.

When religionists (and, sadly, a few atheists) think about the relation between religion and morality, they tend to think in two terms. One is religion as the *source* of morality, possibly in the C. S. Lewis sense of the creator of a moral aptitude or a moral genius in humans (one which even he had to confess yields various and largely unsuccessful results), but more often in the sense of the *author* of specific moral injunctions. Where does the moral principle of not killing come from? *God*, they would answer. Without a god, where would you get a rule against killing, they ask. The fact that pre-Christians (and pre-humans) were just as good — sometimes better — at restraining themselves from killing escapes them.

But scientists and philosophers have found an evolutionary explanation for morality, even if the details are not all settled, and there is no need to resort to supernatural sources. So religionists resort to a second link in the religious *sanction* of morality. That is, they might argue that there is no reason to be moral unless there are supernatural consequences for one's behavior. The god(s) who originated the rules in the first place must back them up with penalties and prizes, rewards and punishments.

It has been commented by others before me that moral choices made for the benefits they accrue or the costs they incur are not really moral at all. By many definitions, 'morality' must be selfless, and religious morality of the divine-reward-and-punishment variety is, in a way, the ultimate egotism: I do good for the good it will do *me* (getting into heaven, *etc.*). A more concrete objection is that there are indeed many consequences for bad or inappropriate behavior: supernatural sanctions would be one kind, but there are legal and professional and personal and all manner of social sanctions available that are definitely more immediate and arguably more effective. In other words, I do not kill because I do not want to go to jail, or lose my job, or lose my property, or face humiliation and dishonor, and so on; in fact, once I have become a fully enculturated member of my society, I do not want to kill at all. In other words, there are plenty of reasons, social and individual, for abiding by the group's morality.

There is a third, more interesting and more frequently overlooked possible link between religion and morality, in which religion is not so much the source or the sanction as the *legitimation* for action. By 'legitimation' we mean justification, authorization, the reason not only why we do it but why it is the right thing to do. The legitimation function can be achieved through sources and sanctions, but it can also be achieved — perhaps more subtly and successfully — through *models* and through *moods and motivations*.

Here, then, is the connection between myth and morality. Myths, as we argued, are not always or fundamentally origin stories, just-so tales of how this or that began. In fact, if Karen Armstrong and even others like Joseph Campbell are correct, myths are not, and are not intended to be, historical accounts of the early days at all, and least of all are they meant to be explanations. Malinowski said it best when he wrote that myth is not a "speculation about origins of things born out of philosophic interest. Neither is it the result of the contemplation of nature — a sort of symbolic representation of its laws" (1948:83–4). Rather,

> Studied alive, myth ... is not symbolic, but a direct expression of its subject matter; it is not an explanation in satisfaction of a scientific interest, but a narrative resurrection of a primeval reality, told in satisfaction of deep religious wants, moral cravings, social submissions, assertions, even practical requirements. Myth fulfills in primitive culture an indispensable function: it expresses, enhances, and codifies belief; it safeguards and enforces practical rules for the guidance of man. Myth is thus a vital ingredient of human civilization; it is not an idle tale, but a hard-worked active force; it is not an intellectual explanation or an artistic imagery, but a pragmatic charter of primitive faith and moral wisdom (101).

In other words, as he asserts a few paragraphs earlier, myth "is not merely a story told but a reality lived. It is not of the nature of fiction, such as we read today in a novel, but it is a living reality, believed to have once happened in primeval times, and continuing ever since to influence the world and human destinies" (100).

Myths, as Malinowski is credited with formulating, are not so much explanations as *charters*. They do not so much tell us what was done then as *what we are to do now*. They are not history because they are not in time but instead timeless. The actions in myth are not historical incidents but what the great historian of religion Mircea Eliade called "paradigmatic acts," behaviors that set the world, natural and social, along a particular course and which serve today as the models or exemplars or paradigms for human behavior.

That people, even modern and smart people, use myths to guide their current actions and decisions is easy and amusing to see. One of the most spectacular examples can be found in the contemporary American debate over gay marriage. Many Christians base their position on (opposition to) gay marriage on religious grounds, sometimes explicitly stating that "God created Adam and Eve, not Adam and Steve." Thus, this 'first marriage' serves as the model and charter for all subsequent marriages. (What is unusually hilarious about this case is that Christians use the *gender* of the first couple as a charter but not any other characteristics about them: perhaps only men and women who are naked should marry each other, or perhaps men should only marry women who are made out of their rib!)

Another example is a more general one, literally, along the lines discussed in Chapter 8, applied to the body of the believer. I am referring to the question that Christians often ask themselves — "What would Jesus do?" — and to their **WWJD** bracelets. Here, the behaviors — or the presumed behaviors — of Jesus serve as the model for his followers: do what the founder did. Of course, other traditions evince the same force: Muslims take Muhammad as a model and use his sayings and decisions as precedents for choosing their own; Buddhists take the Buddha, and so on.

In a certain sense, it does not matter whether these religious models or any models are real or true. Whether or not George Washington ever said, "I cannot tell a lie," it is a good story for conveying the value of telling the truth. *The power of a story does not reside in its factuality.*

The psychologist Alfred Adler went so far as to dub such stories "guiding fictions," and Rollo May explained that the power of such a story is that the individual "refers to this guiding fiction down through the subsequent years as the secret myth of oneself" (1991:69). We are more familiar with the notion of 'role models' these days, but undeniably one can model oneself after a person that one has never met and is unlikely ever to meet (*e.g.*, a celebrity like Oprah or Madonna), a historical figure (*e.g.*, Washington or Lincoln), a fictional character (*e.g.*, Harry Potter or Dagny Taggart from *Atlas Shrugged*), or a purely imaginary entity (*e.g.*, a vampire). As long as the individual adopts the model as the inspiration of his or her own clothing styles or speaking patterns or daily habits or what have you, the model is *effective* and has been *brought to life in the life of the follower or imitator*.

Fictional or imaginary characters work fine as models for oneself, but no doubt real ones work better, and some real ones work better than others. In particular, profoundly effective paradigms or charters probably have three traits — *reality*, *antiquity*, and *proximity to the source of power*. The value of a really-existing model is self-evident: there is a 'true' example to appeal to and conform to. As well, in general, the more ancient the model the more potent it is as a model; this factor plays on what Eliade called "the prestige of the past," because it has worked for a long time and had many followers before (think of that 'old time religion'). Finally, the closer the model sits to the seat of power, the better. This is why Christians and atheists both frequently appeal to the Founding Fathers, since they were there at the beginning and had the superior strength and wisdom that founders always have. If we can emulate what they did, or what they said they were doing, or they meant to do, we can be sure to be 'right.' After all, it was they, the argument goes from either side, who determined what 'right' was in the first place, and they had the authority to do so.

This, then, explains two bedrock qualities about myths. First, they are thought to be true; a false or fictional myth would have much less authority. Second, they involve the *most* real, the *most* ancient, and the *most* powerful beings of all — the non-human, super-human ones. Therefore, if those beings, according to the myths, did something or wanted something done, that is sufficient reason to do it today.

Which brings us back to morality. Morality is what we are supposed to do and as such is construed as right or good behavior (the details of the behavior are quite unimportant for us here, whether one is supposed to smite one's enemies or love one's enemies). The best way to ensure moral behavior is to mold the kind of individuals who are inclined to act in conformity with the standards of morality, the interaction code described above. The best way to accomplish that is to instill in these individuals certain "moods and motivations," as Geertz said, and the best way to do that is to give them grand and (allegedly) true models, in story form, to copy. This perspective all comes together in Geertz' famous definition of religion: "a system of symbols which acts to establish powerful, pervasive, and long-lasting moods and motivations in men by formulating conceptions of a general order of existence and clothing these conceptions with such an aura of factuality that the moods and motivations seem uniquely realistic" (90).

Ultimately, myth presents to the believer a world in which certain things are good to do precisely because they were really done in the past. But myth does one thing more: it takes this creation, this establishment of models and this formation of paradigms, out of human hands and *presents it back to humans as if it is not a human achievement.*

As we said above, humans have invented many ways of living, many interaction codes, which anthropologists call *cultures.* As Geertz expresses it, humanity "is an animal suspended in webs of significance he himself has spun," and "culture is those webs" (5). However, the message of myth is that, yes indeed humans are suspended in webs of significance, but human *have not* spun those webs. Rather, as Marshall Sahlins (1976) stresses, it was the actions of non-humans and super-humans — not just spirits and gods but also plants and animals — that set the pattern for contemporary human reality. What to us atheists and social scientists is *culture* (a human product) becomes in the religious and mythical perspective non-cultural and super-cultural (a non-human and super-human product).

Yet, religion and myth are always *about* humans in the end — who we are and what we are supposed to do. But

Myths and Morals

this 'supposed to do,' this general form of morality, is stolen from culture, from humans, and attributed either to nature or to super-nature. By doing so, culture becomes naturalized and supernaturalized, and nature and super-nature become culturalized — but neither any longer seems to belong to humans. It is all, rather, dictated to and imposed on humans.

The relation between religion and morality, then, is this: religion is the means by which human values become dehumanized. Humans make their own moral codes, what Nietzsche called their "tablets of good and evil." Morality — and the whole culture of which is but a part — is a 'social contract' that humans have drafted for themselves. As such, the specific terms of the contract are much less important than its sheer existence. Every group of humans needs a standard of behavior, a way to live. However, every group of humans needs more: a reason to follow the standard, a justification for its way of life. Voluntary values are not enough, since they seem so relative and optional. So humans turn around and attribute their code and their culture to non-human and super-human sources — something outside, above, and greater than humanity. In short, religion is humanity's method of commanding itself to obey its moral code — a code that it invented — by inventing a non-human authority (literally, an *author*) to command the code. From the religious perspective, morality and culture are anything but a social contract. They are a super-social directive. But this is nothing more than humans commanding themselves indirectly, making their own rules and norms obligatory on themselves by ascribing those rules and norms to a source beyond themselves.

This is why, to make one final point, the details of moral systems can be so diverse while one common thread runs among them — the thread of *obligation*. The 'moral' is what humans are *obligated* to do, or at least what they ought to *feel* obligated to do. Other aspects of the interaction code seem somewhat more voluntary or improvisational (though never totally so), but morality is that part of the code that seems most urgent and mandatory.

Roy Rappaport (1999), in his study of religion and ritual, put his finger on the issue when he asserted that the two key functions of religion and ritual, via myth, are to *establish obligations* and to achieve *acceptance of obligations.* What precisely these obligations are — dietary norms, honoring the Sabbath, wearing a certain kind of underwear, or killing infidels — is less important than the facts that *they are obligatory* and that *they are set down by someone other than those who are to obey them* — i.e., they are "not encoded by the performers." That is, religious morality by definition comes from the outside; it is *about* and *for* humans but it is not *by* humans. This is why morality tends to take the form of imperatives or commands — you shall/shall not do *X*. Morality is not basically about instructing but about ordering: Nielsen said it himself when he asserted that "moral utterances usually involve a *telling to,* not a *telling that*" (83).

Therefore, two last consequences fall out of our analysis. First, humans are not supposed to question and need not even understand the obligations: obligations are not things to *know* but things to *do.* The human prerogative is to accept. The fundamental human obligation is, in a word, to accept one's human obligations. Therefore and second, the worst thing a human can do is to reject obligation. As Rappaport explains, 'immoral' means, if it means anything, 'contrary to obligation.' Whatever a society or religion obligates one to do is moral in its eyes. Whatever breaches this obligation is immoral. Rejection or violation of obligation, he insists, *is* immorality, however senseless, trivial, or even inhumane that obligation might be.

On Atheism, Morality, and the Good Story

To hell with facts! We need stories!
—Ken Kesey

As atheists, we have no choice but to discount myth, since we discount the supernatural in total. As atheists, we have no choice as well but to face the condemnation of certain religionists who find us immoral by definition, since we refuse to accept and perform at least some of what they consider human moral obligation — including or especially recognizing their god. I am untroubled by either.

Myths and Morals

We should and do have a response, however, when we are charged with having no source, no sanction, and no legitimation of our morality. There are many sources of morality, and religion has colonized this domain just as surely and effectively as it has colonized so many others as described in Chapter 8. We must not let them claim morality as their private possession. At the same time, we must not simply ape their view of morality as some mystical, incomprehensible, and unnatural element in human existence. Morality is one of the many things that links us in continuity with the natural non-human world. Morality, like language and like religion itself, is a human product, a diverse one, and an ambiguous one. We may not and need not agree with religionists on what is moral or even what is a moral problem — after all, they do not agree with each other — and we may not and need not agree among ourselves. But we know that as humans we are the kinds of beings who must impose rules upon themselves.

The sanctions for morality are also many and natural. Oneself, one's family, one's neighborhood, one's nation, one's species, and one's world are plenty, and any person who needs more sanction than that is probably a menace to us all. I have heard Christians say that without religion and their god they would run amok. Perhaps they would, but if so then they are actually *less* moral than those of us who control ourselves. More likely, they are living a fantasy here as in so many areas of their lives: sooner or later, even religionists without their gods have to settle down and go to work.

For us, legitimation of morality and any other social norms or institutions is less of a problem than religionists imagine. Humans make rules, and humans establish institutions. And thank goodness for it: Aristotle opined that slavery was a natural institution, and many Christians have thought that it was a divine institution; if either was correct, slavery could never be eradicated. But since humans made it, humans can unmake it. Humans made marriage, and humans can modify it. This hardly means that the course of human affairs ever did or will run smooth; humans will endlessly bicker about this or that rule or norm or moral or institution. But then humans have endlessly bickered about *religious* rules and norms and morals and institutions, so religion seems to offer no relief there.

ATHEISM ADVANCED

Mainly, we should reclaim and re-naturalize morality precisely because it has been stripped away from us and credited to someone or something other than us. To paraphrase a conclusion in *Natural Atheism*, 'morality' as we know it today is humanity estranged from itself, humanity's own struggle to define and order itself alienated and ascribed to the non-human. C. S. Lewis and others may find it nobler that humans are handed a moral law. I find it less noble: the nobility lies in having to make it and defend it for ourselves.

So atheists have nothing to be ashamed of, and much to be proud of, in the arena of morality. However, there is a flip-side to the question of myth and morality. While we happily and rightly embrace morality of a certain sort and reject myth, we often fail to appreciate the power of stories. We atheists, we rationalists, we literalists tend to want the true, the factual, to the exclusion of everything else. But humans cannot live by facts alone. In my earlier work, I stressed that we have a burden not only to be *correct* but to be *convincing*. I think we have additional burdens as well — to be *compelling*, perhaps even to be *comforting*.

Nobody wants to read a laundry-list of factual statements. Nobody (almost) wants to see a sequence of disconnected actions. If Kesey is right, and I think he is, humans need stories, and they need stories with human (or at least human-like) protagonists. Humans need stories because stories provide that arc of meaning, that dramatic coherence, that life as a mere series of events lacks. Some scholars have gone so far as to suggest that myth is not just a second and secondary mental process but an essential mental process, so long as we think of myth not as 'religious story' but as 'guiding fiction.' Rollo May is one such writer, whose *The Cry for Myth,* while perhaps a bit melodramatic, makes a salient point. Myth, by which he means 'grand narrative' and 'guiding fiction,' "is a way of making sense in a senseless world. Myths are the narrative patterns that give significance to our existence" (1991:15). Humans, as we have seen, do not have an innate direction in their lives. They must find and/or make their own direction. This is why sensitive authors in the twentieth century often emphasized 'the search for meaning.'

Myths and Morals

Atheists, like Richard Dawkins, often declaim, even with a certain sense of glee, that the universe is meaningless. No doubt. But *humans* cannot live without meaning. Having stripped them of *religious* meaning and direction, we often adjourn, satisfied that we have done our duty. But, as May points out, left in a meaningless, directionless state, "it is not surprising that frantic people flock to the new cults, or resurrect the old ones, seeking answers to their anxiety and longing for relief from their guilt or depressions, longing for something to fill the vacuum of their lives" (22). We do a disservice to humanity, then, if we deprive it of its stories but give it nothing in return but facts. It would be something like depriving humanity of rich foods but giving it nutrient pills to live on. It would be even more, to use Nietzsche's analogy, like pulling the ground out from under humanity and leaving it hanging in mid-air. A few of us, perhaps, have the courage to live in suspension, but most do not.

Atheists, therefore, as they contemplate reclaiming and reshaping a world left vacated by or vanquished of religion, but still populated by human beings, must begin to imagine what kinds of stories they will tell. Even more, Chip and Dan Heath (2007) emphasize story-telling or narrative as a particularly effective way of getting a message to stick — a revelation that atheists should take better advantage of. We all know that the best scientific writing has a certain personal quality to it, like the work of Carl Sagan, for example. Science need not be dry and cold and impersonal. Atheism too need not and must not be dry and impersonal. But the alternative is not mean-spirited and sarcastic fiction, the likes of which I have seen flowing from atheist pens. Atheists must learn and master the power of metaphor, symbolism, and narrative to establish a new world where the moods and motivations of people lead them to god-less but all the same meaning-full new thoughts, feelings, and actions. Atheism, in a word, must be brought to life and made into the kind of thing human beings can live in.

Chapter 11

Discredism:
Beyond Atheism and Beyond Belief

If there is one thing that everyone — theist and atheist — seems to agree on, it is that *belief* is the key to religion. A religion is a belief-system, and all members of a religion are believers or have beliefs. Some go still further, asserting that *every* position, opinion, or conclusion is a belief, including not only religion but science and atheism itself. More than a few atheists have accepted and echoed the notion that atheism is not only a belief-system but a veritable religion. However, once again, all of these claims are wrong.

Having in this book re-assessed and deconstructed concepts like 'ritual,' 'myth,' 'morality,' and 'religion' itself, it should be no shock that we will and must do the same to 'belief.' We will find, as we proceed below, that there is no essence to the concept of belief and further that the concept may not appear in the same form — *or appear at all* — in any particular religion. As we have come to say, *belief* is neither universal nor unique to religions, and where it does occur, it is not a single, simple thing. Rather, belief as we are familiar with it is a *Christian* concept which is not applicable to all religions; to insist otherwise is to persist in speaking Christian when Christian language is just not relevant.

The re-evaluation of belief will lead us to think differently about religions, but it also has important implications for atheism. Atheism is most assuredly not a belief in any meaningful sense of the word and therefore certainly not a belief-system. In fact, as I have argued before, atheism is not a 'system' at all, since there is nothing systematic about it: it has only one part, namely the lack of any belief in any god(s). But now we should formulate this differently: atheism is not the lack of any *belief* in god(s); it is the lack of any meaningful *concept* or *idea* of 'god(s).' As we established in Chapter 2, the very word *god(s)* is a foreign word to us. We can obviously learn the meaning that the word has for theists, but it is not a word that we use or that has any referent for us (or for anyone else, although they think it does).

But since atheism is not a belief nor a disbelief in god(s), two things become significantly true: first, there is no longer sense or substance in talking about belief in god(s) as a relevant category for atheism and second, atheism emerges as an insufficient notion for dealing with the variety of religious claims or beliefs, let alone non-religious claims or beliefs. It is good and correct to be an atheist, but it is inadequate. *We must go further.*

In this chapter I propose to situate atheism within a broader, more comprehensive project of *non*-belief, of *dis*-belief, or *discrediting* and *discarding* belief, just as theism is situated within a broader and more comprehensive classification of religions, and religion is situated within a broader and more comprehensive classification of beliefs. Atheism, while true at its level, is *only* true at its level: that is to say, there is no such thing as god(s), but what about all of the other supposed religious entities and agents? At the highest level, I assert that religions themselves are nothing but special cases of the global category of 'unfounded things accepted as true,' just as atheism is a special case of the global category of 'rational and naturalistic conclusions about reality.' Therefore, as rationalists generally and atheists specifically, we need to advance beyond a critique of Christianity or of theisms or of religions in general to reject *all* irrational and unsound reality-claims. For this most inclusive rationalist or naturalistic position, I propose the term *discredism*.

Why We Need a New Term

For purposes of rhetoric and polemics, if not outright politics, people are forever introducing new terminology. There is nothing wrong with that practice *per se*, although it may make the language crowded and cumbersome. At the same time, old words sometimes perpetuate old ideas, and it is (as we discussed in Chapter 2) often difficult to say the things one needs to say in the language that one has inherited from other systems with other purposes. Therefore, sometimes it is not only necessary but prudent to start over with new terms.

Discredism

Discredism (pronounced dis-**cred**-ism) is derived from the Latin *credere* for 'to believe,' which also gives us such English words as 'credible,' 'credence,' 'credentials,' 'credit' (and 'discredit'), and of course 'creed.' In its conjugated form (*credo*, 'I believe') it is specifically the first word in the famous and formative Christian dogmas known as the Nicene Creed and the Apostles' Creed. The prefix *dis-* also comes from the Latin for 'apart' or even more actively 'to part,' 'to separate from,' 'to deprive of,' 'to exclude/expel.' (Ironically, *Dis* is also the name of the Roman god of the underworld, perhaps giving the prefix its negative connotations.) Together, the prefix *dis-* and the root *cred* give us the term *discredism*[1] which means 'no belief' or 'without belief' but much more. Discredism suggests not just the passive or indifferent absence of belief but an active, intentional, and principled *dis*missal of and *dis*-respect for belief. It is a deliberate *dis*-connection from the entire notion of belief, *dis*-sociation from the practice of believing, and ideally and hopefully a *dis*-abling of the power of belief. For our purposes it is the position or life-way of being without belief(s).

As with Thomas Huxley's neologism 'agnosticism,' *discredism* is not another belief or creed; it is the *rejection* of beliefs or creeds as such. It is not, then, *something else to believe* but a *reasoned avoidance of belief* on the ground that believing is an unsound and therefore undesirable thing to do. It understands 'believing' to mean specifically 'accepting as true despite the lack of evidence or the existence of contradictory evidence,' which cannot be recommended under any circumstances. Discredism is not a hesitation to believe nor a middle ground between believing and not-believing, but rather a *dismissal of the very concept of belief* as valid.

It should be more than obvious that atheism and discredism are not synonyms. As popularly used, *atheism* often means 'disbelieving in god(s),' although I insist that this is a misleading and ultimately false definition: one cannot and need not 'disbelieve' in anything, and it is possible that the very word

---

1 I want to thank my friend Evert Ford for the suggestion of the specific term 'discredism,' which captures better the meaning that I was trying to express in this chapter than such alternatives as 'acredism' or 'incredulism.'

disbelieve is a nonsense word. Christians do not disbelieve in Zeus or *jukurrpa*; they disregard the first and have probably never even heard of the second. Informed adult Americans do not disbelieve in Santa Claus; they dismiss the notion of Santa Claus as a fairy tale for children.

Discredism recognizes that the burden of proof for any concept, religious or otherwise, is on the believer. If the believer can demonstrate the truth of his or her belief, then the belief is no longer a *belief* but an established *fact*. In other words, if a geographer said that he or she "believed" that the earth was round and could show us the proof of it, we would not then *believe* but *know* that the earth was round. If another geographer said that he or she "believed" that the earth was flat and could not show us any proof of it, we would not even say that he or she has a *belief* but that he or she has *an error*. It would be intolerably foolish of us to embrace a belief which we know is a mistake. In situations where the evidence is inadequate and the question unsettled, it is wise for us to neither believe nor disbelieve but to wait for more information. For instance, if a new drug is being tested for effectiveness against heart disease, until the trials are completed we do not believe that it is effective nor do we disbelieve that it is effective (or believe that it is ineffective). We set aside belief in any form and await further data. Those who think that such patience in the face of unanswered questions is a type of disbelief should rethink their position.

Discredism is, therefore, a quite general and rational approach to questions of all sorts: if the evidence warrants a positive conclusion, accept it as true; if the evidences warrants a negative conclusion, reject it as false; if the evidence warrants no conclusion, postpone arriving at a conclusion while pursuing more information. But *at no point* is belief warranted, necessary, or helpful. Belief can never be anything better than premature arrival at a conclusion (figuratively 'jumping to a conclusion') and can often be much worse, like accepting an unjustified and more-than-likely false conclusion.

Since religions confront us with a number of questions, discredism is particularly applicable to them, at a higher level than atheism. Again, as it is often used in everyday conversation and debate, *atheism* is simultaneously *too broad and too narrow* to get the job done. Theists and atheists alike typically use the term 'atheism' to refer to a position that is opposed to or dismissive of all religion, but this is inaccurate in two ways. First, atheism means 'no/without god(s)' but *implies quite literally nothing about other kinds of religions.* Second and closely related, both theists and atheists in America, when they talk about religion, almost invariably mean *the Christian religion* and sometimes even worse *fundamentalist Christian religion.* Of course, if you think that Christianity is the only religion in the country or in the world, then there can only be one contrary position — *a-* or *anti-*Christianity — and so atheism becomes simultaneously *a-*Christianity, *a-*theism, and *a-*religion. However, we know now that this position in untenable because we know that religion is too diverse.

In other words, atheism is usually conceived of either too generally as 'no/without religion' or too specifically as 'no/without Christianity' or both (on the false assumption that Christianity *is* religion). If we reconsider our discussion from Chapter 1, this is easy to grasp. We identified several types or forms of religion, including theism but also other less familiar manifestations like animism, animatism, ancestor spirits, and ethical non-theism. In any coherent way, *atheism is not an alternative to or a rejection of all of these forms of religion.* In fact, it is not only possible but essential to say that *these other four forms of religion are themselves quite rightly a-theistic,* in the sense that they are 'without god(s).' They are not necessarily hostile to god(s), and it would not even be appropriate to say that they disbelieve in god(s). For the most part, they have never heard of god(s); their religious concepts do not *include* god(s). They lack any such word or idea, or at least have little or no interest in such a word or idea; they have their own words and ideas instead.

So, to represent this state of affairs graphically, we can alter our chart of religions as shown in Figure 4. This image clearly depicts that atheism is on the same level as theism *but only pertains to that level and the subcategories below that level.* In other words, atheism is an alternative to and rejection of theism and subsequently of all specific types of theism — polytheisms, monotheisms, and any other permutations (deism, pantheism, henotheism, *etc.*) and any subtypes of theism

ATHEISM ADVANCED

Figure 4. Atheism as opposed only to theistic religions

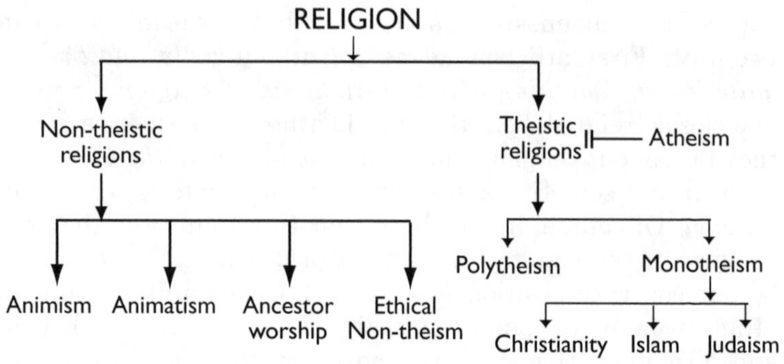

including Christianity and Islam and Judaism and any other permutations (Sikhism, Jainism, Hinduism, and all the rest). Atheism is *not* an alternative to or rejection of *the other types of religions at the same level as theism, nor of religion itself at a higher level.* Atheism does not necessarily reject non-theistic religions. It is fair to say that atheism does not apply to them at all; in fact, as we just explained, in a way atheism *includes* them, since the non-theistic religions are, again, a-theistic in the non-argumentative sense. Like us, they are 'without god(s).'

So, it would be logically consistent for a good American atheist to reject or dismiss — even to savagely criticize — all concepts of god(s) and yet maintain a belief in nature spirits, dead ancestors, supernatural forces, or supernatural ethical systems. These things are not contrary to atheism as it is formally and strictly interpreted. However, I would sincerely hope that all who arrive at their atheism by the standards of reason (scrutiny of the available facts and logical processing of those facts) would find non-theistic religious claims equally unacceptable and unbelievable. Nevertheless, the strict interpretation of atheism does not compel this. One could be — and no doubt many a person is — a committed atheist and still practice *feng shui* or claim to communicate with the dead. Even Raelians consider themselves atheists.

So 'atheism' cannot rightfully be used to refer to rejection or dismissal of all forms of religion, with or without god(s); it pertains to a specific kind of religion. But while we are at it, we realize that a person who critiques and rejects all religions — who is more than without god(s) but without any religious or supernatural concepts or entities — might (and often in reality does) still entertain other non-religious beliefs. 'Beliefs' are not exclusive to religion; there are all kinds of things to believe other than religious things. What I am saying is that *religion* is not a top-level category but actually a subcategory of a higher class of ideas which we could call *beliefs* or *belief-systems*, as depicted in Figure 5.

Figure 5. Belief systems and religion

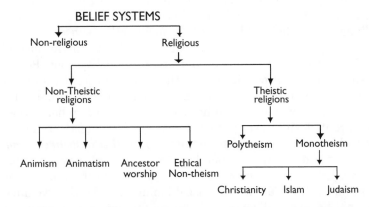

It is not hard to appreciate that the classes and subclasses of non-religious belief could be and almost certainly would be more extensive than the religious ones. There are all manner of things to have beliefs about: monsters, extra-terrestrials, cures, conspiracies, near-death and after-death experiences and entities, and so on indefinitely. Under monsters one might believe in Big Foot or the Loch Ness beast or yetis or what have you. Under extra-terrestrials one might believe in Martians or Alpha Centaurians or beings from another dimension or universe, *etc.* Truly, the claims on our *credulity* (another derivation from the root *credere*) or capacity or tendency to believe, are limitless.

We all know that being an atheist is not a vaccination against all unsubstantiated and false ideas. There are atheists who accept the existence of Big Foot or of space aliens, who subscribe to unproven alternative medical methods, who claim to speak to the dead, or who fear the international conspiracies of the communists or Jews. I am not saying that all of these claims are conclusively false. I am saying that they are not conclusively true, which is reason enough for a rational person to be skeptical of them and even to dismiss them. I am also not saying that atheism inherently implies the rejection of such claims. As we have shown, atheism does not pertain to them; there is nothing inconsistent as such with an atheist thinking that Big Foot exists. Atheism only refers to the non-god(s) position, but on other questions, it is not applicable. Atheism, in other words, is intermediate in its relevance to the classification of beliefs: it pertains to a certain subset of beliefs (namely, god-beliefs) but is silent on any other subset.

But does that mean that we are helpless in the face of all of these other claims on our credulity? I hope not. People who arrive at a conclusion on the god(s)-question rationally (and is therefore necessarily an atheist) hopefully also employ reason to arrive at their other conclusions. Rationalists, when confronted with unsupported claims and assertions — religious or otherwise — do not believe them, *nor do they disbelieve them*. As I stated in my previous book, the rational person simply says, "Show me some evidence for them, or take them away from me." It is a Jamesian false dilemma to insist that we must either believe or disbelieve (let alone that we *should* believe or that we can or should let our emotions settle the dispute for us).

Discredism, which is ultimately nothing more than the courageous and unrelenting application of reason to all questions brought before us, refuses to participate in beliefs at all. There is *knowledge* and there are other kinds of things — opinions, hypotheses, theories, preferences, predictions, hopes, values, and wishes — but belief quite emphatically and thoroughly has no place in our mental world. Discredism says "I don't *do* 'belief.'" It is an alternative to and rejection of all believing. If discredism has one imperative, it is "*Dis*-card and *dis*-allow belief."

Figure 6. Discredism as opposed to beliefs of all kinds.

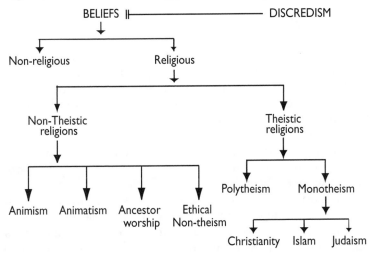

Religion is Not What You Believe

Atheist to theist: "I don't believe in God."
Theist to atheist: "But God believes in you."

Readers are probably familiar with this classic theist retort, which is frequently given with great satisfaction as if it is a knock-out blow to atheism. Really, it is sheer fluff: imagine a Muslim hearing an atheist (or any non-Muslim) say, "I don't believe in Allah" and responding, "But Allah believes in you." Would you be convinced by that? Imagine, even worse, a Warlpiri hearing an atheist (or any non-Warlpiri) say, "I don't believe in *jukurrpa*" and responding, "But *jukurrpa* believes in you." The absurdity becomes obvious.

It is plain to see that any religious member can substitute any religious concept for 'God' here and have the same exchange, which proves absolutely nothing. But there is a more serious point to be made. When one says, "I do/do not believe in God" and "God believes/does not believe in you," one is using 'believe' in two very distinct senses. The same meaning is not being conveyed by the word *believe* in both cases. When the atheist (or anyone from a non-theistic religious tradition), says, "I do not believe in God," he or she is asserting that this God-being does not exist. 'Believe' here means 'to claim/accept the existence of.' When the responder says, "God believes in you," presumably he or she is *not* asserting that God claims/accepts that *you* exist. Your existence is not in dispute, since it is fairly evident that you exist. The theist here has subtly, and for most people imperceptibly, shifted the meaning of the word 'believe' to something like 'trust' or 'love' — which is a different thing altogether.

Before we proceed to talk about religions and the concept of belief, it is incumbent upon us to discuss the concept a bit more, for, as we have seen now, *belief* or *believing* is not a single, simple notion. It is one of those terms which philosophers of language call *polysemous*, that is, possessing several possible meanings. And these are not mutually exclusive meanings: often enough, a person's use of the term may imply or convey more than one meaning simultaneously. Further, as I explored in my previous book, 'belief' as used in English is a gloss for many different psychological and linguistic relations, which might and arguably should be separated into their constituent parts. That is to say (as I did say), statements like 'I believe in god,' 'I believe in love,' 'I believe it is going to rain,' and 'I believe stewed tomatoes are gross' use the same word in vastly different ways. The only thing they have in common, as Wittgenstein would have said, is that they are all part of the English "language game of *belief*." It is entirely possible — and, as we will see below, entirely factual — that other languages and religions do not play the belief-game the same way that English and Christianity do.

I will not repeat my previously published examination of 'belief' here. However, we must identify three central types or dimensions of its meaning and show how this impacts the religious debate and the atheist-discredist project. The first and most transparent meaning of 'belief' is propositional, that is, about true or false states of affairs. If one says, "I believe *X*," one is avowing that one holds *X* to be true. We can call this the dimension of *correctness*. However, as our opening example to this section illustrates, not all belief statements are, or at least are only or primarily, truth-claims. When I say, "I believe that my wife is going to pick me up at the airport," I suppose one could trivially interpret this as "I claim that it is true that my wife is going to pick me up at the airport." But the usual import of the declaration is that I *trust* my wife to pick me up. In other words, this second dimension of 'belief' suggests *confidence* in some state of affairs. Finally, when I say, "I believe in love" or "I believe in democracy," I am neither making a truth-claim (like "I think that love/democracy exists") nor expressing my confidence ("I trust that love/democracy will do this or that") but rather testifying to my values or preferences. Essentially, it is equivalent to saying that I *like* love or democracy, that I think they are good, that I endorse or support them. This third dimension we will call *commitment* and might legitimately be considered *valuing*. This is why the concepts of 'belief' and 'value' often get confused together.

It goes without saying that being correct, being confident, and being committed are radically different things *which may and often do co-occur but which are not dependent on each other in any way*. Of course and frequently, one can be wrong about any or all of these types of belief. For instance, I can believe that my wife will pick me up at the airport, but she never shows up. I can believe in love, although love always lets me down or hurts me. And I can believe in leprechauns or unicorns, although there are no such things.

More critically, my "belief" can be unjustified. If I have asked my wife to pick me up at the airport before, and she has always forgotten or refused, then it is unjustified (indeed, stupid) for me to believe that she will do it this time. Of course, if I was unmarried, or my wife did not exist, it would be particularly unjustified, in fact it would be nonsense, to hold my belief about my ride from the airport or anything else concerning some wife. Therefore, if a belief does not meet the first requirement — that it refer correctly to states of affairs about really-existing entities — then *any other belief-claims* one might make are sheer nonsense (like "God does not exist, but I am confident that God will cure my illness"). So, in an indisputable way, confidence and commitment do depend on the correctness of some beliefs.

Nevertheless, the three dimensions are still independent.

ATHEISM ADVANCED

That is, one could believe that a higher being exists but not have confidence in what that being might do. Many Christians feel that way ("I believe in God, but I am not confident that God will do this or that"). Further, as we saw in an earlier chapter, not all theistic religions have anything like confidence in their gods. Some think that their gods are capricious, some that they are evil, and some that they are just uninterested. So theism, the belief in god(s), does not necessarily imply any particular *attitude toward* god(s). Also, one may believe that some religious agent exists and be confident in its actions but not be committed to it: I assume that most Christians think that the devil exists and are confident that he will do evil but are not thereby committed to the devil.

Before we move on and investigate belief in Christianity and other religions, I want to emphasize the significance of the unpacking of the belief concept that we have just performed. It is interesting and important that we atheists, as rationalists and literalists, have tended to focus on the correctness or propositional aspect of belief largely to the exclusion of the other aspects. Of course, there are reasons for this particular focus. Beliefs as truth-claims are subject to verification and falsification in a way that beliefs are trusts and judgments are not; ideally, we expect that if people are shown that their beliefs are false, they will relinquish their confidence and commitment (but we know that this does not always happen). Beyond this, it is undoubtedly a feature of the Western tradition that we discussed in Chapter 9 to privilege the *idea* part of a culture or religion and to underestimate the *emotional* or *behavioral* parts. However, if we have shown anything in this book, it is that the non-cognitive elements of a religion are at least as important if not profoundly *more* important than the cognitive or intellectual elements, the doctrines or what we usually think of as beliefs.

In fact, the preoccupation with the belief component of religion obscures the reality that many believers do not actually even *know* the beliefs of their religion, and if they know them they do not *understand* them, and if they understand them they do not *accept* them. For instance, surveys have shown that many Christians cannot name all of the Ten Commandments nor are they fluent in all of the assertions in their scriptures. Many

Christians may have heard of doctrines like *transubstantiation* or *rapture* but do not really comprehend their meaning. And all Christians presumably know about the concept of Satan, but a 2002 study by the Barna Group (which does a great deal of research on Christian beliefs and attitudes) found that 59% reject the notion of Satan as an actual being, understanding him merely as a symbol of evil. All in all, the results show what the Barna Groups calls "a smorgasbord of religious beliefs" among American Christians.

These observations highlight the analysis of the anthropologist Melford Spiro (1978:*xiii–xiv*), who used his research on spirit beliefs in Burma as an occasion to reconsider the concept of belief. He found that it is not a one-dimensional but a multi-dimensional notion, with at least five distinguishable layers.

Layer 1 is simple acquaintance or familiarity with the belief, and not all members are even basically acquainted with all supposed beliefs of a religion.

Layer 2 is understanding the belief in the conventional way, which often means either the way that the majority understands it or the way that the experts understand it. Here he makes the often-neglected point that there is no reason "to assume that the meanings attributed to beliefs by religious virtuosi are shared by the other members of the group" (*xv*) — nor, we might add, by all age-groups, genders, classes, and other divisions of society. He also reminds us, *contra* William James from Chapter 7, that religious beliefs *are* conventions and not private or idiosyncratic creations: "religious beliefs are culturally constituted, they are *traditional* beliefs, *i.e.*, they are beliefs that arise and develop in the history of a social group, and that are transmitted from one generation to the next through those social processes that are variously denoted by such terms as 'education' and 'enculturation'" (*xii*).

Layer 3 is holding and promoting the belief as true, which, as we just saw with the Christian/Satan example, is not automatic even when the belief is known and understood.

Layer 4 is embracing the belief as important or central to the individual's life; and finally layer 5 is using the belief as a personally motivational or guiding force. What Spiro finds, then, in his description of Burmese religion, is great diversity among the population in regard to awareness of beliefs, understanding of them, acceptance of them, commitment to them, and employment of them.

What we are saying here is that 'belief' is not a unitary and monolithic thing. In fact, in keeping with our modular model from previous chapters, it is fair to say that belief is not a thing at all but instead a composite of various and strikingly different and independent kinds of notions and actions. If we assert that someone or some group believes something, we have not really said anything clear or concrete just yet. 'Belief' is at best a concept — and therefore quite possibly a culturally and religiously specific concept, not a general or universal one — and perhaps less than a concept but rather a category.

In other words, I suggest that there is no such thing as belief just as there is no such thing as religion or language. There are only religions, languages, and beliefs. One cannot speak a language in general nor have a religion in general; one can only speak a particular language or have a particular religion. Similarly, one cannot believe in general but can only believe particular things in particular ways. And ultimately, one can not-believe at all, that is, lack the concept of belief completely — and I am not just talking about rationalistic atheists and discredits. It is possible that belief is exclusive to certain religious traditions and not others and therefore that one can not only have beliefs without religion but religion without beliefs.

The Evolution of Belief in Christianity

We get our familiar and supposedly meaningful and objective concept of belief from Christianity as it is formulated in the English language. Given all that we have learned in this presentation, we can foresee that this may be a problem. Speaking about belief may not be speaking accurately and objectively about religion but rather may be speaking Christian about Christianity — and too often imposing such Christian thinking on other religions as well.

There is no debate that belief is important, even central, to Christianity. There is, nonetheless, good reason to conclude that belief is not a simple or immutable concept, even in

Christianity. Specifically, as Rodney Needham (to whom we will return below) has phrased it, the contemporary Christian concept of belief "is demonstrably an historical amalgam, composed of elements traceable to Judaic mystical doctrine and Greek styles of discourse" (1972:49). Fortunately, on this subject we have the invaluable assistance of Malcolm Ruel, whose concise but critical essay "Christians as Believers" dismantles the notion of belief in Christianity and identifies four distinct historical manifestations of the idea. According to Ruel, these four phases in the evolution of Christian belief include the early decades of the Christian movement as it arose out of and separated itself from its Jewish roots, the period of the formation of the Church and the official creed of Christianity, the Protestant Reformation, and the modern era (1997:37).

In the first years, perhaps as much as the first century or two, of Christian history, the new religion literally spoke the language of its Hebrew ancestry, because it was initially, in many minds, an extension of, a reform sect of Judaism, or at most a fulfillment of Jewish doctrines and expectations. Needham and Ruel both mention how the Hebrew word *he'min* occurs in the Torah/Old Testament, derived from the root *'mn* meaning 'to be true, reliable, or faithful.' Ruel points out that the Hebrew word *'mn* "express[es] centrally the notion of trust or confidence" (38), that is, that it is not basically propositional ('God exists') as much as emotional or relational ('I put my trust in God'). The existence of their god was not fundamentally a matter of factual disputation but of hope and assurance: will they let go and put themselves in his hands or not? No one, they wanted to suggest, seriously doubted that their god existed; it was just a matter of how much they would submit to him. Essentially, then, at least in early Judaism, religion was more about proper ritual activity, and eventually proper moral action and obedience, and much less about what Christians stress as 'belief.'

But most Christians do not receive their religious language and concepts directly from the Hebrew but rather via the intermediate of Greek and Latin. In early translations of the Torah/Old Testament, and in the New Testament (much if not all of which was composed in Greek), the Greek term *pistis* was used where we read *belief* today. *Pistis*, according to Needham, conveys a range of meanings from certainty or conviction to trust, confidence, and loyalty (47). Ruel, leaning on substantial biblical and linguistic research, argues yet more extensively that *pistis* and its verb form *pisteuo*, 'to believe,' referred to "the trust that a man may place in other men, or gods; credibility, credit in business, guarantee, proof of something to be trusted" — proof not like evidence in an argument but like collateral in a loan (38). *Pisteuo* thus meant "to trust something or someone" and was not essentially religious in nature. The multi-dimensional (and largely non-propositional) quality of *pistis/pisteuo* reflects the same quality of *'mn/he'min* which, if anything, expresses "even more directly a quality of relationship; it was used of the reliability or trustworthiness of a servant, a witness, a messenger, or a prophet, but it also served to characterize the relationship between God and his people, reciprocally trusted and trusting" (38).

However, the propositional or 'correctness' property of *pistis/pisteuo* appeared early in the scriptures and in the debates within Christianity over doctrine. It first emerged "in the sense of to be converted, to become a Christian" (39) — that is, to be convinced by and subscribe to the new message. Converts were called 'those believing' (*hoi pisteuontes*) or 'those of the belief' (*hoi pistoi*). As a noun, *pistis* came to denote those things that Christians were supposed to accept as true, not the least of which was that Jesus was the son of God and had given his life for humanity.

At a certain moment in the evolution of Christianity, "Christian *belief* now begins to part company with Hebrew *trust*" (40). Naturally, Christians trust their god too, but "there is the added confidence or conviction about an event (the resurrection and all that that signifies) that had actually taken place." Ruel insists that "it is but a short step from *belief* as accepting as a fact ... to *belief* as asserting as a proposition" — which is what atheists and Christians alike typically mean by 'belief.'

As we noted briefly in our discussion of Tertullian (Chapter 9), the early Church was in a constant state of agitation over doctrine and heresy; perhaps this is why belief and *orthodoxy* — literally, 'right opinion' — were so crucial to the new religion. Tertullian and others quarreled continuously and furiously about the actual events, the correct interpretations, and the necessary actions of Christianity. This would lead almost inevitably to statements of belief or *creeds*, in various forms for various purposes, as well as rituals of commitment and initiation like baptism and confirmation of new members. Once the idea of creeds crystallized, there was a need to settle on one which would become the official or orthodox belief of Christianity. One of the first such creeds or avowals of belief, something like an oath that a member must utter, was the Apostles' Creed, which coalesced in the second half of the second Christian century (around 150–175 CE). It goes:

> I believe in God, the Father Almighty;
> And in Jesus Christ, his only begotten Son, our Lord, who was born of the Holy Spirit and the Virgin Mary, crucified under Pontius Pilate and buried; the third day he rose from the dead, ascended into heaven, being seated at the right hand of the Father, whence he shall come to judge the living and the dead;
> And in the Holy Spirit, holy Church, forgiveness of sins, and the resurrection of the flesh.

There is a great deal contained in that statement which Christians were not only supposed to mouth but to *believe* in all of the senses mentioned by Spiro.

The practice of drafting creeds, the likes of which one does not quite observe in Judaism (or most religions, as we will see below), led eventually to the most famous and influential formulation, the one that was adopted by the Roman Emperor Constantine for the official religion of the empire. Known as the Nicene Creed since it was written at a council of Church leaders at Nicaea (325 CE), it asks all Christians to avow

> I believe in one God, Father Almighty, maker of all things, visible and invisible. And in one Lord Jesus Christ, the Son of God, begotten of the Father, as His only son, that is, from the substance of the Father, God from God, light from light, true God from true God, begotten, not made, of the same substance with the Father, through whom all things in heaven and earth were made; who for us men and our salvation came down and was made flesh, became man, suffered, and rose on the third day, ascended to heaven, and is coming to judge the living and the dead. And in the Holy Spirit.

ATHEISM ADVANCED

Each of these oaths begins with the Latin word *credo*, 'I believe.'

Interestingly, this later creed is much more specific about a number of questions, some of which are not raised in the previous creed at all (what 'substance' is Jesus?) and many of which are not directly addressed in the scriptures themselves. It would be worthwhile to investigate more about how this particular creed came into being, as a response to the particular disputes and controversies of the day, but I leave that for the reader to pursue. (Elaine Pagels in her *The Origin of Satan* [1995] does suggest quite persuasively that each of the Gospels was written under particular political circumstances and is a faithful representation of and response to those circumstances.) What is especially fascinating for us, in view of our consideration of the Western tradition in Chapter 9, is how classical Greek questions of 'substance' and the relationship between substances crept into early Church ruminations. We can only assume that, if some other civilization than the Greco-Roman one had gotten the opportunity to shape Christian doctrine, it would look distinctly different today.

At any rate, with much dissension and bloodshed the thousand-plus years of Christianity from the Nicene Creed to the Reformation (early 1500s) was a period of expected and compulsory affirmation of the official truths or beliefs of the official Church (which was never as unified or official as Christians like to imagine and which had already lost its eastern portion in the 1054 schism that led to the establishment of the 'Orthodox Church' — which obviously considered itself in possession of the *true* beliefs). Martin Luther's Protestant movement was the first successful break *within* Western or Catholic Christendom, and in order to make room for itself, it had to reformulate not only the doctrines of Christianity but the relationship between believers and their religion. To make a complex religious problem simple, Luther moved the attention of religion from the doctrines or propositions (external to the believer) to the condition or experience of 'faith' (internal to the believer). As Ruel mentions, *faith* (from the Latin *fides*, giving such words as 'fidelity') conveys much of the same meaning as 'belief' in the sense of *dependability*, *trust*, and *confidence*.

Luther's achievement, then, was to shift the focus from the

external to the internal, not for the first time in the history of Christianity but crucially at this time. The reasons for this divergence are multiple and complex, but one that we must acknowledge is the political motivation. With Catholic dogma as the official form of Christianity, Luther needed to find a way for the individuals to extricate themselves from the Church yet remain Christians. His trick was to assert individual judgment, or what he called *conscience*, the person's experience of and "subjective appropriation of" the truths of the religion (47). Experience was elevated over creed, if only because it had to be in order to free itself from the Catholic monopoly on creed; this is not to say that creed never crept back in to the Protestant sects. Nevertheless, Luther offers a new paradigm, "the person who possesses belief by being possessed by it: such is the 'faith' that comes from without but signifies a subjective transition from disorganized doubt to clarity, conviction, and a certain kind of personal freedom" (48).

This probably sounds very familiar and comfortable to a twenty-first-century Westerner, for whom religion is voluntary and personal. If so, it only illustrates how deeply Western society and Western Christianity has imbibed the Protestant attitude. Ruel characterizes the modern era as one of "encounter" rather than "belief," or a "belief in belief" rather than an unbending conviction that particular propositions are true and no other (49). Religion even becomes a personal "adventure," a process that the individual traverses individually and heroically and not an automatic acceptance of a body of dogma or a creed. Merely "having belief," whatever that belief might be, has become a satisfactory and almost noble occupation, and individuals are more or less free to believe what and how they want. In the process, though, there is the danger that "the word 'believe' has become so generalized as to have lost most of its content" (50). This goes a long way toward explaining the revival of fundamentalism, as a reaction against this wishy-washy, populist, whatever-you-believe-is-your-truth mentality — a mentality which is definitely *not* the tradition in Christianity.

There is one last matter which is not raised by Ruel but which deserves our attention. Christianity has for most of its history been a religion of creed not only because it rested on a few allegedly factual claims, and not only because the diversity of Christian opinions (*heterodoxy*) called for a resolution of the disputed issues (an *orthodoxy*), but because of two other crucial features of the religion and its culture — absurdity and doubt. As we saw in Chapter 9, thoughtful Christians since Tertullian have not merely understood but reveled in the fact that Christian claims were absurd. That a supernatural, immaterial being could also be a natural, material one; that a human could die and come back to life; that one being could be the same substance as another being; that one being could be three beings but still be one being — these are all patently and conspicuously absurd. Yet Tertullian, and Kierkegaard, and Lewis, and many others before and since, have insisted that this very absurdity is not a weakness but a strength of Christianity; we should quite literally believe it *because* it is absurd (or sometimes I think we should read Tertullian's famous quote as "we can *only* believe it because it is absurd, since we certainly cannot *know* it." In other words, the only way one could hold such an absurd position is by belief — hardly, I think, a rousing endorsement of belief).

Closely related to the problem of absurdity is the problem of doubt. Christianity offers the member many opportunities to doubt, since its claims and propositions are at best doubtable. Any of them, or all of them collectively, might be false, which would, you would think, demolish the religion. The member must then make a valiant stand against doubt by adopting the creed *as* a truth, as a *belief*. Beyond the inherent doubtability of Christianity propositions is the ancient and pervasive Western (*i.e.*, Greek) tradition of doubt, of uncertainty, of questioning and philosophizing about inherited and conventional doctrines. Greek philosophers did the same thing to their own traditional religions — which is, after all, what got Socrates killed.

Doubt has been a perennial problem for Christianity, as manifested in Descartes, although the religion has not only managed to survive it but to thrive in it: I have heard many Christians proclaim that doubt strengthens belief, although it most assuredly should not. At any rate, the absurdity and inescapable doubt intrinsic to Christianity have made the religion particularly self-aware and defensive (even 'apologetic,' in both senses of the word) and necessarily led Christians to separate fact from faith and to elevate the latter over the former. After all, Kant (see Chapter 9) conclusively demonstrated that Christians cannot prove their religious creed by reason, evidence, speculation, or logic but that they could and should still hold it by faith and belief. The fascinating thing is that, despite the fact that the unprovability and absurdity of Christianity have been permanently and irrefutably established, so many Christians continue to advance 'proofs' of their religion or reasons to believe — even arguing that Christianity is a rational religion.

Religion without Belief

> Primitive religion is not so much thought out as danced out.
> —R. R. Marett, *The Threshold of Religion*

Given the fact that belief is not even a single consistent thing over the course of Christianity, and that belief is not exclusive to religion, and that belief seems to be a composite of various concepts and attitudes and not a thing at all, it is truly remarkable that scholarly work and popular discourse — among theists and atheists — have taken the notion so completely for granted. Even my fellow anthropologists, the professional explorers into the mental and social worlds of other peoples, have generally taken belief and "the relationship between belief, ritual practices, emotional expression, and talk about spirits as unproblematic" (Howard 1996:136). In fact, they have explicitly gone in search of the beliefs of other cultures and religions and, when they have found an idea or action in these cultures and religions, they have tagged it as a *belief*.

However, there is more than a possibility that we are finding belief where we want to, not where it really is. Belief is such a powerful and pervasive concept in Christianity — and yet such a complex and confused one — that thinkers reared within the Christian tradition, whether or not they are Christian believers, are liable to think in terms of belief. This is a classic, and our final and most profound, example of speaking Christian. Other religions have their own languages and their own experiences, and it may be as inappropriate to ask about non-Christian belief as it is to ask about Christian reincarnation or *jukurrpa*.

Rodney Needham, whom we introduced above, has put the concept of belief to a harsher cross-cultural test than any writer I know, and his findings are surprising and disconcerting for Christians and all those who unselfconsciously attribute belief to other societies and religions. His attack has two prongs. The first is an analysis of the concept of belief itself, and the second is an account of the empirical variation in or just plain *absence* of belief in many non-Christian traditions.

In our discussion of Spiro's work, we saw that belief in the conventional Western or Christian sense entails not only a proposition but a mental or psychological attitude toward that proposition; that is to say, *belief* presumes both that 'X is true' and 'This person holds that X is true.' To rephrase, Needham insists that claims about the beliefs of other religions "are assertions about the inner states of individuals" (1972:5). If this is the case, then there must be certain distinguishing characteristics of this inner belief-state and there must be some way to observe or measure them. Needham argues that neither is the case. Belief, he explains,

> is not the recognition of a bodily phenomenon, it does not discriminate a distinct mode of consciousness, it has no logical claim to inclusion in a universal psychological vocabulary, and it is not a necessary institution for the conduct of social life. Belief does not constitute a natural resemblance among men (151).

The inevitable conclusion, then, is that "when other peoples are said, without qualification, to 'believe' anything, it must be entirely unclear what kind of idea or state of mind is being ascribed to them" (188). At the very least, we might be talking about any of the four phases of belief in the evolution of Christianity. At the most we might be talking about some phenomenon which is not found in Christianity at all — or worse yet, a phenomenon that is not found in the religion we are studying but which we impose on it nonetheless.

This is the essence of Needham's second criticism of belief, and it is the crux of his argument and of ours. He finds that belief in any recognizable shape simply does not occur in the thinking and speaking of many other religions. That is, if we *stop speaking Christian* and *start speaking a different religious language*, it is often unnecessary, inappropriate, or even impossible to talk about belief. He gives many examples. One of the best known non-Western religions in anthropology is that of the Nuer, a cattle-herding tribe in East Africa. Described by E. E. Evans-Pritchard in his renowned *Nuer Religion* (1956), it comes across as a curiously Christian-like system, with 'sin' and 'god' and all the regular elements. The Nuer have a concept which they call *kwoth* and which Evans-Pritchard translates as 'God,' despite the fact that their notion of *kwoth* shares little in common with most notions of the Christian god. Further, Evans-Pritchard interprets their religion as an "interior state" much like modern Protestant Christianity.

If Nuer religion is an interior religion with 'God' and 'sin' and 'belief,' then it is. However, there is reason to wonder. Evans-Pritchard himself warns us about projecting our own views and concepts on them, including in areas that feel familiar, like 'sin.' But Needham urges much more caution. For instance, he mentions that one of the key Nuer sayings, *Kwoth a thin*, literally '*Kwoth*/God is present,' is not so much a proposition — let alone an article of faith — as an expression of trust, akin to '*Kwoth* is with us/will help us.' *Belief* is not exactly how the Nuer talk about their religion and is not quite a way they *can* talk about their religion; it is doubtful whether they have a concept of "belief." Indeed, Needham declares that "in Nuer, there is no verbal concept at all which can convey exactly what may be understood by the English word 'believe' (37). The problem did not arise until Christian missionaries began to try to translate documents and teachings into Nuer, when they found no precise equivalent to 'belief.' As in all cases, they fished around in the local language for a word that could do the duty, coming up with *liagh* and *ngath*, neither of which quite denotes the same meaning as 'belief' (*ngath* in particular indicates trust instead of propositional correctness).

One case is sufficient to refute the universality of a claim, but Needham mentions several others. In the Penan language of Borneo, he argues that it is impossible to utter a phrase like 'I believe in god' (1). Their word *ayu*, often translated as 'believe,' simultaneously means "'to use,' as of a tool or a weapon; and in addition it means 'to wear,' as of a loincloth or a necklace" (34). The Celebes and Roti languages of Indonesia offer similar challenges. The Roti word *hele*, in addition to conveying 'trust,' can mean 'to pick up,' 'to select,' 'bird-song,' 'to hinder, obstruct, weary,' and 'tight, strong, firm, to make fast, fix, appoint, determine, agree upon' (34) — hence its association with trustworthiness. In Celebes, the same word can mean to believe, to trust, to hold dear — the three English senses of 'believe' — as well as 'to take or use,' 'to accept,' 'to suppose,' 'to hope,' and others.

A few additional examples will make the point. In Navajo, "there is no word by which the English 'believe' ... can be exactly translated" (32). On the other hand, Hindi contains several words, such as *visvas, nischay, sachchai*, and *pratiti* with similar or overlapping meanings, sometimes "in the sense of belief as evidence or assurance," sometimes as 'faithfulness' (33). The Guatemalan language of Kikchi uses the same word for 'believe' and 'obey,' whereas Tagalog and other Philippines languages have different words to distinguish 'belief' from 'trust.' The Uduk of Ethiopia use a phrase that translates as 'to join God's word to the body' for the Christian equivalent 'to believe in God,' and the Shipibo say 'to be strong on God' in the same circumstances.

Some other societies and religions actually *do* have a conception of belief, more or less like the English or Christian one; Feinberg, for example, discovers that the Anutans of the Solomon Islands have a native belief concept. "The word *pakatonu*, literally 'make straight,' is used in almost precisely the manner of the English 'to believe.' Anutans are very much concerned with truth and falsity. After relating a story or an incident, they ask each other whether they 'believe' (*pakatonu*) the narrative's assertions" (1996:107). Conversely, Howard concludes that inhabitants of Rotuma had no word for belief prior to missionization, when the missionaries had to coin a new word, *pilifi* (a corruption of *belief*), to represent the Christian idea (1996:135).

Not wishing to become tiresome about this, nevertheless it is clearly the case that some languages and religions have more words or fewer words for 'belief' — and sometimes no word at all. The cross-cultural religious evidence, as Needham maintains, "has undermined the category of belief as a term of universal application" (206). Not all religions or languages

Discredism

— or *religious languages* — talk about belief or experience their religious world in terms of belief. I can assure the reader from my own fieldwork with a radically different religion, that if one were to ask the Warlpiri what they believe, they would consider the question quite odd. They would most likely respond, "I don't know what you mean," and if they ventured an answer at all, it would be something along the lines of, "I know about the *jukurrpa*" and "I can tell you this story" or "I must do this ceremony" and so on. To say that the Warlpiri believe in *jukurrpa* is to mistreat their religious experience. They do not talk that way, and to put such words in their mouths is to force them to speak Christian. Or, in Needham's words, "we are not sharing their apprehension and are not understanding their thought if we foist this typically western distinction on to them" (175).

I want to make one final point before we end this book, which puts belief ultimately and thoroughly in its place — which is a place of only local and minor importance. As the quotation from Marett above indicates, most religions most of the time do not formulate an explicit creed at all. Marett spoke specifically of "primitive religions," but as we have seen throughout this book, there is much less distance between 'primitive' and 'modern' or 'world' religions than the latter like to think. Even in Christianity, much of the religion is either informal or non-doctrinal. And there are many religious things to do other than believe.

Anthropologists, who specialize in the primitive or small-scale religions, have long reported that the religious ideas of a society are often informal, fuzzy, and even contradictory. S. F. Nadel has only echoed what we all see, which is that most religions do not have a formal creed (1954:8), just as they often lack a formal or elaborate mythology or ritual or prayer, *etc*. Some, like the Dogon in Africa, do have a very intricate 'religious knowledge,' but even then it might be inadvisable to call it *belief*. But most religions depend mostly on an unstructured, unarticulated, implicit or tacit kind of knowledge that gets the job done — a sort of religious common sense which is not and need not be codified and is seldom written down.

Clifford Geertz is one of the few to take seriously the notion of common sense as a cultural repository of knowledge and motivation. In his insightful essay "Common Sense as a Cultural System," he pointed out that much human knowledge is an unorganized, thumb-nail, pragmatic assortment of truths and truisms. The whole point of common sense is that it is *not* formal or organized, let alone creed-like: it is not 'something to believe' but rather 'what everyone knows.' As Geertz states it, from the member's perspective "its tenets are immediate deliverances of experience, not deliberated reflections upon it" (1983:75). In other words, it is precisely the kind of thing that does not require belief.

As Geertz puts it, common sense has much in common with religion; in fact, much of religion *is* common sense as far as the members are concerned. Just as every American knows that you should come in out of the rain or that you should starve a cold and feed a fever (or *vice-versa?*), so the Azande know that misfortune is caused by witches and the Nuer know that you should sacrifice an ox to cleanse sin — and Christians know that God answers prayers and that Jesus died for their sins. No Azande or Nuer is ever asked to commit to a creed; it is just what everyone knows and does. Geertz goes so far as to assert that common sense "is as totalizing as any other [system of thought]: no religion is more dogmatic, no science more ambitious, no philosophy more general" (84). It is what everyone takes for granted, what is self-evidently true, and what requires no speculation.

To be more precise, Geertz suggests that common sense has five characteristics. First, it seems natural and simple: "An air of 'of-courseness,' a sense of 'it figures' is cast over things" (85). Second, it is "practical"; it gets thing done. Third, it is "thin"; it is what it appears to be and nothing more. Fourth, it is "immethodical," that is, not theoretical or thought out but *ad hoc* and spur-of-the-moment. Fifth, it is "accessible," meaning that anybody with a brain should be able to understand it. Taken together, common sense "represents the world as a familiar world, one everyone can, and should, recognize, and within which everyone stands, or should, on his own feet" (91).

What I want to impress upon the reader is that *this is precisely the charge and, usually, the accomplishment of religion.* For most people in most religions, including most Christians, their religion amounts to their learned and inherited common sense. It is self-evidently true, which is why they do not need to be persuaded of it and can hardly be persuaded out of it. It is as natural as the air; in fact, they think that the air and everything else they see around them speaks their religious 'truth.' It is *not* highly thought out; there are those who *have* thought about it a lot, but most believers are utterly unfamiliar with this work (how many American Christians have read Karl Barth and Hans Küng, let alone Tertullian and Kant?). When scriptures exist in a religion — and no religion had them prior to a few thousand years ago, although all recent religions have them — many believers have not completely read them, do not completely understand them, and do not completely agree with them. *But scriptures, creeds, and beliefs are not where the power of religion comes from; they are not where religion 'lives.'*

Rather, as we noted particularly in Chapter 8 but also in Chapters 2 and 9 and 10, and arguably throughout this book *as the main thesis of this book*, religion is embodied and inscribed in many aspects and potentially every aspect of the individual member's life and the society's collective institutions and experience. Even without a formal doctrine, a creed, a set of propositions to which the individual is supposed to assent, a religion works its effects. Radcliffe-Brown said that the "function of a religion is independent of its truth or falsity" (1965:154), and he could not have been more correct. But we can and must go further: the function, the power, the efficacy of a religion is independent of whether it is believed to be true or false or of whether it is believed at all.

We know now that religion, like all of culture, is less about thinking than about *doing*. As long as humans are doing the things that religion seems to impel, command, and obligate them to do, religion is working. It does not matter whether these things include congregating, singing, marching, hanging wreaths, collecting canned food, condemning homosexuals, burning witches, or — as Marett suggested — dancing. As long as they are 'doing religion,' they are *doing* religion. Religion is not so much about belief as about discipline — being the kind of person who performs certain actions and is prone to certain experiences and interpretations of experience. Belief is optional and trivial in comparison.

ATHEISM ADVANCED

If Religion Can Do Without Belief, Why Not Atheism?

Believing is not thinking.
> —Ludwig Wittgenstein, *Philosophical Investigations*

Religion can live without belief. Belief can live without religion. Atheism can live without both.

Atheism is not 'disbelief' in god(s). *Disbelief* is not the opposite of 'belief.' Disbelief is another form of belief, a 'belief-not,' a belief that '*X* is not true' or that '*X* does not have *Y* properties.' Atheism is, if I am correct, being 'without god(s),' lacking the very concept of god(s). But atheism is not necessarily without other kinds of beliefs and concepts, religious or otherwise. However, when the principles and processes that produce atheism are applied more generally, to questions other than the existence or properties of god(s), the result is *discredism*.

Let me give a case in point. A year or two ago, I was invited to be the guest-evolutionist at a church youth group. The group was amiable, and they were indulging in many of the non-belief practices of religion that we have addressed in this book — rock music, games, snack foods, videos, and so on. The leaders were a savvy bunch, who realized that religion cannot live by belief alone. Anyhow, I was interviewed in front of the youngsters, off of a list of prepared questions. Two of the questions were "Do you believe that the universe is billions of years old?" and "Do you believe that dinosaurs lived millions of years before humans?" I am sure that the answer they expected from me to both was "Yes." Instead, to their surprise, I said, "No." I went on to explain that I do not *believe* anything about those two questions. It would be a misrepresentation of knowledge to say that any scientifically educated person "believes" such claims. Rather, as I expounded, the best and most preponderant evidence leads us to conclude that the universe is billions of years old and that dinosaurs existed millions of years ago. There is no belief involved at all. Believing is, I maintained, what you do when you do *not* have evidence — or when you do not have evidence *on your side.*

When it comes to matters of the Big Bang, dinosaurs, extraterrestrials, ESP, alternative medicine, the abominable snowman, and of course gods and spirits and supernatural forces, I am a discredist. I neither believe nor disbelieve. I find no need and no place for belief. There are some things I know with certainty (2 + 2 = 4, the earth is round), some things that I know with less certainty, and some things that I do not know. There are some things that I hypothesize, some things that I theorize, some things that I guess, *but nothing that I believe.*

'Belief' is one of those words that I recommend atheists, as discredists-of-god(s), to purge from their vocabulary *completely.* There are no occasions on which it is advisable to use the word. This includes all three of the dimensions of the everyday English usage of the term; in fact, this is critically important, since using 'belief/believe' when you do not mean propositional correctness is not only confusing but strengthening of the religious usage.

When I mean 'trust' or 'confidence,' I say "trust" or "confidence." It is not only wiser but more accurate to say, "I am confident that my wife will pick me up at the airport" than "I believe that my wife will pick me up at the airport."

When I mean 'commit' or 'value,' I say "commit" or "value." It is not only wiser but more accurate to say, "I value/am committed to democracy" than "I believe in democracy."

As for the propositional sense of belief — accepting something as true without evidence or in the face of contradictory evidence — you should say "belief/believe" if you *mean* that, *but a thinking person should never mean that.* How much more revealing it would be if believers spoke clearly and honestly, confessing, for instance, that "I believe in God, but there is no evidence for it and plenty of evidence against it." I think that, rather than applauding such belief, most thinking people would respond, "Why in the world would you do *that*?"

As a propositional claim, a claim of factual correctness, 'belief' is *always* invalid and unsound, even when it happens to get it right — which would be purely accidental. Beliefs are not always false, *but you can never tell whether they are true or false*, so why bother? However, I want to stress adamantly that atheists have accentuated far too strongly the propositional aspect of belief. This is partly because we recognize the invalid and/or false quality of the beliefs around us and we object to them. This is partly because we are thinkers, and thinkers dwell in the realm of propositions; we love to argue, and argumentation exists at the level of propositions. Also, it is partly because we are all still victims of the Western tradition of valorizing ideas over everything else, including especially emotions and actions and the body itself. Again, Christianity did not invent the disparaging of the body and of bodily experience that we find in that religion. Plato and other philosophers taught that lesson long before, and Christianity largely inherited it (Judaism did not and does not despise the body so completely, and most other religions do not either).

This preoccupation, this obsession, with facts and propositions, has led us to tragically overlook the power and efficacy of the non-propositional dimensions of belief, of religion, and of ordinary human life. We should have long ago noticed the relative ineffectiveness of our argumentation with theists and adjusted our course. People do not get argued out of religion *because they do not get argued into religion in the first place.* For most members of a religion, the propositions or creed of that religion are comparatively unimportant; there are a few key ones that most members know and accept, but most of the doctrines and the history of their own religion are either unknown or vaguely known to them. And it does not make the religion any less real or any less important to them. This is because, as we have seen throughout this book, as the one recurring theme of this book, religion is not only or perhaps mostly about doctrines or creeds or ideas or beliefs.

What is a religion, then? It is primarily a way of talking and secondarily a set of things to talk about. The 'language' of a religion makes it possible and necessary to say certain things, impossible and unnecessary to say other things, and highly likely to say yet other things. Religion is also *practices* more than it is ideas. It is *things to do*, and it does not particularly matter what those things are. These activities can consist of praying and reading scriptures, or singing, eating, not eating, marching, kneeling, or playing bingo. The important things are *that they be done together* and *that they be done because they must be done.*

These practices (and the ideas or propositions or creeds that underlie them) become the charter for a way of life for the collectivity, 'the way we do things around here.' They become virtually the group's learned common sense, their notion of how things work and what humans can (and cannot) do about it. The individual, almost never an author of these religious elements, is rather authored by them. Religious individuals are inundated with religion — often from early in life and continuously thereafter, in every medium that the religion can master. They are surrounded, permeated, saturated with religion, not merely or mostly convinced by it as much as in-*structed* and trans-*formed* by it. They are imbued with those Geertzian 'moods and motivations' appropriate and necessary to the religion, whether or not they understand them or the religion from which they emanate. In fact, it might be better if they do not.

Since propositions and creeds are apparently a minor part of the religious experience, arguing about and against religious propositions and creeds must become a minor part of the atheist and discredist experience. As we concluded in Chapter 8, we must *begin with our words* and *proceed to our worlds*. Atheism and discredism must stop speaking religion (in particular in the American context, 'speaking Christian') and must develop its own way of formulating its own experience. This experience must be expressed in stories, codified into institutions, and inscribed in our collective reality so that we can see it reflected back to us. And it must be *beautiful* — not in the sense of 'pretty' and definitely not in the sense of self-delusion that denies the difficulty and ugliness in the world, like death and disease — but in the sense of 'grand' and 'profound.' It must be *attractive* in that it can attract — that it offers something to attract — people of thought, people of feeling, and people of action.

Atheism has always had its logic, its epistemology, its metaphysics (or perhaps lack thereof). It has bickered about ethics. But has it ever had an aesthetics? In my previous book, I implored atheists to think about "the art of atheism" — what kind of world they would make, what a holistic atheism would look like, what atheism can offer to the person of mind, the person of heart, and the person of body. In this book, I have given some clues as to how religion provides these experiences and how atheism might claim them back. There is no single final form for an atheist world, just as there is no single human culture. What we are talking about is creating an atheist culture — or many atheist cultures. The one thing I am sure of is that this future atheist culture will be beyond religion — and beyond belief.

Bibliography and References

Allport, Gordon. 1979. *The Nature of Prejudice.* Reading MA: Addison-Wesley Publishing Company.

Ammerman, Nancy T. 1987. *Bible Believers: Fundamentalists in the Modern World.* New Brunswick New Jersey and London: Rutgers University Press.

Armstrong, Karen. 2000. *The Battle for God.* New York: Ballantine Books.

Asay, Elder Carlos E. 2006. "The Temple Garment: An Outward Expression of an Inward Commitment." Http://library.lds.org/nxt/gateway.dll/Magazines/Ensign/1997.htm/ensign%20august%20 1997.htm/the%20temple%20garment%20an%20outward%20 expression%20of%20an%20inward%20commitment.htm?f=templa tes$fn=documentframe.htm$3.0$q=$x= | The. Accessed November 22, 2006.

Asser, Seth M. and Rita Swan. 1998. "Child Fatalities from Religion-Motivated Medical Neglect." *Pediatrics,* v101, pp. 625–9.

Atran, Scott. 2002. *In Gods We Trust: The Evolutionary Landscape of Religion.* Oxford: Oxford University Press.

Austin, J. L. 1962. *How To Do Things with Words.* Oxford: Clarendon.

Avalos, Hector. 2005. *Fighting Words: The Origins of Religious Violence.* Amherst NY: Prometheus Books.

Baker, Don. 2002. "The Andrea Yates Case: The Christian God 0 vs. Christianity Meme 3." Http://www.christianitymeme.org/yates. shtml. Accessed January 12, 2006.

Barbour, Ian G. 1997. *Religion and Science: Historical and Contemporary Issues.* New York: HarperCollins Publishers.

Barfield, Thomas. 1997. *The Dictionary of Anthropology.* Oxford: Blackwell.

Basso, Keith H. 1970. *The Cibecue Apache.* New York: Holt, Rinehart, and Winston.

ATHEISM ADVANCED

Baudrillard, Jean. 1983 [1978]. *In the Shadow of the Silent Majorities*. Paul Foss, John Johnston, Paul Patton, and Andrew Berardini, trans. New York: Semiotext(e).

Baumeister, Roy. 2001 *Evil: Inside Human Violence and Cruelty*. New York: Barnes & Noble Books.

Beidelman, T. O. 1971. *The Kaguru: A Matrilineal People of East Africa*. New York: Holt, Rinehart, and Winston.

Bell, Catherine. 1992. *Ritual Theory, Ritual Practice*. New York: Oxford University Press.

Benokraitis, Nijole. 1993. *Marriages and Families*. Englewood Cliffs NJ: Prentice-Hall.

Berger, Peter. 1967. *The Sacred Canopy*. Garden City New Jersey: Doubleday.

Bloom, Howard. 1995. *The Lucifer Principle: A Scientific Expedition into the Forces of History*. New York: The Atlantic Monthly Press.

Bloom, Paul. 2004. *Descartes' Baby: How the Science of Child Development Explains What Makes Us Human*. New York: Basic Books.

Boyer, Pascal. 2001. *Religion Explained: The Evolutionary Origins of Religious Thought*. New York: Basic Books.

Buechler, Hans C. and Judith-Maria Buechler. 1971. *The Bolivian Aymara*. New York: Holt, Rinehart, and Winston.

Bulbulia, Joseph. 2006. "Nature's Medicine: Religiosity as an Adaptation for Health and Cooperation." In Patrick McNamara, ed. *Where God and Science Meet: How Brain and Evolutionary Studies Alter Our Understanding of Religion. Vol. 1: Evolution, Genes, and the Religious Brain*. Westport CT and London: Praeger, pp. 87–121.

———. 2004. "The Cognitive and Evolutionary Psychology of Religion." *Biology and Philosophy* 19, pp. 655–86.

Burke, Kenneth. 1969. *A Rhetoric of Motives*. Berkeley and Los Angeles: University of California Press.

Bibliography and References

Burkert, Walter. 1983 [1972]. *Homo Necans: The Anthropology of Ancient Greek Sacrificial Ritual and Myth.* Peter Bing, trans. Berkeley: University of California Press.

Campbell, Joseph. 1972. *Myths to Live By.* Toronto: Bantam Books.

Canetti, Elias. 1963 [1960]. *Crowds and Power.* Carol Stewart, trans. New York: The Viking Press.

Carroll, Michael P. 2002. *The Penitente Brotherhood: Patriarchy and Hispano-Catholicism in New Mexico.* Baltimore and London: The Johns Hopkins University Press.

Cassirer, Ernst. 1954. *An Essay on Man: An Introduction to a Philosophy of Human Culture.* Garden City New York: Doubleday & Company, Inc.

Collins, Francis S. 2006. *The Language of God: A Scientist Presents the Evidence for Belief.* New York: The Free Press.

Comaroff, John L. and Jean Comaroff. 1991. *Of Revelation and Revolution: The Dialectics of Modernity on a South African Frontier,* v.2. Chicago and London: The University of Chicago Press.

Counts, Dorothy Ayers. 1999. "'All Men Do It': Wife Beating in Kaliai, Papua New Guinea." In Dorothy Ayers Counts, Judith K. Brown, and Jacquelyn C. Campbell, eds. *To Have and to Hit: Cultural Perspectives on Wife Beating.* Urbana Illinois: University of Illinois Press, pp. 73–86.

Darwin, Charles. 1882 [1871]. *The Descent of Man and Selection in Relation to Sex,* 2nd ed. London: John Murray.

Dawkins, Richard. 2006. *The God Delusion.* Boston and New York: Houghton Mifflin.

———. 1986. *The Blind Watchmaker: Why the Evidence of Evolution Reveals a Universe without Design.* New York: W. W. Norton & Company.

De Waal, Frans. 2006. *Primates and Philosophers: How Morality Evolved.* Princeton and Oxford: Princeton University Press.

———. 2001. *The Ape and the Sushi Master: Cultural Reflections of a Primatologist.* New York: Basic Books.

Dees, Morris with James Corcoran. 1996. *Gathering Storm: America's Militia Threat.* New York: HarperCollins Publishers.

Den Boer, E. 1998. "The Frequency of Original Metaphors in Literary and Nonliterary Texts." Paper presented at the biannual conference of the Internationale Gesellschaft für Empirische Literaturwissenschaft, Utrecht University, Utrecht, The Netherlands.

Denton, Lynn Teskey. 2004. *Female Ascetics in Hinduism.* Albany: State University of New York Press.

Dickeman, M. 1975. "Demographic Consequences of Infanticide in Man." *Annual Review of Ecology and Systematics,* 6, pp. 107–37.

D'Onofrio, Brian M. *et al.* 1999. "Understanding Biological and Social Influences on Religious Affiliation, Attitudes, and Behaviors: A Behavior Genetic Perspective." *Journal of Personality* 67 (6), pp. 953–84.

Downs, James F. 1972. *The Navajo.* New York: Holt, Rinehart, and Winston.

Droge, Arthur J. and James D. Tabor. 1992. *A Noble Death: Suicide and Martyrdom Among Christians and Jews in Antiquity.* New York: HarperSanFrancisco.

Dugdale Pointon, T. 2005. "Ikko-Ikki." Http://www.historyofwar. org/articles/weapons_ikko.html. Accessed January 18, 2006.

Dundes, Alan. 1965. "What is Folklore?" In Alan Dundes, ed. *The Study of Folklore.* Englewood Cliffs NJ: Prentice-Hall, Inc., pp.1–3.

Durkheim, Emile. 1965 [1915]. *The Elementary Forms of the Religious Life.* New York: The Free Press.

Dussart, Françoise. 2000. *The Politics of Ritual in an Aboriginal Settlement: Kinship, Gender, and the Currency of Knowledge.* Washington DC and London: Smithsonian Institution Press.

Eller, Cynthia. 1993. *Living in the Lap of the Goddess: The Feminist Spirituality Movement in America.* New York: Crossroad Publishing Company.

Eller, David. 2004. *Natural Atheism.* Cranford NJ: American Atheist Press.

Bibliography and References

Eller, Jack David. 2005. *Violence and Culture: A Cross-Cultural and Interdisciplinary Approach.* Belmont CA: Wadsworth Publishing.

———. 1999. *From Culture to Ethnicity to Conflict: An Anthropological Perspective on International Ethnic Conflict.* Ann Arbor: University of Michigan Press.

Evans-Pritchard, E. E. 1962. *Social Anthropology and Other Essays.* New York: The Free Press.

———. 1956. *Nuer Religion.* New York and Oxford: Oxford University Press.

———. 1937. *Witchcraft, Oracles, and Magic Among the Azande.* New York: Oxford University Press.

Falkenberg, Lisa. 2004. "Religiosity Common Among Mothers who Kill Children." *San Antonio Express-News*, December 14.

Feinberg, Richard. 1996. "Spirit Encounters on a Polynesian Outlier: Anuta, Solomon Islands." In Jeannette Marie Mageo and Alan Howard, eds. *Spirits in Culture, History, and Mind.* New York and London: Routledge, pp. 99–120.

Festinger, Leon, Henry W. Riecken, and Stanley Schachter. 1964 [1956]. *When Prophecy Fails: A Social and Psychological Study of a Modern Group that Predicted the Destruction of the World.* New York: Harper & Row, Publishers.

Fortes, Meyer. 1959. *Oedipus and Job in West African Religions.* Cambridge: Cambridge University Press.

Freke, Timothy, and Peter Gandy. 1999. *The Jesus Mysteries: Was the "Original Jesus" a Pagan God?* New York: Harmony Books.

Frend, W. H. C. 1967. *Martyrdom and Persecution in the Early Church: A Study of a Conflict from the Maccabees to Donatus.* Garden City New York: Anchor Books.

Freud, Sigmund. 1969 [1921]. *Group Psychology and the Analysis of the Ego.* James Strachey, trans. New York: Bantam Books.

Gardiner, Patrick. 1988. *Kierkegaard: A Very Short Introduction.* Oxford: Oxford University Press.

Gardner, Howard. 1983. *Frames of Mind: The Theory of Multiple Intelligences.* New York: Basic Books.

Geertz, Clifford. 1983. *Local Knowledge: Further Essays in Interpretive Anthropology*. New York: Basic Books.

———. 1973. *The Interpretation of Cultures*. New York: Basic Books.

Gelles, Richard J. and Murray A. Straus. 1988. *IntimateViolence*. New York: Simon and Schuster.

Gellner, Ernest. 1988. *Plough, Sword, and Book: The Structure of Human History*. Chicago: The University of Chicago Press.

Gill, Sam D. 1981. *Sacred Words: A Study of Navajo Religion and Prayer*. Westport Connecticut: Greenwood Press.

Gilsenan, Michael. 2000 [1982]. *Recognizing Islam: Religion and Society in the Modern Middle East*. London and New York: I. B. Taurus Publishers.

Girard, Rene. 1977. *Violence and the Sacred*. Patrick Gregory, trans. Baltimore: The Johns Hopkins University Press.

Glasner, Peter E. 1977. *The Sociology of Secularisation: A Critique of a Concept*. London: Routledge & Kegan Paul Ltd.

Gonzalez, Justo L. 1984. *The Story of Christianity, Volume 1: The Early Church to the Dawn of the Reformation.* New York: HarperSanFrancisco.

Gorski, Eric. 2006. "Church Looks to Find its Next Life." *The Denver Post*, November 24, 2006.

Gould, Stephen Jay. 1999. *Rock of Ages: Science and Religion in the Fullness of Life*. New York: The Ballantine Publishing Group.

Green, Maia. 2003. *Priests, Witches, and Power: Popular Christianity after Mission in Southern Tanzania*. Cambridge: Cambridge University Press.

Green, Miranda Aldhouse. 2002. *Dying for the Gods: Human Sacrifice in Iron Age and Roman Europe*. Gloucestershire and Charleston South Carolina: Tempus Publishing.

Bibliography and References

Hallowell, A. Irving. 1976. "Ojibwa Ontology, Behavior, and World View." In Paul Radin, ed. *Contributions to anthropology: selected papers of A. Irving Hallowell*. Chicago: University of Chicago Press, pp. 357–390.

Hamer, Dean H. 2004. *The God Gene: How Faith Is Hardwired into Our Genes*. New York: Doubleday.

Harpham, Geoffrey Galt. 1987. *The Ascetic Imperative in Culture and Criticism*. Chicago and London: The University of Chicago Press.

Harvey, Graham. 2006. *Animism: Respecting the Living World*. New York: Columbia University Press.

Hatfield, Elaine, John T. Cacioppo, and Richard L. Rapson. 1993. "Emotional Contagion." *Current Directions in Psychological Science* v2, n3, pp. 96–9.

Haught, James. 1995. *Holy Hatred: Religious Conflicts of the '90s*. Amherst New York: Prometheus Books.

———. 1990. *Holy Horrors: An Illustrated History of Religious Murder and Madness*. Amherst New York: Prometheus Books.

Heath, Chip and Dan Heath. 2007. *Made to Stick: Why Some Ideas Survive and Others Die*. New York: Random House.

Hefner, Robert. 1993. "Introduction: World Building and the Rationality of Conversion." In Robert Hefner, ed. *Conversion to Christianity: Historical and Anthropological Perspectives on a Great Transformation*. Berkeley: University of California Press, pp.3–44.

Heider, Karl. 1979. *Grand Valley Dani: Peaceful Warriors*. New York: Holt, Rinehart, and Winston.

Herskovits, Melville J. 1938. *Dahomey: An Ancient West African Kingdom*, v2. New York: J. J. Augustin, Publisher.

Hoffer, Eric. 1966 [1951]. *The True Believer: Thoughts on the Nature of Mass Movements*. New York: HarperPerennial.

Holy, Ladislav. 1991. *Religion and Custom in a Muslim Society: The Berti of Sudan*. Cambridge: Cambridge University Press.

Horton, Robin. 1960. "A Definition of Religion, and its Uses." *The Journal of the Royal Anthropological Institute of Great Britain and Ireland*, v90, n2, pp.201–226.

Howard, Alan. 1996. "Speak of the Devils: Discourse and Belief in Spirits on Rotuma." In Jeannette Marie Mageo and Alan Howard, eds. *Spirits in Culture, History, and Mind*. New York and London: Routledge, pp. 121–45.

Hubbard, L. Ron. 1999 [1950]. *Dianetics: The Modern Science of Mental Health*. Los Angeles: Bridge Publications, Inc.

Hughes, Dennis D. 1991. *Human Sacrifice in Ancient Greece*. London and New York: Routledge.

Huntington, Samuel. 1996. *The Clash of Civilizations and the Remaking of World Order*. New York: Simon & Schuster.

James, William. 1958 [1902]. *The Varieties of Religious Experience: A Study in Human Nature*. New York: The New American Library.

Jaynes, Julian. 1976. *The Origin of Consciousness in the Breakdown of the Bicameral Mind*. Boston: Houghton Mifflin Company.

Juergensmeyer, Mark. 2000. *Terror in the Mind of God: The Global Rise of Religious Violence*. Berkeley: University of California Press.

Jung, Carl G. 1949 [1916]. *Psychology of the Unconscious: A Study of the Transformations and Symbolisms of the Libido*. Beatrice M. Hinkle, trans. New York: Dodd, Mead and Company.

Kant, Immanuel. 1990 [1781]. *Critique of Pure Reason*. J.M. D. Meiklejohn, trans. Amherst New York: Prometheus Books.

Katz, Richard. 1982. *Boiling Energy: Community Healing Among the Kalahari Kung*. Cambridge and London: Harvard University Press.

Kaufmann, Walter. 1961. *The Faith of a Heretic*. Garden City NY: Doubleday & Company.

Kiefer, Thomas M. 1972. *The Tausug: Violence and Law in a Philippine Moslem Society*. New York: Holt, Rinehart, and Winston.

Bibliography and References

Kimball, Charles. 2002. *When Religion Becomes Evil.* New York: HarperSanFrancisco.

Kirkpatrick, Lee. 2005. *Attachment, Evolution, and the Psychology of Religion.* New York: The Guilford Press.

Krakauer, Jon. 2003. *Under the Banner of Heaven: A Story of Violent Faith.* New York: Doubleday.

Kurtz, Paul, ed. 2003. *Science and Religion: Are They Compatible?* Amherst New York: Prometheus Books.

Lakoff, George. 2004. *Don't Think of an Elephant: Know Your Values and Frame the Debate — The Essential Guide for Progressives.* White River Junction Vermont: Chelsea Green Publishing Company.

Lakoff, George and Mark Johnson. 1980. *Metaphors We Live By.* Chicago: The University of Chicago Press.

Langer, Suzanne K. 1942. *Philosophy in a New Key: A Study in the Symbolism of Reason, Rite, and Art.* New York: Mentor Books.

Le Bon, Gustave. 1896. *The Crowd: A Study of the Popular Mind.* New York: The Macmillan Company.

Lee, Richard B. 1984. *The Dobe !Kung.* New York: Holt, Rinehart, and Winston.

Lessa, William A. 1966. *Ulithi: A Micronesian Design for Living.* New York: Holt, Rinehart, and Winston.

Lester, Tory. 2002. "Oh, Gods!" *The Atlantic Monthly* (February), pp. 37–45.

Lewis, C. S. 1960 [1943]. *Mere Christianity.* New York: Collier Books.

Levy, Leonard W. 1993. *Blasphemy: Verbal Offense against the Sacred, from Moses to Salman Rushdie.* New York: Alfred A. Knopf.

Levy, Robert I., Jeannette Marie Mageo, and Alan Howard. 1996. "Gods, Spirits, and History: A Theoretical Perspective." In Jeannette Marie Mageo and Alan Howard, eds. *Spirits in Culture, History, and Mind.* New York and London: Routledge, pp. 11–27.

Lienhardt, Godfrey. 1961. *Divinity and Experience: The Religion of the Dinka.* Oxford: Clarendon Press.

Lohman, Roger Ivar. 2003. "The Supernatural is Everywhere: Defining Qualities of Religion in Melanesia and Beyond." *Anthropological Forum*, 13 (2), pp. 175–85.

Luntz, Frank. 2007. *Words That Work: It's Not What You Say, It's What People Hear.* New York: Hyperion.

Mackay, Charles. 1980 [1841]. *Extraordinary Popular Delusions and the Madness of Crowds.* New York: Harmony Books.

Malinowski, Bronislaw. 1948. *Magic, Science, and Religion and Other Essays.* Garden City New York: Doubleday Anchor Books.

Martin, Michael. 1990. *Atheism: A Philosophical Justification.* Philadelphia: Temple University Press.

Matos Moctezuma, Eduardo. 1984. "The Templo Mayor of Tenochtitlan: Economics and Ideology." In Elizabeth Boone, ed. *Ritual Human Sacrifice in Mesoamerica.* Washington DC: Dumbarton Oaks Research Library and Collection, pp. 133–64.

May, Rollo. 1991. *The Cry for Myth.* New York: Delta Publishing.

May, Thomas S. 2006. "Terms of Empathy: Your Pain is my Pain — If You Play a Fair Game." *Brain Work* v16 (May–June), pp. 4–8.

McTernan, Oliver. 2003. *Violence in God's Name: Religion in an Age of Conflict.* Marknoll New York: Orbis Books.

Meigs, Anna S. 1984. *Food, Sex, and Pollution: A New Guinea Religion.* New Brunswick New Jersey: Rutgers University Press.

Milgram, Stanley. 1963. "Behavioral Study of Obedience." *Journal of Abnormal and Social Psychology*, 67, pp. 371–8.

Miller, Lisa. 2002. "Why We Need Heaven." *Newsweek* August 12, pp. 44–51.

Moore, G. E. 1963 [1912]. *Ethics.* London: Oxford University Press.

Morgan, Lewis Henry. 1978 [1877]. *Ancient Society.* Palo Alto CA: New York Labor News.

Bibliography and References

Morimoto, Ryo and Shannon Wills. 2004. "Differences in Moral Reasoning Between Religious and Non-Religious Groups." Unpublished manuscript.

Nadel, S. F. 1954. *Nupe Religion.* Glencoe Illinois: The Free Press.

Needham, Rodney. 1972. *Belief, Language, and Experience.* Chicago: The University of Chicago Press.

Newberg, Andrew, Eugene d'Aquili, and Vince Rause. 2002. *Why God Won't Go Away: Brain Science and the Biology of Belief.* New York: Ballantine Books.

Nielsen, Kai. 1989. *Why Be Moral?* Buffalo: Prometheus Books.

———. 1982. *An Introduction to the Philosophy of Religion.* New York: St. Martin's Press.

Nisbett, Richard. 2003. *The Geography of Thought: How Asians and Westerners Think Differently...And Why.* New York: The Free Press.

O'Connell, S. M. 1995. "Empathy in Chimpanzees: Evidence for Theory of Mind?" *Primates,* 36, pp. 397–410.

Obeyesekere, Gananath. 1981. *Medusa's Hair: An Essay on Personal Symbols and Religious Experience.* Chicago: University of Chicago Press.

Ohnuki-Tierney, Emiko. 1974. *The Ainu of the Northwest Coast of Southern Sakhalin.* New York: Holt, Rinehart, and Winston.

Ortiz, Alfonso. 1969. *The Tewa World: Space, Time, Being, and Becoming in a Pueblo Society.* Chicago and London: The University of Chicago Press.

Ortner, Sherry B. 1973. "On Key Symbols." *American Anthropologist* 75 (5), pp. 1338–46.

Overing, Joanne. 1986. "Images of Cannibalism, Death, and Domination in a 'Non-Violent' Society." In David Riches, ed. *The Anthropology of Violence.* Oxford: Basil Blackwell, pp.86–102.

Pagels, Elaine. 1995. *The Origin of Satan.* New York: Random House.

Parks, Douglas. 1996. *Myths and Traditions of the Arikara Indians.* Lincoln and London: University of Nebraska Press.

Paulson, Steve. 2006. "Religious Belief Itself is an Adaptation." *Salon.com.* Http://www.salon.com/books/int/2006/03/21/wilson/index.html. Accessed July 26, 2007.

Perkins, Judith. 1995. *The Suffering Self: Pain and Narrative Representation in the Early Christian Era.* London and New York: Routledge.

Persinger, Michael. 1987. *Neuropsychological Bases of God Beliefs.* Westport, Connecticut: Praeger Publications.

Pinker, Steven. 1995 [1994]. *The Language Instinct: How the Mind Creates Language.* New York: HarperPerennial.

Plantinga, Alvin. 1997. "Methodological Naturalism, Part 2." *Origins and Design*, 18, 2 (Fall), pp. 22–34.

Poirier, Sylvie. 1993. " 'Nomadic' Rituals: Networks of Ritual Exchange between Women of the Australian Western Desert." *Man* (n.s.), 27, pp. 757–76.

Prothrow-Stith, Deborah. 1991. *Deadly Consequences.* New York: The Free Press.

Radcliffe-Brown, A. R. 1965 [1952]. *Structure and Function in Primitive Society.* New York: The Free Press.

Rael (Claude Vorilhon). 1998. *The Final Message.* London: The Tagman Press.

Ranstorp, Magnus. 2003. "Terrorism in the Name of Religion." In Russell D. Howard and Reid L. Sawyer, eds. *Terrorism and Counterterrorism: Understanding the New Security Environment.* Guilford CT: Mc-Graw Hill/Dushkin, pp.121–36.

Rappaport, Roy. 1999. *Ritual and Religion in the Making of Humanity.* Cambridge: Cambridge University Press.

———. 1992. "Ritual." In Richard Bauman, ed. *Folklore, Cultural Performances, and Popular Entertainments: A Communications-Centered Handbook.* New York and Oxford: Oxford University Press, pp. 249–60.

Bibliography and References

Redfield, Robert. 1957 [1953]. *The Primitive World and its Transformations.* Ithaca NY: Cornell University Press.

Ruel, Malcolm. 1997. *Belief, Ritual, and the Securing of Life: Reflexive Essays on a Bantu Religion.* Leiden: E. J. Brill.

Rushkoff, Douglas. 1996. *Media Virus: Hidden Agendas in Popular Culture.* New York: Ballantine Books.

Ryle, Gilbert. 1970 (1949). *The Concept of Mind.* Harmondsworth UK: Penguin Books.

Sahlins, Marshall. 1976. *The Use and Abuse of Biology: An Anthropological Critique of Sociobiology.* Ann Arbor: University of Michigan Press.

Schaffer, Matt and Christine Cooper. 1980. *Mandinko: The Ethnography of a West African Holy Land.* New York: Holt, Rinehart, and Winston.

Scott, Eugenie C. 2003. "My Favorite Pseudoscience." *Reports of the National Council for Science Education* 23, 1, 11–6.

———. 1996. "Creationism, Ideology, and Science." In Paul R. Gross, Norman Levitt, and Martin W. Lewis, eds. *The Flight from Science and Reason.* New York: The New York Academy of Sciences, pp. 505-22.

Selengut, Charles. 2003. *Sacred Fury: Understanding Religious Violence.* Walnut Creek California: AltaMira Press.

Shermer, Michael. 2004. *The Science of Good and Evil: Why People Cheat, Gossip, Care, Share, and Follow the Golden Rule.* New York: Times Books.

Skorupski, John. 1976. *Symbol and Theory: A Philosophical Study of Theories of Religion in Social Anthropology.* Cambridge: Cambridge University Press.

Smart, Ninian. 1996. *Dimensions of the Sacred: An Anatomy of the World's Beliefs.* London: HarperCollins.

Smith, George. 1989. *Atheism: The Case Against God.* Amherst, New York: Prometheus Books.

Smith, Huston. 2001. *Why Religion Matters: The Fate of the Human Spirit in an Age of Disbelief.* New York: HarperCollins Publishers.

Smith, Lacey Baldwin. 1997. *Fools, Martyrs, Traitors: The Story of Martyrdom in the Western World.* New York: Alfred A. Knopf.

Sommerville, C. John. 1992. *The Secularization of Early Modern England: From Religious Culture to Religious Faith.* New York and Oxford: Oxford University Press.

Sosis, Richard and Candace Alcorta. 2003. "Signaling, Solidarity, and the Sacred: The Evolution of Religious Behavior." *Evolutionary Anthropology* 12, pp. 264–74.

Spence, Jonathan D. 1996. *God's Chinese Son: The Taiping Heavenly Kingdom of Hong Xiuquan.* New York and London: W. W. Norton & Company.

Sperber, Dan. 1975. *Rethinking Symbolism.* Alice L. Morton, trans. Cambridge: Cambridge University Press.

Spiro, Melford. 1978 [1967]. *Burmese Supernaturalism*, expanded edition. Philadelphia: Institute For the Study of Human Issues.

Staal, Frits. 1979. "The Meaninglessness of Ritual." *Numen* 26, pp. 2–22.

Steffen, Lloyd. 2003. *The Demonic Turn: The Power of Religion to Inspire or Restrain Violence.* Cleveland: The Pilgrim Press.

Stenger, Victor. 2002. *Has Science Found God? The Latest Results in the Search for Purpose in the Universe.* Amherst New York: Prometheus Books.

Stern, Jessica. 2003. *Terror in the Name of God: Why Religious Militants Kill.* New York: HarperCollins Publishers Inc.

Strobel, Lee. 1998. *The Case for Christ: A Journalist's Personal Investigation of the Evidence for Jesus.* Grand Rapids Michigan: Zondervan.

Suarez-Orozco, Marcelo. 1992. "A Grammar of Terror: Psychocultural Responses to State Terrorism in Dirty War and Post-Dirty War Argentina." In Carolyn Nordstrom and JoAnn Martin, eds. *The Paths to Domination, Resistance, and Terror.* Berkeley: University of California Press, pp. 219–59.

Bibliography and References

Summers, Randal W. and Allan M. Hoffman, eds. 2002. *Domestic Violence A Global View*. Westport CT: Greenwood Press.

Swinburne, Richard. 1977. *The Coherence of Theism*. Oxford: Clarendon Press.

Taleqani, Ayatullah Sayyid Mahmud. n.d. "Beliefs and Practices: Jihad and Shahadat." Http://www.al-islam.org/beliefs/philosophy/jihadandshahadat.html. Accessed January 16, 2006.

Tajfel, Henri. 1981. *Human Groups and Social Categories: Studies in Social Psychology*. Cambridge: Cambridge University Press.

———. 1978. *Differentiation between Social Groups*. London: Academic Press.

Tambiah, Stanley J. 1970. *Buddhism and the Spirit Cults in Northeast Thailand*. London: Cambridge University Press.

Tillich, Paul. 1952. *The Courage to Be*. New Haven and London: Yale University Press.

Trigger, Bruce G. 1969. *The Huron: Farmers of the North*. New York: Holt, Rinehart, and Winston.

Turner, Victor. 1981 [1968]. *The Drums of Affliction: A Study of Religious Processes among the Ndembu of Zambia*. London: Hutchinson University Library for Africa.

Valeri, Valerio. 1985. *Kingship and Sacrifice: Ritual and Society in Ancient Hawaii*. Paula Wissig, trans. Chicago and London: The University of Chicago Press.

Vecsey, Christopher. 1996: *On the Padres' Trail*. South Bend: University of Notre Dame Press.

Von Fuerer-Haimendorf, Christoph. 1969. *The Konyak Nagas: An Indian Frontier Tribe*. New York: Holt, Rinehart, and Winston.

Wade, Wyn Craig. 1987. *The Fiery Cross: The Ku Klux Klan in America*. New York: Touchstone.

Wallace, Anthony F. C. 1966. *Religion: An Anthropological View*. New York: Random House.

———. 1956. "Revitalization Movements." *American Anthropologist* 58, 2, pp. 264–81.

441

ATHEISM ADVANCED

Wegner, Daniel M. 1989. *White Bears and Other Unwanted Thoughts: Suppression, Obsession, and the Psychology of Mental Control.* New York: Viking.

Werner, Susan Jayne. 1981. *Peasant Politics and Religious Sectarianism: Peasant and Priest in the Cao Dai in Vietnam.* New Haven: Yale University Southeast Asia Studies.

Wheelwright, Philip, ed. 1966. *The Presocratics.* New York: The Odyssey Press, Inc.

Williams, Thomas Rhys. 1965. *The Dusun: A North Borneo Society.* New York: Holt, Rinehart, and Winston.

Wilson, David Sloan. 2002. *Darwin's Cathedral: Evolution, Religion, and the Nature of Society.* Chicago: The University of Chicago Press.

Wilson, E. O. 1978. *On Human Nature.* Cambridge: Harvard University Press.

———. 1975. *Sociobiology: The New Synthesis.* Cambridge: Belknap Press of Harvard University Press.

Winnick, Pamela R. 2005. *A Jealous God: Science's Crusade against Religion.* Nashville: Nelson Current.

Worsley, Peter. 1968. *The Trumpet Shall Sound: A Study of "Cargo Cults" in Melanesia.* New York: Shocken Books.

Zamorska, Julia. 1998. "Modernity in a Different Way: Cargo Cults in Melanesia as Creative Response to Modernisation." Http://www.geocities.com/southbeach/lagoon/ 3638/ anthro2.html. Accessed March 3, 2004.

Zimbardo, Philip. 2000. "The Psychology of Evil." *Psi Chi* 5, pp. 16–9.

General Index

General Index

General Index

Elema, people of Papua, Vailala madness in relation to, 133
Elementary Forms of the Religious Life, The, of Emile Durkheim, 77, 219, 252
Eliade, **Mircea**, on hierophanies, 278, on myths as paradigmatic acts, 386, on prestige of the past, 114
Eller, **Cynthia**, on syncretism in modern movements, 124
Eller, **David**, *Natural Atheism* of, all humans born as atheists as central thesis of, 36, on what an atheistic world would look like, 293, violence in relation to, 156
Elohim, plural epithet of Yahweh, 17, race of aliens in Raelian religion, 150
E-meter, Scientologists' use of, 142
Empiricism, Immanuel Kant in relation to, 330
Enemies, group need to conceive as 'devil', 248
Enemyway, Navajo ceremony, 50
England, as case of decolonization, Henry VIII in relation to, 297, secularization of, 298
Epicurus, doubts existence of the gods, 222
Epilepsy, temporal-lobe, religiosity in relation to, 83
Epiphenomenon, religion evolving as, 98

Equinox, religious colonization of time in relation to, 281
Essay on Man, An, of Ernst Cassirer, 361
Essenes, as religious movement, 119
Essentialism, as core error of Western civilization, 309, inference systems in relation to, 93, in Paul Tillich, 346
Ethical Non-theism, discussed, 11
Ethics, G. E. Moore on morality and, 365
Ethno-religious Conflict, discussion of, 185
Etiquette, interaction code in relation to, 380
Euhemerus, claimed gods to be deified humans, 70
Euthyphro, theory of moral behavior in Plato's, 321
Evans-Pritchard, **E. E.**, *Nuer Religion* of, 417, on Azande witchcraft, 230, on ethics in Nuer religion, 371, on moral neutrality of Azande god Mbori, 14, on Nuer lack of creation myth, 354
Evara, his role in Vailala madness, 134
Evil, myth of pure, 160, problem of, in various religions, 172, theodicy and monotheistic problem of, 18
Evil: Inside Human Violence and Cruelty, of Roy Baumeister, 160

Evil, **Problem of**, Theognis on, 222
Evolution, compatibility and incompatibility with various religions, 205, of Christian belief, 408, of morality, 372
Experience, more important than belief in religious identity, 269, religious colonization of, 267
Experience and reason, Kant's two sources of knowledge, 337
Explanation, analysis of the process, 226
Extraordinary Delusions and the Madness of Crowds, of Charles Mackay, 239
Eynan, Neolithic burial site, 71

F

Faith, Kierkegaard on, 337, 338
Faith, **leap of**, of Kierkegaard, 337
Family, violence in, 168
Farming, Christianization of, 272
Fasting, during Ramadan, 288
Fear and Trembling, of Kierkegaard, 337
Feinberg, **Richard**, on animistic world view of Anutans of Solomon Islands, 6
Feng shui, in arrangement of living space, 7
Festinger, **Leon**, *When Prophecy Fails* of, 124
Final Message, The, of Rael (Claude Vorilhon), 150

General Index

Hypnosis, Durkheim likens relation between individual and religious group as, 261, group violence in relation to, 164, mutual, as condition of groups, 245

I

Ialulep, Ulithi god who holds the thread of life, 16

Idealization, in Freudian theory, 245

Idea of the Holy, The, of Rudolph Otto, 74

Ideologies, strengthened if unverifiable, 170, violence in relation to, 170

Ideology, violence in relation to, 169

Immutability, as core error of Western civilization, 311, illusion of, in perceptions of religions, 111

Imperatives, morality and myth in relation to, 383

Imperial Wizard William Joseph Simmons, on religious tenets of Ku Klux Klan, 185

Index of Banned Books, many scientific books included, 200

Inference systems, templates in operation of, 93

Initiation, of Warlpiri, religious colonization of life in relation to, 277, self-mortification in relation to, 181

Innovation, in religion, problems in explaining it, 115

Inoculation, Rev. Edmund Massey's sermon against, 200

Inquisition, for combatting heresy, 184

Instinct, religious, as social instinct, 92, violence in relation to, 163

Institutions, violence in relation to, 167

Intellectualist theories, of religion, 73

Intelligence, Howard Gardner's studies of, 88, in non-human animals, 318, modular nature of, Pascal Boyer on, 93

Intelligent Design, speciousness of, 203

Interaction Code, morality in relation to, 378

Interests, of groups, 168, violence in relation to, 168

Intolerance, of monotheisms, 19

Iraq, Sunni conflict with Shi'ites in, 186

Ireland, Northern, religious conflict in, 186

Iron Age, of ancient Greece, 72

Irrationality, of groups, 264

Irredentism, as revitalization movement, 126

Isaac, Abraham's near sacrifice of, 337

Isaiah, valorization of suffering in relation to, 178, Yahweh as origin of peace and evil in, 19

Islam, atheism vs., x, civilization shaped by, 306, evolutionary position of, 119,

good and bad gods of, 19, holy war conceived as defense in, 191, knowledge of, 2, martyrdom in, 180, not really a monotheism, 3, Shi'a form of, 24, Sunni form of, 24, violence in relation to, 154

Islamic civilization, 306, in Samuel Huntington's theory, 305

J

Jains, (religious group), violence in relation to, 158

James, William, importance and philosophy of, 338, *The Varieties of Religious Experience* of, 237, 340, *The Will to Believe* of, 338

Japanese, culture, 305

Jaynes, Julian, his historical theory of religion, 71

Jealous God, A, of Pamela Winnick, 199

Jehovah, x

Jerome of Prague, persecuted by Inquisition, 184

Jerusalem, and Athens, Tertullian's comments on, 324

Jesus, as manifestation of Yahweh, x, Christian origins in relation to, 323, divinity of, as blasphemy, 19, 'Do' of Heaven's Gate is analog of, 143, Lessing on proof of divinity of, 336, no basis for Dec. 25 birth of, 23, time of alleged birth of, 109, 'What would Jesus do?', 115, wine

General Index

General Index

Lutheranism, 26, conscience in relation to, 238, lateness of formation of, 109

Luther, Martin, 95 theses of, 25, argued religion was a matter of conscience, 238, enemy of science and reason, 201, in evolution of Christian beliefs, 412, in Protestant Reformation, 184, Nietzsche on, 334

M

Macarthur, General Douglas, xi

Maccabees, political-military movement of, 119

Maccabees, Books of, self-sacrifice in, 178

Made to Stick, of Chip and Dan Heath, 58

Magic, in religion, opinion of William James, 341

Magisteria, non-overlapping, claim of Stephen Jay Gould, 209

Magnetic field, stimulation of brain by, 83

Mahayana, as later development in Buddhism, 12

Malinowski, Bronislaw, disagreement with Radcliffe-Brown, 78, emotionalist nature of his work, 74, on legitimating function of myths, 385, on religion as part of human toolkit, 74

Mana, Polynesian animatistic concept of, 7

Mandinko, of Africa, concept of four-part human nature of, 10

Marching, Hermann Rauschning on utility of, 263

Marett, R. R., on lack of creeds in most religions, 419, *The Threshold of Religion* of, quotation from, 415

Margulis, Lynn, *Microcosmos: Four billion Years of Microbial Evolution* of, 375

Marital rape, recentness of concept, 157

Marriage, religious colonization of life in relation to, 276

Mars, Roman god of war, 16

Martin, Michael, his *Atheism: A Philosophical Justification*, 41, critique of god-talk, 44

Martyrdom, at Masada and early Christianity, 179, in Islam, 180, Origen and Tertullian on, 179, Tertullian's view on, 326

Marx, Karl, historical and sociological theory of religion of, 72, sociological theory of religion of, 76

Maryland Toleration Act of 1649, toleration only of Trinitarians, 184

Masada, martyrdom in relation to, 179

Massey, Rev. Edmund, sermon against inoculation, 200

Matzo, as Passover food, 288

Maya, human sacrifice practiced by, 176, kings of, delayed burial of, 71

May, Rollo, on stories as guiding fictions, 387, *The Cry for Myth* of, 392

Mbori, as special god of the Azande, 18, Azande god, moral neutrality of, 14, not all-good god, 42

McTernan, Oliver, *Violence in God's Name* of, 153

Meaning, problem of, in religious language, 42

Meaninglessness, of religious language, 41, 45

Mecca, city of Muhammad, 278

Media Virus, of Douglas Rushkoff, 57

Meditation, brain function during, 82

Mediums, functions of in Cao Dai, 147

Meigs, Anna, on food regulations in New Guinea, 288

Mentality, is there a mythical?, 357

Mere Christianity, of C. S. Lewis, 343

Metaphor, importance of in language and thought, 361, in religious and common language, 51

Methodism, lateness of formation of, 109

Methodological naturalism, Eugenie Scott explains, 209

Michigan, Battle Creek, as headquarters for Seventh Day Adventism, 140

Microcosmos: Four Billion Years of Microbial Evolution, of Lynn Margulis, 375

General Index

intertribal trading of, 117, Roy Rappaport on, 257, Thomas Barfield on, 257, Victor Turner on, 257

Ritualization, of interaction behaviors in humans and other species, 380

Robertson, Pat, on divine preference for Israel against Palestinians, 186

Rock of Ages, of Stephen Jay Gould, 229

Roman Catholicism, as variant of Christianity, 1

Routinization, segmentation and secularization in relation to, 296

Ruby Ridge, Randy Weaver's home at, 196

Ruel, Malcolm, on four phases in evolution of Christian beliefs, 409

Rushkoff, Douglas, *Media Virus* of, 57

Ryle, Gilbert, on mind and meaning, 361, on nature of thought, 359

S

Sabbath, religious colonization of time in relation to, 282

Sacred, concept of the, sacrifice in relation to, 174, Emile Durkheim theory of, 77, religious marking of spaces that are, 278, science shows that nothing is, 220

Sacrifice, human, in ancient Greece and Europe, 175, in the Bible, 175, of blood, 176, violence in relation to, 174

Sagan, Carl, quality of scientific writing of, 393

Sahlins, Marshall, on role of myth, 388

Saigon, Ngo Minh Chieu proselytization at, 145

Saints, in supposedly monotheistic religions, 3

Samsara, Hindu concept, 'speaking Christian' in relation to, 33

Santa Claus, in non-Western cultures, 23

Sapolsky, Robert, on temporal-lobe epilepsy and religiosity, 83

Sarin, nerve gas release in Tokyo subway, Shoko Asahara in relation to, 147

Satan, as bad god, 19, Barna Group poll on belief in existence of, 407, in supposedly monotheistic religions, 3

Satanism, knowledge of, 2

Schaffer and **Cooper**, on Mandinko four-part human nature concept, 10

Schisms, in religious evolution, discussed, 20

Science, and religion compared, 215, as a-theistic (without gods), 208, atheism at heart of, 199, breaks religion to reveal truth about religion, 234, Christianity and origins of, 314, Eastern vs. Western, 318, necessary spiritlessness of, 207

Science and Religion: Are They Compatible?, of Paul Kurtz, 203

Scientology, 23, importance and discussion of, 141, language of, 41, lateness of formation of, 109, syncretism in, 124

Scott, Eugenie, explains methodological naturalism, 209, explains philosophical naturalism, 210, on science and religion, 205, on varieties of creationism, 204, refutation of her claim of science-religion compatibility, 217

Scripts, as language category, 54

Scriptures, Judeo-Christian, myths in, 353

Sculpture, religious colonization of arts in relation to, 285

Second Advent, The, Millerite publication, 139

Sects, in classification of religions, 27

Secularization, atheists need to promote, 294, of England, 298, Peter Glasner on, 294

Segmentation, Peter Glasner on, 295

Selengut, *Sacred Fury: Understanding Religious Violence* of, 153

Self-defense, as justification for violence, 170

Self-Mortification, religious violence in relation to, 178

463

General Index

U

UFO cults, syncretism in relation to, 124

Ulithi, of Micronesia, lacking creation story, 14, lack of creation gods among, 355, polytheism of, 16

Understanding, not needed for religion to be effective, 46

Under the Banner of Heaven, of Jon Krakauer, 194

Unification Church, lateness of formation of, 109, the Moonies, 110

Unitarianism, as Christian heresy, 25

Unitarians, expelled from Massachusetts, 184

Universalizability, of moral assertions, 369

Unverifiability, of doctrines, as requirement for effectiveness, 170

V

Vailala madness, Elema cargo cult of Papua in relation to, 133

Valeri, Valerio, on sacrifice in Hawaii, 177

Van Impe, Jack, joy contemplating end of the world, 125

Varieties of Religious Experience, The, of William James, 237

Vatican, site of alleged death of St. Peter, 279

Vecsey, Christopher, on techniques of Catholic missionary priests, 267

Vedas, sacrifice in relation to, 175

Venezuela, Piaroa tribe of, cannibal god Kuemoi of, 42

Via Dolorosa, as Christian holy site, 278

Violence, brain function in relation to, 160, in families, 168, in nature, 163, problems in defining, 158, religion-based, 171, religion in relation to, 153, religious explanations and justifications of, 172, understanding the causes and nature of, 156

Violence and the Sacred, of Rene Girard, 177

Vishnu, atheism vs., xi, major Hindu god, 16

Vitalism, in religious evolution, 126

VMAT2, as 'god gene', 82

Vocabulary, of religions, 38

Von Fuerer-Haimendorf, Christoph, on Konyak Nagas of India, 10

Vorilhon, Claude, French journalist who becomes Rael, 150

W

Waal, Frans de, on evolutionary benefit of cooperation, 375, on morality in non-human animals, 378, on perception of intelligence in non-human animals, 317, *Primates and Philosophers: How Morality Evolved* of, 374

Waco, Texas, Branch Davidians of, 140

Wailing Wall, as site of Temple of Yahweh, 278

Waldo, Peter, persecuted by Inquisition, 184

Wallace, Anthony, on new religious movement failure statistics, 132, on revitalization movements, 120, on modular theory of religion, 89, on supernatural principle in religion, 100

War, as eruption of two crowds, 248

Ward, Nathaniel, critical of toleration, 231

War, Holy. *See* **Holy War**

War, Just, Christian theory of, 190

Warlpiri, animistic world view of, 4, characteristics of religion of, 69, culture, 305, Françoise Dussart on perceived immutability of religion of, 116, localness of religion of, 129, religion of, 253, trying to 'speak Christian', 33

Wartime, social cohesiveness increased during, 251

Weaver, Randy, home at Ruby Ridge, 196

Week, religious colonization of time in relation to, 282

Wegner, Daniel, *White Bears and Other Unwanted Thoughts* of, 58

Werner, Susan, on Cao Dai religious movement, 145

Wernicke's area, of brain, modular na-

467